"*A Women's Lectionary for the Whole Church* challenges the androcentric landscape of our most common readings, upending customary theological constructs to uncover the presence of the feminine Divine. Such upending reveals space in our sacred text not only to see the stories of these women but also to see more deeply our own."

—Rev. Traci D. Blackmon, Associate General Minister,
Justice & Local Church Ministries, The United Church of Christ

"Reading Wil Gafney's work is not unlike listening to a gifted jazz musician. She knows the tradition yet has the ability to weave multiple genres together to create a powerful and beautiful new song."

—Rev. Otis Moss III, Senior Pastor,
Trinity United Church of Christ, Chicago, Illinois

"Dr. Gafney has written a series of volumes that laypeople and clergy can read easily and be blessed by mightily as their souls cry out in ecstasy, "Finally comes the poet!" I commend her work to those who will use this Lectionary. And I encourage you to read it carefully and prayerfully."

—The Rev. Dr. Jeremiah A. Wright Jr., Pastor Emeritus,
Trinity United Church of Christ, and author of *What Makes You So Strong?*

"I did not know how much my soul needed *A Women's Lectionary for the Whole Church* until I began reading it, but now I suspect that I will never prepare another sermon or devotional without consulting it. Every pastor, indeed every Christian, needs this among their collection."

—Chanequa Walker-Barnes, PhD,
author of *I Bring the Voices of My People: A Womanist Vision for Racial Reconciliation*
and *Too Heavy a Yoke: Black Women and the Burden of Strength*

"As someone who has learned so much from the Rev. Dr. Wil Gafney, I commend it to every congregation and classroom. It is a prime example of revolutionary scholarship."

—Brian D. McLaren,
author of *Faith After Doubt*

"I could sit at the feet of Wil Gafney for days and soak up her wisdom and knowledge. She has offered the church a treasure in this *Women's Lectionary*, and we would do well to make use of it quickly and thoroughly."

—Rev. Nadia Bolz-Weber, author

"*A Women's Lectionary for the Whole Church* is not only a resource for liturgy and preaching. I believe it is also a tool for contemplation on the mighty works of God on behalf of all people."

—The Rt. Rev. C. Andrew Doyle, Episcopal Bishop of Texas
and author of *Embodied Liturgy*

"This resource will be a great blessing and useful to all who seek to loose the shackles and set free the voices of the religiously oppressed and suppressed."

—Rev. Dr. Yvette A. Flunder, Presiding Bishop,
The Fellowship of Affirming Ministries,
and Senior Pastor, City of Refuge UCC in Oakland, California

YEAR
B

A WOMEN'S LECTIONARY FOR THE WHOLE CHURCH

A WOMEN'S LECTIONARY FOR THE WHOLE CHURCH

WILDA C. GAFNEY

CHURCH
PUBLISHING
INCORPORATED

Church Publishing
19 East 34th Street
New York, NY 10016
www.churchpublishing.org

Cover art by Pauline Williamson
Cover design by Dylan Marcus McConnell, Tiny Little Hammers

A record of this book is available from the Library of Congress.

ISBN 978-1-64065-570-6 (paperback)
ISBN 978-1-64065-571-3 (ebook)

For those who have searched for themselves is the scriptures
and did not find themselves in the masculine pronouns.
May these words of mine please you. *

---

* Psalm 104:35, *BCP*, adapted.

CONTENTS

ACKNOWLEDGMENTS

This Volume

Many thanks to the Rev. Dr. Mark Bozzuti-Jones and Ms. Summerlee Staten for the hospitality of the Trinity Retreat Center. I am grateful for the reading and consultation of Bishop Yvette Flunder, the Rev. Dr. Pamela Lightsey, the Rev. Dr. Martha Spong, and the Rev. Dr. Eric Thomas as I remain ever mindful of the sacred responsibility to write for all of God's children. Particular thanks to the Rev. Leah Jordan for early editorial work.

Previous Volumes

I would like to thank the Louisville Institute for the 2019 Sabbatical Grant for Researchers; the trustees, administration, faculty, and staff of Brite Divinity School for a twelve-month sabbatical in 2019; and the rector, Mike Kinman, vestry, and members of the All Saints Episcopal Church in Pasadena for ongoing material, spiritual, and temporal support during this project and for committing to a year-long trial use of the lectionary in 2020–2021.

Special thanks to the former RevGalBlogPal community and Martha Spong for an early hearing of the work and a collaborative digital space in which to try out lesson and translation choices. For valuable feedback, support, and inspiration, many thanks to the women, nonbinary persons, and men who attended collaborative consultation sessions across the country, including Martha Simmons of the African American Lectionary Project. Thanks to Alicia Hager for administrative support in the first year and to NaShieka Knight, my research assistant at Brite.

I remain grateful for translations and translators that have inspired me to take up the text: Marcia Falk, Everett Fox, Hugh Page, and Joel Rosenberg. I am appreciative of the *Wisdom Psalter* by Laura Grimes; it was an early resource, and she an early collaborator. The psalms in these volumes are shaped by that interaction.

I am deeply grateful for all who have expressed support and encouragement, and impatience for delivery in person, through correspondence, and on social media. I am profoundly grateful for all of you who have purchased, given, recommended, and assigned *A Women's Lectionary for the Whole Church, Year A* and *Year W*.

Lastly, I mourn those who will not see this project, especially those who died due to Covid-19 and its complications. They are legion.

ABOUT THE COVER IMAGES

I first saw Wil Gafney in chapel at Candler School of Theology in October of 2016, during a service where Leea Allen read an amazing poem, "Heart Matters," and Dr. Gafney preached a sermon entitled "Love God Herself," drawn from Beyoncé's song "Don't Hurt Yourself." I was inspired. I didn't have anything that day other than a regular piece of paper and my colored pens—this was before I unapologetically carted my markers into services because I do most of my work in situ—but I drew the image of a woman standing proud, brown face crowned with locks of dark hair, clothed in green, and holding up the world. She speaks to me of triumph.

This was not the last time that Dr. Gafney's words would inspire my art.

In a Queer and Feminist Theology course I took, we read Dr. Gafney's article "Don't Hate the Playa, Hate the Game." In it, she refocused our attention on the fullness of Delilah's story, teasing out details and possibilities of connection that reframed both Delilah's motivations and power. If you haven't read it, I suggest you do. It spoke to me of honey, and fire, and memory, and love, and retribution, and these things all shaped the piece I created in response: "Remembering the Fire."

Since then, I've been inspired many times over.

When I was beginning a Lenten series, I read Dr. Gafney's article "Ritualizing Bathsheba's Rape" and drew, in response, "In the Ashes." The piece depicts Bathsheba sitting by a fire in ashes, weeping and cradling her dead child while David laments outside. I also did a series of pieces of the women in Saul's life that were inspired by what Dr. Gafney wrote in her incredible *Womanist Midrash*. Time and time again, I know that if I want to be schooled in a text, brought closer to the nuances and truths contained therein, and inspired by those truths, I will find that wisdom in Dr. Gafney's works. Without a doubt, the volume you currently hold in your hands contains this wisdom, and I hope you are similarly inspired.

My pieces for the *Women's Lectionary* were created in the same theme and seek to center and lift up the power that Black Women have in these stories of salvation. I drew "Queen of Heaven" (the cover image for Volumes A, B, and C) in June of 2017 using Tombow Watercolor Markers on Bristol Vellum paper. It shows Mary, enthroned and crowned with all the planets of the solar system and the wonders of the Universe bearing witness, clothed in life and light, and holding the Christ Child in her arms. She is the guardian and the bearer of God—Theotokos; she is the creation honored by the Creator.

The next work, "No Longer Lost" (the cover image for Volume W), speaks of the parable where God is imaged as a woman, the woman who loses her coin and finds it. She celebrates with all of her neighbors as God celebrates with the host of heaven when the lost ones come home. Surrounding her in these coins are us, connecting, praying, studying, dancing. You can also see the dove, and the lost sheep, and the broom, because some things need cleaning up, not the least of which are our misconceptions and our preconceived notions, which have grown dusty as we have let them sit.

Let the words of the Rev. Dr. Wil Gafney clear up some of those misconceptions and open windows to shed light on truth in a way you have never before seen. Sit with these words. Let them sink in. Feel their power and be empowered by the story of the Good News told in ways you may have never experienced before. May the luminous wisdom of the Word find a home within you, and may it spark your inner fire.

Pauline Williamson, creating as *Seamire*

ABBREVIATIONS

Alter	*The Hebrew Bible: A Translation with Commentary*, trans. Robert Alter
AYBD	*Anchor Yale Bible Dictionary*
BigS	*Bibel in gerechter Sprache*
BDAG	*A Greek-English Lexicon of the New Testament and Other Early Christian Literature*, revised and edited by Frederick William Danker
BDB	*Brown-Driver-Briggs Hebrew and English Lexicon*
CEB	*Common English Bible*
DCH	*Dictionary of Classical Hebrew*
DSS	Dead Seas Scrolls
Fox	*The Five Books of Moses*, trans. Everett Fox
GSJPS	*A Gender-Sensitive Adaptation of the JPS Translation*
HALOT	*Hebrew and Aramaic Lexicon of the Old Testament*
IB	*The Inclusive Bible*
JPS	Jewish Publication Society *TANAKH*
KJV	King James Version
LXX	Septuagint
MT	Masoretic Text
NRSV	New Revised Standard Version
RCL	Revised Common Lectionary
SP	Samaritan Pentateuch

BIBLICAL RESOURCES

Original Language Texts

Dead Sea Scrolls
Hebrew Masoretic Text
Nestle-Aland Greek New Testament, 28th ed.
Peshitta (both testaments)
Samaritan Pentateuch
Septuagint
Targums
Vulgate

Bibles in Translation

Bishops Bible, 1568
Common English Bible, 2011
Dead Sea Scrolls Bible, 1999
Douay-Rheims Bible, 1582 (NT), 1610 (HB)
The Early Prophets: Joshua, Judges Samuel, Kings, Everett Fox, 2014
The Five Books of Moses, Everett Fox, 1995
A Gender Sensitive Adaptation of the JPS Tanakh, 2006
Geneva Bible, 1599
The Hebrew Bible: A Translation with Commentary, Robert Alter, 2018
Inclusive Bible, 2007
Jewish Publication Society Tanakh, 1985
King James Version, 1611
A New English Translation of the Septuagint, 2000
New Revised Standard Version, 1989
Revised Standard Version, 1971
Tyndale's (incomplete) translation, 1525
Wycliffe Bible, 1384

Commentaries

Hermeneia
Jewish Publication Society Torah Commentary
The Torah, A Women's Commentary
The Wisdom Commentary
Women's Bible Commentary
The Yale Anchor Bible Commentary

INTRODUCTION

What does it look like to tell the Good News through the stories of women who are often on the margins of scripture and often set up to represent bad news? How would a lectionary centering women's stories, chosen with womanist and feminist commitments in mind, frame the presentation of the scriptures for proclamation and teaching? How is the story of God told when stories of women's brutalization and marginalization are moved from the margins of canon and lectionary and held at the center in tension with stories of biblical heroines and heroes? More simply, what would it look like if women built a lectionary focusing on women's stories? These were my initial questions when I sat down to draft a proposal for a women's lectionary, a lectionary designed by women—or an individual woman—for the whole church. I do not imagine that my questions and perceptions are the questions and perceptions of all other women. But I do believe that my questions and perceptions invite women, men, and nonbinary readers and hearers to engage the scriptures in new ways, and in that engagement, they might find themselves and their questions represented.

The lectionary is a catechetical tool. There are more than two billion Christians in the world, according to the Pew Research Center's Forum on Religion and Public Life (Global Religious Landscape).* As of 2018, there were nearly 2.3 billion Christians representing slightly more than 31 percent of the world's total population. With Roman Catholics making up an estimated 1.2 billion and accounting for Orthodox Christians, Anglicans, Episcopalians, Methodists, Presbyterians, Lutherans, and other Reformed traditions along with some Baptist and congregational churches that use a lectionary, the overwhelming majority of Christians receive their scripture mediated through a lectionary; that would be nearly 1.4 billion persons whose customary exposure to the scriptures occurs through a lectionary. Based on the numbers in the Pew Research Center's May 12, 2015, report, "America's Changing Religious Landscape," as many as 60 percent of American Christians attend services in churches that use lectionaries.**

The scriptures are androcentric, male-focused, as are the lectionaries dependent upon them. Those lectionaries are not simply *as* androcentric as are the scriptures, but in my experience as a congregant and priest, women are even less well represented in them than they are in the biblical text. For example, there are at a minimum

---

* The Pew Center's report can be accessed here: https://www.pewresearch.org/religion/2012/12/18/global-religious-landscape-exec/.

** The section of the Pew Center report on data pertaining to Christians can be found here: https://www.pewresearch.org/religion/2012/12/18/global-religious-landscape-christians/

one hundred and eleven named women in the Hebrew Scriptures—which is itself underrepresented in preaching lectionaries and not always preached upon or even read—and that reckoning does not account for the numbers of unnamed women and girls. Yet not many of my students or parishioners can name even ten women in the Hebrew Scriptures or even the entire biblical canon. The extant lectionaries do not introduce us to even a tithe of them. As a result, all many congregants know of the Bible is the texts they hear read from their respective lectionary.

As a biblical scholar, it is my hope to see congregants exposed to the Bible more broadly and deeply and see them equipped to engage the sacred texts of their tradition critically, and with nuance. As a Hebrew biblical scholar, it is my hope to see congregations embrace the Hebrew Scriptures as a full and sufficient canon of scripture, revealing God and her word in conversation with, but not subject to, the Christian scriptures that follow honoring the ancient texts and *their* contexts. As a professor, priest, and preacher, I am keenly aware that it is the stories of women and girls, female characters and their names (when given), that are most likely to be unknown by congregants and seminarians, and all too often, clergy. A more expansive, more inclusive lectionary will remedy that by introducing readers and hearers of scripture to "woman story" in the scriptures. (Adapted from April D. Westbrook, *"And He Will Take Your Daughters . . .": Woman Story and the Ethical Evaluation of Monarchy in the David Narrative.*)

Biblical women are often generalized as a monolith of oppressed biblical womanhood. In my years teaching in theological classrooms and Jewish and Christian congregations, I find scripture readers unfamiliar with women prophets (the subject of my first book, *Daughters of Miriam: Women Prophets in Ancient Israel*) or the more than twenty named Israelite and Judean queens preserved in the text (addressed in my most recent monograph, *Womanist Midrash: A Reintroduction to the Women of the Torah and the Throne*), or the female assassins who execute their would-be rapists, or many other texts in which women have unexpected power and agency. A significant aim of this project is to increase biblical literacy, beginning with scripture's most neglected population.

Recognizing that the scriptures are an androcentric collection of documents steeped in patriarchy, this lectionary grapples with the gender constructs of the text rather than romanticizing admirable heroines. Indeed, it questions "admirable" constructs of womanhood rooted in birthing and mothering. The extent to which women's narratives uphold the patriarchal agendas of the scriptures is held in tension with those passages in which women demonstrate agency, wielding power and authority. Sometimes those are the same texts. The degree to which the scriptures are (and are not) liberating for all of their characters and claimants will be, hopefully, more accessible to preacher and reader and other interpreters and exegetes.

Biblical values and norms around gender occupy a central place in biblical interpretation, providing opportunity for preachers to engage them and their impact on the construction of gender norms in the world in which these texts are interpreted. I believe it is crucial to reframe the texts so that women and girls are at the center of the story, even though they are, to one degree or another, literary creations of premodern men. It is important that women who are often second-class citizens in the text and in the world in which the text is interpreted have a text selection and reading paradigm that centers the interests and voices of women in the text, no matter how constructed. The task of preachers is to proclaim a word—of good news, of liberation, of encouragement, of prophetic power, of God-story, and sometimes, of lament, brokenness, and righteous rage. These lectionaries will provide a framework to do that and attempt to offer some balance to the register in which the word has often been proclaimed.

A significant aspect of the work of shaping a lectionary and preaching from it is hermeneutical. I was (and remain) convinced it ought to be possible to tell the story of God and God's people through the most marginalized characters in the text. That is my practice as a preacher. This project, *A Women's Lectionary for the Whole Church*, intends to do that in a three-year lectionary accompanied by a standalone single-year lectionary. The three-year cycle, Years A, B, and C, will feature the Gospels of Matthew, Mark, and Luke, respectively, with John interwoven, as is the case in the Revised Common Lectionary (RCL) and Episcopal Lectionary (similar to the RCL but with the inclusion of deuterocanonical texts not deemed canonical by churches outside of the Anglo-Catholic and Orthodox streams). Year W (for "Women") covers all four Gospels.

Specifically, the *Lectionary* includes:

1. companion texts in the traditional four-fold model, first lesson, generally Hebrew Bible, Psalm (or other Canticle), Christian Testament lesson, and Gospel appropriate to the liturgical season;
2. fresh translation of the lessons for each Sunday, the Principal Feasts, Holy Week, and the Feasts of the Ever-Blessed Virgin Mary and Mary Magdalene, using gender-expansive language and, in the case of the Psalms, explicitly feminine God-language (see "About the Translations");
3. brief text commentaries on each day's lections; and
4. brief preaching commentaries on each day's lections.

The lectionary *does not* include collects. The lack of collects—prayers that tie together the readings that open the Liturgy of the Word—is intentional, that clergy and lay liturgists might develop their own in conversation with the lectionary.

A final word about gendered language: as a women's lectionary, this project specifically and intentionally makes women visible in these lectionary texts. This will inevitably seem strange to some hearers and readers. Some will find it welcome and a signifier of inclusion. Some will find it discordant, and I invite those to think deeply about what that discomfiture signifies. These responses may well be multiplied when reading and hearing the psalms using feminine pronouns. And some will find the language in these volumes insufficiently inclusive, particularly with regard to nonbinary and agender persons. While there is nonbinary language for human and divine subjects, the purpose of this project is to make women and girls more visible. Nonbinary and inclusive language can obscure women and girls. The commitment to the visibility of women and girls is not in conflict or competition with the commitment to the visibility of nonbinary persons; this language, my language, like all language, is simply inadequate to express the fullness of God in and beyond the world or even in human creation.

Most simply, these translations seek to offer and extend the embrace of the scriptures to all who read and hear that they might see and hear themselves in them and be spoken to by them. Similarly, taking seriously that we are all created in the image of God, these translations seek to display a God in whose Image we see ourselves reflected and reflecting.

TEXT SELECTION

I crafted lectionaries that centered the telling of the stories of scripture on the stories of women and girls in the text, without regard to whether they are named or voiced in the text or whether their experiences of and with God support the narrative and theological claims made by and on behalf of the text or not. Specifically, I prioritize passages in which women and girls are present whether named or not, whether speaking or not. In addition, I selected passages in which women and girls are present but obscured in plurals and other groupings, e.g., "children," "Israelites," "people," "believers," etc. As is the case with all lectionaries, some passages recur and others are omitted all together. None of the extant Christian lectionaries offers comprehensive reading of any of the canons of scripture. This lectionary is no exception.

My methodology was broadly as follows:

1. First, I established a female canon within the broader canons of scripture by using Accordance Bible Software to identify passages in which there is explicit language for female persons. I designed a Boolean search to capture as many terms as possible in singular and plural constructions and varied grammatical forms (mother* <or> daughter* <or> sister* <or> wom*n <or> wife <or> wives <or> widow* <or> *maid* <or> mistress* <or> lady <or> ladies <or> prostitute* <or> prophetess* <or> princess* <or> queen* <or> sorceress* <OR> womb <OR> pregnan* <or> midwi*e*). My search terms were not necessarily exhaustive, but they were more than sufficient for the task. I used the *Dictionary of Women in Scripture,* edited by Carol Meyers et al., to supplement this list.

2. Then, beginning with the liturgical season and its themes, I identified Hebrew biblical or deuterocanonical texts from the female canon. (Year W does not use the deuterocanonical texts apart from select readings during one or more of the Principal Feasts, such as Judith during the Great Vigil of Easter).

3. Next, I looked for readings that shared thematic language or specific words that related to the liturgical season and first lesson. I saved my Boolean search results in text groups: Hebrew Bible, Psalms, books that make up the New Testament lesson—Acts, the Epistles, and Revelation—and the Gospels. That meant I did not have to search the entire canon each time I worked on a specific reading. One nontraditional aspect of these lectionaries is that I occasionally use the Acts of the Apostles as the New Testament lesson, expanding the options for readings with female characters.

4. Sometimes a specific passage in a Gospel, psalm, or Epistle would suggest itself. Other times, I would move through the lesson categories looking for connective language. Most often the selection sequence was Hebrew Bible followed by a psalm then the Gospel and the New Testament lesson last.

Text selection was one of the most time-consuming aspects of the project, second only to translating the text. I was greatly facilitated in this work by collaboration circles, in person in Atlanta, Chattanooga, Chicago, Dallas, Fort Worth, Pasadena, Richmond (VA), and in Kapaa, Kilauea, and Wailua, Kauai (HI) in addition to international trips to Managua (Nicaragua) and a continuing education event for clergy on a Central and South American cruise where the *Lectionary* was one of the teaching topics. There is also an ongoing digital collaboration through a closed Facebook working group.

My conversation partners included sixty-three participants from across the United States, United Kingdom, Scotland, Canada, and New Zealand in one setting, Episcopal parishes in Kauai and Pasadena during separate one-month residencies, and a series of individual and small group consultations, some seventeen collaborations, some of which were composed of multiple sessions. Denominations represented included: African Methodist Episcopal, Anglican, Baptist (of various sorts), Disciples of Christ, Episcopal, the Fellowship of Affirming Ministries, Lutheran, Presbyterian, Unitarian Universalist, United Church of Canada, United Church of Christ, United Church of Scotland, and United Methodist.

I deliberately engaged potential users of the *Lectionary,* including clergy, seminarians, and lay leaders, with a range of gender identities and expressions. I also held a specific session for queer-identifying and nonbinary readers and hearers of the text focusing on the use and implications of binary language, even in service to womanist/feminist work, in an increasingly postbinary world.

I am beyond grateful for the contributions, questions, and suggestions of all of these conversation partners, including their assessment for wording and translation choices in addition to text pairings.

USING *A WOMEN'S LECTIONARY*

T he *Women's Lectionary* is designed for congregational and devotional life. It will also serve well in theological classrooms in preaching, worship arts, liturgy, and spiritual formation. The *Lectionary* is also suitable for clergy lectionary study groups. Individuals and congregations will have a number of options for use. Each set of readings is accompanied by text and translation notes and a preaching commentary. In addition, the *Lectionary* comes with a list of the divine names and titles used for God in these translations that might be used in public liturgy and private prayer. There is also an index of all the passages of scripture in the lectionary, making them available for individual study. Suggested practices for public reading follow in the "About the Translations" section.

CONGREGATIONAL USE

The gender-expansive translations throughout the *Women's Lectionary* and explicit feminine God language in the psalter provide an opportunity for Christian education and formation on matters of biblical authority and translation issues, oft-neglected conversations in congregations (beyond creedal statements).

- Adopt the *Lectionary* fully, Years A, B, and C for three years using these lessons in this translation.
- Adopt the *Lectionary* for a single year, using Year W for representation from all four Gospels. This would be especially suitable for churches that do not use a multiyear lectionary.
- Adopt the *Lectionary* to replace a year in the three-year lectionary currently in use.
- Adopt the *Lectionary* readings using another translation of the scriptures for public proclamation. (This may be a useful option in a congregation that might balk at hearing feminine pronouns used for God in scripture proclamation.)
- Use the *Lectionary* for substitute readings for the same day and liturgical season in a particular year (for example, when the Episcopal or RCL lessons are unsatisfactory).
- Use the *Lectionary* for Bible study, whether preaching from the *Lectionary* or not. The preaching prompts may be used as conversation starters.
- Use the list of divine names and titles for God to enrich the theological language of the community in liturgy, corporate, and personal prayer.

DEVOTIONAL USE

The *Lectionary* is designed for oral reading; read it out loud. Use the *Lectionary* for devotional reading, daily or weekly, whether your congregation uses the *Lectionary* or not. The four lessons can be read together every day of the week in their liturgical setting or spread out over the course of the week. The index can be used to identify individual passages for study and the list of divine names in the appendix can be used to augment the vocabulary of prayer.

THEOLOGICAL EDUCATIONAL USE

As a resource in the theological classroom, the *Lectionary* offers a much-needed alternative to the long-standing Episcopal and Revised Common Lectionaries for the study of liturgy and worship planning, offering a relevant and expansive vocabulary at a time when many clergy, congregations, and denominations are looking for liturgical alternatives and some are considering revisions of prayer books and hymnals for this very purpose.

These translations make a specific contribution to the oft-neglected but necessary conversation about the nature, function, and scope of biblical translation beyond the standard rubric of formal literalism and dynamic flexibility.

ABOUT THE TRANSLATIONS

Gender matters. Gender matters in the text, in the world, in the world of the text, and in the world of the translator. Gender matters to me and to countless numbers of women hearers and readers of the biblical text for whom it is Scripture. Gender matters significantly to those who have been and are marginalized because of gender, especially when it is done in the name of God, appealing to the Scriptures. And gender matters to men. Gender matters to hearers and readers of the Scriptures who are privileged to share the gender of the dominant portrayal of God, the majority of biblical characters, the majority of biblical characters who have speaking parts, the majority of translators of biblical texts, and the majority of interpreters of biblical texts.

(Wilda Gafney, *Womanist Midrash*, p. 289)

While prompted in part by my experience of hearing the scriptures read and proclaimed in nearly exclusively masculine language, multiplied in effect by equally, if not more, male liturgical language, this *Women's Lectionary* is a lectionary for the whole church. Androcentrism, sexism, and misogyny in the scriptures, in their translation and in their preaching and liturgical use, hurts men and boys and nonbinary children and adults as much as it does women and girls. Exclusively masculine language constructs and reinforces the notion that men are the proper image of God and women are secondary and distant. Further, the simple reality that men and boys have always heard their gender identified with God cannot be overlooked as a source of power and authority and security in terms of their place in the divine household and economy. Many, if not most, women and girls have not heard themselves identified their gender as and with the divine and for those who have had that experience, it has been profoundly moving, rare, and even sometimes profoundly disturbing. The translation choices employed in the *Women's Lectionary* offer an opportunity to hear the scriptures in public and private settings in a different timbre, a feminine vocal register. Specific translation choices are annotated in the text notes that follow each set of readings.

The *Women's Lectionary* is a multilayered work. In addition to the compilation of entirely new lectionary readings for the three-year cycle and composite single year, the production of entirely new gender-expansive translations and explicitly feminine translations in the Psalms distinguish this lectionary. Gender-expansive means expanding collections of people, e.g., Israelites, children, nations, and even "people" to reflect gendered subgroups such as "the women, children, and men of

Israel." (These translations generally place women before men in translation.) In every place where it can be reasonably inferred a group is composed of persons of more than one gender, I reflect that in the translation. Where gender neutral or inclusive language is used, it is used for male subjects; for example, "child" is used preferably to "son."

In genealogies, gender expansiveness means that lineages are presented matrilineally. For example, rather than "the God of Jacob," the *Lectionary* uses "the God of Rebekah's line." When supplemental language is added to establish the maternal genealogy, it is placed in brackets, i.e., "[Rachel-born] Benjamin." In each case, the original reading and translation choices are clearly identified in the text notes. For this project, explicitly feminine language is preferable to inclusive and neuter language, which obscures and erases women and girls. In addition, singular neuter gender and inclusive plurals do not disrupt the learned gender patterns, as many readers and hearers interpret them through their previously learned gender pattern and experience them as male. There is also some nonbinary language for human beings and God throughout the *Lectionary*; erasure of any gendered minority is contrary to the aims of this project.

Because so many readers pray the Psalms devotionally, I wanted to offer an opportunity to hear those compositions speaking to, by, and about women and girls primarily and to encounter God in explicitly feminine language so readers of all genders will have the experience of praying to God in the feminine gender. Therefore, these translations of the Psalms use feminine pronouns for God primarily, supplemented by nonbinary pronouns.

Following the practice of translators before me, I have adopted the practice of choosing descriptive expressions for the name of God and other divine names and titles. Given the most commonly used title for God in the Hebrew Scriptures, LORD (with the large and small caps indicating it is a substitutionary word for God's unpronounceable Most Holy Name represented by the letters YHWH) is the common male human slave holding title; it is not used for God in the *Lectionary*. The *Lectionary* preserves the ancient biblical and rabbinical practice of substituting something that can be said for that which cannot. (In some places the Hebrew Masoretic text uses Elohim, "God," as a substitute). In rabbinic and subsequent practice, *HaShem*, "the Name," is a common substitution; there are others.

Dr. Joel Rosenberg of Tufts University translated selected psalms for the Kol Haneshamah Reconstructionist prayer book. He renders the divine name using choices such as "THE ETERNAL, "THE ONE," and in Psalm 29, "THE ONE WHO CALLS over many waters." I was deeply impacted by these translations during the time I spent as a member of the Dorshei Derekh Reconstructionist minyan of the Germantown Jewish Centre in Philadelphia and adopted and expanded the practice in my own translations for teaching, preaching, and publication. The translations in the *Lectionary* draw from a robust list of options for naming God listed in an appendix. Some examples include: ARK OF SAFETY, DREAD GOD, FIRE OF SINAI, ROCK WHO GAVE US BIRTH, SHE WHO IS HOLY, etc. The list numbers more than one hundred and twenty. I preserve "Lord" for human beings, as that is the origin of the title, respectful address, and functionally the title refers to a slaveholder or other hierarchical role.

Similarly, in the Second Testament, I also reserve "Lord" for human beings—apart from Jesus. There are two sets of divine names and titles for the Christian Testament in the appendix. For Jesus I use: Anointed, God-born, Messiah, Rabbi, Redeemer, Savior, Son of Woman, Teacher, and Woman-Born. Son of Woman and Woman-Born both derive from the expressions previously and commonly translated as "son of man" (in the KJV) and more recently as "Mortal" or "the Human One" in translations like the NRSV and CEB. The underlying Greek expression, *huios tou anthropou*, means "son [male offspring] of a human" ("person of either sex" according to the standard authoritative BDAG lexicon); it also means "humankind" collectively. Whether one speaks or writes from a human, biological perspective or a theological one, the humanity of Jesus stems from his mother. Grammatically, Son of Woman and Woman-Born are both correct. Inasmuch as generic "man" is no longer used to represent humanity in totality, an argument can be made that Son of Woman is more theologically correct. The expression *huios tou anthropou* is not *de novo* to the Second Testament; it occurs in the First Testament in both Hebrew as *ben adam* and the same Greek expression in the LXX. *Ben adam* means son (and generic child) of humanity. In the First Testament and deuterocanonical books, I use woman-born where it is a human title signifying mortality. In at least one occurrence, in a poetic text, I translate it as "children of earth and Eve," given that the root of *adam* is *adamah*, "earth" (soil).

There is a second list of divine titles for God (apart from Jesus) used in the Second Testament. Those names and titles are: Creator, Creator of All, Dread God, Faithful One, Father, Holy One, Living God, Majesty, (our) Maker, Most High, One Parent, Provider, Shepherd-of-All, Sovereign, and Weaver (of lights). While I do preserve "Father" in some places, I employ it much less frequently than it occurs in the text. I reserve it for places where the parentage of Jesus is being addressed specifically. As it pertains to God's whereabouts and way of being in this world and the world beyond this one, I eschew "king" and "kingdom" in the *Lectionary*. As with all human attempts to describe God, monarchal language is inadequate; it is particularly unsuitable in that it stems from a rather brutal human system of governance that is unnecessary in the space where God is. Instead, I utilize "reign" and "realm" individually or in combination and "majesty." (The latter is feminine in Greek and functions as a divine title in Heb. 1:3 and 8:1.) When translating from the Hebrew Bible and deuterocanonical texts, I use "ruler" preferentially.

I take special care with translation choices for the Christian Testament because of the long history of anti-Judaism and anti-Semitism in biblical translation and interpretation and, in some cases, in the texts themselves. This lectionary intentionally excludes texts that blame Jews for the death of Jesus. The expression "the Jews" in Christian literature, including scripture, and in broader Christian discourse is very often negative. In the Greek New Testament, *Ioudaioi* can mean Jews, Judeans (people from Judea), or Jewish Christians in distinction from Gentile Christians. I use Judeans preferentially. In addition, because "scribes" can be easily misunderstood as simple copyists, I translate them as "biblical scholars" to make their underlying expertise more readily apparent.

Because scripture is read and heard and understood contextually, I am mindful of the ways in which the scriptures has been read and heard and understood in the broader Western and specifically American contexts. Across both testaments and the writings in between, slavery is ubiquitous, including on the lips of Jesus. While many translations use "servant" preferentially, I find that to be dishonest given that the persons so named were owned, controlled, raped, impregnated, bred, sold, maimed, and killed. Even when the bondage was of short *durée* or to pay off a debt, the lord and master had complete control of the subjugated person's body and sometimes retained their children after their liberation. So while it is certain to produce discomfort in the reader and hearer, I preserve "slave" and invite the reader and preacher to wrestle with that term and its influence on and in crafting and defending the American slavocracy. Minimizing the footprint of slavery in the scriptures weakens the link between them and subsequent slaveholding societies and the churches that unite them and us. Readers are welcome to replace the word "slave" with "servant," knowing that doing so writes over the degree to which the scriptures are slaveholding texts with no imagination of the possibility of abolition. I would encourage congregations to talk about that language and why they will or will not retain it.

Also bearing in mind the American context in which these translations were produced and the related contexts in which they will be read, I chose to disrupt the traditional biblical language of light and white to mean good and dark and black to mean something negative or even evil. While there is no concept of race in the Hebrew Bible or Christian Testament and people and nations are not assessed based on skin color and physical characteristics, that language has been mapped onto human bodies in the postbiblical world, justifying dehumanizing treatment, including slavery and legalized discrimination, including in the Church. Not all dark/black language in the biblical text is negative. Where it indicates something positive or holy, I retain it; for example, "God dwells in thick darkness" throughout the scriptures

As I move to complete Year C and make final edits to Year B, I return to my early definition of translation as "art and science," more specifically, as a "mysterious

and nearly indefinable process, which is both art and science" and, as *poiesis*,* creation of a new text in a new language out of the elements of the original text, its
original language content and context/s and, out of the receiving language and
context/s of the intended reader hearers—including the translator. I find translation to be a dance between all of these components. Language is not static, thus
translation is fluid—hence so many translations of the biblical text and other classic volumes and their revisions. What that means for this project is that successive
iterations of individual passages may be revised between volumes and some small
number were, challenging the recent (in millennial terms) insistence on a literal
inflexible unchanging text and singular interpretation for all time, common among
evangelical and fundamentalist strains of Christianity that cast a long shadow. In
these translations I dance with the Spirit, following her lead acknowledging that
this dance is not the only dance; indeed I dance other dances in other projects.

In sum, the translations in the *Lectionary*:

- Identify original language and translation choices in accompanying text notes.
- Identify supplemental expansive translations with brackets.
- Expand people groups to make the presence of women and girls explicit.
- Use feminine and nonbinary pronouns for God in the Psalms.
- List genealogical information maternally.
- Use expansive descriptive language for the name of God instead of "Lord."
- Limit use of "Father" to texts addressing Jesus's parentage.
- Replace "kingdom" with "reign" and "realm" or with "majesty" (ruler is used preferentially in the Hebrew Bible).
- Use "Judeans" rather than "Jews" preferentially where appropriate.
- Maintain slave language rather than weaken or minimize with "servant."
- Modulate "dark/black" negative language as "shadow" and "bleak/ness."

It is my hope that this lectionary will enrich the experience of hearing and reading scripture and invite readers and hearers into deeper study of the scriptures, their
translation, and interpretation. It is also my hope that liturgy, the work of the people in service to God, will be a place where all people can experience themselves as
fully created in the image of God whose words they hear through the scriptures,
and in prayer and preaching.

---

* *Poiesis* is Greek for creation out of some kind of starting material, particularly the creation of art and poetry, out of words. Contemporarily it is used to name the creation of the blood cells out of material within the human body, hematopoiesis. I develop this concept in the appendix "A Note on Translating" in *Womanist Midrash: A Reintroduction to the Women of the Torah and of the Throne*, Louisville: Westminster/John Knox Press, pp 281-284.

THE LESSONS WITH COMMENTARY
Year B

ADVENT I

In the second year, B, of the three-year lectionary cycle, this series will read through the Gospel of Mark as entirely as possible and as sequentially as possible. This will require the preacher and the person reading devotionally to think more deeply about not just where are the women in the text, but also what are the implications of these texts for women, nonbinary persons, and other marginalized communities and community members. This will also result in longer Gospel readings. Readers and preachers seeking more traditional Advent readings for all four Sundays of Advent will find them in Years A, C, and W of the *Lectionary*.

Isaiah 12:1–5; Psalm 65:1–13; Romans 1:7–8, 14-17; Mark 1:1–13

Isaiah 12:1 You will say in that day,

"I will give thanks to you, REDEEMING ONE,
for though you were angry with me,
your anger turned away,
then you comforted me.
² Behold! God is my salvation;
I will trust and I will not fear,
for Yah [She Who Is] GOD is my strength and my might
and has become my salvation."
³ Then you all shall with joy draw water from the wells of salvation.
⁴ And you all shall say in that day,
"Give thanks to the GOD OF OUR SALVATION,
call on God's name;
acclaim God's deeds among the nations;
make known that God's Name is exalted."
⁵ Sing praises to the MIGHTY GOD, who has done gloriously;
let this be made known in all the earth.

Psalm 65:1–13

¹ To you silence is praise, God in Zion;
and to you vows shall be performed,
² You who answer prayer!
To you shall all flesh come.

³ When deeds of iniquity overwhelm us,
you forgive our transgressions.
⁴ Happy are those whom you choose and bring near
to dwell in your courts.
We shall be satisfied with the goodness of your house,
your holy temple.
⁵ Through wondrous deeds you answer us with deliverance,
O God of our salvation,
hope of all the ends of the earth
and of the farthest seas.
⁶ You established the mountains through your might;
you are girded with strength.
⁷ The one who silences the roaring of the seas,
the roaring of their waves,
the rumble of the peoples.
⁸ They who live at the farthest reaches are awed by your signs;
you make the dawnings of morning and evening sing for joy.
⁹ You attend the earth and water her,
you enrich her greatly;
the river of God is full of water;
you provide the people with grain,
thus you have established it.
¹⁰ Irrigating earth's furrows,
smoothing her ridges,
softening her with showers,
and blessing her growth.
¹¹ You crown the year with your goodness;
your paths overflow with fatness.
¹² The pastures of the wilderness overflow,
and with joy the hills gird themselves.
¹³ The meadows are clothed with flocks,
the valleys arrayed in grain,
indeed they, shout for joy.

Romans 1:7 To all who are in Rome, God's beloved, who are called to be saints:
Grace to you all and peace from God our Creator and the Messiah Jesus Christ. ⁸ First, I thank my God through Jesus Christ for all of you, because your faith is proclaimed throughout the world. ¹⁴ To Greeks and to barbarians, to the wise and to the foolish am I a debtor, ¹⁵ thus my eagerness to proclaim the gospel to you all who are in Rome. ¹⁶ Indeed I am not ashamed of the gospel; it is the power of God for salvation to everyone who has faith, to the Jew first and even to the Greek. ¹⁷ For the righteousness

of God is revealed in it through faith for faith; as it is written, "The one who is righteous will live by faithfulness."

Mark 1:1 The beginning of the gospel of Jesus Christ, [the Son of God].

2 As it is written in the prophets,
"Look! I am sending my messenger ahead of you,
who will prepare your way;
3 *the voice of one crying out in the wilderness,*
'Prepare the way of the Holy One,
make straight the paths.'"

4 John the baptizer was in the wilderness proclaiming a baptism of repentance for the forgiveness of sins. 5 And people from all the Judean countryside and all the people of Jerusalem were going out to him and were baptized by him in the River Jordan, confessing their sins. 6 Now John was wearing camel's hair, with a leather belt around his waist, and he ate locusts and wild honey. 7 He proclaimed, "There is one coming after me who is more powerful than am I; whose sandal thongs I am not worthy to stoop down and untie. 8 I have baptized you in water; but that one will baptize you in the Holy Spirit."

9 And it was in those days that Jesus came from Nazareth of Galilee and was baptized by John in the Jordan. 10 And just as he was rising up out of the water, he saw the heavens torn apart and the Spirit descending like a dove on him. 11 And a voice came from heaven, "You are my beloved Son; with you am I well pleased." 12 Then the Spirit suddenly drove Jesus out into the wilderness. 13 He was in the wilderness forty days, tempted by Satan, and he was with the wild beasts, and the angels waited on him.

PROCLAMATION

Text Notes

"Yah" (as in "hallelujah/hallelu-yah") is, according to grammatical form, feminine, though it takes masculine verbs in biblical Hebrew and successive literature. In some contemporary Jewish feminist practices and prayer, it is used as a feminine name for God with the grammar modified accordingly. It is also the first syllable of the unpronounceable divine name, the Tetragrammaton, YHWH, which when translated "I AM/WILL BE WHO I AM/WILL BE"; there are no strictures on pronouncing the one syllable. In Isaiah 12:2 I offer a feminine reading option in brackets for those who so choose.

In Romans 1:17, Greek *pistis*, like its Hebrew antecedent *'emunah*, has primarily meant "faithfulness" and referred more to action than belief. In fact, trust is not always a significant part of faithfulness in the Hebrew Bible; they are distinct terms. In the New Testament, the concept narrowed to come to mean belief in Jesus. This narrowing does not replace the earlier semantic range; rather, it adds to it.

There is significant variability among the Markan manuscripts. The modifier "of Jesus Christ" in the first verse seems to have been added very early, i.e., after Sinaiticus, one of the earliest and most well-attested manuscripts of the New Testament. Yet it is present in others that are well regarded. The Isaiah citation in the first verse is incorrect and lacking in many manuscripts; I follow Alexandrinus (another extremely well regarded very early manuscript) in correcting it to "the prophets" along with other witnesses. The quoted material in Mark 1:2 is a combination of Exodus 23:20 and Malachi 3:1. The quoted material in verse 3 is from Isaiah 40:3; all of this material corresponds to the shape of these texts in the LXX. The baptisms of verse 8 can be understood grammatically and conceptually as both "in" water and the Holy Spirit and "with" water and the Spirit.

Traditions vary as to whether Jesus should be understood as "my son, the Beloved" or "My beloved son" in Mark 1:11. "You are my son" is a quote from Psalm 2:7; in the song, it is royal adoption language common between gods and monarchs (of both genders) in the Afro-Asiatic world.

In the Israelite cultural and literary context, "angels," as in verse 11, are really "messengers." The word is used for both human and divine beings; both senses endured into the New Testament. However, in both Psalm 91 and the wilderness sojourn of Jesus in Mark 1, divine beings are clearly meant, and there is a particular sentimental attachment to angels in both of these passages.

Preaching Prompts

This year's Advent theme is "salvation." In the Hebrew Scriptures, salvation is corporate. Though some individuals, notably in the psalms, experienced individual deliverance from difficulty and danger, salvation was understood as deliverance for the whole community, the entire people. This is true even when a singular address is used, as in the first lesson. The "I" is the nation speaking collectively. Isaiah 12 is the praise song of a people looking forward to the day of their liberation, imagining the song they will sing on that day. They are so certain of their redemption, they are already writing the lyrics to their redemption song. Were women and children, widow and orphan, landless and poor, and the immigrants who made their home among them to pen their verses of the song of salvation, what would the song sound like then?

The psalmist celebrates a God who hears and answers prayers, including prayers for deliverance. She is also aware that she and her people are prone to transgression, and rather than being cut off from the saving grace of God, they find themselves the beneficiaries of God's gracious forgiveness.

Paul likewise has an expansive understanding of God's embrace in Romans 1. However, he expresses this openness in ethnocentric terms, starting with himself and his people and inferring that it is remarkable that God would include people beyond his community. His language is not generous. "God welcomes barbarians and even Greeks! That's a good and generous God. Am I right?" Paul sounds like the leader of a dominant culture enclave patting themselves on the back for having one black family join, one out person on the vestry or church council, but not too many and no need for any more. These readings invite us to ask if our welcome and inclusion are as expansive and generous as possible, imitating God's radical inclusion and welcome to her saving grace and embrace. They also remind us that those who are best suited to answer the question are often swallowed up in a corporate body that does not always speak to and for them.

The broad framework of Advent is preparing for the return of Christ by contemplating his first advent. In other years lectionaries begin with the infancy Advent and Christmas stories. Mark's advent story begins with the moment all questions about the identity and paternity of Jesus are answered by the highest source. Like the nativity stories, there is the power of the Holy Spirit, and there are bands of angels framing the advent of the son of God (which, for Mark, is the advent of his ministry). The year of Mark begins with the words of scripture (remembering that the evangelists and authors of the Epistles and Apocalypse did not understand themselves to be contributing to a canon they likely considered closed). Mark's Gospel begins with a "new" reading of the ancient texts through the life, teaching, miracles, death, and resurrection of Jesus. They read the scriptures with new eyes and found new ways of interpreting and understanding them in their current context. As we preserve their interpretive work, we must not neglect to do our own, for our context is ever-changing.

Thus, we enter Advent on the heels (prayerfully) of a global pandemic mourning the loss of perhaps 1 million persons in the United States, and many times more around the world. And in the first week of Advent, we heed the prophet's call to repentance and baptism and its renewal, not because our sin has brought calamity upon us, but because in our calamity, we have discerned and cultivated a desire for internal transformation liberation while we await the salvation and redemption of the world around us.

ADVENT II

Genesis 16:7–13; Psalm 48:1–3, 9–14; Romans 10:9–13; Mark 1:14–28

Genesis 16:7 Now the messenger of the ALL-SEEING GOD found Hagar by a spring of water in the wilderness, the spring on the way to Shur. [8] And the messenger said, "Hagar, slave-girl of Sarai, from where have you come and where are you going?" And she said, "From my mistress Sarai am I fleeing." [9] The messenger of the INSCRUTABLE GOD said to her, "Return to your mistress, and subject yourself to her."

[10] The messenger of the WELLSPRING OF LIFE said to Hagar, "Greatly will I multiply your seed, so they cannot be counted for multitude." [11] Then the messenger of the FOUNT OF LIFE said to her,

> "Look! You are pregnant and shall give birth to a son,
> and you shall call him Ishmael (meaning God hears),
> for the FAITHFUL ONE has heard of your abuse.
> [12] He shall be a wild ass of a man,
> with his hand against everyone,
> and everyone's hand against him;
> and he shall live in the sight of all his kin."

[13] So Hagar named the LIVING GOD who spoke to her: "You are El-ro'i"; for she said, "Have I really seen God and remained alive after seeing God?"

Psalm 48:1–3, 9–14

> [1] Great is the AGELESS GOD and greatly praised,
> in the city of our God is God's holy mountain.
> [2] Beautiful in elevation, the joy of all the earth,
> Mount Zion, in the far north,
> is the city of the great Sovereign.
> [3] Within her citadels God
> has made herself known as a bulwark.
> [9] We contemplate your faithful love God,
> in the midst of your temple.
> [10] Like your Name, God, your praise,
> reaches to the ends of the earth.
> Your right hand is filled with righteousness.
> [11] Let Mount Zion be glad,
> let the towns of Judah rejoice
> because of your judgments.
> [12] Go about Zion, go all around her;
> count her towers.
> [13] Set your hearts upon her ramparts;
> go through her citadels,
> that you may recount to the next generation:
> [14] For this God is our God, our God forever and ever.
> She will be our guide until we die.

Romans 10:9 If you confess with your lips that Jesus is Sovereign and believe in your heart that God raised him from the dead, you will be saved. [10] For with the heart a woman or man believes and is made righteous, and with the mouth a person confesses and so is saved.

[11] Indeed, the scripture says, *"one who believes in him will not be put to shame."* [12] For there is no distinction between Jew and Greek because the same Sovereign is sovereign over all and is generous to all who call on him. [13] For, *"Everyone who calls on the name of the Sovereign shall be saved."*

Mark 1:14 Now after John was arrested, Jesus came to Galilee, proclaiming the gospel of God, [15] and saying, "The time is fulfilled, and the reign of God has come near; repent, and believe in the gospel." [16] And as Jesus passed along the Sea of Galilee, he saw Simon and his brother Andrew throwing a net into the sea, for they were fisherfolk. [17] And Jesus said to them, "Follow me and I will make you fish for people." [18] Then immediately they left their nets and followed him. [19] As he went a little farther, he saw James son of Zebedee and his brother John, who were in their boat mending the nets. [20] Then immediately Jesus called them and they left their father Zebedee in the boat with the laborers and followed him. [21] And they went to Capernaum and when the sabbath came Jesus entered the synagogue and taught.

[22] The women and men [in the synagogue] were astounded at his teaching, for he taught them as one having power, and not as the scholars. [23] Immediately after [Jesus finished teaching] there was in their synagogue [at Capernaum] a person with an unclean spirit, [24] who cried out, "What have you to do with us, Jesus of Nazareth? Have you come to destroy us? I know who you are, the Holy One of God." [25] But Jesus rebuked the spirit, saying, "Be silent, and come out!" [26] Then the unclean spirit, convulsing the person and crying with a loud voice, came out. [27] And the women and men in the synagogue were all amazed, and they kept on asking one another, "What is this? A new teaching—with power! He commands even the unclean spirits, and they obey him." [28] And his fame immediately began to spread throughout the surrounding region of Galilee.

PROCLAMATION

Text Notes

The language of Hagar's annunciation parallels the promise to Abraham in Genesis 13:16 closely; each is promised that their "seed" (or offspring) will be numerous beyond counting. Hagar is the first woman in scripture granted an annunciation; the unnamed mother of Samson follows in Judges 13:3–7, followed in turn by Mary, the mother of Jesus. Hagar and Rebekah (Gen. 24:60) are the only women in the canon credited with their own seed/offspring; the language is usually reserved for men. (Rebekah's seed is blessed by her matrilineal family; her father Bethuel ben Milcah bore his mother's name, not his father's.) Notably, God speaks to Abraham *about* Sarah in Genesis 17:15–16, as do the divine messengers in Genesis 18:9–10; even when she is within hearing, none speak to her.

Hagar's abuse or affliction, more rightly, Sarah's abuse of Hagar in verse 11, is articulated with a verb that encodes both physical and sexual violence; the verb is also used for the abuse the Israelites suffered at the hands of the Egyptians. The divine demand that Hagar "subject herself" to Sarah is communicated with a reflexive form of the same verb; she is told to subject herself to more potential violence. Some translate Ishmael's fate in verse 12 as living "in opposition," i.e., conflict, with his kin rather than "opposite," i.e., in their sight or presence; the verb has both senses.

In Psalm 48, Zion's superlatives hail from other cultures identifying their God as God of all the earth using the specific vocabulary of surrounding nations: *noph* signals "elevation" but is also the Egyptian name of Memphis, the capital city (and may also mean "fair," see JPS). Zaphon is the home of the Canaanite gods and is in the farthest northern reach, unlike Zion/Jerusalem. In verse 14, God will be our God "until death"; "until we die" makes clear that it is not God who will die.

Romans 10:11 quotes Isaiah 28:16 from the LXX, and verse 13 quotes Joel 2:32 (3:5 Heb), which is the same in both versions.

Mark 1:22 has "they were astounded." I have expanded the plural to account for the presence of women who might otherwise be presumed to be absent. *Exousia* can mean authority or power. "Power" fits better with the exorcism narrative that follows, where *exousia* is repeated in Mark 1:26. (That passage is assigned for Epiphany I.) I use "scholars" rather than scribes to preserve the sense of them as legal and biblical scholars and avoid the suggestion they were copyists.

Preaching Prompts

In the Gospel, Jesus goes into full-time ministry at full throttle, preaching, teaching, traveling, and calling his first disciples. Mark will not reveal female disciples, yet we know from the larger tradition that Jesus was surrounded by women, children, and men. The advent of the reign of God is at hand and he has come to prepare the way that none might be lost. Advent is an urgent business in this Gospel.

Names were powerful in the ancient world, to the point of magic. For some of the peoples surrounding ancient Israel, to know a true name was to potentially have power over a person, a deity, or other supernatural entity. In this context Hagar's imposition of a name on the Israelite deity that was accepted is extraordinary. In the Hebrew Scriptures, God's most holy name was YHWH—not pronounced, replaced with an acceptable word such as LORD (not used here), the HOLY ONE, etc.—what is considered the essence of their being. It was God's name that dwelt above the ark in the temple (Deut. 12:11; 14:23; 16:2, 6, 11; 26:2; Ps. 74:7) and in Shiloh before that (Jer. 7:12). In Psalm 48:10, this Name stretches to the ends of the earth accompanied by praise. After some torturous exegesis in the earlier portion of Romans 10 in which Paul replaces "the commandment" (meaning all of the commandments as a single body) in Deuteronomy 30:12–13 with Jesus, he transforms an Isaiah text (28:16) about trusting in God to having faith in Jesus and concludes by likewise transforming a text (Joel 2:32/3:5 Heb) about the power of the Name of God to save to one about invoking the name of Jesus for salvation. In the Gospel, the unclean spirit knows that Jesus has a name, an identity, beyond the one everyone knows. Before it can reveal even more, Jesus silences and expels it.

What's in a name? How we name God matters when the names we have inherited and those we choose reflect the identities of some in our communities and in our world while excluding others. How we name each other matters when some take it upon themselves to determine how others will be named, from white priests determining that the names of enslaved children were too dignified and baptizing them with more servile names to social, cultural, and legal systems that reject the names and identities of trans and gender-nonconforming people.

ADVENT III

Genesis 20:1–7, 9, 11–12, 14, 17; Psalm 147:1–7;
Acts 16:16–24; Mark 1:29–45

Genesis 20:1 Abraham journeyed toward the region of the Negeb and settled between Kadesh and Shur and he sojourned in Gerar. ² Now Abraham said about his woman Sarah, "She is my sister." And Abimelech, king of Gerar, sent and took Sarah. ³ Then God came to Abimelech in a dream at night and said to him, "Beware! You are about to die on account of the woman whom you have taken; she is a married woman." ⁴ Now Abimelech had not approached her so he said, "Mighty One, will you slay an innocent people? ⁵ Did he not himself say to me, 'She is my sister'? And she say herself, 'He is my brother'? In the integrity of my heart and the innocence of my hands did I do this." ⁶ Then God said to him in the dream, "I know myself that in the integrity of your heart you did this, and it was I myself who restrained you from sinning against me. Therefore I did not let you touch her. ⁷ And now, restore the man's woman for he is a prophet and will pray for you and you shall live. But if you do not restore her, know that you shall surely die, you and all that is yours."

⁹ Then Abimelech called Abraham and said to him, "What have you done to us? How have I sinned against you that you have brought upon me and upon my realm such great guilt? Things which ought not be done have you done to me." ¹¹ Then Abraham said, "It was because I thought, surely there is no fear of God in this place, and they will kill me because of my woman. ¹² Also, she truly is my sister; she is the daughter of my father but not the daughter of my mother, and she became my woman. ¹⁴ Then Abimelech took flocks and herds and enslaved women and men and gave them to Abraham, and returned to him his woman Sarah. ¹⁷ And Abraham prayed to God and God healed Abimelech and his woman and also healed the women enslaved to him so that they gave birth.

Psalm 147:1–7

1 Praise the LIVING GOD!
How good it is to sing praise to our God;
for God is gracious and a song of praise is a delight.

2 The ARCHITECT OF HEAVEN builds up Jerusalem,
and gathers the outcasts of Israel.

3 She heals the brokenhearted,
and binds up their sorrows.

4 She numbers the number of the stars;
giving to all of them their names.

5 Great is our Sovereign, and abundant in power;
her understanding is beyond measure.

6 The FAITHFUL ONE lifts up the oppressed;
she casts the wicked to the ground.

7 Sing to the JUST ONE with thanksgiving;
make melody to our God on the lyre.

Acts 16:16 One day, as we were going to the place of prayer, we met an enslaved girl who had a spirit of divination and brought her masters a great deal of money by fortune-telling. 17 While she followed after Paul and us, she cried out, "These persons are slaves of the Most High God, who proclaim to you a way of salvation." 18 This she did for many days. But it bothered Paul, who turned and said to the spirit, "I order you in the name of Jesus Christ to come out of her." And it came out that hour.

19 Now when her masters saw that their hope of financial gain was gone, they seized Paul and Silas and into the marketplace they dragged them before the authorities. 20 When they had brought them before the magistrates, they said, "These persons are disturbing our city; they are Judeans 21 and are preaching traditions that are not right for us to follow as Romans." 22 The crowd joined against them, and the magistrates had them stripped of their clothing and ordered them to be beaten with batons. 23 After they had laid many blows on them, they threw them into prison and commanded the jailer to keep them securely. 24 Receiving these instructions, he put them in the innermost cell and their feet he fastened in the stocks.

Mark 1:29 Immediately after [Jesus and the disciples] left the synagogue, they entered the house of Simon and Andrew, with James and John. 30 Now the mother of Simon's wife was in bed with a fever, and immediately they told Jesus about her. 31 Jesus came and lifted her up, taking her by the hand. Then the fever left her and she ministered to them. 32 As it was becoming evening, when the sun was setting, they brought to Jesus all who were sick or demon-possessed. 33 And the whole city was gathered around the door. 34 And Jesus cured many who were sick with various diseases and cast out many demons, and he would not permit the demons to speak, because they knew him.

[35] Now in the morning [of the day after Jesus healed Peter's mother-in-law], while it was still dark, he got up and went out to a deserted place and there he prayed. [36] And Simon and those [the women and men] with him chased after Jesus. [37] And they found him and said to him, "Everyone is searching for you." [38] Then Jesus replied to them, "Let us go on to the neighboring towns, so that I may proclaim the message there; for that is what I came out to do."

[39] So Jesus went throughout Galilee, proclaiming the message in their synagogues and casting out demons. [40] Now a person with a skin disease came to Jesus begging him, and kneeling said to him, "If you choose, you can restore me." [41] Moved with compassion, Jesus stretched out his hand and touched the person and said, "I do choose. Be restored!" [42] Immediately the skin disease left and the person was restored. [43] And after a stern warning Jesus sent the person away at once, [44] saying, "See that you say nothing to anyone; rather, go show yourself to the priest and offer for your cleansing what Moses commanded, as a testimony to them." [45] However, the person went out and began to proclaim it freely, and to spread the word so that Jesus could no longer go into a town openly; rather he stayed out in the country and people came to him from every side.

PROCLAMATION

Text Notes

Because biblical Hebrew does not have a distinct word for "wife," I use "woman" every place allowable by English grammar. In addition to representing the lexical world of the language, it also serves to keep some distance between contemporary notions of marriage and the variety of conjugal relationships in the biblical text in the ancient world. Curiously, the adjective "married" and its corresponding noun "marriage" are seldom used in the text.

The textual tradition behind Genesis 20 is unique in considering Abraham a prophet, though the story exists in several forms. In Genesis 12, it is Abram and Sarai and the Pharaoh who takes her and does have sex with her, which should be considered nonconsensual, a rape. In Genesis 26, it is Isaac and Rebekah who is protected from the (here) Philistine king, Abimelech. Today's version in Genesis 20 explicitly protects Sarah from rape, a likely intentional revision.

Where grammatically and rhetorically possible, I translate the language "slavery" to reflect what was done to persons—being enslaved—rather than identify them by their state as in Genesis 20 and Acts 16.

In Acts, the divining spirit is called a "python," a reference to the python guarding the Delphi Oracle, which then became a euphemism for all sorts of vocal performances, including divination and ventriloquism. The word translated as "fortune-telling" can also be translated as "divination" or "prophecy."

The healing of Peter's (invisible) wife's mother varies slightly among the synoptic Gospels: in Mark 1:29–31 the disciples *tell* Jesus about her; he takes her by the hand and lifts her up. In Matthew 8:14–15, Jesus sees her and touches her, and she gets up on her own. In Luke 4:38–39, the disciples *ask* Jesus about her; he rebukes the fever without touching her, and she gets up on her own. After her healing, in Matthew 8:15, Peter's mother-in-law ministers to Jesus, while in Mark, she ministers to "them," the (other) disciples.

Preaching Prompts

In these readings, women are vulnerable to the whims of men and the forces of nature and disease. In the first lesson, God is manifest to a foreign king through imposition of harm and its subsequent healing, protecting Sarah and Abraham, though in the world of the text, it is Abraham's honor that is at stake with Sarah's body; her protection is secondary. In the psalm, God is the one who gathers the outcasts and binds up the brokenhearted. One might imagine Sarah asynchronously praying this prayer. But one must remember there was no deliverance for the enslaved women (or men) either in Abimelech's realm or those he gave to Abraham who would be counted among the "blessings" with which God enriched him. Note the amount of time it would take for the queen and enslaved women to be diagnosed with infertility and have that attributed to Sarah's kidnapping.

Jesus is manifest as God in human flesh through the same power to heal God wields in Genesis. To a lesser degree than in Genesis, Peter's wife's mother is also healed for the benefit of the men in her life. Peter illustrates that God's power is still in the world, but its human bearers lack the graciousness and majesty of God. After having been the corecipient of Jesus's healing ministry in Mark, Peter becomes transformed to heal in Acts but heals the enslaved girl whose origin is unknown not out of concern for her, but because he is vexed by her. In two of these texts, the manifestation of God's awesome power is eclipsed by the banality of unchallenged slavery.

The Gospel of Mark repeats all-inclusive terms like "all" or "the whole city [or region]." Who is missing from our ministry efforts? What do authentic healing ministries look like in the church of this century (when excluding charlatans and the potential for abuse)? It will be important to note that the almost magical quality of divine healing found throughout the scriptures is not the lived reality of most people and is not so because of a lack of faith.

ADVENT IV

Isaiah 52:7–10; Psalm 118:14–26; 1 Peter 1:10–12; Luke 1:26–38

Isaiah 52:7 How beautiful upon the mountains
   are the feet of one who brings good news,
   proclaiming peace,
   bringing good news,
   proclaiming salvation,
   who says to Zion, "Your God reigns, daughter."
 8 Daughter, the sound of your sentinels, lifting their voice!
   As one they sing for joy;
   for from one eye to another they see
   the return of the HOLY ONE OF SINAI to Zion.
 9 Revel! Raise a song together,
   you ruins of Jerusalem.
   For the HOLY ONE OF OLD has comforted God's people,
   God has redeemed Jerusalem.
 10 The MIGHTY GOD has bared a holy arm
   before the eyes of all the nations;
   and all the ends of the earth shall see
   the salvation of our God.

Psalm 118:14–26

 14 The MIGHTY GOD is my strength and my might
   and has become my salvation.
 15 The sound of song and of salvation is in the tents of the righteous:
   "The right hand of the MOST HIGH is mighty;
 16 the right hand of the MIGHTY GOD is exalted;
   the right hand of the MOST HIGH is mighty."
 17 I shall not die, but I shall live,
   and recount the deeds of the ANCIENT OF DAYS.
 18 The MERCIFUL GOD has punished me severely,
   but to death did not hand me over.
 19 Open to me the gates of righteousness,
   that I may enter through them
   and give thanks to the FOUNT OF JUSTICE.
 20 This is the gate of the LIVING GOD;
   the righteous shall enter through it.
 21 I thank you for you have answered me
   and have become my salvation.

²² The stone the builders rejected
   has become the chief cornerstone.
²³ This is the MIGHTY GOD's doing;
   it is marvelous in our eyes.
²⁴ This is the day that the CREATOR OF ALL has made;
   let us rejoice and be glad in it.
²⁵ Save us, we pray, SAVING ONE!
   GENEROUS ONE, we pray, grant us prosperity!
²⁶ Blessed is the one who comes in the name of GOD WHO IS HOLY.
   We bless you from the house of the EVER-LIVING GOD.

1 Peter 1:10 Concerning this salvation, the women and men who prophesied of the grace that was to be yours made searched diligently and inquired earnestly, ¹¹ discerning with regard to the time that the Spirit of the Messiah within them made known when testifying before time of the sufferings and following glory of the Messiah. ¹² It was revealed to the women and men who prophesied that they were serving not themselves but you all, in regard to the things that have now been announced to you through those who brought you good news—gospel—by the Holy Spirit sent from heaven; these are things into which angels long to look!

Luke 1:26 In the sixth month the angel Gabriel was sent by God to a town of Galilee, Nazareth, ²⁷ to a virgin betrothed to a man whose name was Joseph, of the house of David. And the name of the virgin was Mary. ²⁸ And the angel came to Mary and said, "Rejoice, favored one! The Most High God is with you." ²⁹ Now, she was troubled by the angel's words and pondered what sort of greeting this was. ³⁰ Then the angel said to her, "Fear not, Mary, for you have found favor with God. ³¹ And now, you will conceive in your womb and give birth to a son, and you will name him Jesus. ³² He will be great and will be called the Son of the Most High, and the Sovereign God will give him the throne of his ancestor David. ³³ He will reign over the house of Jacob forever, and of his sovereignty there will be no end." ³⁴ Then Mary said to the angel, "How can this be, since I have not known a man intimately?" ³⁵ The angel said to her, "The Holy Spirit, She will come upon you, and the power of the Most High will overshadow you; therefore the one born will be holy. He will be called Son of God. ³⁶ And now, Elizabeth your kinswoman has even conceived a son in her old age, and this is the sixth month for she who was called barren. ³⁷ For nothing will be impossible with God." ³⁸ Then Mary said, "Here am I, the woman-slave of God; let it be with me according to your word." Then the angel left her.

PROCLAMATION

Text Notes

Addresses to Zion and Jerusalem are often in the feminine as they are here. I use "daughter" to make the occurrences visible to the English reader where it is not explicit. Verses 7 and 8 address the feminine singular daughter Zion, and in verse 9, it is the plural "ruins of Jerusalem" that are addressed. In verse 8, "sentinels" is a synonym for prophets.

Verses 14–16 quote Miriam's song in Exodus 15:2 and are also found in Isaiah 12:2. The assonant and alliterative poetry of Psalm 118:25 (the "Hosanna") is difficult to reproduce: *Ana Ya hoshia na; Ana Ya chatzlicha na.* The "hosanna" pronunciation comes from the Greek transliteration of the Hebrew. "God's faithful love endures forever" is one of the oldest liturgical refrains in the Hebrew Bible: see the opening and closing of this psalm and Psalm 118.

Given the presence of women and men among the prophets in testaments, I have expanded "prophets" in 1 Peter 1:10 and in verse 12 to reflect that.

In Mary's linguistic and cultural world, in Hebrew and Aramaic, the Spirit is feminine; the Syriac text uses a feminine verb for the Spirit in Luke 1:35. Also, in her world, there was no distinction between servant and slave. Mary is not saying she will wait on God hand and foot in verse 38; she is giving God ownership of her body, ownership slaveholders claimed without consent. This volume uses "slave" normatively, reflecting the troubling language in the scriptures and their contexts.

Preaching Prompts

For the fourth week of Advent, we leave Mark for a moment for a more traditional Advent set of readings. In addition to salvation, the theme of reversal is prominent. Israel's fortunes are reversed. The exile is returned. The captive is set free. The lament is turned into praise.

The poet-prophet continuing Isaiah's work proffers a vision of salvation that brings both light and life to Jerusalem configured as God's daughter. This salvation is rooted in the experience of exile and its end, a return that was perceived as a second exodus, a new beginning. This redemption is for Jerusalem representing Israel, yet it is performed in the sight of all the nations, with "eyes" and "seeing" prominent, setting the stage for a more expansive proclamation of salvation. The psalm continues the theme of Isaiah as a celebration of God's salvation.

The author of 1 Peter revisits the prophetic scriptures of his people and sees in their promise of a messiah, Jesus. It is important to remember that the Hebrew Scriptures offer a number of messianic visions, the nation as a messiah, the immediate reestablishment of the Judean monarchy led by a messiah king, one or more figures all suffer and die on behalf of the nation, and David and Cyrus named as God's messiahs.

Mary takes on the language of enslavement, subjecting herself to God and God's will. Yet, there is a question in the mind of some readers as to whether Mary actually had the option to consent, given Gabriel tells her what *will* happen to her and to her body. It is unclear what would have happened had she demurred. Yielding herself to God, Mary joins the ranks of those deemed "servants," or slaves of God: Moses, David, Paul, James. Through her yielding, the first Advent comes to us.

CHRISTMAS I

Isaiah 26:16–19; Psalm 68:4–11; 1 Thessalonians 4:13–18; Luke 2:1–14 or 2:1–20

Isaiah 26:16 HOLY ONE, in distress they sought you,

>they pressed out a whispered prayer
>when your chastening was on them.

17 Just as an expectant mother
>writhes-in-labor and cries out in her pangs
>when her birthing time is near;
>thus were we because of you, Holy One.

18 We too were expectant, we writhed-in-labor,
>but it was as though we birthed only wind.
>No victories have we won on earth,
>neither do the inhabitants of the world fall.

19 Your dead shall live; their corpses shall rise.
>Awake and sing for joy you who dwell in the dust!
>For your dew is a radiant dew,
>and the earth shall release those long dead.

Psalm 68:4–11

4 Sing to God, sing praises to her Name;
>exalt her who rides upon the clouds;
>HOLY is her Name, rejoice before her!

5 Mother of orphans and defender of widows,
>is God in her holy habitation!

6 God settles the solitary in a home bringing prisoners into prosperity;
>while the rebellious shall live in a wasteland.

7 God, when you marched before your people,
>when you moved out through the wilderness,

8 the earth shook, even the heavens poured down,
>at the presence of God, the One of Sinai,

at the presence of God, the God of Israel.

⁹ Rain in abundance, God, you showered abroad;
  when your heritage grew weary you prepared rest.

¹⁰ Your creatures found a dwelling in her;
  God, you provided in your goodness for the oppressed.

¹¹ The AUTHOR OF LIFE gave the word;
  the women who proclaim the good news are a great army.

1 Thessalonians 4:13 Now we do not want you to be ignorant, sisters and brothers, about those who have fallen asleep, so that you might not grieve as those do who have no hope. ¹⁴ For since we believe that Jesus died and rose, even so they who sleep, will God by Jesus, bring with him. ¹⁵ For this we declare to you by the word of the Most High God, that we who are alive, who remain until the coming of Jesus, will not precede those who have fallen asleep. ¹⁶ For Jesus himself, with a command, in the voice of the archangel and with the trumpet of God, will descend from heaven, and the dead in Christ will rise first. ¹⁷ Then we who are alive who are left, together with them, will be caught up in the clouds to meet Jesus in the air; and so we will be with Jesus forever. ¹⁸ Therefore comfort one another with these words.

Luke 2:1 Now it happened in those days that a decree went out from Caesar Augustus that all the world should be registered (for taxation). ² This was the first registration and occurred while Quirinius was governor of Syria. ³ So all went to be registered; each to their own towns. ⁴ Joseph also went up from Galilee, out of the city of Nazareth into Judea, to the city of David called Bethlehem, for he was from the house and heritage of David. ⁵ He went to be registered with Mary, to whom he was betrothed and who was pregnant. ⁶ So it was, that, while they were there, the time came for her to birth her child. ⁷ And she gave birth to her firstborn son and swaddled him, and laid him in a manger, because there was no place for them in the inn.

⁸ Shepherds were in that region there staying in the fields, keeping watch over their flock by night. ⁹ Then an angel of the Most High God came upon them, and the glory of the Living God shone around them, and they were greatly terrified. ¹⁰ But the angel said to them, "Fear not. Look! For I proclaim to you good news of great joy for all the people: ¹¹ For there is born to you this day a Savior who is the Messiah, the Sovereign God, in the city of David. ¹² This will be a sign for you: you will find a baby swaddled and lying in a manger." ¹³ And immediately there was with the angel a multitude of the heavenly array, praising God and saying,

¹⁴ "Glory to God in the highest heaven,
  and on earth peace among peoples whom God favors!"

¹⁵ And it happened when the angels had departed from them into heaven, the shepherds said to one another, "Let us go now to Bethlehem and see this thing that has come to

be, which the Sovereign God has made known to us." [16] So they came hurrying and found Mary and Joseph, and the baby lying in the manger. [17] Now seeing this, they made known what had been spoken to them about this child. [18] And all who heard marveled at what was spoken by the shepherds to them. [19] But Mary preserved all these words and pondered them in her heart. [20] The shepherds returned, glorifying and praising God for all they had heard and seen, it was just as it had been told them.

PROCLAMATION

Text Notes

The psalm portion ends with women proclaiming the good news of deliverance using the verbs that will come to mean "proclaim the gospel" in Hebrew and Greek (the LXX uses *euaggelizo*). Unfortunately, NRSV, RSV, CEB, and KJV obscure that this "company of preachers" is exclusively female.

The Epistle uses "Lord" repeatedly in such a way that it is not clear whether the author means God or Jesus. The translation above seeks to clarify the referents; however, the reader should be aware of the likely intentional ambiguity.

Preaching Prompts

The Hebrew Scriptures offer a variety of positions on life after death, including "sleep" to which all succumb, and none rise (see Job 14:10–12, 14). This unit of Isaiah uses the language of pregnancy and birth to speak of life beyond death. This first reading for Christmas brings images of a heavily pregnant woman into conversation with the heavily pregnant and laboring Virgin in the Gospel—though the text and tradition gloss over or minimize her travail. The pregnant woman is the people who have not been able to deliver themselves or have someone to deliver them—rather than a deliverer, they have only produced wind. God is perhaps midwife here. Because of God's response to her people's prayers across the ages, the equally heavily pregnant earth will one day give birth to the dead.

In both the first lesson and psalm, there is water that renews and refreshes dry places. In the regendered psalm, God is the mother of orphans (fatherless children in Hebrew idiom), protector of widows, and provides homes (families) for the lonely. She is also sovereign of the skies, source of rain, and shepherd of her people. The women who functioned as town criers, proclaiming good news of victory in times of war, proclaim the good news of God's providence.

The Epistle takes up the theme of the dead rising and makes it a promise guaranteed by Jesus's own resurrection. Each of these texts with its focus on birth, life, and life beyond frames the Gospel and its presentation of the good news of Mary's child and the portents of his birth which she pondered.

CHRISTMAS II

Isaiah 66:10–13; Psalm 103:1–17; 1 Peter 1:22–2:3;
Luke 2:15–20 or 2:1–20

Isaiah 66:10 Rejoice with Jerusalem, and celebrate with her
all you who love her;
rejoice with her in joy,
all who mourn deeply over her;
¹¹ in order that you all may nurse and be satisfied
from her comforting breast;
that you all may drink deeply and delight yourselves
from the glory of her breast.
¹² For so says the HOLY ONE OF OLD:
Watch! I will extend to her flourishing like a river,
and the wealth of the nations like an overflowing stream;
and you all shall nurse and be carried on her arm,
and you all shall be bounced on her knees.
¹³ As a mother comforts her child,
so will I comfort you all;
you all shall be comforted in Jerusalem.

Psalm 103:1–17

¹ Bless the FOUNT OF WISDOM, O my soul,
and all that is within me, bless her holy Name.
² Bless the FOUNT OF WISDOM, O my soul,
and forget not all her benefits.
³ She forgives all your sins
and heals all your infirmities;
⁴ She redeems your life from the grave
and crowns you with mercy and loving-kindness;
⁵ She satisfies you with good things,
and your youth is renewed like an eagle's.
⁶ SHE WHO IS WISDOM executes righteousness
and judgment for all who are oppressed.
⁷ She made her ways known to Miriam and Moses
and her works to the children of Israel.
⁸ WISDOM's womb is full of love and faithfulness,
slow to anger and overflowing with faithful love.
⁹ She will not always accuse us,
nor will she keep her anger forever.

¹⁰ She has not dealt with us according to our sins,
  nor rewarded us according to our wickedness.
¹¹ For as the heavens are high above the earth,
  so indomitable is her faithful love upon those who revere her.
¹² As far as the east is from the west,
  so far has she removed our sins from us.
¹³ As a mother's love for her children flows from her womb,
  so too does WISDOM's love for those who revere her flow from her womb.
¹⁴ For she herself knows whereof we are made;
  She remembers that we are but dust.
¹⁵ Our days are like the grass;
  we flourish like a flower of the field;
¹⁶ When the wind goes over it, it is gone,
  and its place shall know it no more.
¹⁷ But the faithful love of SHE WHO IS WISDOM endures forever
  on those who revere her,
  and her righteousness on children's children.

1 Peter 1:22 Now that you have purified your souls by your obedience to the truth so that you have the love without pretense of children raised together; from a pure heart love one another persistently. ²³ You have been born again, not of corruptible seed but of incorruptible seed through the living and enduring word of God. ²⁴ For:

  "All flesh is like grass
  and all its glory like the flower of grass.
  The grass withers,
  and the flower falls,
  ²⁵ but the word of the Living God abides forever."

This is the word that was proclaimed to you as good news. ²:¹ Lay aside, therefore, all malice, and all deceit, pretense, envy, and all slander. ² Like newborn babies, long for the pure spiritual milk, so that by it you may grow into salvation—³ if you have tasted that the Sovereign God is good.

See Gospel Reading in Christmas I.

PROCLAMATION

Text Notes

The poet responsible for Isaiah 66 seems to have reached beyond the Hebrew language for the expression "glory of her breast" in verse 11. The underlying expression "teat" or "udder" of glory may well have come from Akkadian and has an Arabic cognate (see the corresponding entry in the *Dictionary of Classical Hebrew*).

In verse 12, "flourishing" is a better, less-materialistic reading of *shalom* than "prosperity."

The one comforted by their mother in Isaiah 66:13 is a man; the grammar of his passive comforting relegates his mother to the end of the sentence and makes him the focus: "As a man is comforted by his mother. . . ." Common convention (JPS, NRSV, CEB) inverts the sentence, "as a mother comforts. . . ." Mother-love in Psalm 103:13 is attributed to a father: "As a father mother-loves his children" (using the verbal form of the noun "womb"). The verse could be translated: "As a father loves his children with a mother's love. . . ." As with Isaiah 66, the maternal image, here womb-love, is also attributed to God.

1 Peter 1:22 uses *philadelphia*, sibling-love, where I have translated "children raised together" rather than "sisters and brothers" to avoid excluding reader-hearers who do not identify with a binary understanding of gender. The divine mother's milk is described as "spiritual," a somewhat elliptical rendering of *logikos*, which has to do with "carefully thought-through, thoughtful" deliberations particularly in religious contexts. It also connotes "spiritual" in contrast with "literal." (See the corresponding entry in *A Greek-English Lexicon of the New Testament and Other Early Christian Literature* [known as BDAG for its authors]).

Preaching Prompts

These Christmas lessons center an image rarely proffered in liturgy or preaching but common in art and culture: the nursing mother as an icon of love. In Isaiah 66:11, Jerusalem is the nursing mother with abundant "comforting" breasts that are her "glory." (In the CEB she is full-breasted.) In Psalm 103, God's love is womb-love suggesting but not articulating an accompanying abundance of breastmilk (vv. 8, 13). In 1 Peter 2:2–3 God's children are to long for the gospel as babies long for milk and at the breast of God "taste and see that God is good"—offering a new way to hear that very common refrain. In Luke 2 the newly delivered Virgin Mother nurses her holy child through the visits of mortals and angels without notice in the text.

In Isaiah 66:13, the poet-prophet uses the image of a mother—clearly nursing in light of the earlier verses—as an image of God. This intersects in interesting ways with the parental image in the psalm; mother-love of human and divine parents in verses 8 and 13 provide the lexicon for divine imagery. Even with some masculine grammatical language in the texts, the dominant divine images are feminine, rooted in birthing, nursing, and mothering, a reversal of the more common dominant masculine and male imagery. Similarly, the Gospel presents a woman-born Sovereign God swaddled in human flesh, nourished at his mother's breast. Of all the changes that the Christmas miracle births into the world, the ability to experience and name God more richly can be easily neglected.

The imagery of pregnancy, birthing, nursing, and mothering is integral to the Christmas story. It is also the primary trope for women in the scriptures, often reducing them to one dimension. It is not, however, the universal experience of women, and biblical portrayals of women can be painful for those who cannot mother, were not mothered, or were poorly mothered. These images can also be frustrating for these who choose not to mother.

CHRISTMAS III

Wisdom 9:1–6, 9–11; Psalm 33:1–9; Colossians 1:15–20; John 1:1–14

Wisdom 9:1 "O God of my ancestors and Author of mercy,
  who have made all things by your word,
² and by your wisdom have formed humankind
  to govern the creatures you have made,
³ and oversee the world in holiness and righteousness,
  and renders judgment as the soul of righteousness:
⁴ Give me the wisdom that sits by your throne,
  and do not reject me from among your children.
⁵ For I am your slave, the child of your slave girl,
  one who is weak and short-lived,
  with little understanding of judgment and laws;
⁶ for even one who is perfect among human beings
  will be regarded as nothing without the wisdom that comes from you.
⁹ With you is Wisdom, she who knows your works
  and was present when you made the world;
  she knows what is pleasing in your sight
  and what is right according to your commandments.
¹⁰ Send her forth from the holy heavens,
  and from your throne of glory send her,
  that she may labor with me,
  and that I may learn what is pleasing to you.
¹¹ For she knows and understands all things,
  and she will guide me wisely in my actions
  and guard me with her glory.

Psalm 33:1–9

¹ Rejoice in the ALMIGHTY, you righteous;
  it is good for the just to sing praises.
² Praise SHE WHO IS MAJESTY with the harp;
  play to her upon the psaltery and lyre.

3 Sing for her a new song;
   sound a fanfare with all your skill upon the trumpet.
4 For the word of WISDOM is right,
   and all her works are sure.
5 She loves righteousness and justice;
   the faithful love of the MOTHER OF ALL fills the whole earth.
6 By the word of WISDOM were the heavens made,
   by the breath of her mouth all the heavenly hosts.
7 She gathers up the waters of the ocean as in a water-skin
   and stores up the depths of the sea.
8 Let all the earth revere SHE WHO IS WISDOM;
   let all who dwell in the world stand in awe of her.
9 For she spoke, and it came to pass;
   She commanded, and it stood fast.

Colossians 1:15 Jesus is the image of the invisible God, the firstborn of all creation; [16] for in him all things in the heavens and on earth were created, things visible and invisible, whether thrones or dominions or rulers or powers—all things have been created through him and for him. [17] Jesus himself is before all things, and in him all things hold together. [18] Jesus is the head of the body, the church; he is the beginning, the firstborn from the dead, so that he might come to have preeminence in everything. [19] For in Jesus all the fullness of God was well pleased to dwell, [20] and through Jesus God was well pleased to reconcile to Godself all things, whether on earth or in heaven, by making peace through the blood of his cross.

John 1:1 In the beginning was the Word, and the Word was with God, and the Word was God. [2] The Word was with God in the beginning. [3] Everything came into being through the Word, and without the Word not one thing came into being that came into being. What has come into being [4] in the Word was life, and that life was the light of all people. [5] The light shines in the bleakness, and the bleakness did not overtake it.

[6] There was a man sent from God, whose name was John. [7] He came as a witness to testify to the light, so that all might believe through him. [8] He himself was not the light, but he came to testify to the light. [9] The true light, which enlightens everyone, was coming into the world.

[10] He was in the world, and the world was created through him; yet the world did not know him. [11] To his own he came and his own did not receive him. [12] But to all who did accept him, who believed in his name, he empowered to become children of God—[13] that is, those who were born, not of blood or of the will of the flesh or of the will of a human person, but of God.

[14] And the Word became flesh and lived among us, and we have seen his glory, glory as of a parent's only child, full of grace and truth.

PROCLAMATION
Text Notes

The Greek word *pais* used in Wisdom 9:4 means both child and enslaved person. I choose the easier reading here and preserve the slave language in the following verse where two different words for an enslaved person occur.

Colossians uses the masculine pronoun repeatedly and does not include the name of Jesus in the Greek text. I have substituted it for some of the pronouns for smoothness and clarity.

Preaching Prompts

Today's Christmas readings focus on Wisdom and the Word. Both are invoked in the creation of the world; Wisdom in Wisdom 9:2 and Psalm 33:6, and the Word in John 1:1–2. Jesus is the word incarnate, unnamed in the Gospel portion. The Colossians reading names Jesus explicitly and links him to the creation of the world. This Sunday has traditionally focused on the preexistent Christ of John's Gospel, a concept expressed in grammatical gender (masculine for the Word and feminine for Wisdom in a similar portrayal), but ontologically beyond gender. These lessons present an opportunity to think about why we and our spiritual ancestors, our languages and theirs, gender things the way we do and what that really means.

The Wisdom reading also offers an opportunity to discuss the ubiquity of slavery in the biblical world and text. The scriptures use the language of slavery as more than a metaphor. Its normalcy is something with which we must contend. Many translations soften slave language to "servant." That seems dishonest given the total control—physical, sexual, reproductive, financial—over the lives and bodies of the persons at stake. Yet, it is hard to use slave language in scripture, prayer, and liturgy; doubly so for Black folk.

FIRST SUNDAY AFTER CHRISTMAS

Isaiah 40:1–8; Psalm 69:30–36; Galatians 4:1–7; Luke 2:25–38

(These texts can also be used for the Feast of the Presentation.)

Isaiah 40
[God speaks to heaven and earth]
1. "Comfort [them], comfort my people!" says your God.
2. "Speak heart-tender to Jerusalem, and cry to her
   that her term of service is fulfilled, that her iniquity is absolved,
   that she has received from the hand of the Righteous Judge double for all her sins."
3. A [heavenly] voice cries out:

"In the wilderness clear the way of the EVERLASTING GOD,
make smooth in the desert a highway for our God.
4 Every valley shall be lifted up,
and every mountain and hill made low;
the rugged ground shall become level,
and the rough places a plain.
5 Then the glory of the MAJESTY OF THE AGES shall be revealed,
and all people shall see it together,
for the mouth of the THUNDER OF SINAI has spoken."
6 A [heavenly] voice says, "Cry out!"
And I said, "What shall I cry?"
[The voice replied] All people are grass,
their fidelity is like the flower of the field.
7 The grass withers, the flower fades,
when the breath of the FIRE OF SINAI blows upon it;
surely the people are grass.
8 The grass withers, the flower fades;
but the word of our God will stand forever.

Psalm 69:30–36

30 I will praise the Name of God with a song;
I will magnify her with thanksgiving.
31 This will please the SAVING GOD more than an ox
or a bull with horn and hoof.
32 Let the oppressed see it and be glad;
you who seek God, let your hearts revive.
33 For the FAITHFUL ONE hears the needy,
and the prisoners who are hers, she does not despise.
34 Let heaven and earth praise her,
the seas and everything that moves in them.
35 For God will save Zion
and rebuild the cities of Judah;
and they shall dwell there and take possession of it.
36 And the children of her servants shall inherit it,
and those who love her Name shall dwell in it.

Galatians 4:1 I say that as long as heirs are minors, they are no better than slaves, though they are the masters of all; 2 but they remain under guardians and trustees until the time set by the father. 3 So also for us; while we were minors, we were enslaved by the constitutive elements of the world. 4 But when the fullness of time had come, God sent God's own Son, born of a woman, born under the law, 5 to redeem those who were under the law, so that we might receive adoption like children. [6] And because you are children, God has sent the Spirit of God's own Son into our hearts, crying, "Abba! Father!" [7] So you are no longer a slave but a child, and if a child then also an heir, through God.

Luke 2:25 Now, there was a man in Jerusalem whose name was Simeon; this man was righteous and devout, waiting to welcome the consolation of Israel, and the Holy Spirit, she rested upon him. [26] It had been revealed to him by the Holy Spirit that he would not see death before he had seen the Messiah of the Most High God. [27] Led by the Spirit, Simeon came into the temple. When the parents brought in the child Jesus, to do for him what was customary under that which was taught, [28] Simeon took him in his arms and praised God, saying,

> [29] "You release now your slave in peace, Master,
>   according to your word;
> [30] for my eyes have seen your salvation,
> [31] which you have prepared in the presence of all peoples,
> [32] a light for revelation to the Gentiles
>   and for glory to your people Israel."

[33] And the child's mother and father were amazed at what was being said about him. [34] Then Simeon blessed them and said to his mother Mary, "This child is set for the falling and the rising of many in Israel, and to be a sign provoking contention; [35] also, your own soul a sword will pierce so that the true hearts of many will be revealed."

[36] There was also a prophet, Anna the daughter of Phanuel, of the tribe of Asher. She was of a great age, having lived with her husband seven years after her marriage, [37] then as a widow to the age of eighty-four. She never left the temple but worshiped there with fasting and prayer night and day. [38] At that moment she came and began to praise God, and to speak about the child to all who were looking for the redemption of Jerusalem.

PROCLAMATION

Text Notes

An alternative opening for Simeon's prayer is, "Sovereign, now you are dismissing your servant. . . ." However, that mitigates the explicit slaveholding rhetoric. "Master" here is *despotos*: lord, master, slaveholder.

In general, these volumes will preserve "Father" in the Gospel when Jesus says it or when it pertains specifically to his Sonship/paternity. Likewise, these volumes will not whitewash slavery in the text and its world by softening it to servitude. That the enslaved could be beaten, killed, raped, and forced to breed more enslaved persons makes clear that slavery and its vocabulary is the appropriate translation for the assorted terms across the canons. The implications of slave language as normative in the text is something with which readers and hearers must wrestle honestly, particularly in light of the transatlantic trafficking of human persons and legacy of the American slavocracy, including in churches and denominations (discussed further below).

Most translations place the line about the trauma Mary will experience after the significance of Jesus as an afterthought. The syntax of the text includes her trauma as part of what unmasks human hearts.

Preaching Prompts

The temple scene involves a creative reading of Israelite traditions: Luke presents the earlier ritual restoration of Mary as "their" restoration, counter to the Torah, which requires the ritual for the new mother and portrays a "presentation" that has no biblical antecedent. Anna's residence in the temple makes sense in light of later rabbinic teaching that there was a special chamber on the temple campus in which women wove the temple curtains. (See *Carta's Illustrated Encyclopedia of the Holy Temple in Jerusalem,* which has a useful section on women's participation in the life of Israelite sanctuaries over time.)

These Christmastide lessons end with the good news of Jesus's birth being preached by an elderly female prophet and the joy of his birth tempered by a word of warning from another elder who is not styled as a prophet. This good news comes at a high cost.

The beautiful words of the poet-prophet in Isaiah 40 speak to a nation devastated and decimated by invasion, occupation, subjugation, exile, and virtual enslavement. This is not the experience of the American church writ large. And yet, these words still speak comfort to a church that has more often been the oppressor or on the side of the oppressor. It may be useful to invite dominant culture congregations and individuals with social and cultural privilege to hear this text spoken to those who lack it in response to them and the privilege they enjoy and its consequences.

Slave language in the Gospels and Epistles is ugly. It is tempting to soften it to servant, woman servant, maidservant, etc. The blood of more than six million Africans spilled in the Middle Passage cries out with the blood of every other enslaved person across time and space. We must confront slavery in the text and in the churches and institutions built on it and its rhetoric. We can retain the image of being adopted by God without a straw comparison to an enslaved person—who cannot even be considered a child according to Paul's rhetoric—to establish our relative worth.

FEAST OF THE HOLY NAME, JANUARY 1

Isaiah 7:3–16; Psalm 89:1–8, 14; Philippians 2:5–11; Luke 2:15–21

Isaiah 7:3 The HOLY ONE said to Isaiah, "Go out now to meet Ahaz, you and She'ar-jashub your son, at the end of the conduit of the upper pool on the highway to the Fuller's Field, [4] and say to him, 'Watch, hush, and fear not, and let not your heart faint on account of these two smoldering stumps of firebrands, because of the rage of Rezin and Aram or the son of Remaliah. [5] For indeed, Aram has plotted evil against you—with Ephraim and the son of Remaliah—saying, [6] 'Let us go up against Judah and cut off Jerusalem and conquer it for ourselves and make the son of Tabeel king in it;' [7] therefore thus says the Sovereign GOD:

'It shall not stand,
and it shall not come to pass.
[8] For the head of Aram is Damascus,
and the head of Damascus is Rezin.'

(In abut sixty-five years Ephraim will be shattered, no longer a people.)

[9] The head of Ephraim is Samaria,
and the head of Samaria is the son of Remaliah.
If you do not stand firm in faith,
you shall not stand firm at all.'"

[10] Again the HOLY ONE spoke to Ahaz, saying, [11] "Ask a sign of the HOLY ONE your God; from the deep of Sheol or the height of what lies above." [12] Yet Ahaz said, "I will not ask, and I will not test the HOLY ONE." [13] Then Isaiah said, "Hear now, House of David! Is it not enough that you exhaust mortals, that you must exhaust my God also? [14] Therefore the self-same Creator will give you a sign. See, the young woman is pregnant and she shall give birth to a son, and she shall name him Immanu-El. [15] He shall eat curds and honey when he knows how to refuse the evil and choose the good. [16] For before the child knows how to refuse the evil and choose the good, the land before whose two kings you dread will be deserted.

Psalm 89:1–8, 14

[1] I will sing of the faithful love of the FOUNT OF LIFE forever;
with my mouth I will make known your faithfulness from across the generations.
[2] When I declare that your faithful love is established forever;
your faithfulness is established in the heavens,
[3] [you responded,] "I have inscribed a covenant with my chosen one;
I have sworn an oath to the descendants of Bathsheba:
[4] 'I will establish your line forever,
your throne that I will build, will be to all generations.'"
[5] The heavens confess your wonders, O WOMB OF CREATION,

and to your faithfulness in the congregation of the holy ones;
6 For who in the skies can be compared to the WOMB OF LIFE?
who is like the MOTHER OF ALL among the children of the gods?
7 a dread God in the council of the holy ones,
great and terrible above all who surround her.
8 WARRIOR PROTECTRIX, who is mighty like you?
YOU WHO ARE, your faithfulness surrounds you.
14 Righteousness and justice are the foundations of your throne;
enduring love and faithfulness go before your face.

Philippians 2:5 Let the same mind be in you all that was in Christ Jesus,
6 who, though he was in the form of God,
did not regard equality with God
as something to be seized,
7 but emptied himself,
taking the form of a slave,
being born in human likeness;
then being found in human form,
8 he humbled himself
and became obedient to the point of death,
even death on a cross.
9 Therefore God also highly exalted Jesus
and gave him the name
that is above every name,
10 so that at the name of Jesus
every heavenly and earthly knee should bend,
along with those under the earth,
11 and every tongue should confess
that Jesus Christ is Savior,
to the glory of God the Sovereign.

Luke 2:15 And it happened when the angels had departed from them into heaven, the shepherds said to one another, "Let us go now to Bethlehem and see this thing that has come to be, which the Sovereign God has made known to us." 16 So they came hurrying and found Mary and Joseph, and the baby lying in the manger. 17 Now seeing this, they made known what had been spoken to them about this child. 18 And all who heard marveled at what was spoken by the shepherds to them. 19 But Mary preserved all these words and pondered them in her heart. 20 The shepherds returned, glorifying and praising God for all they had heard and seen, it was just as it had been told them.
21 After eight days had passed, it was time to circumcise the child; and he was called Jesus, his name was the name given by the angel before he was conceived in the womb.

PROCLAMATION

Text Notes

Isaiah's son's name means "a remnant will survive." He is a prophetic sign in the text. The stem that means "cut off" in Isaiah 7:6 also means "terrorize." Hebrew hearers would have recognized both meanings. The young woman, an *almah*, in 7:14 is not identified as a virgin, *betulah*. The text does not even stipulate that this is her first child. Many scholars, myself included, consider it possible that she was also the mother of Isaiah's (other) children with equally portentous names, She'ar Yashuv in 7:4 and Maher Shalal Hash Baz in 8:4. The woman's pregnancy is contemporaneous with Isaiah; she *is* pregnant, a descriptive adjective. The word "virgin" and the use of a future tense come from the LXX, rather than the Hebrew text, effectively transforming the text to read more easily as a prediction of Jesus.

In the traditional language of Psalm 89:3, God swears an oath to "David, my servant." Note that Bathsheba indeed has her own throne, symbolically if not literally, passed down to the Judean Queen Mothers (see 1 Kings 2:19). The children of the gods refer to any number of divine or semidivine beings, from other gods to angels depending on the age and redaction of the text. Warrior Protectrix in verse 8 is God of "hosts" or warriors.

Preaching Prompts

Biblical prophecy can include prediction; it is at its heart contemporaneous, interpreting the present and speaking to the people for God as well as speaking to God on behalf of the people. While the framers of the New Testament, and likely the followers of Jesus, interpreted Isaiah 7:14 with reference to Jesus, they did not negate its original meaning in its original context. They interpreted it in their contemporary context as we ought, affirming both interpretations.

Read in context, Isaiah 7:14 is not a prediction but a demonstration of God's reliable fidelity, available in each generation. The young woman in Isaiah is already pregnant. By the time her child is eating soft foods, the two nations threatening Judah will be gone. The presence of Isaiah's son "A Remnant Shall Survive" is a promise that Judah will not be destroyed while those two nations decline. The promise is faithful as is the God who made it.

Psalm 89 celebrates the eternal faithfulness of God, in this translation, expressing that *through* Bathsheba rather than *to* David. Such a reading does not redeem her rape; it does keep her centered in the story in which she continues to play a part.

Philippians 2 and Luke 2 are each traditional readings for the Feast of the Holy Name of Jesus observed on January 1. They celebrate the majesty of the name given by angels and the humble majesty of its bearer.

SECOND SUNDAY AFTER CHRISTMAS

Hosea 11:1–4, 7–9; Psalm 71:15–23;
2 Thessalonians 2:13–17; Matthew 2:13–18

Hosea 11:1 When Israel was a child, I loved them,
    and out of Egypt I called my child.
  2 They, the Baals, called to them,
    they went out to the Baals;
    they sacrificed and to idols,
    they offered incense.
  3 Yet it was I who walked toddling Ephraim,
    taking them by their arms;
    yet they did not know that I healed them.
  4 I led them with human ties,
    with bonds of love.
    I was to them like those
    who lift babies to their cheeks.
    I bent down to them and fed them.
  7 My people are bent on backsliding away from me.
    To the MOST HIGH they call,
    but God does not bring them up altogether.
  8 How can I give you up, Ephraim?
    How can I hand you over, Israel?
    How can I give you up like Admah?
    How can I make you like Zeboiim?
    My heart recoils within me;
    my compassion grows altogether warm.
  9 I will not release my raging fury;
    I will not again destroy Ephraim;
    for I am God and not a mortal,
    the Holy One in your midst,
    and I will not come in wrath.

Psalm 71:15–23

  15 My mouth will recount your righteousness,
    all day long [recount] your salvation,
    though I cannot know their counting.
  16 I come with the mighty deeds of the Sovereign GOD,
    I recall your righteousness, yours alone.
  17 God, you have taught me from my youth,

and even now I yet proclaim your wonders.

18 And yes, even to old age and gray hair;
God, do not forsake me until I proclaim your might
to the generation to come, and your power.

19 Your righteousness God is as the highest.
You who have done great things, God, who is like you?

20 You who have let me see many troubles and adversities
will restore me, bringing me to life;
from the depths of the earth
you will restore me bringing up.

21 You will magnify my greatness,
and turn and comfort me.

22 I, even I will praise you with the harp
for your faithfulness, my God;
I will sing praise to you with the lyre,
Holy One of Israel.

23 My lips will shout for joy as I sing praise to you;
even my soul which you have redeemed.

2 Thessalonians 2:13 Now we are bound to give thanks to God always on your account, sisters and brothers, beloved by the Messiah, because God chose you as the first fruits for salvation through sanctification by the Spirit and through belief in the truth. 14 For this purpose God called you through our proclamation of the gospel that you may obtain the glory of our Savior Jesus Christ.

15 Now then, sisters and brothers, stand firm and hold fast to the traditions that you were taught by us, either by [spoken] word or by our letter. 16 And now, may our Savior Jesus Christ himself and God our Maker, who loved us and through grace gave us eternal comfort and good hope, 17 comfort your hearts and strengthen them in every good work and word.

Matthew 2:13 Now after the sages had left Herod, an angel of God appeared to Joseph in a dream and said, "Get up, take the child and his mother, and flee to Egypt, and stay there until I tell you; for Herod is about to seek the child, to destroy him." 14 Then Joseph got up, took the child and his mother, and went to Egypt at night, 15 and was there until the death of Herod. This was to fulfill what had been spoken by God through the prophet,

"Out of Egypt I have called my son."

16 When Herod saw that he had been tricked by the sages, he was utterly infuriated, and he sent and killed all the children in Bethlehem and around it who were two years old or under, according to the time that he had learned from the sages. 17 Then was fulfilled what had been spoken through the prophet Jeremiah who said:

¹⁸ "A voice was heard in Ramah,
wailing and great lamentation,
Rachel weeping for her children,
and she refused to be consoled, because they are no more."

PROCLAMATION

Text Notes

Inconsistencies in the Hebrew, shifts between first and third person, have led to widely variant translations of Hosea 11:2–3. Some shift all the pronouns to "I/my" since God is speaking. Yet the text is sensible, as it is in most cases; where it is, I will preserve it. At this point in Israel's story, Ephraim refers to the separate Northern nation.

The number and gender of the sages or magi are indeterminate: grammatically, there is more than one, and only one of that number need be male. Matthew 2:15 quotes Hosea 11:1 and verse 18 quotes Jeremiah 31:15. "Tricked" in verse 16 can also mean "mocked."

The verb is missing from the second line of Psalm 71:15; I have repeated the first verb for clarity.

Preaching Prompts

Hosea offers a tender vision of Mother God cuddling and teaching her nursing toddler to walk and worrying about them when they go astray. The teenaged nation turns away from the wisdom and comfort of the divine parent who resolves to forestall her anger. In the psalm, the now mature nation has learned to appreciate the faithfulness of their holy parent. The Epistle can be read as pedagogy reinforcing the lesson of the psalm. Psalm 71:20 is one of the very few Hebrew biblical texts that can be read as having an understanding and expectation of resurrection. (It can also be read as the restoration to hell of a person at the brink of death.) While Hosea speaks longingly of the exodus, Matthew sees the journey of the holy family. As in the exodus, there is mortal peril to the baby boys of the Israelite people, a harbinger of genocide. Yet the God who restores and preserves life in the psalm is with the little family and through their lives, life will be extended to all.

FEAST OF THE EPIPHANY

Isaiah 60:1–6, 11; Psalm 67; 2 Timothy 1:5–10; Matthew 2:1–12

Isaiah 60:1 Arise daughter, shine daughter; for your light has come, daughter,
and the glory of the Holy One has risen upon you daughter.

2 For—watch now daughter!—Bleakness shall cover the earth,
  and thick bleakness the peoples;
  and upon you daughter, the Holy One will arise,
  and over you daughter, God's glory will appear.
3 Nations shall come to your light daughter,
  and monarchs to the brightness of your dawn daughter.
4 Lift your eyes round about daughter, and see;
  all of them gather, they come to you daughter;
  daughter, your sons shall come from far away,
  and your daughters shall be carried on their nurses' hips.
5 Then daughter, you shall see and be radiant;
  your heart, daughter, shall tremble and swell,
  because the abundance of the sea shall turn towards you daughter,
  the wealth of the nations shall come to you daughter.
6 A multitude of camels shall cover you daughter—
  young camels of Midian and Ephah—
  all those from Sheba shall come.
  They shall bring gold and frankincense,
  and shall proclaim the praises of the Holy One.
11 Your gates shall always be open daughter;
  day and night they shall not be shut,
  so that nations shall bring you their wealth daughter,
  being led by their monarchs.

Psalm 67

1 May God be merciful to us and bless us,
  show us the light of her countenance and come to us.
2 Let your ways be known upon earth,
  your saving health among all nations.
3 Let the peoples praise you, O God;
  let all the peoples praise you.
4 Let the nations be glad and sing for joy,
  for you judge the peoples with equity
  and guide all the nations upon earth.
5 Let the peoples praise you, O God;
  let all the peoples praise you.
6 The earth has brought forth her increase;
  may God, our own God, give us her blessing.
7 May God give us her blessing,
  and may all the ends of the earth stand in awe of her.

2 Timothy 1:5 Considering the recollection of your faith without pretense, a faith that lived first in your grandmother Lois and your mother Eunice, now I am persuaded that faith lives in you. [6] For this reason I remind you to reignite the gift of God that is within you through the laying on of my hands; [7] for God did not give us a spirit of cowardice, but one of power and of love and of self-control.

[8] Be not ashamed, then, of the testimony of our Savior or of me Christ's prisoner, rather share in suffering for the sake of the gospel, do so through the power of God, [9] who saved us and called us with a holy calling, not according to our works rather according to God's own purpose and grace which was given to us in Christ Jesus before the ages began. [10] Now it has now been revealed through the appearing of our Savior Christ Jesus, who negated death and brought life and immortality to light through the gospel.

Matthew 2:1 Now Jesus was born in Bethlehem of Judea in the days of King Herod, suddenly sages from the East came to Jerusalem, [2] asking, "Where is the one born king of the Judeans? For we have seen his star at its ascent and have come to reverence him." [3] When King Herod heard this, he was shaken, and all Jerusalem with him; [4] then calling together all the chief priests and religious scholars of the people, he inquired of them where the Messiah would be born. [5] They said to him, "In Bethlehem of Judea; for it has been written by the prophet:

[6] 'And you, Bethlehem, in the land of Judah,
  by no means are least among the rulers of Judah;
  for from you shall come a ruler
  who is to shepherd my people Israel.'"

[7] Then Herod secretly called for the sages and learned from them the time when the star had appeared. [8] Then he sent them to Bethlehem, saying, "Go, search diligently for the child, and when you have found him bring me word so that I may also go and reverence him." [9] When they had heard the king, they left, and there suddenly was the star that they had seen at its ascent going before them until it stopped over the place where the child was. [10] When they saw that the star had stopped, they rejoiced; their joy was exuberant. [11] On entering the house, they saw the child with Mary his mother; and they fell down and reverenced him. Then, opening their treasure, they offered him gifts of gold, frankincense, and myrrh. [12] And having been warned in a dream not to return to Herod, they left for their own country by another road.

PROCLAMATION

Text Notes

Isaiah 60 speaks to a feminine entity, Zion, Jerusalem frequently styled as God's daughter; each "you" and "your" is explicitly feminine and singular, rhythmic and repetitive in Hebrew. I have added "daughter" each place this occurs for the English speaker-reader-hearer. The daughters in verse 4 were already delineated; "hips" here is actually "side."

Bleakness: The thick bleakness of Isaiah 60:2 is the same (word) as the thick darkness in which God is veiled in other texts, i.e., Exodus 20:21; Deuteronomy 4:11, 5:22; 2 Samuel 22:10; 1 Kings 8:12.

"Spirit of fear" is a familiar and common translation of 2 Timothy 1:7. *Deilia* is cowardice; an important distinction. Fear is not a failing. It is a natural and healthy response. It is harmful to tell folks not to feel what they feel. What matters is how folk respond to fear.

Grammatically speaking, not all of the *magoi* need be male, only one; note: no number of sages is specified. "Religious scholars" is preferable to scribes, which can suggest copyists. The Gospel famously quotes Micah 5:2 that a ruler with ancient origins shall come from Bethlehem of Judah. There is a variant to that text which states that out of Bethlehem of Judah "one shall not come forth" to rule. It is worth considering that both traditions were known at the times of the setting and production of the Gospel. The line "least among the rulers" is specific to the Gospel; it is among the "thousands," i.e., clans in Hebrew and Aramaic (Targum and Peshitta). A different word for ruler is used in the LXX, *archon* vs. *hegemon*.

The word *Ioudaioi* is regularly translated "Jews" but also means "Judeans" in an age where an ethic name referred to a people, their land, language, and religion(s). "Judean" is often a preferable reading to "Jew" or "the Jews," which in contemporary discourse have often become an epithet in the mouths of anti-Semites. Further, the distinction is a helpful reminder that the Gospels refer to the Judeans of its world and not the Jewish communities of ours.

Preaching Prompts

These lessons frame a number of epiphanies: God's self-revelation and that of Christ to the world beyond Israel in Isaiah 60 and Psalm 67, in the traditional Epiphany Gospel, Matthew 2, and in 2 Timothy 1. These epiphanies are manifest in or accompanied by light, sometimes set in opposition to darkness, sometimes paired with it, requiring thoughtful exegesis in a world in which darkness and blackness are regularly equated with black and brown people set in opposition to whiteness and white people.

In the commentary on Isaiah 60 in the *Jewish Study Bible,* Benjamin Sommer observes a shift from the traditional pattern centering on a male monarch as a royal figure. Rather God's daughter-city Zion is the locus of liberation wrought by God without human delegation. This is a helpful alternative to the common veneration of monarchy and the fallible members of David's lineage. Similarly, it is God and not a human who judges women and men, "the peoples," with equity, in the psalm.

It is worth asking how the women in and behind these texts experienced and articulated their epiphanies. The promises of restoration and reunification to daughter Jerusalem can be heard as the promises to the daughters of Jerusalem, the mothers, wives, sisters, and daughters of those who are in exile and captivity. Lois and Eunice in 2 Timothy have their own stories of faith. What might they have told us in their own Epistle if they had not been relegated to grandmother and mother? (Note the absence of Timothy's male lineage.) These texts offer an opportunity to proclaim the ways in which God is manifest in the world in and beyond the scriptures, in old ways and new.

EPIPHANY I

Isaiah 51:4–8; Psalm 85; Hebrews 2:1–11; Mark 2:1–12

Isaiah 51:4 Listen to me, my people,
     and my nation, to me give heed;
     for a teaching shall from me go forth,
     and my justice for a light to the peoples.
     I will do so suddenly.
  5 My deliverance is near,
     my salvation has gone forth
     and my arms will govern the peoples;
     for me the coastlands wait,
     and upon my arm they await.
  6 Lift up your eyes to the heavens,
     and look to the earth below.
     For the heavens like smoke will vanish,
     the earth like a garment will wear out,
     and those who live on it will die like gnats;
     yet my salvation will be forever,
     and my deliverance will never be broken.
  7 Listen to me, you who know righteousness,
     you people who have my teaching in your hearts;
     fear not the reproach of others,
     and when they revile you, do not be dismayed.
  8 For like a garment a moth will devour them,
     and like wool a worm will consume them;
     yet my deliverance will be forever,
     and my salvation to all generations.

Psalm 85

1 FAITHFUL GOD, you have shown favor to your land;
  you turned around the captivity of Rebekah's line.
2 You lifted the iniquity of your people;
  you forgave all their sin. *Selah*
3 You withdrew all your wrath;
  you turned away from the fury of your rage.
4 Turn us around again, God of our salvation,
  and destroy your anger toward us.
5 Will you be angry with us forever?
  Will you extend your wrath from generation to generation?
6 Will you not turn us about again that we might live,
  so that your people may rejoice in you?
7 Show us your faithful love, LIVING GOD,
  and grant us your salvation.
8 Let me hear what God the SAVING ONE will speak,
  for she will speak peace to her people, to her faithful ones,
  let them not turn back to folly.
9 Surely her salvation is at hand for those who revere her,
  that her glory may dwell in our land.
10 Faithful love and truth will meet;
  righteousness and peace will kiss each other.
11 Truth from the ground will spring up,
  and righteousness from the heavens will look down.
12 The GRACIOUS GOD will give what is good,
  and our land will yield her produce.
13 Righteousness will go before her,
  and will make a path for her steps.

Hebrews 2:1 We must pay even more attention to what we have heard, so that we do not drift away from it. 2 For if the word spoken through angels was sure and every transgression or disobedience received a just penalty, 3 how can we escape if we neglect so great a salvation first spoken through the Anointed One and confirmed to us by those who heard him, 4 while God testified at the same time by signs and wonders and various miracles and by gifts of the Holy Spirit distributed according to God's will?

5 Now God did not subject the coming world, about which we are speaking, to angels.
6 But someone has testified somewhere,

"What is humanity that you remember them,
  or the woman born, that you care for them?

⁷ You have made them a little lower than the angels;
   you have crowned them with glory and honor,
⁸ subjecting all things under their feet."

Now in subjecting all things to them, God left nothing ungoverned. Now we do not yet see everything in subjection to them, ⁹ but we do see Jesus, who was made a little lower than the angels, now crowned with glory and honor because of the suffering of death, so that by the grace of God he might taste death for everyone.

¹⁰ It was fitting for God because of whom and for whom all that is, is, in bringing many daughters and sons to glory, to make the pioneer of their salvation perfect through sufferings. ¹¹ For the one who sanctifies and those who are sanctified are all of one. For this reason Jesus is not ashamed to call them sisters and brothers.

Mark 2:1 Now when Jesus returned to Capernaum after some days, it was reported that he was at home. ² And so many gathered around that there was no longer room for them, not even in front of the door, and he was speaking the word to them. ³ Then some women and men came, bringing to him a paralyzed person, carried by four of them. ⁴ And when they were not able to bring the person to Jesus because of the crowd, they uncovered the chamber above Jesus and, after having dug through it, they let down the mat on which the paralyzed person lay. ⁵ Now when Jesus saw their faith, he said to the paralyzed person, "Child, your sins are forgiven." ⁶ Now some of the scribes were sitting there, questioning in their hearts, ⁷ "Who is this speaking? [It is] Blasphemy! Who is able forgive sins but God alone?" ⁸ And at once Jesus knew in his spirit that they were discussing these questions among themselves and he said to them, "Why do you question in your hearts? ⁹ What is easier, to say to the paralyzed person, 'Your sins are forgiven,' or to say, 'Stand up and take your mat and walk'? ¹⁰ Yet so that you may know that the Son of Woman has authority on earth to forgive sins"—Jesus said to the paralyzed person: ¹¹ "To you I say, stand up, take your mat and go to your home." ¹² And the person stood up, and immediately took the mat and went out before all of them so that they were all amazed and glorified God, saying, "Nothing like this have we ever seen!"

PROCLAMATION

Text Notes

The Hebrew MT text presents two different forms of "captivity" in Psalm 85:1 supported by the LXX; NRSV, JPS, and Alter revise to "fortunes." "The line of Rebekah" replaces "Jacob." In verse 8, NRSV abandons the MT for the LXX, so there is no reason to do so. I preserve the Hebrew reading along with JPS and Alter.

Hebrews 2:6–8 quotes Psalm 8:4–6.

Mark 2:3 has "they came." Grammatically, the group could be a mixed-gender group, so that is how I render it. A subgroup of that group carries in the paralyzed person; even were that smaller group all male, that would not negate the possibility of women being included in the larger group. For that matter, there could have well been children following along, watching what was already a spectacle. Verse four has a noun that can mean "roof" or "chamber" and a verb that means uncover; uncovering the chamber makes more sense than uncovering the roof. Jesus uses the gender-neutral "child" in verse 5, which NRSV renders as "son." (The narrator's previous descriptions of the person have all used masculine gender.) Blasphemy appears in verse 7 as an exclamation and accusation. If the reader does not modulate your voice appropriately, it may help to have the introductory phrase, "it is." This lectionary project uses "Son of Woman" in lieu of "Son of Man," given that the latter expression is inclusive and refers to humanity in Greek, Hebrew, and English and that the marvel of the Incarnation is that Jesus did not have a human father, rather, that he is mortal, descending from Eve through Mary.

Preaching Prompts

These lessons link physical salvation and restoration of the people with forgiveness of sins in the first lesson and in the psalm with a wider salvation that transforms death through the death of Jesus in the Epistle with the healing and saving touch of Jesus, accompanied by the forgiveness of sin.

The poet writing in Isaiah's name envisions God's restoration of Israel, and for those who struggled to see the vision, she reminds them of who God is—the one who waters the wilderness—and what God has done. God promises a salvation that will endure when even the earth crumbles away. That salvation is national and corporate and not individual, generally meaning deliverance from the physical threats of individuals and nations.

The psalm is a plea for Israel's deliverance; it is set in a period when Israel is subject to the vicious whims of the Assyrians. Unfortunately, the dominant theology to which they subscribe is that their national difficulties were their punishment for their sins. Yet even within those parameters, they know that God is a God who continues to forgive, and so God is worthy of their trust.

The Epistle and Gospel both wrestle with Jesus as something more than human and woman-born at the same time. Jesus, who would taste death as do we all, changed it for the rest of us and, while we yet live, offers the forgiveness of sins, a divine prerogative at home in his human-yet-more flesh. This last is Mark's epiphany for the day.

EPIPHANY II

Proverbs 4:1–13; Psalm 25:4–12; Galatians 1:6–12; Mark 2:13–28

Proverbs 4:1 Listen, children, to the instruction of a parent,
and be attentive to know understanding.
2 For I give you good instruction;
do not forsake my teaching.
3 I was still a child with my father,
and my mother's only [child].
4 And I was taught, and it was said to me,
"Let your heart hold fast my words;
keep my commandments and you shall live.
5 Acquire wisdom, acquire understanding:
Do not forget, nor turn away
from the words of my mouth.
6 Do not forsake her, and she will keep you;
love her, and she will preserve you.
7 The beginning of wisdom is this:
Acquire wisdom, and whatever else you acquire, acquire insight.
8 Esteem her and she will exalt you;
she will honor you if you embrace her.
9 She will place on your head a graceful garland;
she will present to you a glorious crown."
10 Hear my child and receive my words,
that the years of your life may be many.
11 In the way of wisdom have I taught you;
I have led you in the paths of uprightness.
12 When you walk, your step will not be hindered;
and when you run, you will not stumble.
13 Hold fast to instruction; do not let go;
guard her, for she is your life.

Psalm 25:4–12

4 Make known to me your ways, Ageless God;
teach me your paths.
5 Guide me in your truth, and teach me,
for you are the God of my salvation;
for you I wait all day long.
6 Remember your maternal love, O Womb of Life,
and your faithful love,
for they have been from of old.

7 The sins of my youth and my transgressions remember not;
   according to your faithful love remember me,
   for the sake of your goodness, GRACIOUS ONE.
8 Good and upright is the FOUNT OF WISDOM,
   therefore she instructs sinners in the way.
9 She guides the humble in what is just,
   and teaches the humble her way.
10 All the paths of the WISDOM OF THE AGES are faithful and true
   for those who keep her covenant and her decrees.
11 For your Name's sake, LOVING GOD,
   pardon my guilt, for it is great.
12 Who are they that revere the HOLY ONE OF OLD?
   She will teach them the way that they should choose.

Galatians 1:6 I marvel how quickly you all have turned from the one who called you in the grace of the Messiah and are turning to a another gospel. 7 Not that there is another but, there are some who are confusing you all, wanting to distort the gospel of the Messiah. 8 But even if we or a messenger from heaven should proclaim to you all a gospel other than what we proclaimed to you, let that one be accursed! 9 As we have said before, so now I repeat, if anyone proclaims to you a gospel contrary to what you received, may they be cursed!

10 For am I now seeking to persuade the woman-born or God's approval? Or am I seeking to please the children of Eve? Were it the woman-born I was pleasing, I would not be a slave of Christ. 11 For I want you to know, sisters and brothers, that the gospel that was proclaimed by me is not from the children of earth and Eve. 12 for I did not receive it from a human person nor was I taught it, rather I received it through a revelation of Jesus the Messiah.

Mark 2:13 Now Jesus went out again beside the sea and the whole crowd gathered around him and he taught them. 14 And as he was walking along he saw Levi son of Alphaeus sitting at the tax booth and he said to him, "Follow me." And he got up and followed him.

15 Then as Jesus reclined to eat in Levi's house, many tax collectors and sinners were also reclining to eat with Jesus and his disciples, for there were many who followed him. 16 Now when the biblical scholars among the Pharisees saw that Jesus was eating with sinners and tax collectors, they said to his disciples, "Why does he eat with tax collectors and sinners?" 17 And when Jesus heard this, he said to them, "The women and men who are well have no need of a physician, rather those who are sick do; not to call the righteous have I come but rather sinners."

18 Now John's disciples and the Pharisees were fasting and people came and said to Jesus, "Why do John's disciples and the disciples of the Pharisees fast, but your disciples do not fast?" 19 And Jesus said to them, "The attendants of the bridal chamber cannot fast while the bridegroom is with them, can they? As long as they have the bridegroom with

them, they cannot fast. ²⁰ Yet the days will come when the bridegroom is taken away from them and then they will fast on that day. ²¹ No one sews a piece of unshrunk cloth on an old garment lest the patch pulls away from it, the new from the old, and a worse tear is formed. ²² And no one puts new wine into old wineskins lest the wine burst the skins and the wine is lost with the wineskins rather, one puts new wine into fresh wineskins."

²³ Now it was that Jesus was going through the grainfields on the sabbath and as his disciples began the path, they were plucking heads of grain. ²⁴ Then the Pharisees said to him, "Look, why are they doing what is not permissible on the sabbath?" ²⁵ And Jesus said to them, "Have you never read what David did when he was in need and hungry and his companions along with him? ²⁶ How he entered the house of God when Abiathar was high priest and ate the bread of the Presence which it is not permissible for any but the priests to eat, and gave some to his companions?" ²⁷ Then Jesus said to them, "The sabbath was made for the woman-born and not the woman-born for the sabbath. ²⁸ Thus the Woman-Born Son is sovereign, even of the sabbath."

PROCLAMATION

Text Notes

Supplying "parent" in Proverbs 4:1 in lieu of "father" provides balance with the mention of father and mother in verse 3.

To "wait" in Psalm 25:5 also includes hoping; the psalmist waits with expectation. God's maternal love in verse 6 emanates from her womb, which provides the grammatical root for this love.

In Galatians 1:10–11, I translate anthropos, "human," variably in the passage: as "children of Eve" and "children of earth and Eve" based on the Hebrew origin of the phrase, *ben adam* in which *adam* shares a root with the ground, *adamah* from which humanity was created. I also employ "woman born" in verse 10.

In Mark 2:24 and verse 26, "permissible" more accurately conveys the sense of "what is right" than the NRSV translation of "lawful," which may lead the reader/hearer to an unnecessary binary understanding of law and gospel. In verse 27, I use "woman-born" for humanity, and in verse 28, "Woman-Born Son" for Jesus. Historically, other translations have included "son of man," used in both testaments in KJV, deceptively reserved for the NT in the NRSV where mortal is used in the HB as it is in JPS. (Deceptively in that it misleads readers to think that the title "Son of Man" is a New Testament title that applies solely to Jesus.)

Preaching Prompts

The epiphanies of the day come through teaching. The teaching of children in the Hebrew wisdom tradition is a bit more egalitarian than other literature streams in the Hebrew Bible. The wisdom and teaching of mother and father are often exhorted in Proverbs. Wisdom and understanding are feminine nouns; both are personified here and frequently throughout the Hebrew Bible, Deuterocanonical and postbiblical literature, and to a small degree in the New Testament. The psalm declares that it is out of God's goodness and love that she teaches humanity a better way in order that they not sin. The Epistle and Gospel elevate the teaching of Christ. In the Epistle, the divine origins of the Gospel are emphasized. In the Gospel, Jesus is the living embodiment of the wisdom of God with us in the world.

This week's sermon could focus on the breath of wisdom ways, ways of learning, understanding, and teaching in the text and in the world and it reads the text. One might emphasize folk wisdom and motherwit that can be for androcentric ways of learning that hit traditional knowledge against Western knowledge, lay midwives against medical professionals, cultural knowledge against anthropological studies, etc. One might invoke the mother who may have taught Jesus scripture and raised him to be the kind of man he was, nurtured his compassion, and taught him wisdom and understanding according to the model in Proverbs, and perhaps, taught him to interpret the scriptures with nuance.

FEAST OF THE PRESENTATION, FEBRUARY 2

(The Feast falls variably in early Epiphany. For simplicity and consistency, it is placed after the Second Sunday of Epiphany in these volumes.)

Leviticus 12:1–8; Psalm 48:1–3, 9–14; 1 John 5:1–5; Luke 2:22–38

Leviticus 12:1 The HOLY ONE OF SINAI spoke to Moses, saying: ² Speak to the women and men of Israel, saying:

When a woman conceives and gives birth to a male, she shall be taboo seven days; as during the days of her menstruation, she shall be taboo. ³ On the eighth day the flesh of his foreskin shall be circumcised. ⁴ Then, thirty and three days shall she sit in blood purification; she shall not touch any holy thing, or come into the sanctuary, until the days of her restoration are fulfilled. ⁵ Now, if she gives birth to a female, she shall be taboo two weeks, as in her menstruation; her time of blood purification shall be sixty-six days.

⁶ On completing the days of her purification for a daughter or for a son she shall bring a yearling lamb for a burnt offering—and a pigeon or a turtledove for a sin offering—to the priest at the entrance of the tent of meeting. ⁷ Then he shall offer it before the FIRE OF SINAI and make atonement on her behalf and she shall be restored from her flow of blood. This is the teaching for the woman who gives birth to a female or male. ⁸ If she cannot afford a sheep, she shall take two turtledoves or two pigeons, one for a burnt offering and the second for a sin offering; and the priest shall make atonement on her behalf, and she shall be restored.

Psalm 48:1–3, 9–14

¹ Great is the AGELESS GOD and greatly praised,
  in the city of our God is God's holy mountain.
² Beautiful in elevation, the joy of all the earth,
  Mount Zion, in the far north,
  is the city of the great Sovereign.
³ Within her citadels God
  has made herself known as a bulwark.
⁹ We contemplate your faithful love, God,
  in the midst of your temple.
¹⁰ Like your Name, God, your praise,
  reaches to the ends of the earth.
  Your right hand is filled with righteousness.
¹¹ Let Mount Zion be glad,
  let the towns of Judah rejoice
  because of your judgments.
¹² Go about Zion, go all around her;
  count her towers.
¹³ Set your hearts upon her ramparts;
  go through her citadels,
  that you may recount to the next generation:
¹⁴ For this God is our God, our God forever and ever.
  She will be our guide until we die.

1 John 5:1 Everyone who believes that Jesus is the Messiah is born of God, and everyone who loves the parent loves the child of the parent. ² By this we know that we love the children of God, when we love God and undertake God's commandments. ³ For the love of God is this, that we keep God's commandments. And God's commandments are not difficult, ⁴ for anything born of God conquers the world. And this is the victory that conquers the world, our faith. ⁵ Who is it that conquers the world but the one who believes that Jesus is the Son of God?

Luke 2:22 Now when the days of their purification were fulfilled according to the teaching of Moses, they brought Jesus up to Jerusalem to present him to the Holy One: ²³ As it is written in the teaching of the Sovereign God, "Every male who opens the womb [as firstborn] shall be called holy to the Sovereign One." ²⁴ So they offered a sacrifice according to what is stated in the teaching of the Holy One, "a pair of turtledoves or two young pigeons."
²⁵ Now, there was a man in Jerusalem whose name was Simeon; this man was righteous and devout, waiting to welcome the consolation of Israel, and the Holy Spirit, she rested on him. ²⁶ It had been revealed to him by the Holy Spirit that he would not see death before

he had seen the Messiah of the Most High God. [27] Led by the Spirit, Simeon came into the temple. When the parents brought in the child Jesus, to do for him what was customary under that which was taught, [28] Simeon took him in his arms and praised God, saying,

[29] "You release now your slave in peace, Master,
according to your word;
[30] for my eyes have seen your salvation,
[31] which you have prepared in the presence of all peoples,
[32] a light for revelation to the Gentiles
and for glory to your people Israel."

[33] And the child's mother and father were amazed at what was being said about him. [34] Then Simeon blessed them and said to his mother Mary, "This child is set for the falling and the rising of many in Israel, and to be a sign provoking contention; [35] also, your own soul a sword will pierce so that the true hearts of many will be revealed."

[36] There was also a prophet, Anna the daughter of Phanuel, of the tribe of Asher. She was of a great age, having lived with her husband seven years after her marriage, [37] then as a widow to the age of eighty-four. She never left the temple but worshiped there with fasting and prayer night and day. [38] At that moment she came and began to praise God, and to speak about the child to all who were looking for the redemption of Jerusalem.

PROCLAMATION

Text Notes

The traditional language "clean" and "unclean" is deeply implicated in biased treatment of women and girls, particularly after the onset of menstruation. The language lends itself easily to a debased understanding of women and girls that is inconsistent with full humanity and the image of God. These two distinct words, which are not antonyms, have the sense of being temporarily taboo, not ready to rejoin community, and restoration to a communally appropriate state (see Ilona Rashkow's *Taboo or Not Taboo*). The "purification" requires time, ritual bathing, and an offering. The use of the word "atonement" in verse 8 has made it easier to construct women's bodies and reproductive acts as in some way tainted. However, even moderating the language does not ameliorate the ways in which women and their bodies and reproductive biology are treated as dangerous and in need of control.

In the world of the Hebrew Scriptures, women are impregnated; in verse 2, the Hiphil verb is causative, "she is seeded/caused to bear seed." Contemporary translations tend to use "conceive," reflecting subsequent understanding.

In Psalm 48, Zion's superlatives hail from other cultures identifying their God as God of all the earth using the specific vocabulary of surrounding nations: *nof* signals "elevation" but is also the Egyptian name of Memphis, the capital city (and may also mean "fair," see JPS). Zaphon is the home of the Canaanite gods and is in the farthest northern reach, unlike Zion/Jerusalem. In verse 14, God will be our God "until death"; "until we die" makes clear that it is not God who will die.

Luke 2:22 makes Mary's obligation under the Torah "theirs": Joseph's as well; this is counter to the text and practice between Leviticus and Luke and subsequent rabbinic and contemporary Jewish practice.

Preaching Prompts

When overlaid with the androcentrism, patriarchy, and occasional misogyny of the text, the ritual and language for the restoration to the community sounds harsh and discriminatory to many contemporary and non-Jewish ears. It is helpful to remember that biblical Hebrew has a much smaller vocabulary than English and uses some words in ways that extend far beyond their literal meaning. In Leviticus 12, "purify," "atone," and "sin offering" apply to cleansing the woman and her physical spaces, including the sanctuary, from blood taboo, which was not a matter of sin or transgression. Arguably this period afforded the new mother rest and bonding time; the additional time for the female infant may account for the occasional vaginal discharge (or appearance of such) observable in newborn girls.

The "Churching of Women" is a Christian rite likely derived from these Leviticus and Luke texts, previously practiced in Catholic and Anglican congregations where a new mother refrained from attending church for four to six weeks and upon her return prayed a prayer of thanksgiving and received a blessing. However, some women experienced isolation and stigma, treated as unclean until they were "churched." The ritual has fallen into disuse.

While all spilled blood requires purification with both ritual and hygienic components, women and girls were subject to blood taboo and purity regulations. Contemporarily, our society seems obsessed with which bodies bleed and bear which organs to categorize and gender and assign identities and restrooms. Without either passing judgment on another culture or co-opting the specific practice of another religion, we can make physical and ritual space for human bodies in all of their life-stage changes and welcome and rewelcome folk to and back to the community upon and after significant transitions. This text can provide an opportunity to think about how we reintegrate a transperson into the congregation.

EPIPHANY III

2 Kings 5:1–4, 9–14; Psalm 103:1–17;
1 Corinthians 12:1, 4–11; Mark 3:1–12

2 Kings 5:1 Naaman, commander of the army of the ruler of Aram, was a great man in the sight of his master and highly esteemed, because through him the HOLY ONE had given victory to Aram. The man, a great warrior, was diseased in his skin. ² Now Aramean troops went out and took captive from the land of Israel a young girl, and she was placed before Naaman's wife. ³ She said to her mistress, "If only my lord were with the prophet who is in Samaria! He would take his skin disease away." ⁴ So Naaman went in and told his master the girl from the land of Israel had said this and this.

⁹ Then Naaman came with his horses and chariot and stood at the entrance of Elisha's house. ¹⁰ Elisha sent a messenger to him, who said, "Go, wash in the Jordan seven times, and your flesh shall be restored, and you shall be unblemished." ¹¹ But Naaman became angry and left, saying, "Look here! I thought that for me he would surely come out and stand and call on the name of the MOST HIGH, his God, and would wave his hand over the spot, and take away the skin disease! ¹² Are not Abana and Pharpar, the rivers of Damascus, better than all the waters of Israel? Could I not wash in them, and be restored?" Then he turned and went away in a rage. ¹³ But his slaves approached and said to him, "My father, were it a great thing the prophet told you to do, would you not have done it? How much more, when what he said to you was, 'Wash, and be restored?" ¹⁴ So he went down and immersed himself seven times in the Jordan, according to the word of the man of God; his flesh was renewed like the flesh of a little boy, and he was restored.

Psalm 103:1–17

¹ Bless the FOUNT OF WISDOM, O my soul,
  and all that is within me, bless her holy Name.
² Bless the FOUNT OF WISDOM, O my soul,
  and forget not all her benefits.
³ She forgives all your sins
  and heals all your infirmities;
⁴ She redeems your life from the grave
  and crowns you with mercy and loving-kindness;
⁵ She satisfies you with good things,
  and your youth is renewed like an eagle's.
⁶ SHE WHO IS WISDOM executes righteousness
  and judgment for all who are oppressed.
⁷ She made her ways known to Miriam and Moses
  and her works to the children of Israel.

⁸ WISDOM's womb is full of love and faithfulness,
    slow to anger and overflowing with faithful love.
⁹ She will not always accuse us,
    nor will she keep her anger forever.
¹⁰ She has not dealt with us according to our sins,
    nor rewarded us according to our wickedness.
¹¹ For as the heavens are high above the earth,
    so indomitable is her faithful love upon those who revere her.
¹² As far as the east is from the west,
    so far has she removed our sins from us.
¹³ As a mother's love for her children flows from her womb,
    so too does WISDOM's love for those who revere her flow from her womb.
¹⁴ For she herself knows whereof we are made;
    She remembers that we are but dust.
¹⁵ Our days are like the grass;
    we flourish like a flower of the field;
¹⁶ When the wind goes over it, it is gone,
    and its place shall know it no more.
¹⁷ But the faithful love of SHE WHO IS WISDOM endures forever
    on those who revere her,
    and her righteousness on children's children.

1 Corinthians 12:1 Now about spiritual gifts, sisters and brothers, I do not want you to be ignorant. ⁴ Now there are diversities of gifts, but the same Spirit. ⁵ And there are diversities of ministries, but the same Sovereign. ⁶ And there are diversities of works, but it is the same God who works all of them in everyone. ⁷ To each person is given the manifestation of the Spirit for mutual good. ⁸ To one woman or man through the Spirit is given a word of wisdom, and to another a word of knowledge according to the same Spirit: ⁹ To another faith by the same Spirit, to another gifts of healing by the one Spirit, ¹⁰ to yet another working miracles, to another prophecy, to yet another discernment of spirits, to another families of tongues, to another the translation of tongues. ¹¹ All these are activated by one and the same Spirit, who allots to each one individually just as the Spirit chooses.

Mark 3:1 Now Jesus returned to the synagogue and a person was there who had a withered hand. ² And the women and men in the synagogue were watching him carefully to see whether he would cure the person on the sabbath so that they might accuse him. ³ Then Jesus said to the person who had the withered hand, "Come up to the middle." ⁴ Then Jesus said to the women and men in the synagogue, "Is it permissible to do good or to do evil on the sabbath, to save life or to kill?" But they were silent. ⁵ And looking around at them with anger Jesus was grieved at their hardness of heart and said to the person, "Stretch out your hand." And the person stretched it out and their hand was restored. ⁶ Then the Pharisees went out with the Herodians and immediately began to conspire against Jesus, how they might destroy him.

⁷ Then Jesus with his disciples departed to the sea and a great multitude from Galilee followed, and from Judaea, ⁸ Jerusalem, Idumea, beyond the Jordan, and the region around Tyre and Sidon, hearing all that he was doing, they came to him. ⁹ And he told his disciples to have a boat at hand for him because of the crowd of women, children, and men lest they crush him. ¹⁰ For he had cured many, so that as many as had diseases pressed upon him to touch him. ¹¹ And the unclean spirits, when they saw him, they fell down before him and shrieked, "You are the Son of God!" ¹² But Jesus rebuked them strongly not to make him known.

PROCLAMATION

Text Notes

The word "lord/master" is used for persons who enslave other persons and for God in the scriptures; it will only be used for human beings in this work. "Lord" appears as the title of Naaman, his commander, the enslavers of the girl in Acts, and God in verse 6 of the psalm.

In 2 Kings 5:3, "take away" the disease is literally "gather." The language "clean/unclean" can be stigmatizing and does not accurately convey their wider meanings. In verse 14, the renewal of his flesh is "turned [into] the flesh of a little boy." The specific skin disease mistranslated as leprosy throughout the scriptures does not result in loss of extremities but does infect houses and walls, counter to leprosy.

Mother-love in Psalm 103:13 is attributed to a father: "As a father mother-loves his children" (using the verbal form of the noun "womb"). The verse could be translated: "As a father loves his children with a mother's love. . . ." Maternal love, here womb-love, is attributed to God.

The generic "they" in the Gospel is expanded to reflect the women and men who would've been present in the synagogue, similarly the crowd in verse 9. "Permissible" in Mark 3:5 is "what is right"; it is not about what is codified as legal in civil or religious law.

Preaching Prompts

In these lessons, God's power is manifest through healing, first of the Gentile, Syrian military commander—a beneficence that is not restricted to Israelites, then the praying soul in the psalm and all those Jesus encounters in Mark. The Epistle offers pedagogy on the ongoing work and fruit of the spirit, including healing.

It may be worthwhile to consider why Mark frames the introduction of Jesus as the enfleshed power of God with this extended series of healing miracles. It demonstrates a concern for the immediate contextual physical well-being of God's children. This is a gospel of transformation and restoration, not some far-off heavenly salvation. Rather than focus on the miraculous healings which are not a regular feature of the lived experience of most Christian communities, there is an opportunity to focus on the ways in which the church and her people can affect healing, restoration, and transformation in the actual lived lives and sometimes bodies of the peoples in our communities.

What kinds of healing can we bring to women and children who make up the majority of the underhoused and underfed that will have a direct impact on their physical health as well as their spiritual well-being? What can we do as church to safeguard the vulnerable lives of bullied children, teens, and younger children coming to terms with and articulating their sexual and gender identities? Lastly, "disciples" is more fulsome and inclusive term than "apostles." The former most certainly includes women even if they are not articulated in Mark, while the latter is restricted to men—but only in the Gospels.

EPIPHANY IV

Jeremiah 9:17–22; Psalm 34:1–14; Romans 16:1–16; Mark 3:13–35

Jeremiah 9:17 Thus says the SOVEREIGN of the Vanguard of Heaven:
Reason within yourselves, and call for the keening women
and they shall come;
send for the wise, skilled women
and they shall come.

18 Let them quickly raise a wailing over us,
so that our eyes may run down with tears,
and our eyelids flow with water.
19 For a sound of wailing is heard from Zion:
"How we are ruined! We are utterly shamed,
because we have left the land,
because they have cast down our dwellings."
20 Hear now women, the word of SHE WHO THUNDERS,
and let your ears receive the word of God's mouth;
teach to your daughters a wailing,
each woman her neighbor-woman a keening:
21 "Death has come up into our windows,
it has entered our palaces,
to cut off the children from the streets
and the young women and young men from the squares."

²² Thus says the DREAD GOD:

"The corpses of the woman-born shall fall
like dung upon the open field,
like sheaves behind the reaper,
and no one shall gather them."

Psalm 34:1–14

¹ I will bless SHE WHO IS GOD at all times;
her praise shall ever be in my mouth.

² I will glory in SHE WHO IS STRENGTH;
let the humble hear and rejoice.

³ Proclaim with me the greatness of SHE WHO IS EXALTED
and let us exalt her Name together.

⁴ I sought SHE WHO SAVES, and she answered me
and delivered me out of all my terror.

⁵ Look upon her and be radiant,
and let not your faces be ashamed.

⁶ I called in my affliction and SHE WHO HEARS heard me
and saved me from all my troubles.

⁷ The messenger of SHE WHO SAVES encompasses those who revere her,
and she will deliver them.

⁸ Taste and see that SHE WHO IS DELIGHT is good;
happy are they who trust in her!

⁹ Revere SHE WHO IS GOD, you that are her saints,
for those who revere her lack nothing.

¹⁰ The young lions suffer want for food and starve,
but those who seek SHE WHO PROVIDES lack no good thing.

¹¹ Come, children, listen to me;
I will teach you the reverence of SHE WHO IS MAJESTY.

¹² Who is the woman or man that desires life,
and would love long days to enjoy good?

¹³ Keep your tongue from evil,
and your lips from speaking deceit.

¹⁴ Turn from evil, and do good;
seek peace, and pursue it.

Romans 16:1 I commend to you all our sister Phoebe, a deacon of the church in Cenchreae, ² so that you all may receive her in Christ as is worthy of the saints, and stand by her in whatever thing she may need of you, for she has been a benefactress of many, and of myself as well.

³ Greet Prisca and Aquila, my coworkers in Christ Jesus, ⁴ and who for my life risked their necks, to whom not only I give thanks, but also all the churches of the Gentiles, ⁵ and the church in their house. Greet Epaenetus my beloved, who was the first fruit in Asia for Christ. ⁶ Greet Mary, who has worked much among you all. ⁷ Greet Andronicus and Junia, my kin and my fellow prisoners; they are eminent among the apostles, and they were in Christ before I was. ⁸ Greet Ampliatus, my beloved in Christ. ⁹ Greet Urbanus, our coworker in Christ, and Stachys my beloved. ¹⁰ Greet Apelles, who is proven in Christ. Greet those who belong to Aristobulus. ¹¹ Greet Herodion, my kinsman. Greet those who belong of Narcissus in Christ. ¹² Greet Tryphaena and Tryphosa who toil in Christ. Greet the beloved Persis who has worked much in Christ. ¹³ Greet Rufus, chosen in Christ, and greet his mother who is also mine. ¹⁴ Greet Asyncritus, Phlegon, Hermes, Patrobas, Hermas, and the sisters and brothers who are with them. ¹⁵ Greet Philologus and Julia, Nereus and his sister, and Olympas, and all the saints with them. ¹⁶ Greet one another with a holy kiss. All the churches of Christ greet you.

Mark 3:13 Now Jesus went up the mountain and called those he wanted to him and they came to him. ¹⁴ And he appointed twelve whom he also named apostles in order to be with him, and to be sent out to preach ¹⁵ and to have authority to cast out demons. ¹⁶ So Jesus appointed the twelve: Peter (he gave Simon the name Peter), ¹⁷ James son of Zebedee and John the brother of James (and he gave them the name Boanerges, that is, Sons of Thunder); ¹⁸ and Andrew, and Philip, and Bartholomew, and Matthew, and Thomas, and James son of Alphaeus, and Thaddaeus, and Simon the zealot, ¹⁹ and Judas Iscariot who also betrayed him.

²⁰ Later, Jesus went into a house and the crowd of women, children, and men came together again, so that they could not even eat [a morsel of] bread. ²¹ And when his family heard it, they went out to restrain him, for they were saying, "He has gone out of his mind." ²² And the biblical scholars who came down from Jerusalem said, "He has Beelzebul, and it is by the ruler of the demons that he casts out demons." ²³ And calling them to him, he spoke to them in parables, "How can Satan cast out Satan? ²⁴ If a realm is divided against itself, that realm cannot stand. ²⁵ And if a house is divided against itself, that house will not be able to stand. ²⁶ And if Satan has risen up against itself and is divided, it will not be to stand; rather, its end has come. ²⁷ On the contrary, no one can enter a strong person's house and plunder their property without first tying up the strong person and then [the robber] will plunder the house.

²⁸ "Truly I tell you all that all things will be forgiven the woman-born, their sins and as many blasphemies as they blaspheme. ²⁹ But whoever blasphemes against the Holy Spirit can never have forgiveness rather, is guilty of an eternal sin." ³⁰ For they had said, "He has an unclean spirit."

³¹ Then the mother of Jesus and his siblings came and standing outside, they sent for him and called him. ³² Now a crowd of women, children, and men was sitting around him

and they said to him, "Look! Your mother and your sisters and brothers are outside, asking after you." ³³ And Jesus replied, "Who are my mother and [my sisters] and my brothers?" ³⁴ And looking at those around him sitting in a circle, he said, "Here are my mother and my siblings! ³⁵ Whoever does the will of God is my [sibling, my] sister and brother and mother."

PROCLAMATION

Text Notes

Biblical Hebrew does not have a word that means simply "divine winged being," what many conceive when they read or hear the word "angel." Instead, Hebrew uses a word, *mal'akh,* which means "messenger," whether the one bearing the message is human or divine. Further, these messengers are distinct from cherubim and seraphim—consider them different species; they are never interchanged—and as in the story of Jacob's ladder, do not have wings. Greek *aggelos* has the same sense of human or divine messenger, and none of the angels of the New Testament are described with wings. There is one distinct angel among the host of heaven, the angel of God (or the Lord) in other translations, here in Psalm 34:7, the angel of Wisdom. Many scholars understand this angel to be God in disguise so that she can be among her people without her holiness harming them. (I say it is God in drag.)

In Mark 3:16 I have duplicated "Peter" outside the parentheses to match the rhetorical formatting of the naming sequence. Simon the Cananaean means Simon the Zealot, likely a reference to his current or former membership in a resistance organization. The spelling and pronunciation of Cananaean may mislead readers and hearers to misinterpret his origins as a Canaanite or being from Cana, so translation is preferable to transliteration here, see BDAG.

In verses 20 and 32, I have expanded "crowd" to make its composition more visible. In verse 21, the identity of the second "they" cannot be identified with certainty. It may be either in a crowd or the family of Jesus. NRSV eliminates the possibility that it is his family, and appropriately so.

Satan is presented in verse 26 as an "it" signifying the degree to which it is outside human parameters in the world of the text.

In verses 31–35, Jesus's family is represented in a number of ways. First, in verse 31, the expression that is translated as "family" means most properly those who are close to him, with him, alongside of him. Since the grammar of the passage indicates this is a separate group than the disciples, and specific family groups will be mentioned in this unit, the dominant understanding is that these are relatives of Jesus. (See Joel Marcus in the Anchor Yale Bible Commentary on Mark.) The passage uses the language of both "brothers, *adelphoi*" and "brothers and sisters, *adelphoi kai adelphai.*" However, *adelphoi* can mean "siblings," "brothers," and "sisters and brothers." I use all of these terms, including adding "sibling" in verse 35, to accommodate the diversity of those who will read and hear this passage.

Preaching Prompts

These lessons present a God who is manifest through teaching and discipling. The sorrowful tone of the first lesson may seem at odds with the rest of the readings. It is one of the few, if not the only, places where God teaches women. These women and their daughter disciples, whether kin or initiates or both, comprise the professional mourners guild responsible for public and private lamentation. The chronology of Jeremiah, a notoriously difficult passage, can be identified thematically as a prophetic response to the Babylonian invasion and its aftermath.

The juxtaposition of the first lesson with this psalm is jarring. The psalmist extols a God who provides and protects, not the experience of the women of Judah mourning their dead at the hand of invaders. The psalm is didactic, teaching the reverence (fear) of God in verses 9 and 11, and a way of life intended to protect the pious from harm and evil in verses 12 and 13. Together these readings provide an opportunity to respond to theological questions about the promises of God in the scriptures at times of crisis, grief, and peril when a person's lived experience is not reflected in those passages.

The Gospel and Epistle are about the "peopling" of the leadership of the Jewish Jesus movement and early church. They tell two different stories, or perhaps the same story in two different ways. Mark's story is about the men, and only men, Jesus called to follow him directly and individually to learn from his teaching and then go out and teach others. Paul's postscript is about the women and men of the next generation of the Way who shared in his teaching ministry as "coworkers" in Romans 16:3, including the female apostle Junia in verse 7.

At one point the teaching of Jesus causes concern for his well-being and sanity. He uses that provocation to expand the boundaries and embrace of his personal family to include all those who follow his teachings doing the will of God. God is present in all of these teaching moments and paradigms, all of which hold the potential for transformation and community building and healing.

EPIPHANY V

Isaiah 6:1–10; Psalm 119:33–40; 1 John 5:18–20 ; Mark 4:1–20

Isaiah 6:1 In the year that King Uzziah died, I saw the HOLY ONE sitting on a throne, high and exalted; and the trailing edges, as of God's garment, filled the temple. [2] Seraphs stood attending God—six wings!—each had six wings! With two they covered their faces, and with two they covered their groins, and with two they flew. [3] And this one called to that one and said:

"Holy, holy, holy is the MARSHALL of heaven's armies;
the whole earth is full of God's glory."

4 The doorposts of the thresholds shook at the voices of those who called, and the house was filled with smoke. 5 And I said: "Woe is me! I am wrecked, for I am a person of unclean lips, and I live among a people of unclean lips; yet my eyes have seen the Sovereign, the COMMANDER of the heaven's vanguard!"

6 Then one of the seraphs flew to me, and in its hand a hot coal that with tongs had been taken from upon the altar. 7 It touched my mouth with it and said: "Look! Now that this has touched your lips, your guilt has turned aside and your sin atoned."

8 Then I heard the voice of the Thundering God saying, "Whom shall I send, and who will go for us?" And I said, "Here am I; send me!" 9 And God said, "Go and say to this people:

'Listen well, but do not comprehend;
Look well, but do not understand.'
10 Close off the heart of this people,
and stop their ears,
and blind their eyes,
so that they may not look with their eyes,
and listen with their ears,
and understand with their hearts,
and turn and be healed."

Psalm 119:33–40

33 Make known to me, HOLY ONE, the way of your statutes,
and I will observe it to the end.
34 Grant me understanding and I shall safeguard your teaching
and shall observe it with my whole heart.
35 Lead me in the path of your commandments,
for in it I delight.
36 Turn my heart to your decrees,
and not to unjust gain.
37 Avert my eyes from seeing falsity;
in your ways give me life.
38 Establish to your slave your promise,
which is for those who revere you.
39 Avert the disgrace that I fear,
for your ordinances are good.
40 Look! I have longed for your precepts;
in your righteousness grant me life.

1 John 5:18 We know that everyone born of God sins not, rather the one begotten of God keeps them and the evil one does not touch them. ¹⁹ We know that we are of God and that the whole world lies lays down for the evil one. ²⁰ And we know that the Son of God has come and has given us understanding so that we may know the one who is true and we are in the one who is true, in God's Child Jesus Christ. This is the true God, and eternal life.

Mark 4:1 And again Jesus began to teach beside the sea and there gathered around him such a large crowd of women, children, and men that he boarded a boat sitting there on the sea while the whole crowd was beside the sea on the land. ² And he taught them much in parables, and then in his teaching he said to them: ³ "Listen up! Look, a sower went out to sow. ⁴ And as the sower sowed, some fell on the path and birds came and devoured. ⁵ And the other fell on the rocky ground where it did not have much soil, and immediately it sprang up because it did not have deep soil. ⁶ Now when the sun rose, it was scorched and since it had no root, it withered. ⁷ And other seed fell among thorns and the thorns grew up and choked it and it produced no grain. ⁸ Other seed fell into good soil and brought forth grain, growing up and increasing and producing thirty and sixty and a hundredfold." ⁹ Then Jesus said, "Let anyone with ears to hear listen!"

¹⁰ Now when Jesus was alone, those women and men who were around him along with the twelve asked him about the parables. ¹¹ And he said to them, "To you has been given the mystery of the majesty of God, but for those outside, everything comes in parables; ¹² in order that they:

'Look well, but do not understand,
listen well, but do not comprehend;
so that they may not turn again and be forgiven.'"

¹³ Then Jesus said to them, "Do you not understand this parable? Then how will you understand all the [rest of the] parables? ¹⁴ The sower sows the word. ¹⁵ These are on the path where the word is sown; when they hear immediately Satan comes and takes away the word that is sown in them. ¹⁶ And these are on rocky ground; when they hear the word, they immediately with joy receive it. ¹⁷ Yet they have no root in them and endure only for a while; then, when there is affliction or persecution on account of the word, immediately they stumble. ¹⁸ And those sown among the thorns; these are the ones who hear the word, ¹⁹ and the cares of the world and the deceitfulness of wealth, and the desire for other things come in and choke the word and it becomes fruitless. ²⁰ And these are sown on the good soil: they hear the word and receive it and bear fruit, thirty and sixty and a hundredfold."

PROCLAMATION

Text Notes

Isaiah 6:1 uses the word for seeing with one's eyes to articulate how Isaiah encountered God. It does not use the separate word for "envisioning a vision." The text does not identify the source of God's trailing edges, hems, or trains, just that they are plural. A garment or its semblance is inferred.

The language of slavery is normative and casual in all canons of the scriptures. In Psalm 119:38, the petitioner abases herself before God, taking the lowliest social position available, an enslaved person.

In the Gospel reading throughout the *Lectionary* volumes, "crowd" is expanded to reveal the women and children who were present. In Mark 4:10, "those who were around" Jesus are distinguished from the twelve primarily male disciples, thus I include women in that larger group. Mark 4:12 cites Isaiah 6:9–10 inverting the sequence of the lines about looking and listening. In addition, either Jesus or the evangelist reinterprets "turn and be healed" as "turn and be forgiven." Both MT and LXX have "heal"; the quote generally follows the MT.

Preaching Prompts

These lessons offer two very different epiphanies. Isaiah's immersive visionary experience presents the most dramatic multisensory epiphany, a visit into the presence of the living God. And Jesus, citing the most opaque portion of Isaiah's experience, proffers a veiled epiphany, a practically Gnostic one. What begins as a familiar text from Isaiah for many quickly becomes disturbing, as God tells the prophet to communicate in such a way that people will not understand God's message. Jesus uses those verses in the same way in Mark chapter 4. It is God who decides whether we humans will have access to the word of God or even the capacity to understand it. In between, the psalmist's prayer is a plea for a personal epiphany. The author of the Epistle rests secure in what it is we can know about ourselves in our relationship to God without need for an epiphany. Together these passages present the scope of the ways God is made manifest to us from the majestic and mysterious to the mundane.

EPIPHANY VI

Job 38:1–3, 8–11, 16–18, 28–29; Psalm 107:1–3, 19–32;
James 1:2–6 Mark 4:30–41

Job 38:1 The GOD WHO THUNDERS answered Job from the whirlwind and said:

2 "Who is this who obscures counsel by words without knowledge?

3 Gird up your loins like a warrior,
   I will question you and you shall make it known to me."

8 "Now, who enclosed the sea with doors
   when it gushed forth from [my] womb,

9 when I settled the clouds as its garment,
   and thick darkness its swaddling band?

¹⁰ Or when I set breakers around it, my statute,
and set bars and doors,

¹¹ and said, 'To here shall you come, and no more,
and here shall your proud waves be stopped'?"

¹⁶ "Have you gone into the springs of the sea,
or searched the deep, walking about?

¹⁷ Have the gates of death been uncovered for you,
and the gates of the shadow of death, have you seen [them]?

¹⁸ Do you comprehend the expanse of the earth?
Say so, if you know all this."

²⁸ "Does the rain have a father,
or who has caused the drops of dew to be born?

²⁹ From whose womb did the ice come forth,
and who has given birth to the frost of heaven?"

Psalm 107:1–3, 19–32

¹ Give thanks to SHE WHO IS MAJESTY, for she is good,
and her faithful love endures forever.

² Let the redeemed of SHE WHO SAVES proclaim
that she redeemed them from the hand of the foe.

³ And she has gathered them from [all] the lands;
from the east and from the west, from the north and from the south.

¹⁹ They cried to the MOTHER OF ALL in their trouble,
and she delivered them from their distress.

²⁰ She sent forth her word and healed them
and saved them from their pits.

²¹ Let them give thanks to the WOMB OF LIFE for her faithful love
and wonderful works for the woman-born.

²² Let them sacrifice sacrifices of thanksgiving
and tell of her acts with shouts of joy.

²³ Some went down to the sea in ships,
working their trade on the mighty waters.

²⁴ They saw the works of the MAKER OF ALL,
her wonderful works in the deep.

²⁵ For she spoke and raised the stormy wind,
which raised up the waves of the sea.

²⁶ They went up to the heavens, they went down to the deeps;
their very soul melted away at their catastrophe.

²⁷ They reeled and staggered like a drunkard,
and all their wisdom was confused.

28 Then they cried to the GOD WHO HEARS in their trouble,
   and she brought them out from their distress.
29 She made the storm be silent,
   and she hushed the waves.
30 Then they were glad for [all] was quiet,
   and she brought them to the refuge of their desire.
31 Let them thank the ARK OF SAFETY for her faithful love,
   for her wonderful works to the woman-born.
32 Let them exalt her in the congregation of the people,
   and in the assembly of the elders, praise her.

James 1:2 Count it all joy my sisters and brothers, whenever you confront trials of any kind. ³ For you all know that the testing of your faith produces endurance. ⁴ And let endurance mature in its work, so that you may be mature and complete, lacking nothing. ⁵ Now, if you are lacking in wisdom, ask God who gives to all generously and without reproach, and it will be given. ⁶ But ask in faith, not doubting, for the one who doubts is like a wave of the sea, windswept and blown away.

Mark 4:30 Jesus also said, "With what can we represent the realm of God, or in what parable shall we put it? ³¹ It is like a mustard seed, which, when sown upon the earth, is smaller than all the other seeds on earth. ³² Yet when it is sown it grows up and becomes bigger than all other shrubs, and produces large branches, so that the birds of the heavens can nest in its shade." ³³ Now with many such parables he spoke the word to them, as they were able to hear. ³⁴ And Jesus did not speak to them except in parables however, privately, he explained everything to his disciples.

³⁵ And that day as evening was coming, he said to them, "Let us go across to the other side." ³⁶ And sending the crowd of women, children and men away, they took him with them in the boat, just as he was, and other boats were with him. ³⁷ And a great windstorm arose, and the waves crashed into the boat, so that the boat was soon swamped. ³⁸ Yet Jesus was in the stern on a cushion sleeping and they woke him up and said to him, "Teacher, do you not care that we are perishing?" ³⁹ He was awakened and rebuked the wind and said to the sea, "Cease! Be silent!" Then the wind stopped and there was a great calmness. ⁴⁰ And he said to them, "Why are you all afraid? Do you not yet have faith?" ⁴¹ And they were terrified with great terror and said to one another, "Who then is this, that even the wind and the sea obey him?"

PROCLAMATION

Text Notes

Note: Even with longer readings and moving sequentially through the Gospel, not every verse of Mark will be included, though it is a short Gospel. The parable of the mustard seed may be omitted from these readings that focus on the power of God and Jesus to control the sea.

In Job 38:17, the shadow of death is the familiar expression from Psalm 23. In verse 8, I emphasize the divine womb with "my" rather than "the." The Hebrew of verse 10 is unclear, involving the verb "to break," "I [will] break" here and "my statute."

In Psalm 107:21 and in verse 31, "woman-born" renders the euphemism for humanity, "human children/children (or sons) of men." In verse 26, "catastrophe" is "evil." In verse 29, the silence is the same as the "sheer silence" Elijah heard, traditionally known as the "still small voice" in 1 Kings 19:12.

The "they" and "them" of the Gospel reading is either the disciples, a larger, gender-inclusive group that surrounded Jesus, or the twelve male apostles. In Mark 4:10, there is "the people around Jesus" and the twelve. There is no clarifying intervening language.

"Peace! Be still!" in Mark 4:39 is a beloved translation. However, both of the verbs Jesus uses pertain to silence.

In both Hebrew and Greek, the verbs that communicate "fear" also communicate "awe," which is often preferable when dealing with God or Jesus. In Mark 4:40, Jesus addresses the fear of those in the boat with him. It makes more sense to translate their experience as fear in keeping with his language.

Preaching Prompts

The calming of the sea is one of the most dramatic epiphanies in the Gospels. In this action Jesus lives into the example of his God and parent. In the ancient Afro-Asiatic world of the scriptures, the God who exercised sovereignty over the sea was the mightiest of gods. That is why the creation stories begin with God creating cosmic harmony out of the churning waters of chaos. That creation narrative is rearticulated in Job, where God is explicitly the mother and father of creation in the Hebrew text. Likewise, the psalmist celebrates the Maker of storms and she who keeps souls safe in the midst of the storm. The Gospel uses the sea and its waves as a metaphor for unstable faith, easily disrupted. And it is faith that Jesus finds lacking with his disciples, faced with the might of an untamed sea.

These lessons all point to a God of incredible power whose works continuously testify to her power and to the full presence of that power in Jesus. The evidence of our faith is all around us. These texts also remind us of what we have no need to be reminded, that storms come, and that we are never alone in those storms. Finally, a word about the mustard seed and its tree. The mustard tree (or bush) is a vision of the expansiveness of heaven with room and welcome for all. And perhaps, an invitation to reconsider our language once more. The mustard tree of heaven is at hand.

EPIPHANY VII

Isaiah 38:16–20; Psalm 30:1–5, 8–12; 2 Corinthians 4:7–12; Mark 5:21–43

Isaiah 38:16 SAVING ONE, on account of these things do people live,

and in all of this is the life of my spirit,

that you restore me to health and make me live!

[17] Truly, rather than well-being I had great bitterness;

but you secured my life from the pit of destruction,

for you have cast behind your back all my sins.

[18] For Sheol does not thank you,

Death does not praise you;

those who go down to the Pit do not hope

for your faithfulness.

[19] It is the living, the living who thanks you,

just as do I this day;

parents will make known to children

your faithfulness.

[20] GOD WHO HEALS will save me,

and we will make music

all the days of our lives,

at the house of the GOD WHO IS LIFE.

Psalm 30:1–5, 8–12

[1] I will exalt you, AGELESS GOD, for you have drawn me up,

and did not let my enemies rejoice over me.

[2] SAVING ONE my God, I cried to you for help,

and you have healed me.

[3] MERCIFUL GOD, you brought up from Sheol my soul,

preserving me from among those gone down to the Pit.

[4] Sing praises to the SHE WHO IS WORTHY you her faithful ones,

and give thanks to her holy Name.

[5] For a moment her anger [endures], a lifetime her favor;

through the night weeping may linger, yet in the morning, joy.

[8] To you, the GOD WHO HEARS, I cried,

and to my sovereign I begged favor:

[9] "What profit is there in my lifeblood descending to the Pit?

Will the dust praise you? Will it tell of your faithfulness?

[10] Hear, HOLY ONE, and be gracious to me!

HEALING ONE, be my help!"

¹¹ You have turned my wailing into dancing;
  you have unfastened my sackcloth
  and clothed me with joy
¹² so that my soul may praise you and not be silent.
  MAJESTIC ONE my God, forever will I give thanks to you.

2 Corinthians 4:7 Now we have this treasure in earthen vessels, so that this supreme power is God's and not of us. ⁸ In every way are we oppressed, but not crushed; perplexed, but not in despair; ⁹ persecuted, but not forsaken; knocked down, but not destroyed; ¹⁰ always bearing forth in the body the death of Jesus, in order that the life of Jesus might also be revealed in our bodies. ¹¹ Always, for as long we live, we are being given up to death for the sake of Jesus, so that the life of Jesus may be revealed in our mortal flesh. ¹² Thus death is at work in us, but life in you all.

Mark 5:21 Now When Jesus had crossed again in the boat to the other side, a great crowd of women, children, and men gathered around him; he was on the shore. ²² Then one of the leaders of the synagogue whose name was Jairus came, and when he saw Jesus, fell at his feet ²³ and implored him repeatedly, "My little daughter is at the end [dying]. Come and lay your hands on her, so that she may be saved and live." ²⁴ So Jesus went with him. And a large crowd of women, children, and men followed him and pressed against him.

²⁵ And there was a woman who had been suffering from [vaginal] hemorrhages for twelve years. ²⁶ And she had suffered much under many physicians, and had spent all that she had and she was not benefitted but rather, she was worse. ²⁷ She had heard about Jesus and came up behind him in the crowd of women, children, and men and touched his clothing, ²⁸ for she said, "If I just touch his clothes, I will be saved." ²⁹ Immediately her flow of blood stopped and she knew in her body that she was healed of her affliction. ³⁰ Also immediately, Jesus perceiving within himself that power had gone forth from him, turned back and forth in the crowd and said, "Who touched my clothes?"

³¹ And his disciples said to him, "You see the crowd—women, children, and men—pressing against on you and you say, 'Who touched me?'" ³² Jesus looked all around to see who had done it. ³³ But the woman fearing and trembling, knowing what had happened to her, came, fell down before him, and told him the whole truth. ³⁴ Jesus said to her, "Daughter, your faith has saved you; go in peace, and be whole [free] of your affliction."

³⁵ While Jesus was still speaking, some people came from the leader's house to say, "Your daughter is dead. Why still trouble the teacher?" ³⁶ But Jesus ignoring the word they spoke, said to the leader of the synagogue, "Fear not, only believe." ³⁷ And he permitted no one with him to follow him except Peter, James, and John, the brother of James. ³⁸ Then they came to the house of the leader of the synagogue, Jesus saw a commotion, women and men weeping and wailing loudly. ³⁹ And as he had entered, he said to them, "Why are you making commotion and weeping? The child is not dead but sleeping." ⁴⁰ And they laughed at him. Then he threw them all out and took the child's mother and father and those who

were with him and went in where the child was. [41] And taking the hand of the child he said to her, "Talitha cum," which is interpreted as, "Girl, to you I say, get up!" [42] And immediately the girl got up and began to walk about—she was twelve years of age. At this they were overcome with great amazement. [43] Jesus strictly ordered them that no one should know this, and told them to give her something to eat.

PROCLAMATION

Text Notes

These verses in Isaiah 38 are from the prayer of Hezekiah after his healing. The Hebrew is torturous in places as evidenced by greatly diverse translations. For example, in verse 16, Robert Altar refers to the "stubborn unintelligibility" of clauses that "defy reconstruction." Verse 20 employs musical terms that are also variously understood. Throughout this project, I specify the women and children that are the often unnamed and unnoticed members of public gatherings as is the case of the crowds in Mark. In Mark 5:21, the boat is only mentioned in some manuscripts; in Greek Jesus is literally "beside the sea." Verse 23 uses a euphemism similar to "she's terminal."

The source of the woman's hemorrhage is not identified in the text because of the shame associated with menstrual blood. The reader may wish to specify "vaginal" in conjunction with a sermon that aims to destigmatize women's bodies and reproductive health and associated diseases. The language about the "flow of her blood" in verse 29 has corollaries in the Torah (Lev. 12:7; 15:19–33; 20:18) that address vaginal discharges in hemorrhages.

"Bearing forth" in 2 Corinthians 4:10 has the sense of carrying something around and displaying it. Also, in verses 10 and 11, "be revealed," *phanerōthē*, evokes an epiphany with its shared root.

In the gospel reading, verses 23, 28, and 34 all use *sozo*, "to save or preserve"; NRSV's and CEB's "make well" and "healed" reserve too little of the full semantic range. In verse 41, Jesus speaks in Aramaic.

Preaching Prompts

These lessons mark the fragility of life and our dependence on God for our very existence, and when our bodies fail, for healing. The power to heal, save, even restore life to the dead is one of the most dramatic expressions of God's power. Power that has been seen in the life of Israel through its prophets Elijah and Elisha. The miracles that Jesus performs will place him in that tradition, but he will go beyond. Jairus and the bleeding woman knew that Jesus was the embodiment of that power. The woman knew that the power Jesus possessed could not be contained and even the touch of his clothing was sufficient to communicate it. Yet, Jesus placed the onus of her healing on her own faith.

We no longer live in the world of miracles, yet we are every bit as fragile as our iron age ancestors even with medical technologies that would be the stuff of miracles for them. We are equally dependent on God for life and health. But we need not fear what is on the other side of death; in the words of Blessed Archbishop Tutu, "Death is not the worst thing that can happen to a Christian." Too many pray for healing and are told their failure to be healed or cured is their own fault—they lack sufficient faith.

These lessons are an opportunity to discuss desperate access to healthcare along lines of race and class. There is opportunity to discuss the shame that is still attended upon women's reproductive health and diseases and stigma around menstruation. And there is the significant peril Black mothers face during pregnancy and childbirth that is disproportionate to the peril faced by other mothers. Lastly, one might address the difficulty finding medical care many trans persons experience.

EPIPHANY VIII

This Sunday in Epiphany is optional pending the fall of Easter.

Proverbs 23:22–26; Psalm 111; 1 John 5:18–21; Mark 6:1–13

Proverbs 23:22 Listen to your father who begot you,

and do not despise your mother when she is old.
23 Truth, buy and do not sell it;
wisdom, instruction, and understanding as well.
24 The parent of the righteous will greatly rejoice;
the one who produces a wise child will be glad in her.
25 Let your mother and father be glad;
let her who birthed you rejoice.
26 My child, give me your heart,
and let your eyes keep watch over my ways.

Psalm 111

1 Praise the LIVING GOD!
I will give thanks to the ONE GOD with my whole heart,
in the assembly of the upright, in the congregation.
2 Great are the works of GOD,
contemplated by all who delight in them.
3 Splendor and majesty are her work,
and her righteousness stands forever.
4 She has gained renown for her wonderful deeds;
the WOMB OF LIFE is gracious and abounds in mother-love.

⁵ She provides fresh meat for those who revere her;
  she remembers her covenant perpetually.
⁶ She has declared the strength of her works to her people,
  giving them the heritage of the nations.
⁷ The works of her hands are truth and justice;
  trustworthy are all her precepts.
⁸ They stand fast forever and ever,
  Executed in truth and uprightness.
⁹ She sent redemption to her people;
  she has ordained her covenant forever.
  Holy and awesome is her name.
¹⁰ Awe of the AGELESS GOD is the beginning of wisdom;
  all those who do have good understanding.
  Her praise endures forever.

1 John 5:18 We know that all who are born of God sin not; rather the One who was born of God protects them and the evil one does not touch them. ¹⁹ We know that we are of God and that the whole world submits to the power of the evil one. ²⁰ And we know that the Child of God has come and has given us understanding so that we may know the One who is true, and we are in the One who is true, in God's Child, Jesus the Messiah who is the true God and life eternal. ²¹ Little children, keep yourselves from idols.

Mark 6:1 Now Jesus left that place and came to his hometown, and his disciples followed him. ² On the sabbath he began to teach in the synagogue, and many women and men who heard him were astounded, saying, "Where did this man learn this?" And "What wisdom has been given him?" And "Such deeds of power, work done by his hands! ³ Is not this the carpenter, the son of Mary and brother of James and Joses and Judas and Simon, and are not his sisters here with us?" And they were scandalized by him. ⁴ Then Jesus said to them, "Prophets are not without honor, except in their hometown, and among their own kin, and in their own house." ⁵ And he could do no deed of power there, except on a few sick people, laying hands and curing them. ⁶ And Jesus was amazed at their unbelief. Then, he went about among the villages teaching.

⁷ Now Jesus called the twelve and began to send them out two by two and he gave them authority over the unclean spirits. ⁸ Thus he instructed them so that they would take nothing for their journey except a staff only: no bread, no bag, no coin in their moneybelts. ⁹ Rather, they should fasten on sandals and not put on two tunics. ¹⁰ Then Jesus said to them, "Wherever you all enter a house, there stay until you leave the place. ¹¹ And if any place will not receive you and they refuse to hear you, in your leaving from there, shake off the dust that is on your feet as a witness against them." ¹² So they went out and proclaimed that people should repent. ¹³ And many demons they cast out, and anointed with oil many who were sick and healed them.

PROCLAMATION

Text Notes

Throughout these readings the order of the gendered parents is reversed so that mother comes before father.

Proverbs 23:24 is "He (or the one who) begets a wise one (masculine singular, missing son/child) will rejoice in him." I use "parent" and "produce" instead. In addition, I provide "her" as the generic person; wisdom is rarely but occasionally credited to women.

In Psalm 111:10, I use "awe" rather than the more common "fear" of God; the underlying word includes both.

In 1 John 5:19, "submit to" renders "lies down in."

I have made the presence of women in the synagogue explicit in "many" in Mark 6:1. Not only did women participate in religious life at synagogue and temple, inscriptional evidence identifies women in leading positions, including *archisyna-gogos*, "leader of the synagogue" (the same title as the male leaders in Matt. 9:18; Mark 5:36, 38; Luke 8:41; 13:14; see Bernadette Brooten, *Women Leaders in the Ancient Synagogue* and Kate Cooper, *Band of Angels: The Forgotten World of Early Christian Women*). Paul would go on to arrest women and men at synagogues who followed Jesus in Acts 9:2. We don't know how many sisters Jesus had; "all" is more than one and likely more than two.

In Mark 6:2, the question of the congregants is fractured and lacking a verb, "where this (one) this (knowledge/teaching)?" Sometimes imagining accompanying gestures helps with such a construction: "Where did this one [points at Jesus] learn this [waves hands around]?" "One" can also be "person" or "man" in this context. In verse 3, "carpenter" includes more than woodworking, extending to "building" and "construction" from other materials.

Preaching Prompts

This last week of epiphany reveals Jesus to be a local boy about whom the neighbors have some questions. Their questions are rooted in their knowledge of him as one of them, a young Jewish man about whom they had certain expectations and assumptions. Their expectations are shaped by what they know, or believe they know, about his family. In the Hebrew Bible, as illustrated by the Proverbs lesson, parents are the first teachers responsible for teaching their children the ways of wisdom, including the reference for and awe of God. The Epistle presents the church as the home in which God's children are nurtured in the ways of wisdom. The psalm makes the case for why God is worthy of that awe which is the beginning of wisdom. In the Gospel, Jesus is the embodiment of that wisdom-provoking awe of various kinds.

The wisdom of Jesus reflects the Greek literary context of the Christian Testament and is rooted in his teaching, teaching that transcends expectations based on what his hometown neighbors know about his family of origin. Their astonishment is a bit of a knock on Jesus's family as is their identification of him by his mother and not his father, raising the possibility there was some question about his parentage in their eyes. (However, in the Hebrew Bible individual men and families were named through the mother quite regularly and there was no offense or scandal.) English translations of the New Testament regularly diminish the Jewishness of Jesus, his family, and followers by anglicizing their names: Mariam (Miriam/Mary), Iakobos (Jacob/James), Ioseph (Joseph), Simon (Simeon), and Ioudas (Judah/Judes or Jude), but ancestral figures from the scriptures with the same names are not treated that way, i.e., Rebekah's son Jacob does not become "James." Names matter and how and why we change them matter tremendously beyond the anti-Jewishness of this practice.

It is unfortunate that the sisters of Jesus get lost in the scriptures and subsequent tradition. With them, we have the image of Jesus as a big brother and then later an uncle. In this lesson they are at the synagogue, active Jewish learners whether they're to hear Jesus or as part of their regular weekly practice; whether as young unmarried girls or as women with their own families. They show up for their brother.

LAST WEEK OF EPIPHANY (TRANSFIGURATION)

Judges 5:1–7; Psalm 102:12–21; 2 Peter 1:16–21; Mark 9:1–13

Judges 5:1 Now Deborah sang on that day [she defeated the enemy] and Barak son of Abinoam was with her, she sang:

2 "When locks are neglected in Israel,
   when the people offer themselves willingly,
   bless the EVER-LIVING GOD!
3 "Hear, you royals; give ear, you rulers;
   to the MIGHTY ONE will I sing,
   I will craft hymns to the MAJESTIC ONE, the God of Israel.
4 "THUNDERING GOD, when you went out from Seir,
   when you marched from the field of Edom,
   the earth trembled,
   and the heavens dripped,
   even the clouds dripped water.
5 The mountains quaked before the INCANDESCENT ONE, the One of Sinai,
   before the FIRE OF SINAI, the God of Israel.

6 "In the days of Shamgar son of Anath,
   in the days of Jael, caravans ceased
   and travelers traversed the byways.
7 The unwalled villages ceased in Israel,
   they ceased, because you arose,
   Deborah, arose as a mother in Israel.

Psalm 102:12–21

12 You, MAJESTY, are enthroned forever;
   your renown, from generation to generation.
13 You will rise up and mother-love Zion,
   for it is time to show favor to her;
   the appointed time has come.
14 For your bondslaves cherish her stones,
   and tenderly regard its dust.
15 The nations will fear the Name of the GOD WHOSE NAME IS HOLY,
   and all the monarchs of the earth your glory.
16 For the COMPASSIONATE ONE will build up Zion;
   she will appear in her glory.
17 She will regard the prayer of the destitute,
   and will not despise their prayer.
18 Let this be engraved for a generation to come,
   so that a people yet unborn may praise the WISDOM OF THE AGES:
19 that she looked down from her holy height,
   from heaven the CREATOR OF ALL beheld the earth,
20 to hear the groaning of the prisoner,
   to set free those who were condemned to die;
21 so that the Name of the HOLY GOD may be recounted in Zion,
   and her praise in Jerusalem.

2 Peter 1:16 For we did not follow sophisticated mythologies when we made known to you all the power and coming of our Redeemer Jesus Christ, rather we had been eyewitnesses of his majesty. 17 For Christ from God the Sovereign received honor and glory, a voice came to him from the Majestic Glory, saying, "This is my Son, my Beloved, with whom I am well pleased." 18 And we ourselves heard this voice that came from heaven, while we were with him on the holy mountain.

19 Thus we have a sure prophetic word; you would do well to be attentive to this as to a lamp shining in a shadowy place, until the day dawns and the morning star rises in your hearts. 20 First this you must understand, that of all written prophecy, none is a matter of individual interpretation. 21 For not by human will ever came any prophecy, rather women and men moved by the Holy Spirit spoke from God.

Mark 9:1 And he said to them, [the crowd,] "Truly I tell you all, there are some standing here who will not taste death until they see that the majesty of God come in power." ² Six days later later, Jesus took with him Peter and James and John his brother and brought them up a high mountain by themselves, alone. And he was transfigured before them, ³ and his clothes began shining, becoming exceedingly white, such as no cloth refiner on earth could bleach them. ⁴ And then Moses and Elijah appeared to them, talking with him. ⁵ Then Peter said to Jesus, "Rabbi, it is good for us to be here; we will pitch three tents here, one for you, one for Moses, and one for Elijah." ⁶ For he did not know what to say because they were terrified. ⁷ Then a cloud overshadowed them, and from the cloud there came a voice, "This is my Son, the Beloved; listen to him!" ⁸ Suddenly when they looked around, they no longer saw no one with them, but only Jesus himself.

⁹ As they were coming down the mountain, he ordered them so that they would tell no one about what they had seen, until after the Son of Woman had risen from the dead. ¹⁰ So they kept the matter to themselves, questioning what this rising from the dead could mean. ¹¹ And they asked him, "Why do the biblical scholars say that Elijah must come first?" ¹² Thus Jesus said to them, "Elijah is indeed coming first to restore all things. Now, how then is it written about the Son of Woman, that through many sufferings he is to go and be treated with contempt? ¹³ Yet I tell you all that Elijah has come, and they did to him whatever they pleased, just as it is written about him."

PROCLAMATION

Text Notes

The poetic account of the prophet Deborah exists in multiple forms in part due to its age; some of it is nearly indecipherable, generating multiple diverse translations. There are two Septuagint versions, LXX-A (Alexandrinus) and LXX-B (Vaticanus). In both, Deborah is portrayed as God's messenger, a term frequently translated as angel but used for both human and divine messengers. This reading confers additional authority upon the woman who is already prophet and judge, following Moses, to be followed only by Samuel.

The ones who benefitted under Deborah's rule in Judges 5:7 have been translated as "peasants" (NRSV), "warriors" (me previously in *Daughters of Miriam*), "villagers" (CEB, KJV), "deliverance" (JPS), "merchants" (J. Alberto Soggin, *Judges*) and "unwalled cities" (Alter). Some elements of the people interested to Deborah's care and rule "prospered" or "ceased." That is, Deborah's rise was accompanied by the rise in fortunes of her people symbolized by either the least or the greatest, or predations of a warrior class ceased because she arose to protect God's people. Or villages without walls, possibly signified by the similarity of the disputed word, *perazon*, with *perizi*, a village in a town without walls. This reading means that the towns did not need walls because Deborah protected them.

"Mother-love" in verse 13 of the psalm communicates the love of God with a verb whose grammatical root is the womb. "Engrave" in verse 18 reflects the dual meanings of the root, "to write" and "to cut."

Mark 8:34 indicates that Jesus addresses the larger crowd rather than the smaller group of disciples or apostles.

Preaching Prompts

These readings begin with the prophet Deborah on Mount Tabor, long understood to be the Mount of Transfiguration. She sings ancient stories of God from Israelite history and her own. For her, God is a mighty deliverer who partners with humanity, with her, to save the people. The psalm is situated in a time when the mighty acts of Deborah are ancient stories, yet its composer trusts that God is the same God and that though it may take generations, God will again save her people. Though the Epistles are generally regarded as predating the Gospels, there is a suggestion that 2 Peter may well be the final book of the standardized canon to have been produced, perhaps very early in the second century CE. Mark, on the other hand, arguably the first Gospel, would have been written in the middle to the second half of the first century CE. Perhaps as little as 50 or 60 years separate these two accounts of the Transfiguration. This extraordinary epiphany links Jesus with Moses and Elijah and also Deborah. These three prophets evoke the God of miracles, the God of the ancient songs, and the transfiguration establishes that Jesus is in their company but more than that, that Jesus is the woman-born child of this great God.

Deborah's forty-year peace benefited all of her people, women and girls, boys and men. Miriam and Moses lead the Israelite women, children and men to safety. Elijah performed miracles for individual women and men. And Jesus counts women among his disciples and one day, apostles. There is in these prophets and their successor a rich tapestry of God-story prefiguring what the Church could be.

LENT—ASH WEDNESDAY

Joel 2:1, 12–17, 21–22; Psalm 90:1–10, 12;
1 Corinthians 15:45–49; Matthew 6:1–6, 16–18

Joel 2:1 Blow the trumpet in Zion!

> Cry the alarm on my holy mountain!
> Let all the inhabitants of the land quake,
> for the day of the HOLY GOD is coming, it is near.
> ¹² Yet even now, says the HOLY ONE,
> return to me with all your hearts,
> with fasting, with weeping, and with lamenting.

¹³ Tear your hearts and not your clothing.
Return to the HOLY ONE, your God,
for God is gracious and loves as a mother,
slow to anger, and abounds in faithful love,
and reluctant to impose harm.

¹⁴ Who knows whether God will not turn and relent,
and leave a blessing behind,
for a grain offering and a drink offering
to the HOLY ONE, your God?

¹⁵ Blow the trumpet in Zion;
sanctify a fast;
call a solemn assembly.

¹⁶ Gather the people:
Sanctify the congregation;
assemble the aged;
gather the children,
even breastfeeding babies.
Let the bridegroom leave his room,
and the bride her canopy.

¹⁷ Between the portico and the altar
let the priests, the ministers of the HOLY ONE, weep.
Let them say, "Spare your people, HOLY ONE,
and do not offer your heritage as a mockery,
a byword among the nations.
Why should it be said among the peoples,
'Where is their God?'"

²¹ Fear not, O land!
Be glad and rejoice,
for the HOLY ONE has done great things!

²² Fear not, O animals of the field!
For the pastures of the wilderness are green;
the tree lifts up its fruit,
the fig tree and vine give their riches.

Psalm 90:1–10, 12

¹ MOTHER OF THE MOUNTAINS, you have been our refuge
from one generation to another.

² Before the mountains were born,
or you writhed the land and the earth into birth,
from age to age you are God.

³ You turn mortal flesh back to the dust and say,
"Turn back, you who are woman-born."
⁴ For a thousand years in your sight are like yesterday when it is past
and like a watch in the night.
⁵ You sweep them aside; they are an illusion;
In the morning flourishing and in the evening wilting and withering.
⁶ In the morning it is green and flourishes;
in the evening it is dried up and withered.
⁷ For we are consumed in your displeasure;
we are afraid because of your wrathful indignation.
⁸ Our iniquities you have set before you,
and our hidden sins in the light of your countenance.
⁹ When you are angry, all our days are gone;
we bring our years to an end like a sigh.
¹⁰ The span of our life is seventy years, perhaps in strength even eighty;
yet the sum of them is but labor and sorrow,
for they pass away quickly and we are gone.
¹² So teach us to number our days
that we may apply our hearts to Wisdom.

1 Corinthians 15:45 Thus it is written, "The first human, Adam, became a living soul"; the last Adam became a spirit that gives life. ⁴⁶ But it is not the spiritual that is first, but the physical, and then the spiritual. ⁴⁷ The first human was from the earth, dust; the second human is from heaven. ⁴⁸ As was the one of dust, so are those who are of dust; and as is the one of heaven, so are those who are of heaven. ⁴⁹ Just as we have borne the image of the one of dust, we will also bear the image of the one of heaven.

Matthew 6:1 [Jesus said,] "Now, beware of practicing your justness before other people in order to be seen by them; surely, lest you have no reward from your Creator in heaven.

² "So when you give alms, do not trumpet before yourself, as the hypocrites do in the synagogues and in the streets, in order that they may be praised by other people. Truly I tell you, they have received their reward. ³ But when you give alms, do not let your left hand know what your right hand is doing, ⁴ in order that your alms may be secret; and your Creator who sees in secret will reward you.

⁵ "And when you pray, do not be like the hypocrites; for they love to stand and pray in the synagogues and on the street corners, in order that they may be seen by other people. Truly I tell you, they have received their recompense. ⁶ But whenever you pray, go into your room and shut the door and pray to your Creator who is in secret; and your Creator who sees in secret will reward you.

¹⁶ "And when you fast, do not be sullen like the hypocrites, for they disfigure their faces in order to show other people that they are fasting. Truly I tell you, they have received their

reward. [17] But when you fast, put oil on your head and wash your face, [18] in order that your fasting may be seen, not by others, but by your Creator who is in secret, and your Creator who sees in secret will reward you.

PROCLAMATION

Text Notes

Land in Joel 2:1 and 21 is soil, not the nation. The hearts of the people in Joel 2:12–13 form a collective one, "the heart of you all."

In Psalm 90:2, God's grammatical gender is masculine, and the imagery used for God is feminine, birthing imagery (in the cisgender ancient Israelite world), yielding the name for God in verse 1. "Turn" in verse 3 means both "turn around" and "repent." Also in verse 3, "mortal flesh" renders "man," and "woman-born" renders "children/descendants of humanity/humankind" or "mortals."

1 Corinthians 15:47 quotes Genesis 2:7; throughout the passage Paul uses *anthropos*, "human," rather than *aner*, "man," following Genesis where the first earthling is "human," not "man."

In Matthew 6:1, "justness/justice," "uprightness," and "righteousness" are all translations of *dikaiosynēn*. Those righteous acts include far more than the almsgiving, prayer, and fasting in the following verses. The prayer room in verse 6 is an inner one, making one's prayer less likely to be seen.

Preaching Prompts

Joel 2 is a call to solemn assembly in fasting and repentance in response to a locust infestation and resulting economic loss and famine seen as divine punishment. It will be important to unravel the blame language. The text is explicitly inclusive across gender and age categories. The image of God as the mother of the mountains in Psalm 90:2 builds nicely on the maternal imagery present in God's mother-love in Joel 2:13.

The people of the land are to quake at God's power and presence (Joel 2:1), but the land itself (herself) should not fear, verse 21. Notably, God addresses the earth and her creatures in verse 21–22 (excluded from the designated verses in the BCP). God cares for them and whether humanity repents or not, God will care for them.

God's essential characteristics delineated in Joel 2:13—graciousness, loving from her womb (the noun and verb share a root), slow to anger, abounding in faithful love, and being slow to inflict retribution—recur in Exodus 34:6, Deuteronomy 4:31, and Jonah 4:2, and throughout the psalms.

The Epistle makes clear that we are all both earthly dust and the stuff of heaven. We are all equally bearers of the divine image now, and even more so in the age to come. Paul's use of a paradigm distinguishing the spiritual from the physical in 1

Corinthians 15:46 lends itself easily to body/soul dichotomies and hierarchies; it also seems to unhelpfully deemphasize the Incarnation.

As with the Epistle, the implicit gender claims in the Gospel will need to be made explicit. Oiling the head, actually hair, is a common grooming practice for those of African descent like the Afro-Asiatic Israelites and their descendants; it is common in some Asian and other cultures as well. It is less comprehensible in the European culture that has colonized the text and its iconography.

In Matthew 6:6–7, omitted from the reading, Jesus tells his disciples not to pray like Gentiles who essentially babble repeatedly, and in that context introduces the Lord's Prayer. It is worth remembering that Jesus initially understood his ministry to be only to "the lost sheep of the house of Israel." (See Matt. 10:5; 15:24.) After his encounter with the Syro-Phoenician woman, his ministry extended to the Gentiles.

A final note, when reciting Psalm 51 in the liturgy of the day, consider recentering Bathsheba's abduction, rape, and forced impregnation along with the murder of her husband.

LENT I

Judges 5:24–31; Psalm 25:1–7; Romans 12:14–21; Mark 6:14–29

Judges 5:24 [Deborah sang:] "Most blessed of women be Jael,
    the wife of Heber the Kenite,
    of tent-dwelling women most blessed.
²⁵ He asked water and she gave him milk,
    in a princely bowl she brought him curds.
²⁶ She put her hand to the tent peg
    and her right hand to the laborer's hammer;
    she struck Sisera a blow,
    she destroyed his head,
    she shattered and pierced his temple.
²⁷ Between her legs he collapsed,
    he fell, he lay still;
    between her legs he collapsed;
    where he collapsed, there he fell utterly destroyed.
²⁸ "Out of the window she peered,
    the mother of Sisera cried through the lattice:
    'Why is his chariot so long in coming?
    Why so late the hoofbeats of his chariots?'
²⁹ The wisest of her royal women her answer,
    indeed, she turns and speaks to herself:

³⁰ 'Are they not finding and dividing the spoil?—

Woman-flesh, one or two for each soldier;

spoil of dyed cloth for Sisera,

spoil of dyed cloth embroidered,

two pieces of dyed work embroidered for my neck as spoil.'

³¹ "Thus may they be eradicated, all your enemies, DREAD GOD!

But may those who love you be like the sun as it rises in its might.

And the land was quieted for forty years.

Psalm 25:1–7

¹ To you, RIGHTEOUS ONE, I lift up my soul.

² My God, in you I trust;

let me not be put to shame,

let not my enemies exult over me.

³ Even more, let not those who hope in you be put to shame;

let them be ashamed who are treacherous [and] empty.

⁴ Make known to me your ways, AGELESS GOD;

teach me your paths.

⁵ Guide me in your truth, and teach me,

for you are the God of my salvation;

for you I wait all day long.

⁶ Remember your maternal love, O WOMB OF LIFE,

and your faithful love,

for they have been from of old.

⁷ The sins of my youth and my transgressions remember not;

according to your faithful love remember me,

for the sake of your goodness, GRACIOUS ONE.

Romans 12:14 Bless the ones who persecute you; bless and do not curse. ¹⁵ Rejoice with the ones who rejoice, weep with the ones who weep. ¹⁶ With one another, be harmonious; be not arrogant, but associate with the humble. Do not make yourselves [out] to be wiser than you are. ¹⁷ Evil for evil you shall not repay anyone; consider before time what is good in the sight of all. ¹⁸ If possible from your ability, with every human person, live in peace. ¹⁹ Do not avenge yourselves beloved; rather leave space for the wrath [of God]; for it is written, "*To me belongs vengeance; I will repay, says the Holy One.*" ²⁰ No, "*If your enemy hungers, feed them; if they thirst, give them something to drink; for by so doing, burning coals shall you heap on their head.*" ²¹ Do not be overcome by evil rather, overcome evil with good.

Mark 6:14 Now King Herod heard of [the teaching of Jesus], for Jesus's name had become known and some were saying, "John the baptizer has been raised from the dead and that is why these powers work through him." [15] Yet others said, "It is Elijah" while others said, "It is a prophet, like one of the prophets [of old]." [16] But when Herod heard of it, he said, "John, whom I beheaded, has been raised."

[17] For Herod himself had sent men who seized John and bound him in prison because of Herodias, the wife of his brother Philip, for Herod had married her. [18] For John had told Herod, "It is not right for you to have your brother's wife." [19] Now Herodias had a grudge against him and she wanted to kill him. But she could not. [20] This was because Herod feared John, knowing that he was a righteous man and a holy man and he protected him and listened to him, though greatly perplexed; yet it pleased him to listen to him.

[21] Now an opportune time came on Herod's birthday when he gave a banquet for his courtiers and commanders and for the leaders of Galilee. [22] And Herod's daughter Herodias came in and danced, pleasing Herod and his dinner guests. The king said to the girl, "Ask me for whatever you wish, and I will give it to you." [23] And he swore to her repeatedly, "Whatever you ask me, I will give you, even half of my kingdom." [24] And she went out and said to her mother, "What should I ask?" She replied, "The head of John the baptizer." [25] Immediately she returned to the king with haste and asked, saying, "I want immediately for you to give me on a platter the head of John the baptizer." [26] The king was deeply sorry, yet because of his oaths and the guests, he did not want to refuse her. [27] Immediately the king sent a soldier under orders to bring John's head. And he went and beheaded him in the prison. [28] And he brought his head on a platter and gave it to the girl and the girl gave it to her mother. [29] When John's disciples heard, they came and took his body, and laid it in a tomb.

PROCLAMATION

Text Notes

In Judges 5:30 the noun rendered as *woman-flesh* is the term for a female reproductive organ and should be understood as a profane term or a slur in that context though it is the normative term for womb.

To "wait" in Psalm 25:5 also includes hoping; the psalmist waits with expectation. God's maternal love in verse 6 emanates from her womb, which provides the grammatical root for this love.

Romans 12:19 quotes Deuteronomy 32:35 in part by corresponding to the first phrase in Hebrew then loosely following a combination of the LXX and MT. Verse 20 quotes Proverbs 25:21–22, following LXX nearly exactly; the sole divergence is the word used for "hunger."

Preaching Prompts

We come to these readings in Lent largely because this is where the Gospel lands us. The readings are about conflict, interpersonal conflict, and violent conflict between persons and nations. In truth we enter the Lenten season every year in the midst of conflict. There is conflict within our nation and conflict in which our nation is engaged outside of our borders. There is conflict in some of our homes, some of it quite dangerous.

Enmity, especially violent enmity, is often constructed as a male prerogative. In these lessons women use violent means to resolve political and military conflicts as do the men around them. Some biblical scholarship is highly critical of these women for being "unwomanly." Arguably, these women demonstrated the full range of "womanly" behavior in their world as do their corollaries in our world. In the shadow of the Russo-Ukrainian war, it is important to recognize that these larger stories are not figurative or fairytales. Rather, they are illustrative of the universal failure of humanity to govern itself well and relate to others justly. In this light we should, perhaps, listen again to all of those psalms praying for or celebrating victory over one's enemy and recognize that they are not speaking about our conflicts at work or broken relationships.

In Judges 5, the prophet Deborah sings her own victory song. In these lines she celebrates her comrade in arms, Jael, who killed the enemy general, Sisera. The poetic passage in chapter 5 is the older version of the story; the prose of chapter 4 came later. In Judges 5:30 the general's mother comes to the conclusion that her son is late from battle, not because he has died or been killed, but because he is choosing women to rape. Rape has always been a tool of war and genocide. Women suffer disproportionately in war whether there are women on the battlefield, in command, or in the White House.

In the story of Herod, Herodias, and her unnamed daughter, the women in the story demonstrate the concept of kyriarchy, the absolute power of a monarch, which trumps gender peril in the same way white privilege often does. Rather than fulfill the law, the Herods, like most, if not all ancient monarchs, set themselves above the law and take whatever they want. (The marriage of Herod and Herodias is prohibited by Lev. 18:16.) People, their lives, and bodies are disposable playthings to them. Their human monarchy is death-dealing while the majesty of God incarnate in Christ Jesus (absent from the reading yet still looming large) is life-giving.

Paul offers sage counsel for dealing with all kinds of human conflict. Leave vengeance to God, and "with every human person, live in peace"—albeit with caveats. It's not a feasible national or political strategy, thus the current situation of the world. But for all of the interpersonal hurts we experience, including those that have the potential to escalate to violence, his counsel is sound, if hard. These readings may form the basis of a more meaningful Lenten practice.

LENT II

Proverbs 28:20–25; Psalm 50:1–15; 1 Timothy 5:1–4, 8; Mark 7:1–15

Proverbs 28:20 A person who is faithful [has] abundant blessings,

while one who is in a hurry to be rich will not go unpunished.

²¹ The one who shows favoritism is no good—

over a piece of bread will a woman or man do wrong.

²² A person with a covetous eye hastens toward riches

and does not know want is on the way.

²³ The woman or man who rebukes another person

will find favor afterward,

more than one who flatters with the tongue.

²⁴ Anyone who robs mother or father

and says, "That is no transgression,"

is a companion to a vandal.

²⁵ A greedy person stirs up strife,

while a woman or man who trusts in the GOD WHO PROVIDES

will be well provisioned.

Psalm 50:1–15

¹ God of gods, the MAKER OF ALL,

speaks and summons the earth

from the dawning of the sun to its setting.

² From Zion, the perfection of beauty,

God shines forth.

³ Our God comes and does not keep silent,

before her is a devouring fire,

and a whirling [wind] surrounds her.

⁴ She summons the heavens above—

and the earth—in order to judge her people:

⁵ "Gather to me my faithful ones,

who made a covenant with me by sacrifice."

⁶ The heavens declare her righteousness,

for God, she is the one who judges. *Selah*

⁷ "Listen my people and I will speak,

Israel and I will testify against you;

I am God, your God.

⁸ Not for your sacrifices do I rebuke you;

your burnt offerings are continually before me.

⁹ I will not accept a bull from your house,
   or goats from your pens.
¹⁰ For mine is every wild animal of the forest,
   the cattle on a thousand hills.
¹¹ I know every bird of the mountains
   and everything that moves in the field is mine.
¹² Were I hungry, I would not tell you,
   for mine is the world and all that fills it.
¹³ Do I eat the flesh of bulls,
   or the blood of goats drink?
¹⁴ Offer to God a sacrifice of thanksgiving,
   and pay to the Most High your vows.
¹⁵ Then summon me in the day of trouble;
   I will deliver you and you shall glorify me."

1 Timothy 5:1 Do not rebuke an elder man, but speak to them as to a father, to those younger, as brothers, ² to elder women as mothers, to younger women as sisters, in absolute purity. ³ Honor widows who are really widows. ⁴ If a widow has children or grandchildren, let them learn first to show devotion to their own family and make repayment to their parents; for this is pleasing in God's sight.

⁸ And whoever does not provide for their own, and especially for family members, has denied the faith and is worse than an unbeliever.

Mark 7:1 Now there gathered around Jesus Pharisees and some of the biblical scholars who had come from Jerusalem. ² And they saw some of his disciples were eating bread with common hands, meaning unwashed. ³ For the Pharisees, and all Jews, do not eat unless they wash their hands as fists, observing the tradition of the elders. ⁴ Also, when coming from the market, without washing, they do not eat anything. And there are also many other [traditions] that they have taken on: washing cups, pots, and bronze kettles—and beds. ⁵ Now the Pharisees and the biblical scholars asked him, "Why do your disciples not walk according to the tradition of the elders, but eat with common hands?" ⁶ And Jesus said to them, "Well did Isaiah prophesy about you hypocrites, as it is written:

> 'This people honors me with their lips,
>   but their heart is far from me;
> ⁷ and in vain do they worship me,
>   teaching human teaching as commandments.'

⁸ Abandoning the commandment of God and taking on human tradition!"

⁹ Then Jesus said to them, "Well do you all spurn the commandment of God in order to establish your tradition. ¹⁰ For Moses said: *Honor your mother and your father* and: *The one who curses mother or father will certainly be put to death*. ¹¹ But you all say that if anyone

tells mother or father, 'Korban, an offering to God, is whatever of mine that would have supported you,' [12] then you all no longer permit doing anything for a mother or father, [13] making void the word of God through your tradition that you have handed on, and you do many things like this."

[14] Jesus called the crowd again and said to them, "Listen to me, all of you, and understand: [15] There is nothing outside a woman or man that by going into them has the power to defile, rather what comes out of a person is what defiles a person."

PROCLAMATION

Text Notes

The "covetous" eye in Proverbs 28:22 is an "evil" eye.

God summons the heavens and the earth to do her bidding in verses 1 and 4, and empowers her people to summon her in turn in verse 15, all using the same word. Indeed, the divine issues it as a command using the imperative, "Summon me!" Other translations soften it to "call on me." But God is granting permission to be summoned in the same way she summons the elements of the universe. In verse 10, *behemoth*, the plural form of beast (*behemah*), is traditionally translated as cattle here.

In the world of 1 Timothy 5, "widow" signifies more than being bereaved of a husband; it is also a ministerial office in the early church. The term is used both ways in the Epistles (see Annette Bourland Huizenga's discussion in the 1–2 Timothy and Titus volume of the *Wisdom Commentary* and Joanna Dewey's discussion of the passage in the *Women's Bible Commentary*). The ministerial widow could also be a virgin or otherwise unmarried.

Mark 7:15 uses *anthropou*, man or generic human; I have specified women and men, as the teaching would not have applied to minors. My reading understands the word is intended to communicate something about how to hold one's hands when performing the ritual of washing before eating.

Throughout this project "biblical scholars" replaces "scribes," as it communicates more of their actual function in the community. Counter to many established translations such as NRSV and CEB, "impure" and "unclean" are not used in verses 1 and 5. The use of the word *pugme*, "fist," in verse 3 has tested (and vexed) translators across the ages. Verses 6–7 quote Isaiah 29:13; verse 10 quotes the Decalogue in Exodus 20:12/Deuteronomy 5:16 and Exodus 21:17. All of the citations follow the Septuagint.

I preserve "Jews" because the matters under discussion pertain to the practice of Second Temple Judaism.

Preaching Prompts

These readings might well be entitled, "Charity begins at home." As Lenten readings they call us to tend to our families, especially our elders, before engaging in even praiseworthy acts outside the circle of family. There is rare gender parity in women and men equally being in need of their children or other relatives to care for them in their old age. However, men, nearly universally, are expected and enabled to do that providing. These lessons also focus on money, our desire forward, and our stewardship of it. The two frameworks combine in Proverbs 28 with the specter of someone robbing their parents; likely the inspiration for Jesus's teaching in Mark 7. In the psalm, God reminds her human creation that the rest of creation is hers as well, and while she receives them, she has no need of our offerings. In calling our attention to the obligation to care for family, the Epistle condemns those who neglect that duty in the strongest terms reflecting its context—those who fail in this sacred duty are as unbelievers.

In addition to condemning the financial neglect of parents by claiming piety, giving what should be used to support them as an offering, Jesus uses eating and the subsequent production of waste to vividly illustrate that nothing one consumes defiles one, as even kosher food becomes waste. Rather, it is what is in the human heart that defiles. An editorial hand adds that Jesus had declared all foods "clean." It should be noted that this conclusion is in a second voice and is somewhat at odds with the early history of the Church and disputes over Torah observance. As always, the language "the Jews" and "all the Jews" should be considered carefully as bombastic. For example, in his exuberance, the evangelist misrepresents the ritual washing practices as belonging to "all the Jews" when the Sadducees did not share those practices.

As Lenten readings, these passages call us to reflect on and repent for our avarice and greed, and our neglect of our elders, providing an opportunity to discuss and address the vulnerability of our queer elders and others without families.

LENT III

Joshua 6:15–17, 23, 25; Psalm 146; James 2:14–19, 24–26; Mark 7:24–30

Joshua 6:15 And it happened on the seventh day that they rose early, at the break of dawn, and circled the city in the same way seven times. Only on that day that they circled the city seven times. [16] And it was the seventh time, when the priests blew the ram's horns, Joshua said to the people, "Shout! For the FAITHFUL ONE has given you the city. [17] The city and all that is in it shall be devoted to the HOLY ONE. Only Rahab the prostitute, she shall live and all who are with her in her house because she hid the messengers we sent.

[23] So the youths who were the spies went in and brought Rahab out, along with her mother, her father, her sisters and brothers, and all who belonged to her—all her kinfolk they brought out—and set them outside the camp of Israel.

²⁵ And Rahab the prostitute and her ancestral household and all who belonged to her, Joshua let live. She [her descendants] lives in the midst of Israel to this day for she hid the messengers whom Joshua sent to spy out Jericho.

Psalm 146

¹ Halleluyah! Praise the AGELESS ONE, O my soul!
² I will praise the EVER-LIVING GOD all my life;
I will sing praises to my God throughout my living.
³ Put not your trust in the great, nor in any child of earth,
for there is no help in them.
⁴ When they breathe their last, they return to earth,
and in that day their thoughts perish.
⁵ Happy are these for whom the God of Rebekah's line is their help,
whose hope is in the CREATOR OF ALL, their God.
⁶ Maker of heavens and earth, the seas, and all that is in them;
keeping faith forever.
⁷ Bringer of justice to the oppressed,
bringer of bread to the hungry.
⁸ The COMPASSIONATE GOD sets the prisoners free,
the ALL-SEEING GOD opens the eyes of the blind,
the JUST GOD lifts up those who are bowed down.
⁹ The RIGHTEOUS GOD loves the righteous,
the MOTHER OF ALL cares for the stranger,
orphan and widow she bears up,
but confounds the way of the wicked.
¹⁰ The MAJESTIC ONE shall reign forever,
your God, O Zion, from generation to generation.

James 2:14 What benefit is it, my sisters and brothers, if faith you say you have, but do not have works? Is faith able to save you? ¹⁵ If a sister or brother is naked and lacks daily food, ¹⁶ and one of you says to them, "Go in peace; warm yourself and eat your fill," and you all do not provide what is necessary for the body, what is the benefit of that? ¹⁷ And thus faith, if it has no works, is dead by itself.

¹⁸ Yet someone will say, "Faith you have and works I have." Show me your faith separately from your works, and I through my works will show you my faith. ¹⁹ You believe that God is One; you do well. Even the demons believe and they tremble.

²⁴ You see that by works is a woman or man shown to be righteous and not by faith alone. ²⁵ And likewise, was not Rahab the prostitute, by works, also shown to be righteous when she welcomed the messengers and sent them out by another road? ²⁶ For just as the body without the spirit is dead, so then faith without works is also dead.

Mark 7:24 [After teaching] Jesus, getting up, went to the region of Tyre. And he entered a house and did not wish anyone to know. Yet he was not able to escape notice; ²⁵ rather, immediately, a woman whose little daughter had an unclean spirit heard about him and she came and bowed down at his feet. ²⁶ Now the woman was Greek [meaning not Judean], of Syrophoenician ancestry and she asked him to cast the demon out of her daughter. ²⁷ And he said to her, "Let first the children be fed, for it is not right to take the children's bread and cast it to the dogs." ²⁸ But she answered him, "Healer, yet even the dogs under the table eat the crumbs of the children." ²⁹ Then Jesus said to her, "Because of this word, go; the demon has come out of your daughter." ³⁰ And she went to her house, found the child put on the bed and the demon gone.

PROCLAMATION

Text Notes

In Joshua 6:25, what has previously been described as Rahab's household (Josh. 2:1) is now configured as her father's household. That language along with "mother's household" signifies the smallest unit of Israelite society now applied to Rahab and her family. It reads as though a later Israelite editor was trying to fit her household into their social context. Indeed, in verse 27, it is "she" who continues to live among the Israelites, meaning her lineage, not her father's.

In Psalm 146:1, "throughout my living" is derived from "in my continuing" where "continue" is the adverb meaning "longer," *'od*, with the first possessive suffix, "my" attached; a very complex idiomatic saying. The "great" in verse 2 are "nobles," sometimes royal offspring, hence "princes" in other translations. In verse 4 "Rebekah's line" replaces "Jacob." The nature of God's support for widow and orphan in verse 9 is unclear; the verb there is only used there and its derivation is unclear. NRSV's "uphold" derives from the LXX and provides the basis for my "bear up." Similarly, the Peshitta has "nourish/support."

In Mark 7:26, "Greek" is used as the equivalent of "Gentile," demonstrating the categorization of people into a binary: Jewish/Judean and not. The woman "asks" Jesus and does not "beg" as so many others have translated, erasing her dignity. "Healer" replaces "Lord" in verse 28, where it is simply used as a courteous greeting and not as a religious confession. ("Lord" is a slaveholding title that dominates the scriptures as human and divine address; it is used sparingly in this project.) In verse 30, the use of *beblemenon* indicates the little girl is "put" or even "tossed" on the bed (by the demon?).

Preaching Prompts

This week's Lenten readings call us to consider our assumptions about and treatment of those we deem foreign, immigrants, those who do not share our religion and the cultural constructs that emerge from it, and those who have an historic adversarial relationship with us due to national and international politics. These lessons take a critical and uncomfortable look at who is deemed worthy to be safe, saved, and healed, and the reality that there are those who are posited in scripture not to qualify.

Rahab infamously saves her family and her people—that is those who belong to her and are part of her household whether they are kin or not—from the merciless attack on her city. God, through Joshua, destroys every infant, child, adult, and animal along with the architectural beauty and cultural legacy of the city. Of course, Jericho endures as arguably the oldest continuously inhabited city on the planet, and the story is braggadocious and a hermeneutics of imagination and reversal, the way we imagine it was or should have been. (It is important to note that the archaeological record reads against the majority of the conquest stories in Joshua, as do the opening chapters of Judges which state emphatically and repeatedly that the Israelites lived with the Canaanites in the land.) Yet, Joshua has been lionized and with it and him, Rahab as part of a tradition claiming the settled and inhabited land of Canaan as divine promise. It would be opportune to reflect on the lands we as Americans and as the Church have occupied and colonized. Rahab becomes notable as an example of faith in James, in part, because she is a foreign woman. And it is as a foreign woman that a desperate mother is first turned down by Jesus when she asks for healing for her daughter. In conversation with the Gospel, the Epistle reads as the inner monologue Jesus had before deciding to heal the little girl. His response to the foreign woman (though he is in her country) interrupting his seaside retreat is culture-bound and perhaps unwelcome evidence that Jesus is fully human as well as fully divine, and his humanity is not always seamlessly integrated with his divinity. His instinctual response, shaped by his culture and formation, is an opportunity for us to relate to and reflect on the things that shape us and our engagement with those who are different from us. And, it being Lent, repent where necessary, meaning, changing patterns of behavior as steps toward changing our assumptions, biases, instincts, and impulses.

LENT IV

1 Kings 17:8–16; Psalm 145:8–10, 14–19; 1 Corinthians 3:1–9; Mark 8:1–21

1 Kings 17:8 The word of the HOLY ONE to Elijah was, ⁹ "Get up, go to Zarephath, which is part of Sidon, and settle there; watch now, I have commanded a widow woman there to provide for you." ¹⁰ And Elijah got up and went to Zarephath. Then he came to the gate of the town, and look! a widow woman was there gathering sticks; so he called to her and said, "Bring me, please, a little water in a vessel, that I may drink." ¹¹ She went to bring it, and he called to her and said, "Bring me, please, a bit of bread in your hand." ¹² Then she said, "As the HOLY ONE your God lives, if I had a cake. There is only a handful of flour in a jar, and a little oil in a jug. Now look, I am gathering two sticks, then I will go home and prepare the oil and flour for myself and for my child; we will eat it, and we will die." ¹³ Then Elijah said to her, "Fear not; go and do as you have said, only make me a little cake of it and bring it to me first, then make something for yourself and your child afterwards. ¹⁴ For thus says the HOLY ONE the God of Israel: The jar of flour will not empty and the jug of oil will not decrease until the day that the HOLY ONE grants rain upon the earth." ¹⁵ She went and she did as Elijah said, and she and he, and her household, ate for many days. ¹⁶ The jar of flour did not empty and the jug of oil did not decrease according to the word of the HOLY ONE that God spoke through Elijah.

Psalm 145:8–10, 14–19

⁸ Full of grace and a mother's love is the MOTHER OF ALL,
   slow to anger and abounding in faithful love.
⁹ The WOMB OF LIFE is good to all,
   and her mother-love is upon all she has made.
¹⁰ They shall praise you, WELLSPRING OF LIFE, all your works,
   and all your faithful shall bless you.
¹⁴ The MERCIFUL ONE upholds all who fall,
   and raises up all who are bent over.
¹⁵ The eyes of all look to you,
   and you give to them their food at the right moment.
¹⁶ You open your hand,
   and satisfy the desire of every living thing.
¹⁷ The FAITHFUL ONE is righteous in all her ways,
   and loving in all her works.
¹⁸ The EVER-PRESENT GOD is near to all who call on her,
   to all who call on her in truth.
¹⁹ The desire of all who reveres her she fulfills;
   and their cry she hears and delivers them.

1 Corinthians 3:1 Now sisters and brothers, I could not speak to you all as spiritual, but rather as carnal, as infants in Christ. ² I fed you all with milk, not solid food, for you were not yet ready for solid food. Even now you are still not ready, ³ for you all are still carnal. Given there is still jealousy and discord among you, are you not carnal, and going around as merely human? ⁴ For when one says, "I am Paul's," and another, "I am Apollos's," are you not merely human?

⁵ What then is Apollos? What is Paul? Ministers through whom you came to believe, as the Messiah granted to each person. ⁶ I planted, Apollos watered, but God produces growth. ⁷ Therefore neither the one who plants nor the one who waters is anything, rather it is God

who produces growth. [8] The one who plants and the one who waters are alike, and each will receive wages according to their labor. [9] For we are God's coworkers, working together; you are God's cultivation, God's construction.

Mark 8:1 In those days there was again a great crowd of women, children, and men and they did not have anything to eat; Jesus called his disciples and said to them, [2] "I have compassion for the women, children, and men, because they have remained with me for three days already and do not have anything to eat. [3] And if I send them on their way hungry to their homes, they will faint on the way, and some of them have come from far away." [4] His disciples replied, "From where can anyone get loaves to feed these people here in the desert?" [5] Jesus asked them, "How many loaves do you all have?" They said, "Seven." [6] Then he ordered the women, children, and men of the crowd to sit down on the ground and he took the seven loaves, and after giving thanks, he broke and gave them to his disciples in order that they might distribute them, and they distributed them to the women, children, and men. [7] They had also a few little fish and after blessing them, he ordered that these be distributed as well. [8] They ate and were filled; and they took up the broken pieces left over, seven baskets full. [9] Now there were about four thousand women, children, and men. And he sent them on their way. [10] And immediately he got into the boat with his disciples and went to the district of Dalmanutha.

[11] And the Pharisees came and began to debate with Jesus, asking him for a sign from heaven, to test him. [12] And he sighed deeply in his spirit and said, "Why does this generation seek a sign? Truly I tell you all, no sign will be given to this generation." [13] And he left them again getting into the boat, he went across to the other side.

[14] Now they had forgotten to bring loaves of bread and except for one loaf they did not have any with them in the boat. [15] And Jesus instructed them, saying, "Look here! Beware of the yeast of the Pharisees and the yeast of Herod." [16] And they discussed among themselves that because of the lack of loaves he said it. [17] And becoming aware of it, Jesus said to them, "Why are you all discussing having no loaves? Do you still not perceive or understand? Are your hearts hardened?

[18] *Do you have eyes and fail to see? Do you have ears and fail to hear?*

And do you not remember? [19] When I broke the five loaves for the five thousand men, how many baskets full of broken pieces did you collect?" They said to him, "Twelve." [20] "And the seven for the four thousand women, children, and men, how many baskets full of broken pieces did you collect?" And they said to him, "Seven." [21] Then he said to them, "Do you not yet understand?"

PROCLAMATION

Text Notes

Psalm 145 uses the root *rchm,* derived from the womb, *rechem,* to articulate God's feelings for Israel. Accordingly, in verses 8–9, I translate the sentiment as "mother-love" rather than the traditional "compassion," which severs the link between the terms and their semantic range.

In this Gospel reading, "crowd" is amplified with "women, children, and men," the constituent of elements of any crowd without other delimiters. Jesus quotes Jeremiah 5:21 in verse 18. In verse 19, I supply "men" as Mark 6:44 specifies that the crowd of five thousand was entirely comprised of male people.

Preaching Prompts

The fourth Sunday in Lent is often celebrated as *Laetare* (rejoicing) Sunday, derived from the opening words in Latin of Isaiah 66:10, a traditional reading for the day. Many clergy wear rose pink vestments, a color associated with the Virgin Mary; additionally, the Sunday can fall in proximity to the Feast of the Annunciation on March 25. In these readings, the mothering figures include an actual mother, a series of men, Elijah, Jesus, and Paul, and God.

These Lenten lessons speak to the tender maternal love of God and Jesus, both of whom feed us in the wildernesses, ecologically and spiritually. God provides for all her children in 1 Kings 17: the prophet, the "foreign" widow, and her son. (Widow's children were considered orphans because the technical term translated "orphan" actually means fatherless.) The widow is desperate and vulnerable, and not an Israelite. The demand of the prophet of a God that she give him all she has to feed her child could easily have been exploitative. Contemporarily that is often the case.

In the psalm, God is the mother of all creation whose mother-love, more literally "womb love," extends to all she has made.

Paul appears as God's wetnurse, providing milk for spirit-young Christians who cannot tolerate solid food. Unnamed among the men who are also nursing God's children in the living Word of the Jesus movement are the women with whom he works and shares in teaching duties, such as Prisca, Priscilla. Where were his coworkers? The nursing imagery is helpful in that it does not confine care of infants to female people. There is trans-ness in this image and language as it pertains to the biological production of breastmilk. There is also the useful image of a man taking on childcare responsibilities as a metaphor for communicating the gospel and thereby potentially sanctifying it as a practice in the community. And Jesus feeds with solid food, in the words of the Epistle, for body and soul in the Gospel.

FEAST OF THE ANNUNCIATION, MARCH 25

Zephaniah 3:14–20; Canticle 15, the Magnificat (Luke 1:46–55);
2 Corinthians 6:16b–18; Luke 1:26–38

Zephaniah 3:14 Sing aloud, daughter of Zion; shout, all ye Israel!

Rejoice, daughter, and exult with all your heart, daughter of Jerusalem!

[15] The JUDGE OF ALL FLESH has taken away the judgments against you,
and has turned away your enemies, daughter.
The sovereign of Israel, CREATOR OF THE HEAVENS AND EARTH,
is in your midst, daughter; no longer shall you fear evil.

[16] On that day it shall be said to Jerusalem:
Fear not, Zion; do not let your hands grow weak, daughter.

[17] The AGELESS ONE, your God, is in your midst, daughter,
a warrior who will deliver salvation;
who will rejoice over you with gladness, daughter,
God will renew you in love, daughter;
God will exult over you, daughter, with loud singing.

[18] Those who are grieved on account of the festivals,
I will remove from you, daughter,
so, daughter, that you will not bear their reproach.

[19] I will deal with all your oppressors, daughter, at that time.
And I will save the lame and gather the outcast,
and I will change their shame into praise
and renown in all the earth.

[20] At that time I will bring you all home, at the time when I gather all of you;
for I will make you all renowned and praised
among all the peoples of the earth,
when I restore your fortunes before all of your eyes,
says the GOD WHO IS SALVATION.

Canticle 15, the Magnificat, Luke 1:46–55

[46] "My soul magnifies the Holy One,
[47] and my spirit rejoices in God my Savior,
[48] for God has looked with favor on the lowliness of God's own servant.
Surely, from now on all generations will call me blessed;
[49] for the Mighty One has done great things for me,
and holy is God's name.

⁵⁰ God's loving-kindness is for those who fear God
from generation to generation.

⁵¹ God has shown the strength of God's own arm;
God has scattered the arrogant in the intent of their hearts.

⁵² God has brought down the powerful from their thrones,
and lifted up the lowly;

⁵³ God has filled the hungry with good things,
and sent the rich away empty.

⁵⁴ God has helped God's own child, Israel,
a memorial to God's mercy,

⁵⁵ just as God said to our mothers and fathers,
to Abraham and Hagar and Sarah, to their descendants forever."

2 Corinthians 6:16b For we are the temple of the living God; as God said:

"I will dwell in them and walk among them,
and I will be their God,
and they shall be my people."

¹⁷ *Therefore, "Come out from them,*
and be separate from them," says the Holy One,
and "Touch nothing unclean,"
then "I will take you all in."

¹⁸ *and "I will be your parent,*
and you shall be my daughters and sons,"
says the Almighty Everlasting God.

Luke 1:26 In the sixth month the angel Gabriel was sent by God to a town of Galilee, Nazareth, ²⁷ to a virgin betrothed to a man whose name was Joseph, of the house of David. And the name of the virgin was Mary. ²⁸ And the angel came to Mary and said, "Rejoice, favored one! The Most High God is with you." ²⁹ Now, she was troubled by the angel's words and pondered what sort of greeting this was. ³⁰ Then the angel said to her, "Fear not, Mary, for you have found favor with God. ³¹ And now, you will conceive in your womb and give birth to a son, and you will name him Jesus. ³² He will be great and will be called the Son of the Most High, and the Sovereign God will give him the throne of his ancestor David. ³³ He will reign over the house of Jacob forever, and of his sovereignty there will be no end." ³⁴ Then Mary said to the angel, "How can this be, since I have not known a man intimately?" ³⁵ The angel said to her, "The Holy Spirit, She will come upon you, and the power of the Most High will overshadow you; therefore the one born will be holy. He will be called Son of God. ³⁶ And now, Elizabeth your kinswoman has even conceived a son in her old age, and this is the sixth month for she who was called barren. ³⁷ For nothing will be impossible with God." ³⁸ Then Mary said, "Here am I, the woman-slave of God; let it be with me according to your word." Then the angel left her.

PROCLAMATION

Text Notes

Bat Zion (or Jerusalem) can mean both Daughter Zion the city *or* a daughter of Zion, a woman from the city. In Isaiah 40:9, reading "daughter of" reveals a female prophet crying out to Jerusalem (compare NRSV and JPS translations). Because the addressee is feminine, all the verbs to her are also feminine; I reproduce "daughter" in places where English masks the frequency of feminine address. Verse 18 is notoriously difficult to translate: see the discussion in my commentary on Zephaniah in the *Wisdom* series.

In Luke 1:55, the inclusive plural *pateras* can mean ancestors, parents, or fathers. Since God's promises were not just to Abraham and God also made promises to Hagar (Gen. 16:10–13; 21:17–18), and for Sarah (through Abraham in Gen. 17:15–16), I have expanded "Abraham and his descendants" to reflect that. Abraham also had children with Keturah; their offspring would also be beneficiaries of the promises made Abraham; however, God does not make a promise directly to her in the scriptures.

In Mary's linguistic and cultural world, in Hebrew and Aramaic, the spirit is feminine; the Syriac text uses a feminine verb for the spirit in Luke 1:35. Also in her world, there was no distinction between servant and slave. Mary is not saying she will wait on God hand and foot in verse 38; she is giving God ownership of her body, ownership slaveholders claimed without consent.

Preaching Prompts

In its original context, Daughter Zion was most likely the city. Here I suggest hearing it through the experience of the pregnant Virgin reflecting on her scriptures in light of her experience.

The appointed Epistle is a collection of verse fragments strung together, many out of context. The phrases are inexact quotes, whether looking at Hebrew or Greek antecedents, shaped for deployment here. Leviticus 26:11–12 has the same sense as in 2 Corinthians 6:16. Verse 17 of the Epistle links a fragment found in both Ezekiel 20:34 and 20:41 to a line from Isaiah 52:11 calling for a second Exodus from Egypt. Verse 18 takes God's promise to David for Solomon to be his father in 2 Samuel 7:14 and makes it second person plural, "your all" instead of "his," and adds "daughters" to the altered text in Greek.

Angelic lore is largely pseudepigraphal beginning in 2 Esdras. While Gabriel and Michael appear in the Hebrew Bible (Dan. 8:16; 9:21; 10:13, 21; 12:1), they are not identified as angels. However, Raphael is called an angel in Tobit 5:4.

There is some irony in the pains the Gospel takes to connect Jesus to David and the Hebrew Scriptures, and choice of translators to anglicize the names of the holy family and disciples, undermining their Jewish identity. A further irony is that Jesus's Davidic heritage rests on Joseph's genealogy and the supposition that Mary is from the same tribe as was common but not required. Mary's only relative in the text, Elizabeth, is the wife of a priest. Priests married within the priestly line nearly exclusively, making her likely a *bat cohen*, priest's daughter as well. What this means for Mary's heritage and that of Jesus is unclear.

LENT V

Genesis 4:17–24; Psalm 128; 1 Corinthians 7:1–17; Mark 10:1–16

Genesis 4:17 Now Cain knew his woman (intimately) and she conceived and gave birth to Enoch and he built a city and named it Enoch after his child Enoch. [18] Then born to Enoch was Irad, and Irad fathered Mehujael and Mehujael fathered Methushael and Methushael fathered Lamech. [19] Then, Lamech took two women: the name of the one was Adah and the name of the second, Zillah. [20] And Adah gave birth to Jabal; he was the ancestor of those who live in tents surrounded by livestock. [21] And the name of his brother was Jubal; he was the ancestor of all those who take up the lyre and pipe. [22] Then Zillah gave birth to Tubal-Cain who forged every kind of implement of bronze and iron. And the sister of Tubal-Cain was Naamah.

[23] Lamech said to his women:
"Adah and Zillah, hear my voice;
you women of Lamech, hear well what I say:
I have killed a man for wounding me,
and a boy-child for striking me.
[24] If sevenfold Cain is avenged,
then Lamech seventy and seven."

Psalm 128

[1] Happy are all who revere the FOUNT OF LIFE,
walking in her ways.
[2] Of the labor of your hands shall you eat;
you shall be happy and it shall go well with you.
[3] Your woman, a fruitful vine flanking your house;
your children, olive shoots around your table.
[4] Thus shall the person be blessed
who reveres the SOURCE OF LIFE.
[5] The WELLSPRING OF LIFE bless you from Zion
and may you see the prosperity of Jerusalem
all the days of your life.

[6] And, may you see your children's children.

Peace be upon Israel!

1 Corinthians 7:1 Now, about what you have written: It is good for a man not to take hold of a woman. [2] But because of sexual immorality, each man should have his own woman and each woman her own man. [3] For the wife, the husband should do his duty and likewise the wife for her husband. [4] For the wife does not have authority over her own body, rather the husband does; likewise the husband does not have authority over his own body, yet the wife does. [5] Do not ever defraud each another except by agreement for a time to devote yourselves to prayer, and then come together again so that Satan may not tempt you because of your lack of self-control. [6] This I say as a concession, not a command. [7] I wish that all were as I myself am. But each has their own gift from God, indeed one to one and another to another.

[8] To the unmarried and the widows I say that it is good for them to remain so. [9] But if they are not showing self-control, they should marry; for it is better to marry than to burn. [10] To the married I give this command—not I but the Most High—a woman should not separate from her man, [11] though if she does separate, let her remain unmarried or else be reconciled to her man; also a man should not divorce his woman. [12] To the rest I say—I and not the Most High—that if a believer has a woman who is an unbeliever and she agrees to live with him, he should not divorce her. [13] And if a woman has a man who is an unbeliever and he agrees to live with her, she should not divorce him. [14] For the unbelieving man is made holy through his woman, and the unbelieving woman is made holy through her man. Otherwise, your children would be unclean, yet now they are holy. [15] Now if the unbeliever leaves, let them leave; a sister or brother is not bound in such circumstances. It is to peace that God has called you. [16] For woman, how do you know whether you will save your man, and how do you know, man, whether you will save your woman? [17] However let each walk through life as the Holy One has designated and as God has called them. This is what I instruct all the churches.

Mark 10:1 Now Jesus arose from [Capernaum] and went to the region of Judea and beyond the Jordan and crowds of women, children, and men again gathered around him, and as was his custom, again he taught them. [2] Then came Pharisees, asking him if it was permissible for a man to divorce, testing Jesus. [3] But he answered, saying to them, "What did Moses command you?" [4] Now, they said, "Moses allowed writing a document of release and divorce." [5] But Jesus said to them, "Because of your hard-heartedness he inscribed this commandment for you all. [6] But from the beginning of creation, '_God made them female and male._' [7] '_Because of this a man shall leave his mother and father and be joined to his woman,_ [8] _and the two shall become one flesh._' Thus they are no longer two, but one flesh. [9] Therefore what God has joined together, let no mortal separate." [10] Then in the house, again the disciples asked Jesus about this. [11] He said to them, "Whoever divorces his woman and marries another commits adultery against her; [12] and if she divorces her man and marries another, she commits adultery."

13 Also, women and men were bringing him children so that he might hold them and the disciples rebuked them. 14 Yet when Jesus saw he became angry and said to them, "Let the children come to me; do not prevent them. For to such ones the reign of God belongs. 15 Truly I tell you all, whoever does not receive the reign of God as a little child will not enter it." 16 Then he embraced them, blessing them, laying his hands on them.

PROCLAMATION
Text Notes

Neither Hebrew nor Greek has distinct words for wives or husbands. Both languages use the expressions "her man" and "his woman" to indicate conjugal relationships. In 1 Corinthians 7, Paul first says that each *woman or man* should have their own spouse. Then using the same wording, he means that each *wife or husband* should do their duty by their spouse. Paul uses *anthropos,* which means "human" and "man" for man and *aner*, male person, for "husband" while using the most common term for women, *gune*, for both women and wives. Having used *anthropos* for male initially, it is not clear whether Paul means "all males" or "all people" have their own gift of God in verse 7.

Jesus's previous location, Capernaum, is disclosed in Mark 9:33. *Exestin*, "permissible, right, possible" is not "lawful" (NRSV) or "allow[ed]" by "the Law" (CEB). These translations create and contribute to the idea that Jesus is in opposition to his own cultural and religious background, in anti-Semitism and anti-Judaism. Both NRSV in CEB add "wife" to verses 2 and 4. In neither case is the divorced person specified, though certainly understood to be a woman. In verse 6, Jesus quotes Genesis 1:27; in verse 7 he quotes Genesis 2:24. In verse 13, I expand the inclusive "they" to "women and men," and *hapsetai* here means "touch" or "hold." I prefer "whole" because it is more intimate, and the later description in verse 16, "embrace" (lit. "took them in his arms"), corresponds to "hold" more than to "touch." The verb in verse 14 can mean either "to be angry" or "to be indignant." The stronger reading contributes to a portrait of Jesus who feels the full range of emotions and feels them passionately.

Preaching Prompts

This final week of Lent, we engage some of the various forms of "biblical marriage" in conversation with the Markan account of Jesus's teaching on divorce. Matthew's Jesus is more lenient, allowing for divorce in the case of infidelity by either partner (see Matt. 5:32 and 19:9). In an often-overlooked text, Lamech, the largely unknown first patriarch of the scriptures, invents polygamy. Significantly, he is not rebuked by God and the practice becomes normalized. This demonstrates that human beings can and have and continue to modify the social construct we call marriage—a term rarely used in the canon—across the ages.

In 1 Corinthians 7, Paul proscribes the choices of the community when it comes to marriage but allows for different life patterns while promoting his own celibate estate. He is a "naturalist," desiring believers to remain in their current estate, including marriage, virginity, and, more problematically, slavery (vv. 22–23). Paul lays out his preferred pattern of partnering, describing an egalitarian marriage with each belonging to the other, yet within his hierarchal and specifically patriarchal world it is doubtful there was true equality. Religious proclamations that individuals do not have the right to control their own bodies are dangerous. Paul's narrowing of women's bodily autonomy provides sanctified cover for abusive relationships. His teaching does correspond with Jewish teaching that spouses owe each other sexual pleasure. Paul recognizes that people will leave their partners and articulates a framework of accountability. He does so issuing commands from God interspersed with his own commands and preferences.

Jesus's rejection of divorce for any cause in the Markan account is an outlier when read in conversation with Christian Testament and in light of the practices of the early Jesus movement. This passage has often been taught misrepresenting the access to divorce available to Jewish women. In fact, they, particularly with means, could initiate divorce. This is a difficult passage read more difficult for some by the heteronormative framework of intimate relationships and family building. One useful observation from reading these passages in conversation is that each models interpretive flexibility with how we engage God, scripture, culture, and tradition around marriage.

At the same time, as this complex conversation is happening in and out of the text, Jesus directs our attention to the children who are the heart of many families, a tangible reminder partner decisions are larger communal decisions in keeping with the structure of Israelite familial culture.

Lastly, the preacher will have the possibly unwelcome opportunity to talk about how we read and interpret scripture and can faithfully disagree with it.

PALM SUNDAY—LITURGY OF THE PALMS

Matthew 21:1–11; Psalm 118:19–29

Matthew 21:1 Now they had come near Jerusalem and reached Bethphage on the Mount of Olives, then Jesus sent two disciples, [2] saying to them, "Go into the village before you, and immediately you will find a donkey tied, and a colt with her; release them and bring them to me. [3] If anyone says anything to you, just say this, 'The Son of Woman needs them.' And they will send them immediately." [4] This took place to fulfill what had been spoken through the prophet, saying,

⁵ "Tell the daughter of Zion,
   '*Look, your sovereign is coming to you,*
   humble, and mounted on a donkey,
   and on a colt, the foal of a donkey.'"

⁶ The disciples went and did just as Jesus had instructed them; ⁷ they brought the donkey and the colt, and put their cloaks on them, and he sat on them. ⁸ A very large crowd spread their cloaks on the road, and others cut branches from the trees and spread them on the road. ⁹ The crowds that were going before him and the one following were shouting, saying:

"*Hosanna to the Son of David!*
Blessed is the one who comes in the name of the Holy One!
Hosanna in the highest!"

¹⁰ When Jesus entered Jerusalem, the whole city was shook, asking, "Who is this?" ¹¹ The crowds were saying, "This is the prophet Jesus from Nazareth in Galilee."

Psalm 118:19–29

¹⁹ Open for me the gates of righteousness,
   that I may enter them
   and give thanks to the LIVING GOD.
²⁰ This is the gate to the HOLY PRESENCE;
   the righteous shall enter through it.
²¹ I thank you that you have answered me
   and you have become my salvation.
²² The stone that the builders rejected
   has become the chief cornerstone.
²³ This is OUR GOD's doing;
   it is marvelous in our eyes.
²⁴ This is the day that the FONT OF CREATION has made;
   let us rejoice and be glad in it.
²⁵ Ah! HOLY ONE, help, save us!
   Ah! HOLY ONE, haste, deliver us!
²⁶ Blessed is the one who comes in the name of the MOST HIGH GOD.
   We bless you from the house of the HOLY ONE.
²⁷ The FAITHFUL ONE is God,
   and she has given us light.
   Bind the festal offering with ropes of branches,
   up to the horns of the altar.
²⁸ You are my God, and I will give thanks to you;
   you are my God; I will exalt you.

^{29} Give thanks to the HOLY ONE, for she is good,
for her faithful love endures forever.

PROCLAMATION

Text Notes

The text has Jesus use the title "Lord" of himself in Matthew 21:3. In keeping with the aims of this volume, expansive and explicitly feminine language for God and humanity, I employ a translation of the messianic title Jesus often uses for himself here. (See commentary on Advent 1, Year A.) In verse 5 the Gospel quotes Zechariah 9:9, seeming not to understand the poetic parallelism that describes the same animal in two ways; he appears to sit on both in verse 7. The Gospel adds an introduction to "*the* daughter of Zion," adding the definite article not common in this expression in Greek, begging the question to whom it is addressed. In verse 9, the crowd chants Psalm 118:26, a procession psalm for entering the temple also recited during Passover.

The assonant and alliterative poetry of Psalm 118:25 (the "Hosanna") verse, is difficult to reproduce: *Ana Ya hoshia na; Ana Ya chatzlicha na*. The "hosanna" pronunciation comes from the Greek transliteration of the Hebrew. Verse 27 is unclear in a number of places: "bind the feast with clouds." Since portions of sacrificial animals were eaten, "festal offering" is likely; and "ropes" and "branches" are each one letter away from "clouds." "God's faithful love endures forever" is one of the oldest liturgical refrains in the Hebrew Bible, see the opening and closing of this psalm and Psalm 118.

Preaching Prompts

While this is not traditionally a preaching occasion, one may choose to frame the liturgy with a brief preface or blurb in the leaflet, or alternately address it in the subsequent sermon (if the liturgy precedes another service).

The ubiquity of monarchy in the scriptures and the worlds from which they emerge reflect more about the humans who received and recorded, and translate and interpret them, than it does about God who inspired and speaks through them. Monarchs were the most powerful persons in those worlds and they and their power, reigns, and regalia provided a vocabulary for talking about God. Jesus subverts that to some degree by reinterpreting that title in such a way as to perplex even those who knew him best.

These lessons provide an opportunity to talk about our language and imagery for God in and out of the Bible (and this lectionary) and its impact on persons in terms of class, gender, the performance of gender, and sexual orientation.

PALM SUNDAY—LITURGY OF THE WORD

Isaiah 49:5–16; Psalm 22:1–11; Galatians 3:23–4:7;
Mark 14:32–15:47 (or Mark 14:32–52)

Those who prefer to continue the Gospel through the Passion will find the successive verses in the Good Friday readings.

Isaiah 49:5 And now says the AUTHOR OF LIFE,

> who formed me in the womb to be God's slave
> to return Jacob back to God,
> and that Israel might be gathered to God;
> I am honored in the sight of the HOLY ONE OF OLD,
> and my God is my strength.

6 God says,

> "It is too light a thing that you should be my slave
> to raise up the tribes of Jacob [the line of Rebekah],
> and to restore the survivors of Israel [born of Rachel and Leah, and Bilhah and Zilpah]?
> I will give you as a light to the nations,
> for it will be that my salvation reaches to the end of the earth."

7 Thus says the FAITHFUL ONE,

> the Redeemer of Israel, God's holy one,
> to one despised, abhorred by the nations,
> the slave of rulers,
> "Queens and kings shall see and arise,
> princes and princesses, and they too shall prostrate themselves,
> on account of the FIRE OF SINAI, who is faithful,
> the Holy One of Israel, who has chosen you."

8 Thus says the MIGHTY GOD:

> In a favorable time have I answered you,
> on a day of salvation have I helped you;
> I have kept you and given you
> as a covenant to the people,
> to establish the land,
> to apportion the desolate portions;

9 saying to the prisoners, "Go free!"

> to those who are in darkness, "Let yourselves be seen."
> Along the paths they shall pasture,
> and on all the bare heights shall be their pasture.

10 They shall not hunger nor shall they thirst,

neither shall heat nor sun strike them down,
for the one who mother-loves them shall lead them,
and by springs of water shall guide them.

11 And I will turn all my mountains into a pathway,
and my highways shall be raised up.

12 Look! These shall come from far away,
and see! These from the north and from the sea to the west,
and these from the southland of Syene.

13 Sing for joy, you heavens, and exult O earth;
let mountains break forth into singing!
For the TENDER LOVING ONE has comforted God's people,
and will mother-love God's suffering ones.

14 But Zion said, "The EVERLASTING GOD has forsaken me,
my Sovereign has forgotten me."

15 Can a woman forget her nursing child,
or mother-love for the child of her womb?
Even these may forget,
yet I, no, I will not forget you.

16 See, I have engraved you on the palms of my hands;
your walls are continually before me.

Psalm 22:1–11

1 My God, my God, why have you forsaken me?
Why are you so far from my deliverance, from the words of my groaning?

2 My God, I cry by day, and you do not answer;
and by night, and there is no rest for me.

3 Yet you are holy,
enthroned on the praises of Israel.

4 In you our mothers and fathers trusted;
they trusted, and you rescued them.

5 To you they cried, and were freed;
in you they trusted, and they were not put to shame.

6 But I am a worm, and not human;
scorned by humankind, and despised by people.

7 All who see me mock me;
they flap their lips at me, they shake their heads:

8 "Commit yourself to the SAVING ONE; let God rescue
and deliver the one in whom God delights!"

9 Yet it was you who drew me from the womb;
keeping me safe on my mother's breast.

10 On you was I cast from birth,

and since my mother's womb you have been my God.

11 Be not far from me,

for trouble is near

and there is none to help.

Galatians 3:23 Now before faith came, we were garrisoned and guarded under the law until the faith that was coming should be revealed. 24 Therefore the law was our instructor until Christ came, so that we might be justified by faith. 25 But now that faith has come, we are no longer subject to an instructor, 26 for in Christ Jesus you are all daughters and sons of God through faith. 27 So, as many of you as were baptized into Christ are clothed in Christ. 28 There is no Jew or Greek, there is no slave or free, there is no male and female; for all of you are one in Christ Jesus. 29 And if you belong to Christ, then you are Abraham's [and Sarah's] offspring, heirs according to the promise.

4:1 I say that as long as heirs are minors, they are no better than slaves, though they are the masters of all; 2 but they remain under guardians and trustees until the time set by the father. 3 So also for us; while we were minors, we were enslaved by the constitutive elements of the world. 4 But when the fullness of time had come, God sent God's own Son, born of a woman, born under the law, 5 to redeem those who were under the law, so that we might receive adoption like children. 6 And because you are children, God has sent the Spirit of God's own Son into our hearts, crying, "Abba! Father!" 7 So you are no longer a slave but a child, and if a child then also an heir, through God.

[**Mark 14:32** Jesus and his disciples went to a place called Gethsemane and he said to his disciples, "You all sit here while I pray." 33 He took with him Peter and James and John and began to be deeply moved and distressed. 34 And said to them, "My soul is deeply grieved, to the point of death; you all stay here, and stay awake." 35 And going a little farther, he threw himself on the ground and prayed that, if possible, the hour might pass from him. 36 He said, "Abba, Father, all things are possible for you; remove this cup from me; yet, not what I want, but what you do." 37 Jesus came and found them sleeping; and he said to Peter, "Simon, are you sleeping? Could you not stay awake one hour? 38 Stay awake and pray that you all may not come into the time of trial; the spirit indeed is willing, but the flesh is weak." 39 And again he went away and prayed, saying the same thing. 40 And once more he came and found them sleeping, for their eyes were very heavy; and they did not know what to say to him. 41 Jesus came a third time and said to them, "Are you all sleeping, still, and taking your rest? Enough! The hour has come. Look! The Son of Woman is betrayed into the hands of sinners. 42 Get up, let us go. See, my betrayer is at hand."

43 And instantly, while he was still speaking, Judas, one of the twelve, arrived; with him there was a crowd with swords and clubs from the chief priests, the religious scholars, and the elders. 44 Now the betrayer had given them a sign, saying, "The one I kiss is he; seize him and lead him away safely." 45 Then when Judas came, he went up to Jesus immediately and

said, "Rabbi!" and kissed him. ⁴⁶ Then they laid hands on him and took him. ⁴⁷ But one of the bystanders drew his sword and struck the slave of the high priest and cut off his ear. ⁴⁸ Then Jesus said to them, "Is it as for a bandit you all have come out with swords and clubs to seize me? ⁴⁹ Daily I was with you all in the temple teaching, and you did not seize me. But let the scriptures be fulfilled." ⁵⁰ All of them deserted him and fled. ⁵¹ A certain young man was following Jesus, with just a fine cloth on his naked flesh. They caught hold of him, ⁵² but he forsook the fine cloth and ran off naked.]

⁵³ They took Jesus to the high priest; and they assembled all the chief priests, the elders, and the religious scholars. ⁵⁴ Now Peter followed him from afar into the courtyard of the high priest and was sitting with the attendants, warming himself at the fire. ⁵⁵ Now the chief priests and the whole council sought testimony against Jesus to put him to death but found none. ⁵⁶ For many gave false testimony against him, yet their testimony did not agree. ⁵⁷ Some rose and gave false testimony against him, saying, ⁵⁸ "Well, we heard him say, 'I will destroy this hand-made temple, and in three days I will build another, that is not hand-made.'" ⁵⁹ But even on this point their testimony did not agree. ⁶⁰ Then the high priest stood up before them and said to Jesus, "No response? What are they testifying against you?" ⁶¹ But he was silent and answered nothing. Again, the high priest spoke to him, "Are you the Messiah, the Son of the Blessed One?" ⁶² Jesus said, "I am; and

'you will see the Son of Woman
    seated at the right hand of the Power,'
and 'coming with the clouds of heaven.'"

⁶³ Then the high priest tore his clothes and said, "Why do we still need witnesses? ⁶⁴ You all have heard his blasphemy! How does it appear to you?" All of them condemned him, "Guilty! This is death!" ⁶⁵ Some began to spit on him, to blindfold him, and to strike him, saying to him, "Prophesy!" Then the attendants took him and beat him.

⁶⁶ While Peter was below in the courtyard, one of the high priest's enslaved girls came by. ⁶⁷ When she saw Peter warming himself, she stared at him and said, "You were also with the Nazarene, Jesus." ⁶⁸ But Peter denied it, saying, "I do not know or even understand what you are saying." Then he went out into the front courtyard. Then the cock crowed. ⁶⁹ And the enslaved girl, on seeing him, began to say to the bystanders again that this man is one of them. ⁷⁰ But again he denied it. Then after a little while the bystanders said to Peter again, "Certainly you are one of them, for you are a Galilean." ⁷¹ But he began to curse and swore, "I do not know this person you are talking about." ⁷² And suddenly the cock crowed for the second time. Then Peter remembered the thing Jesus had said to him, "Before the cock crows twice, you will deny me three times." And he threw himself down and sobbed.

15:1 As soon as it was morning, the chief priests took a counsel with the elders and religious scholars and the whole council. They bound Jesus, led him away, and handed him over to Pilate. ² Pilate asked him, "Are you the King of the Judeans?" He answered him, saying, "You say so." ³ Then the chief priests accused him of many things. ⁴ But Pilate asked him again, "Have you no reply? See how many charges they bring against you." 5 But Jesus made no further reply, thus Pilate was amazed.

6 Now at the festival Pilate used to release one prisoner to them, whoever they asked. 7 Now there was a man called Barabbas in prison with the rebels who in the rebellion had committed murder. 8 So the crowd came and began to ask Pilate to do for them according to his custom. 9 Then he responded to them, saying, "Do you all want me to release the King of the Judeans to you?" 10 For he recognized that it was out of jealousy that the chief priests had handed him over. 11 Then the chief priests stirred up the crowd that instead Barabbas might be released for them. 12 Pilate again responded to them, "What then do you wish me to do with the one you call the King of the Judeans?" 13 They shouted more [than before], "Crucify him!" 14 Pilate asked them, "Why, for doing what evil?" But they shouted all the more, "Crucify him!" 15 So Pilate, wanting to satiate the crowd, released Barabbas to them; then he handed Jesus over for flogging and to be crucified.

16 Then the soldiers led him into the courtyard of the property, which is the military headquarters, and they called together the entire cohort. 17 And they clothed him in purple, and they put on him thorns woven into a crown. 18 And they began saluting him, "Hail, King of the Judeans!" 19 They struck his head with a reed, spat upon him, and knelt in homage to him. 20 After mocking him, they stripped him of the purple and put his clothes on him. Then they led him away to crucify him.

21 They compelled a passerby, a certain Simon of Cyrene who was coming from the countryside, to carry his cross; he was the father of Alexander and Rufus. 22 Then they brought Jesus to the Golgotha place (which means Skull Place). 23 And they offered him myrrh wine, but he did not take it. 24 And they crucified him, and divided his clothes, casting lots among themselves for what each would take.

25 It was the third hour [past dawn] when they crucified him. 26 The writing above of the accusation against him read, "The King of the Judeans." 27 And with him they crucified two revolutionaries, one on his right and one on his left.

29 The passersby reviled him, shaking their heads and saying, "Ha! You would destroy the temple and build it in three days—30 save yourself, and come down from the cross!" 31 In the same way the chief priests, with the religious scholars, mocked him among themselves and said, "He saved others; himself he is unable to save. 32 The Messiah, the King of Israel! Come down from the cross now that we may see and believe." Those who were crucified with him also demeaned him.

33 Now when it was the sixth hour [of the day, or noon], darkness came over the whole land until the ninth hour [of the day, about three in the afternoon]. 34 At the ninth hour Jesus cried out with a loud voice, "*Eloi, Eloi, lema sabachthani?*" which means, "My God, my God, why have you forsaken me?" 35 When some of the bystanders heard it, they said, "Listen, he is calling Elijah." 36 And someone ran and filled a sponge with vinegary wine, put it on a stick, and gave it to him to drink, saying, "Wait, let us see whether Elijah will come to take him down." 37 Then Jesus gave a great cry and breathed out a final time. 38 And the

curtain of the temple was torn in two, from top to bottom. [39] Now when the centurion, stationed facing him, saw that in this way Jesus breathed out at the end, he said, "Truly this man was God's Son!"

[40] There were also women watching from a distance; among them were Mary the Magdalene, and Mary the mother of James the younger and of Joses, and Salome. [41] These women followed him and ministered to him when he was in Galilee, and there were many other women who had come up with him to Jerusalem.

[42] When evening had come, since it was the day of Preparation—the day before the sabbath—[43] Joseph of Arimathea, a respected member of the council, who himself was also waiting for the reign of God, went boldly to Pilate and requested for the body of Jesus. [44] Then Pilate wondered that Jesus was now dead, and summoning the centurion asked him whether he had been dead for some time. [45] When he learned it from the centurion, he gave the corpse to Joseph. [46] Then Joseph bought a fine cloth, and taking him down, wrapped him in the fine cloth, and put him in a tomb that had been hewn out of rock. He then rolled a stone against the door of the tomb. [47] Mary the Magdalene and Mary the mother of Joses saw where he was put.

PROCLAMATION

Owing to the length of the Palm Sunday Gospel, the commentary section will be longer than for other readings.

Text Notes

The same word is used in Isaiah 49:5 and verse 7, yet NRSV, JPS, and CEB all translate Israel as God's "servant" but the nation as the "slave of rulers." "Servant" occludes the expectation of complete domination/submission, including ability to maim, kill, breed, rape, impregnate, and sell the person without consequence.

Hebrew plurals like "monarchs/kings" and "princes" in Isaiah 49:7 are inclusive. I have expanded both to reflect the presence of female royals in and at the head of some nations. "Go free" in verse 9 uses the primary verb of the exodus. Syene, or Sinim, in verse 12 is an Egyptian town with a record of some Israelite settlement.

In Isaiah 49:5 and 15 "womb" is the more generic "belly" used broadly for women and men; it is also found in Psalm 22:9–10 (verse 10 also uses the more common specific "womb). In Isaiah 49:13–15 it is paired with "mother-love" (the verb whose root is that same word), and children, including one at the breast, in verse 15. Translating this as "compassion" (NRSV), "pity" (CEB), or just "love" (JPS) eviscerates the intentionally crafted portrait of God as a mother, accomplished despite use of masculine forms.

The second phrase in Psalm 22:3 can also be translated as "you are holy, enthroned, the Praise of Israel." In verse 9 the Divine Midwife "extracts" the baby; she does not just "catch" him, perhaps suggesting a difficult birth.

In Galatians 3:23ff translation choices can present the law in an antagonistic and ultimately anti-Jewish manner as "prison" and "disciplinarian" (see NRSV). However, *ephrouroumetha* in verse 23 means to set a guard or garrison; that is a protective action. And in verse 24, a *paidagōgos* is a teacher; *torah* itself means "teaching" and "revelation" more than "law."

One of the verbs that describes Jesus's emotions in Mark 14:33 is only used in that place, making it difficult to define; suggestions range from "amazed" to "gloomy" to "distressed" to "troubled." In verse 34, Jesus expresses his sorrow using the language of Psalms 42:11 and 43:5 in Greek: "my soul is cast down." Similarly, the description of soldiers gambling for Jesus's clothes matches the wording of Psalm 22:18 in Greek. Judas is concerned that Jesus's arrest be done "safely" in verse 44; he is a complex character with mixed motives. The "attendants" in verse 54 can provide a number of services; the word is more "assistant" than "guard," as is commonly translated. The enslaved "girls" in Mark 14:66–69 could be young women. "Girl" is often used to denote their minor legal status. The criminals crucified with Jesus in Mark 15:27 could have been thieves or highway bandits; the root of *lēstēs* is stolen goods. However, the semantic range includes revolutionaries and insurrectionists. This latter understanding may be what is meant given mention of imprisoned rebels (using a different word, *stasiastēs*) in verse 7. The vinegar wine in verse 36 draws on Psalm 69:21. The nature of the women's ministry to Jesus in 15:41 should be understood as wholistic: spiritual and material. Many Greek manuscripts use the more explicit *ptōma*, "corpse," rather than *soma*, "body," for Jesus's remains in Mark 15:44.

Verse 28 is missing from most translations as its origin hails from less well-regarded manuscripts.

Preaching Prompts

As Holy Week begins, one may wish to explore God's sorrow over a world that crucifies as well as over a crucified beloved child, a mother's sorrow as well as a father's. In Isaiah 49, God is the divine mother whose love emanates from her womb, most specifically in verses 13-15.

Contemporary discomfort with slave language should not overshadow the degree to which it was normative in the biblical text and its theologies. For the biblical ear, "slave of God" and "slave of Sarah" were equally acceptable and nonremarkable. The linguistic distinction between being a "servant" of God and being held in slavery is entirely artificial to the text and permits slave-holding societies to embrace servitude of God as pertaining to them while holding others in bondage in a fictive distinct category.

In Psalm 22 the most obvious divine feminine image is God as midwife and lactation guide in verse 9. There is also the birthing mother who has no voice and makes no cry. In verse 10 God seems to have become a foster parent for a perhaps abandoned child; the child is thrown (away?) on to God. God can be both midwife and foster mother here. We do not know if the birth mother cannot or will not keep her child. She can be preached in conversation with the reminder that women do abandon children in Isaiah 49, yet without demonization. In keeping with Palm Sunday, she can be read as giving her child over to God, whatever his fate.

Galatians 3:23–24 describes the law as a protective, not punitive, garrison and guard. Though addressing a Gentile Church on whom the Torah (or *torah* broadly) was never binding, Paul uses "we" regarding the law. In a rhetorical flourish, Paul argues that the particularities that characterize individuals and communities no longer exist "in Christ," yet he continues to operate as though those categories continue and are normative. Our adoption and kinship does not require us to leave ourselves, our identities behind.

There are very few women and girls in the Passion narratives. Here in Luke there are girls or women held in slavery by the chief priest. There is missing the wife of Simon of Cyrene, the Cross-Bearer; he is named with reference to his sons, but no mention is made of their mother.

The Passion narratives on Palm Sunday and Good Friday have been used to incite lethal physical violence against Jewish communities by the Church and its ministers. They have also been used to craft violent, anti-Semitic theologies that blame Jews for the death of Jesus, demean and defame Judaism, and deem it failed and its covenants replaced. It is important to acknowledge that history while repudiating it and repenting of it and affirming God's fidelity to all her covenants and all her peoples. It is essential to be in conversation with our Jewish neighbors and to listen more than speak. I strongly recommend reading the scriptures in conversation with Jewish scholars, for example with the *Jewish Study Bible* and *Jewish Annotated New Testament*.

MONDAY IN HOLY WEEK

Jeremiah 31:8–13; Psalm 22:19–31; Hebrews 1:1–9; John 12:1–7

Jeremiah 31:8 Look! I am going to bring them from the land of the north,

and I will gather them from the farthest parts of the earth,
among them blind and lame, pregnant and birthing, together,
a great assembly, they shall return here.
9 With weeping they shall come,
and with consolations I will lead them back,
I will have them walk by streams of water,
on a straight path, they shall not stumble on it;
for I am a parent to Israel,
and Ephraim is my firstborn.

10 Hear the word of the HOLY ONE, you nations,
     and declare it in the islands far off;
       say, "The One who scattered Israel will gather him,
       and will keep him as a shepherd a flock."
11 For the FAITHFUL ONE has ransomed Jacob [of Rebekah's line]
     and has redeemed him from hands too strong for him.
12 They shall come and they shall sing on the heights of Zion,
     and they shall be radiant over the goodness of the GRACIOUS GOD,
       over the grain, and over the new wine, and over the oil,
       and over the young of flock and herd;
       their souls shall become like a watered garden,
       and they shall never languish again.
13 Then shall young women rejoice in dance,
     and young men and elders together.
       I will turn their mourning to joy;
       I will comfort them, and give them joy for sorrow.

Psalm 22:19–31

19 SAVING GOD, be not far away!
     My strength, hasten to help me!
20 Deliver my soul from the sword,
     my life from the clutch of the dog!
21 Save me from the mouth of the lion!
     For on the horns of the wild oxen you have responded to me.
22 I will tell of your name to my sisters and brothers;
     in the midst of the congregation, I will praise you:
23 You who revere the FOUNT OF LIFE, praise her!
     all the offspring of Leah and Rachel, Bilhah and Zilpah glorify her.
     Stand in awe of her all you of Rebekah's line.
24 For she did not despise or abhor
     the affliction of the afflicted;
     she did not hide her face from me,
     and when I cried to her, she heard.
25 On your account is my praise in the great congregation;
     my vows I will pay before those who revere her.
26 The poor shall eat and be satisfied;
     those who seek her shall praise the MOTHER OF ALL.
     May your hearts live forever!
27 All the ends of the earth shall remember
     and turn to the WELLSPRING OF LIFE;

and all the families of the nations
shall worship before her.
²⁸ For sovereignty belongs to the SHE WHO IS HOLY,
and she rules over the nations.
²⁹ They consume and they bow down,
all the fat ones of the earth before her,
they bend their knees,
all who go down to the dust,
and cannot save their soul.
³⁰ Later descendants will serve her;
future generations will be told about our God,
³¹ they will go and proclaim her deliverance
to a people yet unborn,
saying that she has done it.

Hebrews 1:1 Many times and in many ways God spoke to our mothers and fathers through the prophets, female and male. ² In these last days God has spoken to us by a Son, whom God appointed heir of all there is, and through whom God created the worlds. ³ The Son is the brilliance of God's glory and reproduction of God's very being, and the Son undergirds all there is by his word of power. When the Son had made purification for sins, he sat down at the right hand of the Majesty on high, ⁴ having become much greater than the angels, as the name he inherited is more excellent than theirs.

⁵ For to which of the angels did God ever say,
"You are my Child; today I have begotten you"?

Or this,

"I will be their Parent, and they will be my Child"?

⁶ Then again, when God brings the firstborn into the world, God says,

"Let all the angels of God worship him."

⁷ On the one hand, of the angels God says,

*"God makes winds into celestial messengers,
and flames of fire into God's ministers."*

⁸ But of the Son God says,

*"Your throne, O God, is forever and ever,
and the righteous scepter is the scepter of your realm.*
⁹ *You have loved righteousness and hated lawlessness;
therefore God, your God, has anointed you
with the oil of gladness beyond your companions."*

John 12:1 Now Jesus, six days before the Passover, came to Bethany where Lazarus was who he raised from the dead. [2] There they gave a dinner for him and Martha served while Lazarus was one of those at the table with him. [3] Mary took a pound of a balm made of expensive pure nard, anointed the feet Jesus, and wiped them with her hair. The house was filled with the scent of the perfume. [4] But Judas Iscariot, one of his disciples, the one who was about to betray him, said, [5] "Why was this balm not sold for three hundred denarii and the money given to the poor?" [6] Now he said this not because he cared about the poor, but because he was a thief; he kept the moneybag, and whatever was put into it, he stole. [7] Jesus said, "Leave her alone. It was for the day of my burial that she kept it."

PROCLAMATION

Text Notes

In Jeremiah 31:9, arguably, "consolations" became "supplications," the literal reading, when a letter was dropped.

In Psalm 22:23, "the offspring of Jacob" are identified by their mothers/matriarchs, enslaved and free; similarly, "Rebekah's line" stands in for "the offspring of Israel."

In keeping with the aims of this work, foremothers and female prophets are made explicit in Hebrews 1:1. *Megalōsynēs*, "Majesty," in Hebrews 1:3, as a feminine noun, marks a rare use of feminine language to describe God or her attributes in the New Testament.

The following verses quote the earlier scriptures widely and often out of context: Hebrews 1:5 quotes Psalm 2:7, where the anonymous psalmist says God told them they were God's begotten child, probably initially heard with regard to David. The next quote is from 2 Samuel 7:14 (and its duplicate, 1 Chron. 17:13), where the promise of God to be a parent to a future monarch is to one of David's descendants. Given the difficulty of asserting biological gender for heavenly beings, I use the neuter "child" and "parent" in verse 5. Verse 6 quotes Deuteronomy 32:43 and Psalm 97:7 from Greek, where the original "gods" were replaced by "angels" to correct toward a pure monotheism. Verse 7 quotes Psalm 104:4, playing on the primary meaning of angel, "messenger." Verses 8–9 quote Psalm 45:6–7, where the first verse refers to God, but the second refers to the king whose wedding psalm it is (Ahab, since Jezebel is the only princess of Tyre to marry into Israel).

Preaching Prompts

A second iteration of the woman who anoints Jesus is traditional on Monday of Holy Week, an earlier version having been read on the last Sunday of Lent. Today the woman is Mary, sister of Martha and the resurrected Lazarus in John. The Jeremiah 31 reading offers the hope of consolation for those who mourn, just as Lazarus's resurrected body at the table with Jesus does.

The context of Jeremiah 31 is God's promise to restore Israel after the Babylonian devastation; our reading affirms the faithfulness of God to her people in each generation, building on, not replacing the earliest reading. In some ways, Jeremiah 31 is an answer to the plea for salvation in Psalm 22. It is important to remember that "salvation" in the Hebrew Scriptures is physical salvation from death or other danger, and normally national or corporate. Paraphrased by Jesus (his recitation does not quite match Hebrew or Greek versions in either Matt. 27:46 or Mark 15:34), Psalm 22 became the Psalm of the Cross, a principal text of Holy Week.

Hebrews 1 calls us back to the fidelity of God who spoke through prophecy but now speaks through her Holy Child. (Some have concluded from this that prophecy came to an end; however, prophets appear scattered throughout the New Testament.) The amount of prooftexting in this short section raises the eyebrows of a biblical scholar yet reminds us how flexible ancient interpreters found the scriptures. That flexibility enabled them to reinterpret them in light of Jesus while still holding their previous understandings. Christians have all too often abandoned contextual readings, seizing upon this type of exegesis, neglecting other biblical models.

The last line of the Gospel points us to the tomb where we needs must linger.

TUESDAY IN HOLY WEEK

Isaiah 49:1–6; Psalm 123; Philippians 3:17–21; Matthew 21:12–17

Isaiah 49:1 Listen to me, you coastlands,

give heed, you peoples from far away!
The LIFE-BREATH OF CREATION called me from the womb,
from the innermost parts of my mother God made my name known.

² God made my mouth like a sharp sword,
in the shadow of God's own hand did God hide me;
God made me a polished arrow,
in God's own quiver did God hide me away.

³ And God said to me, "You are my slave,
Israel, the one in whom I will be glorified."

⁴ But I said, "in vain have I labored,
I have spent my strength for futility and vanity;
yet surely my judgment is with the RIGHTEOUS JUDGE,
and my recompense with my God."

⁵ And now says the AUTHOR OF LIFE,
who formed me in the womb to be God's slave
to return Jacob back to God,

and that Israel might be gathered to God:
I am honored in the sight of the HOLY ONE OF OLD,
and my God is my strength.

⁶ God says,
"It is too light a thing that you should be my slave
to raise up the tribes of Jacob [the line of Rebekah]
and to restore the survivors of Israel [born of Rachel and Leah,
and Bilhah and Zilpah]?
I will give you as a light to the nations,
for it will be that my salvation reaches to the end of the earth."

Psalm 123

¹ To you I lift up my eyes,
the one who is enthroned in the heavens!
² See! It is just as the eyes of the enslaved
are toward the hand of their lord,
as the eyes of an enslaved girl
toward the hand of her mistress,
just so our eyes look to the MIGHTY ONE our God,
until God shows us favor.
³ Have mercy upon us, MERCIFUL ONE, have mercy upon us,
for we have had more than our fill of contempt.
⁴ Our soul has had more than its fill
of the scorn of those who are at ease,
of the contempt of the proud.

Philippians 3:17 Become imitators of me together, sisters and brothers, and observe those who walk according to our example. ¹⁸ For many of them—as I have often told you all, and now I tell you even with tears—walk as enemies of the cross of Christ. ¹⁹ Their end is destruction; their god is the belly; and their glory is in their shame; their minds are set on earthly things. ²⁰ But our citizenship is in heaven, and it is from there that we are expecting a Savior, Jesus Christ, our Sovereign, ²¹ who will transform the body of our humiliation that it may bear the likeness of the body of his glory, through the force that also enables him to make all things subject to himself.

Matthew 21:12 Then Jesus entered the temple and drove out all who were selling and buying in the temple, and the tables of the moneychangers he overturned, as well as the station of those who sold doves. ¹³ He said to them, "It is written,

'My house shall be called a house of prayer';
but you all are making it a den of robbers."

[14] And they came to him in the temple, those who were blind and disabled, and he cured them. [15] Now when the chief priests and the religious scholars saw the amazing things that he did, and heard the girls and boys crying out in the temple, "Hosanna to the Son of David," they became angry. [16] They said to him, "Do you hear what these are saying?" Jesus said to them, "Yes; have you never read,

> 'Out of the mouths of infants and nursing babies
> you have prepared praise for yourself'?"

[17] He left them, went out of the city to Bethany, and spent the night there.

PROCLAMATION

Text Notes

In Isaiah 49:4, the poet-prophet speaking in the first person emphasizes redundantly, "I, I said" what she or the unidentified servant about whom she is prophesying said to God upon being commissioned in God's service. Writing long past the time of Isaiah proper, the gender and identity of the prophet is unknown. (I discuss the possibility of the author being a woman in *Daughters of Miriam: Women Prophets in Ancient Israel*.)

Psalm 123 makes explicit the psalmist's understanding that God is a slave-master, and we, women and men alike, are God's slaves. This understanding pervades the scriptures. Linguistically, the human slave-master, "lord," in verse 2 is the same word as "LORD," most often used to represent God's unpronounceable name formed of the letters YHVH. This volume eschews that language while wrestling with its lingering theology. Philippians 3:20 uses the Greek equivalent for lord, *kyrion*, for Jesus.

In Philippians 3:19, the belly, *koilia*, the marks of one of the carnal obsessions of the "earthly" believer, can refer to innards broadly or to the womb, thereby perhaps to gluttony or lust.

Where the Greek text has "children" in Matthew 21:15, I have specified "girls and boys"; girls have extremely low visibility in the scriptures but would have been present in the temple. There is no reason to presume that only boys acclaimed him, given the plural form allows for the presence of girls.

Preaching Prompts

These texts emphasize the sovereignty of God and of Christ, calling attention to the great gulf between God and humanity in troubling and troublesome language. At the same time, they frame the story of the One who crossed and closed that gulf, looking more human than divine this week. We may be helped by remembering the Church writes from a position of vulnerability, believing in faith that it won't always be that way. Paul, in particular, is imprisoned. One might wish to think of the crucified Church looking to its own resurrection.

The various servants in latter Isaiah are sometimes the nation, sometimes a coming monarch, sometimes a messiah, sometimes indeterminate. This passage speaks in messianic terms and was so understood by Christian readers.

As is often the case, the Epistle distinguishes physical, bodily, and earthly from what is spiritual and heavenly. It is worth remembering that there was a widespread belief that Christ's return was imminent, and we would soon have little use for this world. It is our task to interpret this text in light of our continuing reality and the season, Holy Week, in which the physicality of salvation is made manifest.

Matthew 21:13 fuses Isaiah 56:7 and Jeremiah 7:11 into a single citation. Dr. Amy-Jill Levine helpfully reminds us that a "den of robbers" is not a place where there is criminal activity, just as a lion's den is not where lions do their hunting and killing. It is the refuge, or abode, meaning that the moneychangers who were essential to the proper functioning of the temple were not robbing people. She suggests that Jesus's rebuke, like Jeremiah's before him, was that the unrepentant had made the temple a social club rather than a place of prayer; she also notes that the table-turning would have been a rather small demonstration given the scale of the complex (*Entering the Passion of Jesus: A Beginner's Guide to Holy Week*, chapter 2, "The Temple: Risking Righteous Anger").

Individual women are hard to locate in the Gospel reading but would have been among the worshipers, praying and making their own offering; some likely would have been among those Jesus healed. Jesus evokes but does not mention women when citing Psalm 8:2/3 in Greek (verse numbers vary by language): women birthed and nurse the infants who offer praise to God.

WEDNESDAY IN HOLY WEEK

Ezekiel 17:22–24; Psalm 36:5–10; 1 John 2:7–14; Matthew 23:37–39

Ezekiel 17:22 Thus says the Sovereign GOD:

> I myself will take a sprig of cedar
> from its very top;
> and I will place it;
> from the topmost of its most tender branch
> I will pluck it and I myself will plant it
> on a high and lofty mountain.
> 23 On the mountain height of Israel
> I will plant it,
> that it may lift up its boughs and bear fruit,

and become a noble cedar.
Under it every kind of bird shall live;
every kind of winged creature shall nest
in the shade of its branches.

24 All the trees of the field shall know
that I am the CREATOR OF ALL.
I bring low the high tree,
I make high the low tree;
I dry up the green tree
and I make the dry tree sprout buds.
I the AGELESS GOD have spoken;
I will make it so.

Psalm 36:5–10

5 HOLY ONE, throughout the very heavens is your faithful love,
your faithfulness beyond the clouds.

6 Your righteousness is like the eternal mountains,
your judgments are like the mighty deep;
you save humankind and animalkind alike, FAITHFUL ONE.

7 How precious is your faithful love, O God!
All the woman-born take shelter in the shadow of your wings.

8 They feast on the abundance of your house,
and you give them drink from the river of your delights.

9 For with you is the fountain of life;
in your light we see light.

10 Extend your faithful love to those who know you,
and your justice to the upright of heart!

1 John 2:7 Beloved, no new commandment do I write you all, but an old commandment
that you have had from the beginning; that commandment is the word that you have heard.
8 Yet, I am writing you all a new commandment that is true in Christ and in you, because the
shadow is passing away and the true light already shines. 9 Whoever says, "I am in the light,"
while hating a sister or brother, is in shadow still. 10 Whoever loves a sister or brother lives
in the light, and in such a person there is no occasion for stumbling. 11 But whoever hates
another sister or brother is in shadow, walks in shadow, and does not know where to go,
because the shadow dims the eyes.

12 I am writing to you, little children,
because your sins are forgiven on account of Christ's name.

13 I am writing to you, mothers and fathers,
because you know the one who is from the beginning.

I am writing to you, young women and men,
because you have conquered the evil one.
¹⁴ I write to you, children,
because you know the Creator.
I write to you, mothers and fathers,
because you know the one who is from the beginning.
I write to you, young people,
because you are strong
and the word of God abides in you,
and you have overcome the evil one.

Matthew 23:37 "Jerusalem, Jerusalem, that kills the prophets and stones those who are sent to it! How often have I desired to gather your children together as a hen gathers her chicks under her wings, and you were not willing! ³⁸ See, your house is left to you, desolate. ³⁹ For I tell you all, you will not see me again until you say, 'Blessed is the one who comes in the name of the Holy One.'"

PROCLAMATION

Text Notes

In the psalm, the noun *el*, God, is used as an adjective describing the mountains in verse 6.

Preaching Prompts

Today's lessons revolve around Jesus's journey to Jerusalem, where even on the way to his death, he expressed his longing to mother Jerusalem through its violent inclinations. In these lessons, birds function as both images for a sheltering God and images for a huddled humanity and are themselves creatures of the natural world for whom God also cares.

Ezekiel 17:22–24 is a highly allegorical text that can be read as a description of a messianic figure who has noble (lofty) origins but is tender rather than hardened. The community founded around and beneath sheltering branches of this "tree" is diverse and flourishing. As in other prophetic texts, God brings low what is high and exalts what is low.

The psalm echoes the theme of God's faithfulness to bird and tree, extending it to all animals and all humanity. Here, God is winged, sheltering all life within her wings.

The Epistle exhorts us to replicate the love God has for creation for each other. It also offers a hint that the heaviness and shadow of Holy Week will give way to light.

Jesus's embrace of Jerusalem, its history and hopes, ugly realities, looming threats, sacred space, and all of its people, citizens, immigrants, pilgrims, and occupiers was all inclusive. There is room for all in his embrace.

MAUNDY THURSDAY

Exodus 15:11–21; Psalm 136:1–16; Hebrews 11:23–28; Matthew 26:17–56

Exodus 15:11 "Who is like you, MIGHTY ONE, among the gods?
> Who is like you, resplendent in holiness,
> revered praiseworthy, working wonders?
> ¹² You stretched out your right hand,
> the earth swallowed them.
> ¹³ You led, in your faithful love, the people whom you redeemed;
> you guided them by your strength to your holy abode.
> ¹⁴ The peoples heard, they quaked;
> pangs like labor seized the inhabitants of Philistia.
> ¹⁵ Then the chiefs of Edom were dismayed;
> the rulers of Moab, trembling seized them;
> all the inhabitants of Canaan melted away.
> ¹⁶ Terror and dread fell upon them
> by the might of your arm;
> they became still as a stone
> until your people, REDEEMING GOD, passed by,
> until the people whom you acquired passed by.
> ¹⁷ You brought them and planted them on the mountain of your own possession,
> the place, SHELTERING GOD, you made for your dwelling,
> the sanctuary, Most High God, that your hands have established.
> ¹⁸ The EVERLASTING GOD will reign forever and ever."

¹⁹ The horse of Pharaoh and his chariots and charioteers went into the sea, and the MIGHTY GOD turned the waters of the sea back upon them; but the daughters and sons of Israel walked through the sea on dry ground.

²⁰ Then the prophet Miriam, Aaron's sister, took a hand-drum in her hand, and all the women went out after her with hand-drums and with dancing. ²¹ And Miriam sang to them, women and men:

> "Sing to the INDOMITABLE GOD who has triumphed triumphantly;
> horse and rider God has thrown into the sea."

Psalm 136:1–16

1 Give thanks to the FOUNT OF LIFE, who is good,
 for her faithful love is everlasting.

2 Give thanks to the God of gods,
 for her faithful love is everlasting.

3 Give thanks to the Majesty of Majesties,
 for her faithful love is everlasting;

4 who alone does great wonders,
 for her faithful love is everlasting;

5 who through insight made the heavens,
 for her faithful love is everlasting;

6 to the one who spread out the land upon the waters,
 for her faithful love is everlasting;

7 to the one who made the great lights,
 for her faithful love is everlasting;

8 the sun to govern the day,
 for her faithful love is everlasting;

9 the moon and stars to govern the night,
 for her faithful love is everlasting;

10 who struck Egypt through their firstborn daughters and sons,
 for her faithful love is everlasting;

11 and brought Israel out from among them,
 for her faithful love is everlasting;

12 with a strong hand and an outstretched arm,
 for her faithful love is everlasting;

13 who cut the Red Sea in two,
 for her faithful love is everlasting;

14 and made Israel pass over through the midst of it,
 for her faithful love is everlasting;

15 but churned Pharaoh and his army in the Red Sea,
 for her faithful love is everlasting;

16 who walked her people through the wilderness,
 for her faithful love is everlasting.

Hebrews 11:23 By faith Moses was hidden after his birth by his mother and father for three months, because they saw that the child was beautiful; and they were not afraid of the king's commandment. 24 By faith Moses, after he had grown up, refused to be called a son of Pharaoh's daughter, 25 rather choosing ill-treatment with the people of God than enjoyment of the transitory pleasures of sin. 26 He considered abuse for the sake of the Messiah to be greater wealth than the treasures of Egypt, for he was looking ahead to the reward. 27 By faith he left Egypt, unafraid of the anger of the king; for he persisted as though he saw the unseen. [28] By faith he kept the Passover and the sprinkling of blood, in order that the destroyer of the firstborn would not touch the firstborn daughters and sons of Israel.

Matthew 26:17 On the first day of Unleavened Bread the disciples came to Jesus, saying, "Where do you want us to prepare for you to eat the Passover?" [18] He said, "Go into the city to a certain person, and say, 'The Teacher says, My time is near; I will keep the Passover at your house with my disciples.'" [19] So the disciples did just as Jesus instructed them, and they prepared the Passover meal.

[20] When it was evening, he reclined at table with the twelve, [21] and while they ate, he said, "Truly I tell you, one of you will betray me." [22] And they became deeply grieved and each one began to say to him, "Not me, is it Rabbi?" [23] He responded and said, "The one who dipped his hand into the bowl with me will betray me. [24] Indeed, the Son of Woman goes away as it is written of him, but woe to the person by whom the Son of Woman is betrayed! It would have been better for that person not to have been born." [25] Judas, who betrayed him, responded and said, "It wasn't me was it, Rabbi?" He replied, "You said it."

[26] While they were eating, Jesus took a loaf of bread, and blessing it, he broke it, and gave it to the disciples, saying, "Take, eat; this is my body." [27] Then he took a cup, and giving thanks he gave it to them, saying, "Drink from it, all of you; [28] for this is my blood of the covenant, which is poured out for many for forgiveness of sins. [29] I tell you all, I will not drink again of this fruit of the vine until that day when I drink it new with you all in the realm of my Abba." [30] And when they had sung the hymn, they went out to the Mount of Olives.

[31] Then Jesus said to them, "You will all become scandalized to the point of desertion because of me this night; for it is written,

'*For I will strike the shepherd,*
and the sheep of the flock will be scattered.'

[32] But after I am raised, I will go ahead of you all to Galilee." [33] Peter said to him, "Though all become scandalized and desert because of you, I will never desert you." [34] Jesus said to him, "Truly I tell you, this very night, before the cock crows, you will deny me three times." [35] Peter said to him, "Should it be necessary I die with you, I will not deny you." Then likewise said all the disciples.

[36] Then Jesus came with his disciples to a place called Gethsemane, and he said to them, "You all sit here while I go pray there." [37] He took Peter and the two sons of Zebedee and began to be grieved and distressed. [38] Then he said to them, "My soul is deeply grieved, to the point of death; you all stay here, and stay awake with me." [39] And going on a little, he fell on the ground and prayed, saying, "My Father, if it is possible, let this cup pass from me; nevertheless not what I want but what you do." [40] Then he came to the disciples and found them sleeping; and he said to Peter, "So, you all were not strong enough to stay awake with

me one hour? [41] Stay awake and pray that you all may not come into the test; indeed, the spirit is willing, but the flesh is weak." [42] Again, for the second time, Jesus went away and prayed, saying, "My Father, if it is not possible for this to pass lest I drink it, let your will be done." [43] And again he came and found them sleeping, for their eyes were heavy. [44] So leaving them again, he went away and prayed for the third time, saying those words again. [45] Then he came to the disciples and said to them, "Sleep now and take your rest. See, the hour is at hand, and the Son of Woman is betrayed into the hands of sinners. [46] Get up, let us go. Look, my betrayer is at hand."

[47] While Jesus was still speaking, Judas, one of the twelve, came and with him was a large crowd with swords and clubs from the chief priests and the elders of the people. [48] Now the betrayer had given them a sign, saying, "The one I kiss is he; take him." [49] At once he came up to Jesus and said, "Shalom, Rabbi!" and kissed him. [50] Jesus said to him, "Friend, this is why you have come." Then they came and laid hands on Jesus and took him. [51] Suddenly, someone with Jesus reached out with his hand, drew his sword, and struck the slave of the high priest, cutting off his ear. [52] Then Jesus said to him, "Return your sword to its place; for all who choose the sword will perish by the sword. [53] Do you think I am not able to ask my Father, who will at once send me more than twelve legions of angels? [54] How then would the scriptures be fulfilled, which say it must be thus?" [55] At that hour Jesus said to the crowds, "Is it as for a bandit you all have come out with swords and clubs to seize me? Daily in the temple I sat teaching, and you did not arrest me. [56] But all this has happened, so that the scriptures of the prophets may be fulfilled." Then all the disciples deserted him and fled.

PROCLAMATION

Text Notes

In Exodus 15:13, God's holy "abode" can also be understood as a pasture. The instrument Miriam and the other women play in verse 20 is a hand-drum, traditionally played by women across the ancient Afro-Asiatic world. "Tambourine" is anachronistic; they did not yet exist. In verse 21, Miriam exhorts the entire community or just the men—either can be indicated by the plural verb; however, the women are already following her according to the previous verse.

In Matthew 26:18, the grammar used for the person who hosts Jesus is masculine; it may be generic for "person," as translated above. In verse 22 and elsewhere, "Rabbi" replaces "Lord" for direct address. In verse 29, I use "shalom" as the greeting, reflecting the culture of Jesus rather than the literary world of the Greek text.

Preaching Prompts

Passover and Holy Week and Easter are linked seasonally, thematically, and theologically. In some languages, the word for Easter is "Pascha," making the connection more explicit. The two seasons are also connected by violence. In the Exodus and Passover stories, Israel, God's beloved, is saved, and God sends their oppressors to their deaths. Painfully, those deaths are celebrated in psalms and songs. In Holy Week, Jesus, God's beloved, is executed by his—still God's beloved—people's oppressors. His death will also be commemorated in songs of praise. Each offers an opportunity to reflect on who we say God is in conversation with the scriptures.

The necessity for Jesus to observe Passover is just one of many reminders that Jesus was a religiously observant Jew who never broke with Judaism. The singular host in Matthew 26:18 seemingly obscures women from the household who would have done or helped with the actual work: cleaning, shopping, meal preparation, cooking, serving, and hosting. Since the more inclusive "disciples" is used rather than presumptively exclusively male "apostles," it is reasonable to expect the presence of women, particularly since these disciples prepared and served the meal, verse 19. Should female and male disciples have been present, it would be likely that children would be present, given Passover is a family and community meal. (It should be noted that the form of the Passover meal at the time of Jesus, and even in the literary construction of the evangelists, was not a seder, which form developed later.) The mention of "the twelve" in verse 20 does not foreclose the possibility of a larger group at more than one table.

GOOD FRIDAY

Judges 11:29–40; Psalm 22; Hebrews 12:1–4; Luke 22:14–23:56

Judges 11:29 The Spirit of the HOLY ONE, she was upon Jephthah, and he passed through Gilead and Manasseh. He passed on to Mizpah of Gilead, and from Mizpah of Gilead he passed on to the Ammonites. ³⁰ And Jephthah vowed a vow to the HOLY ONE OF OLD, and said, "If you will give the Ammonites into my hand, ³¹ then it shall be that the one who comes out—whoever comes out—of the doors of my house to meet me, when I return having finished with the Ammonites, shall be the HOLY ONE's, I will offer them up as a burnt offering." ³² Then Jephthah crossed over to the Ammonites to fight against them and the HOLY ONE gave them into his hand. ³³ He smote a mighty smiting on them from Aroer until you come to Minnith, twenty towns, and as far as Abel-keramim. So, the Ammonites were subdued before the people of Israel.

³⁴ Then Jephthah came to his home at Mizpah, and there was his daughter coming out to meet him with drums and with dancing. Only she, an only child; he had no son or daughter apart from her. ³⁵ When he saw her, he tore his clothes, and said, "Ah! My daughter, you have knocked me down; you have become my trouble! I—I opened my mouth to the HOLY ONE, and I cannot take back my vow." ³⁶ She said to him, "My father, you have opened your mouth to the HOLY ONE, do to me according to what has gone out of your mouth, after that the HOLY ONE has taken vengeance through you against your enemies, against the

Ammonites." [37] And she said to her father, "Let be done for me this thing: Release me for two months, and I will go and go down among the hills, and weep for my virginity, I and my women-friends." [38] Then he said, "Go," and sent her away for two months. So, she left, she and her women-friends, and wept over her virginity among the hills. [39] And it was at the end of two months, she returned to her father, who did to her what he vowed in his vow. She had never known a man and she became an observance in Israel. [40] Year by year the daughters of Israel would go out to tell the story of the daughter of Jephthah the Gileadite for four days.

Psalm 22

[1] My God, my God, why have you forsaken me?
Why are you so far from my deliverance, from the words of my groaning?

[2] My God, I cry by day, and you do not answer;
and by night, and there is no rest for me.

[3] Yet you are holy,
enthroned on the praises of Israel.

[4] In you our mothers and fathers trusted;
they trusted, and you rescued them.

[5] To you they cried, and were freed;
in you they trusted, and they were not put to shame.

[6] But I am a worm, and not human;
scorned by humankind, and despised by people.

[7] All who see me mock me;
they flap their lips at me, they shake their heads:

[8] "Commit yourself to the SAVING ONE; let God rescue
and deliver the one in whom God delights!"

[9] Yet it was you who drew me from the womb;
keeping me safe on my mother's breast.

[10] On you was I cast from birth,
and since my mother's womb you have been my God.

[11] Be not far from me,
for trouble is near
and there is none to help.

[12] Many bulls surround me,
mighty bulls of Bashan encompass me;

[13] they open wide their mouths at me,
like a lion, ravaging and roaring.

[14] I am poured out like water,
and all my bones are disjointed.
My heart is like wax;
it is melted within my being.

¹⁵ My mouth is dried up like a potsherd,
and my tongue cleaves to my jaws;
in the dust of death you lay me down.

¹⁶ For dogs are all around me;
a conclave of evildoers encircles me.
Like a lion they ravage my hands and feet.

¹⁷ I can count all my bones.
They gloat and stare at me.

¹⁸ They divide my clothes among themselves,
and for my clothing they cast lots.

¹⁹ SAVING GOD, be not far away!
My strength, hasten to help me!

²⁰ Deliver my soul from the sword,
my life from the clutch of the dog!

²¹ Save me from the mouth of the lion!
For on the horns of the wild oxen you have responded to me.

²² I will tell of your name to my sisters and brothers;
in the midst of the congregation I will praise you:

²³ You who revere the FOUNT OF LIFE, praise her!
All the offspring of Leah and Rachel, Bilhah and Zilpah glorify her.
Stand in awe of her all you of Rebekah's line.

²⁴ For she did not despise or abhor
the affliction of the afflicted;
she did not hide her face from me,
and when I cried to her, she heard.

²⁵ On your account is my praise in the great congregation;
my vows I will pay before those who revere her.

²⁶ The poor shall eat and be satisfied;
those who seek her shall praise the MOTHER OF ALL.
May your hearts live forever!

²⁷ All the ends of the earth shall remember
and turn to the WELLSPRING OF LIFE;
and all the families of the nations
shall worship before her.

²⁸ For sovereignty belongs to the SHE WHO IS HOLY,
and she rules over the nations.

²⁹ They consume and they bow down, all the fat ones of the earth before her,
they bend their knees, all who go down to the dust,
and cannot save their soul.

³⁰ Later descendants will serve her;
future generations will be told about our God,

³¹ they will go and proclaim her deliverance to a people yet unborn,
saying that she has done it.

Hebrews 12:1 Therefore, since we are surrounded by so great a cloud of witnesses, let us also put aside every weight and entangling sin, and with endurance let us run the race that is set before us, ² looking to Jesus the originator and perfecter of our faith, who for the sake of the joy that was set before him endured the cross, its shame disregarding, and at the right hand of the throne of God has taken his seat.

³ Consider the one who endured such hostility against himself from sinners, so that you all may not grow weary or your souls grow faint. ⁴ Not to this point have you all in your struggles against sin resisted to the point of shedding blood.

Luke 22:14 Now when the hour came, he took his place at the table, and the apostles with him. ¹⁵ Then Jesus said to them, "I have greatly desired to eat this Passover with you all before I suffer. ¹⁶ For I tell you all, I will not eat it until it is fulfilled in the realm of God." ¹⁷ Then Jesus took a cup, giving thanks. He said, "Receive this and divide it among yourselves; ¹⁸ for I tell you all that from now on I will not drink of the fruit of the vine until the reign of God comes." ¹⁹ Then Jesus took a loaf of bread, giving thanks, he broke it and gave it to them, saying, "This is my body, which is given for you all. Do this in remembrance of me." ²⁰ And he did the same with the cup after supper, saying, "This cup that is poured out for you is the new covenant in my blood. ²¹ Look, the hand of the one who betrays me is with me, on the table. ²² For indeed the Son of Woman is going as it has been determined, but woe to the one by whom he is betrayed!" ²³ Then they began to ask among themselves, which one of them was about to do this.

²⁴ There was also an argument among them as to which one of them should be considered the greatest. ²⁵ But Jesus said to them, "The royals of the Gentiles lord it over them, and those who have power over them are called benefactors. ²⁶ But not so with you all, rather the greatest among you must become like the youngest, and the leader like one who serves. ²⁷ For who is greater, the one who is at the table or the one who serves? Is it not the one at the table? Yet I am among you all as one who serves.

²⁸ "You are the ones who have remained with me in my trials, ²⁹ so then I covenant with you all, just as my Father has covenanted with me, a royal inheritance, ³⁰ so that you all may eat and drink at my table in my realm, and you all will sit on thrones governing the twelve tribes of Israel.

³¹ "Simon, Simon, listen! The Adversary has demanded to sift all of you like wheat, ³² but I have prayed for you in order that your faith not fail, and you, when you have turned back, strengthen your brothers." ³³ Then he said to Jesus, "Rabbi, I am ready to go with you to prison and to death!" ³⁴ But Jesus said, "I tell you, Peter, this day the cock will not have crowed three times, before you deny knowing me."

³⁵ Then Jesus said to them, "When I sent you out without a purse, bag, or sandals, did you lack anything?" They said, "Not a thing." ³⁶ He said to them, "But now, the one who has a purse must take it, and likewise a bag. And the one who does not have one must sell

his cloak and buy a sword. ³⁷ For I tell you, this scripture must be fulfilled in me, '*And he was counted among the lawless,*' and indeed that which pertains to me is coming to its completion." ³⁸ So they said, "Rabbi, see, here are two swords." He replied to them, "It is sufficient."

³⁹ Then Jesus came out and went, as was his custom, to the Mount of Olives and the disciples followed him. ⁴⁰ When he was at the place, he said to them, "Pray that you not enter into testing." ⁴¹ Then he withdrew from them about a stone's throw on bended knee and prayed, ⁴² "Father, if you are willing, take this cup away from me; yet, not my will but yours be done." ⁴³ [Then an angel from heaven appeared to him and strengthened him. ⁴⁴ In agony he prayed more earnestly, and his sweat became like drops of blood falling down upon the ground.] ⁴⁵ When he rose from prayer, he came to the disciples and found them sleeping from grief. ⁴⁶ And he said to them, "Why are you sleeping? Get up and pray that you not enter into testing."

⁴⁷ While he was speaking, suddenly there was a crowd, and the one called Judas, one of the twelve, was leading them. He approached Jesus to kiss him. ⁴⁸ But Jesus said to him, "Judas, is it with a kiss that you betray the Son of Woman?" ⁴⁹ When those around him saw what was happening, they asked, "Rabbi, should we strike with the sword?" ⁵⁰ Then one of them struck a person enslaved by the high priest and cut off his right ear. ⁵¹ But Jesus responded, saying, "Enough of this!" And he grasped his ear and healed him. ⁵² Then Jesus said to ones who had come for him, the chief priests, the officers assigned to the temple, and the elders, "Have you all come out with swords and clubs as if I were a bandit? ⁵³ When I was with you daily in the temple, you did not lay hands on me. But this is your hour, and the power of darkness!"

⁵⁴ Then they seized him and led him away, bringing him into the house of the high priest. But Peter was following from afar. ⁵⁵ They kindled a fire in the middle of the courtyard and sat down together; Peter sat among them. ⁵⁶ Then a slave-girl, seeing him near the fire, looked intently at him and said, "This one also was with him." ⁵⁷ But he denied it, saying, "Woman, I do not know him." ⁵⁸ After a time someone else, on seeing him, said, "You are one of them too." But Peter said, "Man, I am not!" ⁵⁹ Then about an hour later another one insisted, "On the truth, this one was with him too, for he is a Galilean." ⁶⁰ But Peter said, "Man, I do not know what you are talking about!" Immediately, while he was speaking, the cock crowed. ⁶¹ The Savior turned and looked at Peter. Then Peter remembered the word of the Messiah, how he had said to him, "Before the cock crows today, you will deny me three times." ⁶² And Peter went out and wept bitterly.

⁶³ Now the men who were holding Jesus mocked him and beat him; ⁶⁴ they also blindfolded him and asked him, "Prophesy! Who is it that struck you?" ⁶⁵ They yelled much other abuse at him.

⁶⁶ Then when day came, the elders of the people, chief priests and religious scholars, gathered together and brought him to their council. ⁶⁷ They said, "If you are the Messiah, tell us." Jesus replied to them, "If I tell you, you will not believe, ⁶⁸ and if I ask a question,

you will not answer. [69] But from now on the Son of Woman will be seated at the right hand of the power of God." [70] They all asked, "Are you, then, the Son of God?" He said to them, "You say that I am." [71] Then they said, "What further testimony do we need; we have heard it ourselves from his own lips!"

[23:1] Then the assembly rose as a body and brought Jesus before Pilate. [2] They began to accuse him, saying, "We found this man leading our nation astray, forbidding paying taxes to the emperor, and saying that he is a messiah, a king." [3] Then Pilate questioned him, saying, "Are you the king of the Judeans?" He answered, "You say so." [4] Then Pilate said to the chief priests and the crowds, "I find no cause for legal action against this person." [5] But they insisted, saying, "Because he stirs up the people by teaching throughout all Judea, from Galilee to this very place."

[6] Upon hearing this, Pilate asked if the person was a Galilean. [7] Now when he learned that he was under Herod's authority, he sent him to Herod, who himself was in Jerusalem at that time. [8] When Herod saw Jesus, he was extremely glad, for he had wanted to see him for a long time, because he had heard about him and hoped to see him perform some sign. [9] Herod questioned him to his satisfaction, but Jesus answered him nothing. [10] The chief priests and the religious scholars stood by, vehemently accusing him. [11] Herod and his soldiers also treated him with contempt and mocked him, and he put a majestic robe on him, and sent him back to Pilate. [12] That very moment Herod and Pilate became friends with each other; previously they had been each other's enemy.

[13] Pilate then called together the chief priests, the leaders, and the people, [14] and said to them, "You brought me this person for leading the people astray. Look now, I have examined him in your presence and have not found this person guilty of your charges against him. [15] Nor has Herod, for he sent him back to us. Look here, there is nothing deserving death in his case. [16] Therefore whip and release him."

[18] Then they shouted together, saying, "Away with him! Release for us Barabbas!" [19] (Who for a rebellion that had taken place in the city, and for murder, had been put in prison.) [20] Again Pilate addressed them, wanting to release Jesus, [21] but they kept shouting, saying, "Crucify, crucify him!" [22] A third time he said to them, "Why, what evil has he done? I have found nothing deserving death in him; I will, therefore, have him whipped and release him." [23] But they insisted with loud shouts that he should be crucified, and their voices prevailed. [24] So Pilate passed sentence to grant their demand. [25] So he released the one in prison for rebellion and murder who they asked for, and he handed Jesus over as they wished.

[26] As they led Jesus away, they seized Simon of Cyrene who was coming from the country, and they laid on him the cross to carry behind Jesus. [27] A great number of people followed him, and a group of women who were beating their breasts and wailing for him. [28] But Jesus turned to them and said, "Daughters of Jerusalem, do not weep for me, weep only for yourselves and for your children. [29] Look, the days are surely coming when they will say, 'Blessed are barren women, and wombs that have never given birth, and breasts

that have never nourished.' ³⁰ *Then they will begin to say to the mountains, 'Fall on us'; and to the hills, 'Cover us.'* ³¹ For if when the wood is green they do this, when it is dry what will happen?"

³² Now two criminals were also led away to be put to death with him. ³³ And when they came to the place called Skull, there they crucified Jesus there with the criminals, one on his right and one on his left. ³⁴ [And then Jesus said, "Father, forgive them; for they know not what they do."] *They divided his clothing by casting lots.* ³⁵ And the people stood there, watching; but the leaders ridiculed him, saying, "Others he saved; let him save himself if he is the Messiah of God, God's chosen one!" ³⁶ The soldiers also mocked him, coming and offering him vinegar wine, ³⁷ and saying, "If you are the King of the Judeans, save yourself!" ³⁸ There was also an inscription above him, "This is the King of the Judeans."

³⁹ One of the criminals who was hanging there derided him, saying, "Are you not the Messiah? Save yourself and us!" ⁴⁰ But the other rebuked him, saying, "Do you not fear God, since you are under the same death sentence? ⁴¹ And we indeed justly, for what we have done merits what we are receiving, but this one has done nothing wrong." ⁴² Then he said, "Jesus, remember me when you come into your realm." ⁴³ Jesus replied to him, "Truly I tell you, today you will be with me in Paradise."

⁴⁴ And it was now about the sixth hour [of the day, or noon], and darkness came over the whole land until the ninth hour [of the day, about three in the afternoon]. ⁴⁵ The sun's light ceased, and the curtain of the temple was torn in the middle. ⁴⁶ Then Jesus, crying with a loud voice, said, "Father, into your hands I commend my spirit." Saying this then, he breathed out a final time. ⁴⁷ Now when the centurion saw what had happened, he praised God, saying, "This man was indeed innocent." ⁴⁸ And all the crowds that had gathered for this spectacle saw what had happened, beating their breasts, they turned back. ⁴⁹ All those who knew him stood far off; the women who had followed him from Galilee were watching these things.

⁵⁰ Now, take note, there was a man named Joseph, a member of the council, a good man and a righteous one. ⁵¹ He had not agreed with the council and their action. He was from the Judean town of Arimathea, and he was waiting for the reign of God. ⁵² This man went to Pilate and requested the body of Jesus. ⁵³ Then he took it down, wrapped it in a linen cloth, and laid it in a tomb hewn from rock where no one had yet lain. ⁵⁴ It was the day of Preparation, and the sabbath was dawning. ⁵⁵ The women followed, the ones who had come with him from Galilee, and they saw the tomb and how his body was placed. ⁵⁶ Then the women returned, and prepared spices and balms.

On the sabbath they rested according to the commandment.

PROCLAMATION

Owing to the length of the Passion Gospel, the commentary section will be longer than for other readings.

Text Notes

In Judges 11:31, the word *shalom* is used to indicate completion; the verb is used similarly in Modern Hebrew, for example, to complete a purchase or pay the check. In verse 37 and following, virginity symbolizes a stage of life; the grief is about not reaching the full measure of womanhood in her culture, marrying, and mothering. In verse 40, the women gather to memorialize the woman sacrificed by her father; the verb is "recount," not as usually translated, "lament."

The psalmist locates her heart in her "belly" in verse 14. The verb for the violence done to the psalmist's hands and feet is missing. The LXX and traditional Jewish exegesis (Rashi) supply it.

Throughout this passion account in Luke, "Rabbi" replaces "Lord" so as not to further divinize slave language. For third-person references, Messiah, Christ, and Savior will be used. Also, "enslaved person" rather than "slave" distinguishes between a person and their circumstances. The Eucharistic instruction in Luke 22:16 can be translated as "take" or "receive" (this cup). In the Hebrew Scriptures, to judge is to govern, administer, oversee, rule, and render justice. That full sense is intended in Luke 22:30, rather than passing judgment on Israel. The Adversary, the Satan, occurs in verse 31 with the definite article as in Hebrew where the term is a title or description; further contemporary notions of Satan are often postbiblical. Verses 43–44 in chapter 22 and verse 34 in chapter 23 are not present in all manuscripts as indicated by brackets.

In Luke 23:1 and 13, the more common translation "perverting" (rather leading astray here) has an unnecessary sexual connotation in English. Jesus's accusers testify that he says he is *a messiah*; there is no direct object. The term was not unique to Jesus. Hebrew *meshiach* is translated by Greek *christos*; David and Cyrus are each God's messiah, God's christ in the Hebrew and Greek versions of 2 Samuel 23:1 and Isaiah 45:1, which parallel Luke 23:35 where Jesus is disbelieved as the Christ/Messiah of God. The term, otherwise translated "anointed," also applies to monarchs and priests.

The robe with which Jesus was mocked in Luke 23:11 was "bright" or "shiny," suggesting rich embroidery or embellishment. Some less reliable manuscripts include a verse 17 which is generally removed from critical translations: *He had to release one prisoner for them because of the festival.*

Jesus quotes Hosea 10:8, where people ask for the mountains and hills to cover them in Luke 23:30. Verse 34, "Father, forgive them . . ." is missing in many manuscripts. "Into your hands, I commend my spirit" in verse 46 from Psalm 31:5 can also be translated, "Into your hands, I place my life." In verse 49, "those who stood" are a mixed gender as indicated by the text (grammatically, an all-male group is also possible); those who were watching were the women, according to the feminine plural verb, which excludes males. In contrast, the "they" who rested on the sabbath in verse 56 is inclusive.

A final note, the NRSV translation that Joseph of Arimathea, "who, *though* a member of the council," was "good and righteous" in Luke 23:50 excludes the whole of the Sanhedrin from the possibility of being good and righteous normatively. It is more than an uncharitable reading; it is anti-Judaistic and contributes to the anti-Semitic legacy and practices of the Church.

Preaching Prompts

This lectionary pairs the brutal deaths of Jephthah's daughter and Jesus. Each of their deaths is horrific—at one level, unnecessary slaughter—and each death is believed by someone in their respective story to serve a greater good. The disparate portraits and motives of the two fathers in relation to the death of their sole child offer fruitful space to address the crucifixion beyond the limits of atonement theology. Each of these texts requires us to ask who it is we think God is.

Jephthah, taken from his mother, a sex worker, by his father Gilead, was rejected by his brothers and his father's wife. The troubled boy is not unrelated to the troubled man. He is desperate for affirmation. Note that God had already given Jephthah victory over the Ammonites in Judges 11:32, before he makes a vow to "ensure" his win. Jephthah's god is familiar to many: rigid and unyielding, apparently incapable of forgiving a rash vow, making human sacrifice the only acceptable appeasement. Jephthah doesn't test his theology; he doesn't bargain with God like Abraham. He doesn't offer himself as recipient of divine rage; he does not fight for the life of his child. His parenthood, like his theology, leaves much to be desired. As is the case in rigid, fundamentalist, patriarchal systems, women's lives hold little value and are expendable. Is spite of the lethal limits of the system in which she finds herself constrained, Jephthah's daughter carves out space for herself and other women, illuminating and memorializing the deficiencies of a god like Jephthah's.

The psalmist's God is lightyears away from the tyrant Jephthah worships, savior rather than destroyer. The psalmist's God is part nurse, part midwife, trustworthy and praiseworthy. In Matthew and Mark, Jesus turns to this psalm and this God on the cross, making it virtually inseparable from Good Friday. In Luke's Passion, Jesus quotes Psalm 31, which shares the theme of trusting a trustworthy God for salvation.

Hebrews calls us to look to Jesus in the company of the faithful. Luke presents a roster of the faithful where women are more fully present than in other accounts. The spaces where women are missing are also instructive, such as a conversation about who is greater and injunction for the greatest to serve the least with apparently no women in the room. How different would the church have looked if that teaching were applied to systemic structural inequities between genders and cultures as a start.

Women are rendered invisible in the crowds that characterize the narrative, visible as enslaved girls, weeping women who accompany Jesus on his death march, and the women who were family, friends, followers, and disciples—some in more than one category—standing watch until the end. In spite of the gruesome horror, Jesus's female companions and followers, family and friends, watched and did not turn away according to Luke 23:49; the text cannot make the same claim of the male apostles and disciples. These women were faithful in and beyond the horror that seemed to mark the end of their shared journey.

HOLY SATURDAY

Job 14:1–14; Psalm 31; Philippians 2:1–8; Matthew 27:57–66

Job 14:1 "Woman-born,

humankind is short of days and full of turmoil.

² They sprout like a flower and wither,
flee like a shadow and do not endure.

³ Are your eyes, then, open to such a one as this?
Do you bring me into judgment with you?

⁴ Who can make a clean thing out of an unclean thing?
No one.

⁵ If their days are fixed,
the number of their months is in your keeping,
it is because you have set their boundaries that they cannot pass.

⁶ Look away from them, and they sit at ease,
until they complete, like laborers, their days.

⁷ For there is hope for a tree,
if it is cut down, that it will be renewed,
and that its branches will not fail.

⁸ Its root grows old in the earth,
and its trunk dies in the dust.

⁹ At the scent of water it will bud
and put forth branches like a sapling.

¹⁰ Mortals die, and are carried away;
the woman-born perish, and where are they?

¹¹ As waters dissipate from a sea,
and a river dries up and dissipates,

¹² so a person lies down and does not rise again;
until the heavens are no more,
they will not awake or be stirred from their sleep.

¹³ Grant that you would hide me in Sheol,
that you would cover me until your wrath is past,
that you would set for me a boundary, and remember me.
¹⁴ If a person dies, will they live again?
All the days of my service I would wait
until my change come.

Psalm 31

¹ In you, WOMB OF LIFE, I take refuge;
let me not ever be put to shame;
in your righteousness rescue me.
² Incline your ear to me;
quickly deliver me.
Be for me a rock of refuge,
a stronghold to save me.
³ For you are my rock and my stronghold;
for your name's sake lead me and guide me.
⁴ Free me from the net that is hidden for me,
for you are my refuge.
⁵ Into your hand I commit my spirit;
you have redeemed me, ARK OF SAFETY, God of truth.
⁶ I hate those who attend to worthless vanity,
but in the MOTHER OF ALL I place my trust.
⁷ I will exult and I will rejoice in your faithful love,
because you have seen my affliction;
you have studied my soul's sorrows.
⁸ Yet you have not handed me over to the hand of the enemy;
you have set my feet in a broad place.
⁹ Have mercy on me, MOTHER OF MERCY, for I am in distress;
my eyes waste away with angry tears,
my soul and body too.
¹⁰ For my life is spent in sorrow,
and my years in sighing;
because of my iniquity my strength fails,
and my bones waste away.
¹¹ Because of my enemies I am a disgrace to all,
and to my neighbors, more,
an object of dread to those who know me;
those who see me in the street flee from me.

¹² I have been forgotten from the heart like one who is dead;
I have become like a ruined vessel.
¹³ Because I hear the whispering of many,
terror surrounds in their scheming together against me,
as they plot to take my life.
¹⁴ Yet I, in you I trust, FAITHFUL GOD;
I declare, "You are my God."
¹⁵ My times are in your hand;
deliver me from the hand of my enemies and those who hound me.
¹⁶ Let your face shine upon your slave;
save me in your faithful love.
¹⁷ GRACIOUS GOD, let me not be put to shame,
for I call upon you;
let the wicked be put to shame;
let them go silent to Sheol.
¹⁸ Let lying lips be stilled
the ones that speak against the righteous,
arrogant with pride and contempt.
¹⁹ How great is your goodness
that you have secured for those who fear you,
and that you do for those who take refuge in you,
before all the woman-born.
²⁰ In the shelter of your presence you shelter them
from human plots;
you hide them safe under your shelter
from contentious tongues.
²¹ Blessed be the MOTHER OF CREATION,
who is marvelous in her faithful love to me,
a city under siege.
²² Now I, I had said in my alarm,
"I am cut off from your sight."
However, you heard my supplications
when I cried to you for help.
²³ Love GOD WHOSE NAME IS HOLY, all you her godly ones.
The FAITHFUL GOD preserves the faithful,
and repays with interest the one who acts out of pride.
²⁴ Take courage, and she shall strengthen your hearts,
all you who wait for the MOTHER OF ALL.

Philippians 2:1 If then there is any encouragement in Christ, any consolation from love, any communion in the Spirit, any tenderness and compassion, ² make my joy complete. Be wise in the same way, having the same love, united and sharing the same wisdom. ³ Do nothing from self-interest, but in humility regard others as better than yourselves. ⁴ Each of you, look not to your own interests, but rather to the interests of others. ⁵ Let the same wisdom be in you all that was in Christ Jesus,

> ⁶ who, though he was in the form of God,
> did not regard equality with God
> as something to be seized,
> ⁷ but emptied himself,
> taking the form of a slave,
> being born in human likeness;
> then being found in human form,
> ⁸ he humbled himself
> and became obedient to the point of death,
> even death on a cross.

Matthew 27:57 When it was evening, a rich person came from Arimathea, Joseph, who was also a disciple of Jesus. ⁵⁸ He went to Pilate and requested the body of Jesus; then Pilate commanded it to be given to him. ⁵⁹ So Joseph took the body and wrapped it in clean linen, ⁶⁰ and laid it in his new tomb, which he had hewn in rock. Then he rolled a great stone to the door of the tomb and departed. ⁶¹ Mary Magdalene and the other Mary were there, sitting before the tomb.

⁶² Now, the next day, which was after the day of Preparation, the chief priests and the Pharisees gathered before Pilate. ⁶³ They said, "Lord, we remember what that deceiver said while he was still alive, 'After three days I will rise.' ⁶⁴ Command, therefore, the tomb be secured until the third day; otherwise his disciples may go and steal him, and tell the people, 'He has been raised from the dead,' and the last deception would be worse than the first." ⁶⁵ Pilate said to them, "You may have a squad; go, as secure it as you can." ⁶⁶ So they went with the guard and secured the tomb, sealing the stone.

PROCLAMATION

Text Notes

Job 14 begins its reflection on mortality using inclusive language, "those born of women," and "humanity" in verse 1, then shifts to masculine language, "(male) warrior" in verses 10 and 14 and "man" in verse 12. I apply inclusive language to the other human references in the passage. Job's address shifts from second to third person in verse 6 and 13. Verse 13 begins, "Who will grant. . . ." In his book-length legal complaint, Job looks (rhetorically at least) for someone to compel God to do justly by him. That is part of the theological scandal of the book.

In verse 4 of the psalm, "free me" is the "let my people go" verb of the exodus. In verse 9, there is only one "eye" and tears are lacking; "body" is "belly/womb." Somewhat contradictorily, "to go silently to Sheol" can also be "to go weeping to Sheol." "Godly ones" in verse 23 are often translated anachronistically as "saints," importing Christian language and theology into the Hebrew Scriptures.

There is considerable disagreement over the meaning of *eritheian* in Philippians 2:3, translated here as "self-interest"; some other possibilities are: strife, contentiousness, selfishness, or selfish ambition. According to its earlier usage in Aristotle, it may mean "a self-seeking pursuit" for political office in that case. (See the corresponding entry in the *A Greek-English Lexicon of the New Testament and Other Early Christian Literature, BDAG.*)

The use of "Lord" for Pilate serves as a reminder the title was not unique to Jesus, nor a particularly religious one, but one of hierarchy, signifying Pilate's authority as the face of the Roman occupation. Translations like NRSV, which preserve it for Jesus but change it for other characters, are intentionally misleading.

Preaching Prompts

Holy Saturday may be the most liminal space in the Christian liturgical cycle. Passion has become pathos. The death of Jesus stupefies, but the breaking dawn has not dispelled the waking dream. Yet the liturgical remembrance is part of a thousands-year-old cycle, and we know what the next dawn brings. We struggle not to anticipate that dawn. These lessons underscore our finitude, our mortality and that of all living things, and the mortality of Jesus, Son of Woman, Son of God, Child of Earth.

Job's reflection on his own mortality comes in the midst of his address to God in chapters 12–14, responding to Zophar's chapter 11 rebuke, blaming Job for the evil that has befallen him. In this lesson, Job's ruminations on his inevitable death are accompanied by the reminder that death is part of the cycle of life in nature. Without knowing the hope that Christians hold dear, Job expects a "no" to the question of whether a person who has died will live again. He and the psalmist expect all the dead to go to Sheol (Job 14:13; Ps. 22:17). The psalmist commits her fragile life (verse 5) and finite times (verse 14–15) into God's hands, fully aware of her own mortality. The psalm also includes the remembrance of God's fidelity (verse 7, 19–21, 23) and assurance that God hears the cry of her faithful, verse 22.

As a Holy Saturday text, Philippians 2 presents a Jesus as empty of divinity as his body in the tomb was empty of life. Here Jesus humbles himself to experience the finitude of the human experience, mortality, and one of its most common and most horrific occurrences, a violent death at human hands.

We hold all of these things in our hearts as we wrestle with implications, sitting, watching, and waiting with Miriam, Mary of Migdala, and another woman who also bears the name of Israel's first prophet. They knew not for what they waited. Though we know, we keep vigil with them.

EASTER—THE GREAT VIGIL

At least two of the following Lessons are read, of which one is always the Lesson from Exodus. After each Lesson, the psalm or canticle listed, or some other suitable psalm, canticle, or hymn, is sung.

A God-Crafted Creation: Genesis 1:1–2, 26–27; 2:1–4

Genesis 1:1 When beginning he, God, created the heavens and the earth, ² the earth was shapeless and formless and bleakness covered the face of the deep, while the Spirit of God, she, fluttered over the face of the waters.

²⁶ And God said, "Let us make humankind in our image, according to our likeness; and let them rule the fish of the sea, and the birds of the heavens, and the animals, and the whole earth, and over every creeping creature that creeps upon the earth."

²⁷ So God created humankind in God's own image,
  in God's own image, God created them;
  female and male, God created them.

²:¹ And the heavens and the earth were complete, along with all their multitude. ² Then God finished on the seventh day the work that God had done, and rested on the seventh day from all the work that they had done. ³ So God blessed the seventh day and sanctified it, because on it God rested from all the work that God had done in creation.

⁴ These are the generations of the heavens and the earth when they were created.

Canticle of the Three Young Men: Daniel (LXX) 3:52–60

⁵² "Let the earth bless the Creator of All;
  let her sing hymns to God and highly exalt God forever.
⁵³ Bless the Creator of All, mountains and hills;
  sing hymns to God and highly exalt God forever.
⁵⁴ Bless the Creator of All, all that grows in the ground;
  sing hymns to God and highly exalt God forever.
⁵⁵ Bless the Creator of All, seas and rivers;
  sing hymns to God and highly exalt God forever.
⁵⁶ Bless the Creator of All, you springs;
  sing hymns to God and highly exalt God forever.
⁵⁷ Bless the Creator of All, you sea monsters and all that swim in the waters;

sing hymns to God and highly exalt God forever.

58 Bless the Creator of All, all birds of the air;

sing hymns to God and highly exalt God forever.

59 Bless the Creator of All, all wild animals and cattle;

sing hymns to God and highly exalt God forever.

60 Bless the Creator of All, all people on earth;

sing hymns to God and highly exalt God forever."

The Salvation of Hagar and Ishmael: Genesis 21:2, 8–21

2 Sarah conceived and gave birth to a son for Abraham in his old age, at the set time of which God had spoken to him.

8 The child grew, and was weaned, and Abraham made a great feast on the day of Isaac's weaning. 9 Then Sarah saw the son of Hagar the Egyptian woman, whom she had given birth to for Abraham, playing. 10 So she said to Abraham, "Drive out this slave woman with her son; for the son of this slave woman shall not inherit with my son, with Isaac." 11 The situation was evil in Abraham's eyes on account of his son. 12 And God said to Abraham, "See it not as evil in your eyes on account of the boy and on account of your slave woman. In all that Sarah says to you, obey her voice, for it is through Isaac that offspring shall be named for you. 13 Yet even the son of the slave woman I will make a nation also, because he is your offspring." 14 So Abraham rose early in the morning, and took bread and a skin of water, and gave it to Hagar. He placed it on her shoulder, along with the child, and sent her away. Then she walked away and wandered in the wilderness of Beer-Sheba.

15 When the water in the skin was gone, she thrust the child under one of the bushes. 16 Then she went and sat herself down before him some way off, about the distance of a bowshot; for she said, "Let me not see the death of the child." So, she sat before him and she lifted up her voice and she wept. 17 And God heard the voice of the boy, and the messenger of God called to Hagar from the heavens, and said to her, "What troubles you, Hagar? Fear not; for God has heard the voice of the boy where he is. 18 Rise, lift the boy and hold him with your hand, for a great nation of him I will make." 19 Then God opened her eyes and she saw a well of water. She went, and filled the skin with water, and let the boy drink.

20 God was with the boy, and he grew up; he settled in the wilderness, and became an archer. 21 He settled in the wilderness of Paran, and his mother acquired a wife for him from the land of Egypt.

Psalm 27:5–7, 10–14

5 She will shield me in her shelter

when the day is evil;

she will cover me under the cover of her tent;

she will raise me high on a rock.

6 Now my head is raised up

above my enemies surrounding me,

and I will offer in her tent
sacrifices with shouts of joy;
I will sing and make melody to the GOD WHO SAVES.
⁷ Hear my cry, FAITHFUL ONE, when I cry aloud,
be gracious to me and answer me!
¹⁰ If my mother and father forsake me,
the COMPASSIONATE GOD will gather me in.
¹¹ Teach me, RIGHTEOUS ONE, your way,
and lead me on a smooth path
because of my enemies.
¹² Do not give me over to the throats of my foes,
for lying witnesses rise against me,
and they breathe violence.
¹³ If I but believe, I shall see the goodness of SHE WHO IS FAITHFUL
in the land of the living.
¹⁴ Wait for the LIVING GOD;
be strong, and let your heart take courage;
wait for GOD WHOSE NAME IS HOLY!

From Slavery to Freedom: Exodus 14:26–29; 15:20–21

14:26 Now the HOLY ONE said to Moses, "Stretch out your hand over the sea, so that the water may come back upon the Egyptians, upon their chariots and charioteers." ²⁷ So Moses stretched out his hand over the sea and the sea turned back; by the break of dawn it was back to its strength, and the Egyptians fled at its approach. Then the LIVING GOD shook the Egyptians in the midst of the sea. ²⁸ The waters returned and covered the chariots and the charioteers, the whole army of Pharaoh that came after them into the sea; not a single one of them remained. ²⁹ And the women, children, and men of Israel walked on dry ground through the sea, the waters a wall for them on their right and on their left.

¹⁵:²⁰ Then the prophet Miriam, Aaron's sister, took a drum in her hand; and all the women went out after her with drums and with dancing. ²¹ And Miriam sang to them:

"Sing to the GOD WHO SAVES, for God has triumphed triumphantly;
horse and rider God has thrown into the sea."

Song of Miriam and Moses: Exodus 15:1–3, 11, 13, 17–18

¹ Moses and the women and men of Israel sang this song to the HOLY ONE OF OLD:

"I will sing to the GOD WHO SAVES, for God has triumphed triumphantly;
horse and rider God has thrown into the sea.
² The MIGHTY GOD is my strength and my might,
God has become my salvation.

This is my God, whom I will praise,

my mother's God and my father's God, whom I will exalt.

³ The DREAD GOD is a warrior;

TOO HOLY TO BE PRONOUNCED is God's name.

¹¹ "Who is like you, MOST HIGH, among the gods?

Who is like you, majestic in holiness,

awesome in splendor, working wonders?

¹³ In your faithful love you led the people whom you redeemed;

you guided them by your strength to your holy habitation.

¹⁷ You brought them in and planted them on the mountain that is your own possession,

the place, FAITHFUL GOD, that you made your dwelling place,

the sanctuary, SOVEREIGN ONE, that your hands have established.

¹⁸ GOD WHO IS MAJESTY will reign forever and ever."

Rahab's Salvation: Joshua 2:1–14; 6:15–17, 23

²:¹ And Joshua son of Nun sent two men, spies, secretly from Shittim, saying, "Go, surveil the land, surveil Jericho." So, they went, and entered the house of a prostitute—her name was Rahab—and they lay down there. ² Now the king of Jericho was told, "Look now, men have come here tonight from the Israelites to search out the land." ³ Then the king of Jericho sent to Rahab, "Bring out the men, the ones who came to you, who came to your house, for they have come to search out the whole of the land." ⁴ Now the woman had taken the two men and hid them. Then she said, "True, the men came to me, but I did not know from where they came. ⁵ And it was when the gate was to close at dark that the men went out. I do not know where the men went. Hurry, chase after them, for you can reach them." ⁶ However, she had brought them up to the roof and hidden them in the stalks of flax that she had laid out for herself on the roof. ⁷ So the men chased after them along the path of the Jordan up to the fords. The gate was shut as soon as the pursuers had gone out.

¹² [Rahab said,] "Now I bid you all swear to me by the FAITHFUL GOD—for I have done faithfully by you all—that you also will do faithfully by my father's household. Give me a trustworthy sign. ¹³ Now, spare my mother and my father, my sisters and my brothers, and all who belong to them, and deliver our lives from death." ¹⁴ The men said to her, "Our life for yours, even unto death! If you do not tell this our business, then when the FAITHFUL GOD gives to us the land we will deal faithfully and honestly with you."

⁶:¹⁵ And it happened on the seventh day that they rose early, at the break of dawn, and circled the city in the same way seven times. Only on that day that they circled the city seven times. ¹⁶ And it was the seventh time, when the priests blew the ram's horns, Joshua said to the people, "Shout! For the FAITHFUL ONE has given you the city. ¹⁷ The city and all that is in it shall be devoted to the HOLY ONE. Only Rahab the prostitute, she shall live and all who are with her in her house because she hid the messengers we sent.

²³ So the youths who were the spies went in and brought Rahab out, along with her mother, her father, her sisters and brothers, and all who belonged to her—all her kinfolk they brought out—and set them outside the camp of Israel.

Canticle: Wisdom 5:1–5; 6:6–7

⁵:¹ The righteous will stand with great confidence
   in the presence of those who have oppressed them
   and those who make light of their labors.

² When the unrighteous see, they will be shaken with a terrible fear,
   and they will be amazed at the unexpected salvation.

³ They will speak amongst themselves, repenting,
   and out of distress of spirit they will groan, and say,

⁴ "These are persons whom we once held in derision
   and made the meaning of insult—we were foolish.
   We reckoned their lives as madness
   and their end without honor.

⁵ Why have they been numbered among the daughters and sons of God?
   And why is their lot among the holy ones?"

⁶:⁶ For the least may be pardoned in mercy,
   but the mighty will be mightily tested.

⁷ For the Sovereign of all will not draw back from anyone,
   or show respect to greatness;
   because small and great alike God made,
   and God takes thought for all alike.

Deborah Saves the People: Judges 4:1–10, 23

¹ And again the men and women of Israel did what was evil in the sight of the HOLY ONE OF SINAI, for Ehud [the Judge] was dead. ² So the HOLY ONE sold them into the hand of King Jabin of Canaan, who reigned in Hazor; the commander of his army was Sisera, who lived in Harosheth-ha-goiim. ³ Then the women and men of Israel cried out to GOD WHO HEARS; for Jabin had nine hundred chariots of iron, and had oppressed the Israelites with ruthlessness twenty years.

⁴ Deborah, a woman, a female prophet, a fiery woman, she was judging Israel at that time. ⁵ She used to sit under the palm of Deborah between Ramah and Bethel in the hill country of Ephraim; and the women and men of Israel came up to her for judgment. ⁶ She sent and called for Barak ben Abinoam from Kedesh in Naphtali, and said to him, "Did not the MOST HIGH, the God of Israel, command you? Go! March on Mount Tabor, and take ten thousand men from the tribe of Naphtali and the tribe of Zebulun. ⁷ I will march toward you to draw to you by the Wadi Kishon Sisera the commander of Jabin's army, with his chariots and his troops; and I will give him into your hand." ⁸ Then Barak said to her, "If you will go with me, then I will go; but if you will not go with me, I will not go." ⁹ And she

said, "I will surely go with you; however, there will be no glory for you on the path you are taking, for the MIGHTY GOD will sell Sisera into the hand of a woman." Then Deborah got up and went with Barak to Kedesh. ¹⁰ Barak summoned Zebulun and Naphtali to Kedesh; and ten thousand men went up with him; and Deborah went up with him.

²³ And on that day, God subdued King Jabin of Canaan before the women and men of Israel.

Canticle of Deborah: Judges 5:1, 4–7, 12, 24, 31

¹ Then Deborah and Barak ben Abinoam sang on that day, saying:

⁴ "MIGHTY ONE, when you went out from Seir,
   when you marched from the field of Edom,
   the earth and the heavens dripped,
   even the clouds dripped water.
⁵ The mountains melted before the MOST HIGH, the One of Sinai,
   before the ONE GOD, the God of Israel.
⁶ "In the days of Shamgar son of Anath,
   in the days of Jael, caravans ceased
   and travelers traversed the byways.
⁷ The mighty grew fat in Israel,
   they grew fat on plunder,
   until you arose, Deborah,
   you arose as a mother in Israel."
¹² "Awake, awake, Deborah!
   Awake, awake, utter a song!
   Arise, Barak, capture your captives,
   ben Abinoam."
²⁴ "Most blessed of women be Jael,
   the wife of Heber the Kenite,
   of tent-women most blessed."
³¹ "So perish all your enemies, HOLY ONE OF OLD!
   But those who love God will be like the sun rising in its might."

And the land was pacified for forty years.

Jehosheba Saves the King of Judah: 2 Kings 11:1–4, 10–12

¹ Now Athaliah, Ahaziah's mother, saw that her son was dead, she stood up and destroyed all the royal offspring. ² Then Jehosheba, daughter of King Joram, sister of Ahaziah, took Joash, Ahaziah's son, and she stole him away from among the daughters and sons of the king who were being killed; she put him and his nurse in a bedroom. Thus, she hid him from Athaliah, and he was not put to death. ³ [The prince] remained with Ahaziah six years, hidden in the house of the EVER-LIVING GOD, while Athaliah reigned over the land.

[4] But in the seventh year Jehoiada [the High Priest and Josheba's husband] sent for the captains of the Carites and of the bodyguards and had them come to him in the house of the HOLY ONE. He made a covenant with them and had them swear it in the house of the HOLY ONE OF OLD; then he showed them the son of the king.

[10] The priest [Jehoiada] gave to the captains of the hundreds the spears and shields that had been King David's, which were in the house of the LIVING GOD. [11] Then the guards stood, each with his weapons in his hand, from the south of the temple to the north of the temple, next to the altar and the temple, around the king on every side. [12] Then he brought out the son of the king, put the crown on him, and gave Joash the testimony [of royalty]. They made him king and anointed him; they clapped their hands and shouted, "Long live the king!"

Psalm 9:1–2, 7–11, 13–14

[1] I will give thanks to the GOD WHO SAVES with my whole heart;
   I will tell of all your wonderful deeds.
[2] I will rejoice and exult in you;
   I will sing praise to your name, Most High.
[7] GOD WHO IS MAJESTY sits enthroned forever,
   she has established her throne for judgment.
[8] She judges the world in righteousness;
   she judges the peoples with equity.
[9] SHE WHO IS FAITHFUL is a stronghold for the oppressed,
   a stronghold in times of trouble.
[10] They trust you, they who know your name,
   for you do not forsake those who seek you REDEEMING GOD.
[11] Sing praises to the HOLY ONE enthroned in Zion.
   Declare her deeds among the peoples.
[13] Be gracious to me, GRACIOUS ONE.
   See what I suffer from those who hate me.
   You lift me up from the gates of death,
[14] so that I may recount all your praises,
   and in the gates of Daughter Zion,
   rejoice in your salvation.

Judith Saves Her People: Judith 8:9–10, 32–34; 13:3–14, 17–18

[8:9] Now Judith heard the wicked words of the people against the ruler because they were disheartened from lack of water, and when she heard all the words that Uzziah said to them, and how he swore to them to surrender the town to the Assyrians after five days. [10] So she sent her slave-girl, who was set over all she possessed, to summon Uzziah and Chabris and Charmis, the elders of her town.

^{32} Then Judith said to them, "Hear me and I will do a thing that will go down from generation to generation of our daughters and sons. ^{33} You all shall stand at the gate this night and I shall go out, I along with my slave-girl, and within the days which you have promised to hand over the town to our enemies, the Holy One will visit Israel through my hand. ^{34} None of you all should investigate my task; for I will not tell you until I have completed my work."

$^{13:3}$ Now Judith had told her slave-girl to stand outside the bedchamber and to wait for her to come out, as she did other days; for she said she would go out for her prayer. She spoke to Bagoas these same words. ^{4} So everyone went out beyond sight, and no one was left in the bedchamber, either small or great. Then Judith, standing beside his bed, said in her heart, "Holy God of all power, look with care in this hour on the work of my hands for the exaltation of Jerusalem. ^{5} Now is the time to help your heritage and to carry out my intention to destroy the enemies who have risen up against us."

^{6} She came to the bedpost at Holofernes's head, and took down his sword from there. ^{7} Then she came toward his bed, caught the hair of his head, and said, "Give me strength today, Holy God of Israel!" ^{8} And she struck his neck twice with all her might, and cut off his head. ^{9} Then she rolled his body off the bed and snatched the canopy from the post. A little later she went out and gave Holofernes's head to her slave-girl, ^{10} who placed it in her food bag.

Then the two women went out together, according to their custom at the time for prayer. They passed through the encampment, circled the valley, and went up the mountain to Bethulia, and came to its gates. ^{11} From a distance Judith called out to the guards at the gates, "Open! Open the gate! God, our God, is with us, working deeds power in Israel and might against our enemies, as God has done today!"

^{12} And it happened when the men of her town heard her voice, they rushed to come down to the gate of the city and summoned the elders of the city. ^{13} They all ran together, from small to great, for it was extraordinary to them that she returned. They opened the gate and welcomed the women. Then they lit a fire to provide light, and gathered around the women. ^{14} Then Judith said to them with a loud voice, "Hallelujah! Hallelujah! Praise God, who did not withdraw mercy from the house of Israel, but has broken our enemies by my hand this night!"

^{17} All the people were completely astounded. They bowed down and worshiped God, and said with one accord, "Blessed are you our God, who has this day humiliated the enemies of your people." ^{18} Then Uzziah said to Judith, "O daughter, you are blessed by the Most High God above all other women on earth, and blessed be the Holy God, who created the heavens and the earth, who has guided you to cut off the head of the leader of our enemies."

The Song of Judith: Judith 16:1–6, 13

^{1} Judith said:
Begin praise for my God with drums,
sing to my Sovereign with cymbals.
Craft a psalm and a praise for God;
exalt God and call upon God's name.

² For the Holy One is a God who crushes wars,
   whose encampments are in the midst of the people,
   who delivered me from the hands of my pursuers.

³ Assyria came down from the mountains of the north;
   it came with multitudes of its warriors,
   the same multitude blocked up the waterway,
   and their cavalry covered the hills.

⁴ Assyria boasted that it would burn up my territory,
   and kill my young men with the sword,
   and throw my infants to the ground,
   and give my children away as spoils of war,
   and despoil my virgins.

⁵ But the Almighty God dismissed them
   with a feminine hand.

⁶ For their mighty one did not fall by the hands of the young men,
   nor did the sons of the Titans strike him down,
   nor did tall giants lay him out;
   but Judith daughter of Merari
   with the beauty of her person undid him.

¹³ I will sing to my God a new song:
   Holy One, you are great and glorious,
   wonderful in strength, invincible.

Epistle: Acts 16:13–15

¹³ On the day of the sabbath we went out the gate by the river, where we thought there was a place of prayer; and we sat down and spoke to the women who gathered there. ¹⁴ Now a certain woman named Lydia, a merchant of purple cloth from the city of Thyatira, a worshiper of God, was listening to us. The Messiah opened her heart to listen eagerly to what was said by Paul. ¹⁵ As she was baptized along with her household, she urged us, saying, "If you have judged me to be faithful to Christ, come and stay at my home." And she persuaded us.

Gospel: Matthew 28:1–10

¹ After the sabbath, as the first day of the week was dawning, Mary Magdalene and the other Mary went to see the tomb. ² And look! There was a great earthquake, for a messenger of God, descending from heaven, came and rolled away the stone and sat upon it. ³ Its appearance was like lightning, and its clothing white as snow. ⁴ For fear of the messenger, the guards shook and were as though dead. ⁵ But the messenger responded to the women and said, "Fear not; I know that you all are looking for Jesus who was crucified. ⁶ He is not here; for he has been raised, just as he said. Come, see the place where he lay. ⁷ Then go quickly and tell his disciples, 'He has been raised from the dead, and see, he is on to Galilee ahead of

you; there you all will see him.' This is my message for you." [8] So the women left the tomb quickly with fear and great joy and ran to tell his disciples the news. [9] Then, all of a sudden, Jesus met them and said, "Shalom!" And they came to him, took hold of his feet, and bowed down worshiping him. [10] Then Jesus said to them, "Fear not; go and tell my sisters and brothers to go to Galilee; there they will see me."

PROCLAMATION

Text Notes

In the very first lines of Genesis, and therefore of the Bible, Jewish or Christian, both masculine and feminine verbs are used for God, masculine for God, feminine for the spirit. Ultimately God's human creation will reflect their creator as female and male. The translation follows that early pattern and uses pronouns of both genders throughout the passage. In Genesis 2:2, I also use "they" for God, a reminder that God transcends the binary language in which God is disclosed and that some of those created in the image of God are nonbinary.

In Genesis 21:9, the nature of Ishmael's play (or mocking) is not explained. The NRSV and RSV add "with Isaac," which is not in the text, leading to the demonization of Ishmael as a child. Some commentators go so far as to accuse him of sexually abusing Isaac based on this fiction. In verse 11, Abraham finds the situation "extremely evil," though the word encodes a range of negativity. Hagar's motion in putting her child under the tree is explosive: "throw" or "cast." The idiomatic expression in verse 17, "What is with you?" sounds harsher to English-speaking ears than the traditional, "What troubles you?"

In Psalm 27:11, "teach" is the verbal form of *torah,* which is more properly "teaching" or "revelation" than law. In verse 12, "throats" translates *nephesh,* "soul." The usage is rare but occurs in Job 24:7, Jeremiah 4:10, and Habakkuk 2:5. In verse 24, the number of grammatically masculine subjects leave open another possible translation, familiar from the King James Version: "Be of good courage and God will strengthen your heart."

The Canticle of the Three Young Men comes from the Greek version of Daniel in the Septuagint. A larger selection of verses occurs in the Song of the Three Young Men used as a canticle in the Book of Common Prayer. In many Protestant Bibles like the NRSV, translations of Greek portions of Daniel and Esther are published in a separate section with the Deuterocanonical/Apocryphal books. In Catholic Bibles like the Inclusive Bible, the Greek-based portions are woven in, resulting in an alternate set of verse numbers. This passage is verses 74–82 in the *New English Translation of the Septuagint* (NETS). The NETS translation was influential in my own here.

In Exodus 15:2, I add "my mother's God." While Moses will have to ask who God is and what is the divine Name, Moses's mother, Yocheved, Jochebed, bears the

Name in the first syllable of her name and may be the oldest name in the Hebrew Bible including a portion of the Name. In verse 3, God is thoroughly anthropomorphized as "a man of war."

Like Miriam's Song, Judges 5 is one of the oldest works in the Hebrew Bible, replete with translation challenges. In Judges 4:4, Deborah is a woman of *lappidoth*. While many have contrived a husband, the word is the adjective "fiery" or "flaming" with a feminine ending. Further, unlike every male character in the book, *lappidoth* does not have any family information line for Barak, son of Abinoam. The feminine singular verb in 5:1 indicates Deborah led the song, and Barak followed her lead. An earlier version of the translation of Judges 4–5 and detailed translation notes can be found in *Daughters of Miriam: Women Prophets in Ancient Israel*.

Some details of 2 Kings 11 are filled in with the more detailed account in 2 Chronicles 23.

The sense of the story in Judith is that she dines with the enemy general, maintaining her virtue, got him drunk, and assassinated him. In the critical scene, the tent where Holofernes sleeps is confusingly described as hers in 13:3. Previously 12:1 and following indicate she is staying in his dining tent. In 13:14 I use the traditional "Hallelujah" for the Jewish (woman whose name means just that, a Jewish woman).

In Matthew 28 I have translated the divine messenger in neuter terms, since grammatical gender may not be biologically significant—if the category even applies—to a divine messenger.

Preaching Prompts

While these texts may not be preached on Easter, commentary is offered for those who will choose one for the early service on Easter day. Those preparing for non-lectionary sermons may find the lesson/canticle pairings fruitful. For example, Psalm 27 takes on new meaning when heard from the perspective of Hagar and Ishmael.

In the Exodus account, the God who saves Israelite lives takes Egyptian lives. The scriptures celebrate the liberation and often the deaths of the Egyptians, though later texts will acknowledge that the peoples of Egypt and Israel's other adversaries are also God's. The Exodus Canticle is understood by some scholars to have been Miriam's initially, perhaps just the contents of Exodus 15:21. The longer song in Exodus 15:1–18 then derives from the shorter.

Note that in Joshua 2, the spies do not surveil the land or Jericho. They head straight for a brothel and "lay down." That expression is used for sex and for sleeping. "Spend the night" unnecessarily shifts the reader away from the plain understanding of why men go to a brothel. Joshua 6:23 calls them "youth" or "boys," which may contribute to their decision. This text provides an opportunity to talk about sex work and its criminalization and the (often upstanding) men who buy sex. Tying in Jesus's friendships with sex workers may help frame this text in an Easter sermon.

Note that Rahab's father's household in 2:12 is different from her household in 2:1. She seeks the salvation of her entire family, whether they live with her or not, perhaps, no matter what they think about her line of work. In verse 13, "spare" is less than a command and more than a request. She saves all who are in the house with her in verse 17, the ark of safety she offers may well encompass people who are not related to her. Rahab and her family are delivered using the primary verb of the exodus in Joshua 6:17–18.

Selections from Wisdom chapters 5 and 6 pair with the Rahab story, reminding the reader and hearer that God saves and redeems who God wills, including and particularly those who are thought to be sinful and beyond God's reach and care.

Athaliah is the only woman in the Bible to rule Israel or Judah on her own; functionally, she was a king, as neither Israel nor Judah had queens, a title not used by royal wives. Separately, the queen-mothers of Judah were the mothers of the ruling king in Judah and did serve in an official capacity.

While some number of the women who followed Jesus were present at his resurrection in Matthew 28:10, there were certainly more who, like all of his male followers, were not.

EASTER DAY—EARLY SERVICE

The early Easter service traditionally uses lessons from the Great Vigil of Easter. Choose a first lesson from the Vigil and use the psalm, Epistle, and Gospel readings from the Vigil.

EASTER DAY—PRINCIPAL SERVICE

Isaiah 49:1–13; Psalm 18:2–11, 16–19; Hebrews 11:1–2, 23–24, 28–39; Matthew 28:1–10 or John 20:1–10 (11–18)

Isaiah 49:1 Listen you coastlands to me,

> And pay heed, you peoples from afar!
> The CREATOR OF ALL called me from the womb,
> from my mother's belly God made my name known.
> ² God made my mouth like a sharpened sword,
> and in the shadow of God's own hand, hid me;
> God made me like a polished arrow,
> in God's own quiver, hid me.

[3] And God said to me, "You are my slave,
Israel, in you I am glorified."
[4] But I, I said, "In vain have I labored,
I have spent my strength for nothingness and vanity;
surely my judgment is with the FAITHFUL ONE,
and my wages with my God."
[5] And now says the AUTHOR OF LIFE,
who formed me in the womb to be God's slave,
to return Jacob back to God,
and that Israel might be gathered to God;
I am honored in the sight of the HOLY ONE OF OLD,
and my God is my strength.
[6] God says,
"It is too light a thing that you should be my slave
to raise up the tribes of Jacob [the line of Rebekah],
and to restore the survivors of Israel [born of Rachel and Leah, and Bilhah and
Zilpah]?
I will give you as a light to the nations,
for it will be that my salvation reaches to the end of the earth."
[7] Thus says the FAITHFUL ONE,
the Redeemer of Israel, God's holy one,
to one despised, abhorred by the nations,
the slave of rulers,
"Queens and kings shall see and arise,
princes and princesses, and they too shall prostrate themselves,
on account of the FIRE OF SINAI, who is faithful,
the Holy One of Israel, who has chosen you."
[8] Thus says the MIGHTY GOD:
In a favorable time I have answered you,
on a day of salvation I have helped you;
I have kept you and given you
as a covenant to the people,
to establish the land,
to apportion the desolate portions;
[9] saying to the prisoners, "Go free!"
to those who are in darkness, "Let yourselves be seen."
Along the paths they shall pasture,
and on all the bare heights shall be their pasture.
[10] They shall not hunger nor shall they thirst,
neither shall heat nor sun strike them down,

for the one who mother-loves them shall lead them,
and by springs of water shall guide them.

11 And I will turn all my mountains into a pathway,
and my highways shall be raised up.

12 Look! These shall come from far away,
and see! These from the north and from the sea to the west,
and these from the southland of Syene.

13 Sing for joy, you heavens, and exult O earth;
let mountains break forth into singing!
For the TENDER LOVING ONE has comforted God's people,
and will mother-love God's suffering ones.

Psalm 18:2–11, 16–19

2 The ROCK WHO GAVE US BIRTH is my rock,
and my fortress, and my deliverer,
my God, my rock in whom I take refuge,
my shield, and the horn of my salvation, my stronghold.

3 I call upon the HOLY ONE, may she be praised,
and from my enemies I shall be saved.

4 The snares of death encompassed me;
the rivers of wickedness assailed me.

5 The snares of Sheol encircled me;
the snares of death confronted me.

6 In my distress I called upon SHE WHO HEARS;
to my God I cried for help.
From her temple she heard my voice,
and my cry came before her, to her ears.

7 Then the earth shuddered and quaked;
the foundations also of the mountains trembled
and were shaken because of her anger.

8 Smoke went up from her nostrils,
and consuming fire from her mouth;
burning coals blazed forth from her.

9 She spread out the heavens, and descended;
thick darkness was under her feet.

10 She mounted up on a cherub, and flew;
she soared upon the wings of the wind.

11 She made darkness her veil around her,
her canopy dark waters and thick clouds.

16 She reached down from on high, she took me;

she drew me out of the multitude of water.

17 She delivered me from my strong enemy,
and from those who hate me;
for they were too mighty for me.

18 They confronted me in the day of my calamity;
yet the Sheltering God was my support.

19 She brought me out into a broad place;
she delivered me, because she delights in me.

Hebrews 11:1 Now faith is the essence of things hoped for, the conviction of that which is not seen. 2 By faith, indeed, were our ancestors approved.

23 By faith Moses was hidden after his birth by his mother and father for three months, because they saw that the child was beautiful; and they were not afraid of the king's commandment. 24 By faith Moses, after he had grown up, refused to be called a son of Pharaoh's daughter.

28 By faith he kept the Passover and the sprinkling of blood, in order that the destroyer of the firstborn would not touch the firstborn daughters and sons of Israel.

29 By faith they passed through the Red Sea as though on dry land, but when the Egyptians chose to try, they were drowned. 30 By faith the walls of Jericho fell when encircled for seven days. 31 By faith Rahab the prostitute did not perish with those who did not believe, because she had received the spies in peace.

32 And what more should I say? For time would fail me to tell of Gideon, Barak, Samson, Jephthah, of David and Samuel and the prophets, female and male, 33 who through faith conquered realms, administered justice, obtained promises, stopped the mouths of lions, 34 quenched raging fire, escaped the edge of the sword, were made strong out of weakness, became mighty in war, felled foreign armies. 35 Women through resurrection received their dead. Other women and men were tortured, refusing to receive a release, in order to obtain a better resurrection. 36 Yet other women and men received a trial of mocking and whipping, and even chains and imprisonment. 37 They were stoned, they were sawed in two, they were slaughtered by sword; they went about in animal-skins, in sheepskin and goatskin, impoverished, oppressed, tormented. 38 The world was not worthy of them. They wandered in deserts and mountains, and in caves and holes in the ground.

39 And all these, commended for their faith, did not receive what was promised.

Matthew 28:1–10 *is available with commentary in the readings for the Great Vigil of Easter. John 20 is the customary alternative. The reading from the Gospel of John may be read in longer or shorter form.*

John 20:1 Now it was the first day of the week, Mary Magdalene came, early on while it was still dark, to the tomb and saw the stone removed from the tomb. 2 So she ran and went to Simon Peter and to the other disciple, the one whom Jesus loved, and said to them, "They have taken the Messiah out of the tomb, and we do not know where they have laid him." [3] Then Peter and the other disciple came and went to the tomb. [4] The two were running together, but the other disciple ran ahead of Peter and reached the tomb first. [5] And bending down to see, saw the linen wrappings lying there, but he did not enter. [6] Then Simon Peter came, following him, and went into the tomb, and he saw the linen wrappings lying there [7] and the facecloth that had been on Jesus's head not lying with the linen wrappings but rolled up separately in another place. [8] Then the other disciple, who reached the tomb first, went in and saw and believed. [9] Indeed they did not understand the scripture, that it was necessary for Jesus to rise from the dead. [10] Then the disciples returned once more to their homes.

[[11] Now Mary stood outside, facing the tomb, weeping. As she wept, she bent down to see in the tomb. [12] Then she saw two angels in white sitting, one at the head and the other at the feet, where the body of Jesus had been lying. [13] They said to her, "Woman, why do you weep?" She said to them, "Because, they have taken my Savior, and I do not know where they have laid him." [14] Having said this, she turned around and saw Jesus standing, but she did not know that it was Jesus. [15] Jesus said to her, "Woman, why do you weep? For whom do you look?" Thinking that he was the gardener, she said to him, "Sir, if you have carried him away, tell me where you have laid him, and I will take him away." [16] Jesus said to her, "Mary." She turned and said to him in Aramaic, "Rabbouni!" (which means Teacher). [17] Jesus said to her, "Do not hold me, because I have not yet ascended to the Father. Rather, go to my brothers and say to them, 'I am ascending to my Father and your Father, to my God and your God.'" [18] Mary Magdalene went and announced to the disciples, "I have seen the Savior"; and she told them that he had said these things to her.]

PROCLAMATION

Text Notes

Given there is no concrete present tense in biblical Hebrew, it can be difficult to determine whether an imperfect verb should be translated into present or future tense. In Isaiah 49:3, the question of whether God *is* glorified in Israel or *will be* is open. I have chosen the present to suggest that even in their brokenness, or perhaps because of it, God is glorified in her faithful relationship with an often unfaithful partner. A portion of Isaiah 49 read today overlaps with the one read on Psalm Sunday. See textual and preaching commentary there for further notes.

In Psalm 18:2, I draw the divine name from Deuteronomy 32:18, "You neglected the Rock that gave birth to you; you forgot the God who writhed in birth-labor for you."

The Greek word *hypostasis* means the "essence of a thing," as in the relationship between Jesus and God articulated with this same word earlier in Hebrews 1:2–3. In Hebrews 11:1, faith is the essence of that which is hoped for. In 11:2, "to be approved" is the sense of the verb to "be martyred" or "bear witness" when it is the passive voice. The citizens of Jericho in Hebrews 11:31 can be translated as either they who "were disobedient" or "did not believe." Each is problematic in the context of the earlier story. If disobedient, when? To what message? If unbelieving, then to what?

Note that the celestial messengers speak with one voice in John 20:13. In verse 15, Mary addresses Jesus with the honorific given to any man of status or used to show respect, "master" or "lord," also used for those who held slaves. It also signifies Jesus's own authority and sovereignty. Her demand that this unknown person tell her where Jesus has been taken is expressed in the imperative, as a command. Exclamation point or period? Does Jesus exclaim her name or call it softly or plainly in verse 16? I imagine the latter.

Hebrew and Aramaic are recognized as distinct languages now; they were not always so understood; the terms are used interchangeably in the scriptures.

Preaching Prompts

The anonymity of the Servant Songs in Isaiah has led to them being easily interpreted through the story of Jesus. As an Easter reading, the text reminds us of the import of the life Jesus lived, not just the death he died, a life that was shaped and molded by scriptures like Isaiah 49.

The psalmist is delivered from certain death in her time by being saved from her enemies and their traps. Yet that is not the limit of the power of the God who harnesses the clouds as her chariot. Psalm 18 also serves as a response to Psalm 22 in the earlier plaintive liturgies of Holy Week and Good Friday; the pleas for deliverance and trust in God are answered by the fact of deliverance. God is able to deliver. God is faithful to deliver. Even to and through death.

The Epistle to the Hebrews forms a bridge to the Gospel. In this Epistle penned to Jewish, and therefore Hebrew, people, the author links that faith to the faith of their people (and collaborators) across time. Yet the list of heroes in Hebrews 11 that recounts that faith reads like a patriarchal revisionist history. For example, Barak replaces Deborah, and Jephthah, who murdered his own daughter, is included in 11:32. (However, since Deborah ruled and delivered in the period mentioned, and other women prophets followed her, and the plural "prophets" includes both genders, I have specified "prophets, female and male.") Ironically, it will be women's faithfulness to Jesus at the cross and tomb that will lead to the first proclamations of his resurrection. As a second lesson, the last line of this reading points forward to a promise realized in that resurrection and its proclamation.

With all of the alleluias, it is hard to remember that Easter morning begins in sorrow. Grieving and dumbfounded, women make their way to the tomb, where their friend, teacher, and savior lies. They are not singing alleluia. In John's Gospel, their motivation has been erased; they have been reduced to Mary Magdalene and one "we" in verse 2. They do not enter the tomb, counter to other accounts. They fetch men who go first, then Mary follows them. The male disciples leave, and once again, Jesus is attended only by women, now just Mary. He reveals himself to her and sends her as his messenger bearing his word.

She announces, *aggellousa*, the good news that Jesus has appeared to her and has a message for the men who were not present. That "announcement" is related to the words for messengers, human or divine ones sometimes called angels, and their messages; they share a common root. Interpreters have struggled with what to make of Jesus telling Mary not to touch or hold or hold on to him in John 20:17. Some wince at what they hear as harsh language, as when he asks his mother, "Woman, what concern is that to you and to me?" in John 2:4. I wonder if it is that we do not hear "woman" charitably as a form of address. What may be missed are the parallels to Thomas: Mary sees, hears, speaks with, and touches her savior. Having seen his death, what other than the word of the risen Christ could compel her to let go?

EASTER DAY—EVENING SERVICE

Isaiah 25:6–9; Psalm 118:14–26; 2 Timothy 2:8–13; Luke 24:13–35 (or 24:13–27)

Isaiah 25:6 The COMMANDER of heaven's legions will make for all peoples on this mountain,

> a feast of rich food, a feast of well-aged wines,
> of rich food prepared with marrow, of refined well-aged wines.
> 7 And God will destroy on this mountain
> the shroud that shrouds all peoples,
> the veil that veils all nations.
> 8 God will swallow up death forever.
> Then the SOVEREIGN GOD will wipe away tears from every face,
> and will sweep aside the shame of God's people from the whole earth,
> for GOD WHOSE NAME IS HOLY has spoken.
> 9 It will be said on that day,
> Look! This is our God; in whom we hope, and who saved us.
> This is the CREATOR OF ALL in whom we hope;
> let us be glad and rejoice in God's salvation.

Psalm 118:14–26

> 14 The MIGHTY GOD is my strength and my might
> and has become my salvation.
> 15 The sound of song and of salvation is in the tents of the righteous:

"The right hand of the Most High is mighty;

16 the right hand of the Mighty God is exalted;
the right hand of the Most High is mighty."

17 I shall not die, but I shall live,
and recount the deeds of the Ancient Of Days.

18 The Merciful God has punished me severely,
but to death did not hand me over.

19 Open to me the gates of righteousness,
that I may enter through them
and give thanks to the Fount of Justice.

20 This is the gate of the Living God;
the righteous shall enter through it.

21 I thank you for you have answered me
and have become my salvation.

22 The stone the builders rejected
has become the chief cornerstone.

23 This is the Mighty God's doing;
it is marvelous in our eyes.

24 This is the day that the Creator of All has made;
let us rejoice and be glad in it.

25 Save us, we pray, Saving One!
Generous One, we pray, grant us prosperity!

26 Blessed is the one who comes in the name of God Who is Holy.
We bless you from the house of the Ever-Living God.

2 Timothy 2:8 Remember Jesus Christ, raised from the dead, from the line of David [and Bathsheba]; that is my gospel, ⁹ for which I suffer hardship, even to chains, like a criminal. But the word of God is not chained. ¹⁰ Because of this, therefore I endure everything for the sake of the elect, in order that they may also obtain salvation in Christ Jesus with eternal glory. ¹¹ This is a trustworthy saying:

For if we die together, we will also live together;

12 if we endure, we will also reign together;
if we deny [Christ], he will also deny us;

13 if we are faithless, faithful he remains,
for he cannot deny himself.

Luke 24:13 Now see, two of them on that very day [the first day of the week] were going to a village that was seven miles from Jerusalem; its name was Emmaus. ¹⁴ And they talked with each other about all the things that had happened. ¹⁵ And it happened while they were talking and questioning that Jesus himself came near and accompanied them. ¹⁶ Yet their eyes were kept from recognizing him. [17] And Jesus said to them, "What is this conversation you are having with each other while you journey?" They stood in place, sorrowful. [18] Then one of them, whose name was Cleopas, replied to him, saying, "Are you the only foreigner in Jerusalem who does not know the things that have happened there these days?" [19] Jesus asked them, "What kind of things?" They replied, "About Jesus the Nazarene, who was a man, a prophet mighty in deed and word before God and all the people. [20] Also how our chief priests and leaders surrendered him to be sentenced to death and crucified him. [21] But we had hoped that he was the one to soon redeem Israel. Now besides all this, instead, it is now the third day since these things have taken place. [22] Then again, certain women of our community astounded us. They were at the tomb this morning. [23] And when they did not find the body, they came back and told us they had seen a vision of angels who said Jesus was alive. [24] Then some of those who were with us went to the tomb and found it just as the women had said, but they did not see him." [25] Then Jesus said to them, "Oh, foolish souls, and how slow of heart to believe all that the prophets have spoken! [26] Was it not necessary that the Messiah should suffer these things to enter into his glory?" [27] And starting from Moses and from all the prophets, Jesus interpreted to them the things about himself in all the scriptures.

[28] When they came near the village to which they were going, Jesus walked ahead as if he were going on. [29] So they urged him strongly, saying, "Stay with us, because it is almost evening and the day is nearly over." Then he went in to stay with them. [30] When Jesus was at the table with them, he took bread, blessed and broke it, and gave it to them. [31] And their eyes were opened, and they recognized him. And he vanished from before them. [32] They said to each other, "Were not our hearts burning within us while he was talking to us on the way, while he was opening up the scriptures to us?" [33] Now that same hour they rose up and returned to Jerusalem and found the eleven and others with them gathered together. [34] They were saying, "Really! The Savior has risen, and has appeared to Simon!" [35] Then they told what had happened on the way, and how Jesus had been made known to them in the breaking of the bread.

PROCLAMATION

Text Notes

There are regular differences in how biblical passages are broken into verses between translations. In Isaiah 25, the last line of what is verse 7 in some Christian Bibles like NRSV begins verse 8 in Hebrew and in Jewish Bibles and other Christian Bibles, like CEB. I follow the Hebrew and JPS here. In verse 9, the tense of God's salvation can be understood as past or present. God's record of faithfulness makes her trustworthy; pushing these texts into a future time diminishes that past faithfulness.

Psalm 118 is a literary work of art in Hebrew with a lattice of repeating elements that circle from the last line to the beginning. In verse 25, which yields "hosanna," an alternate pronunciation for *hoshia-na* in the psalm.

Many translations of 2 Timothy 2:11–13 add "with him" throughout for poetic balance; the object and preposition are not present. Verse 12 requires an object for the verb; I have supplied "Christ" from verse 10.

In Luke 24:25, Jesus says, "Oh foolish X . . ." There is no noun present; the adjective includes object information, masculine or inclusive plural. Common translations are "foolish men," "ones," or "people."

Preaching Prompts

On this Principal Feast of the Resurrection, the Church proclaims that death is not the end. This notion appears intermittently in the Hebrew Bible: Elisha raises a widow's son from death in 2 Kings 4, and Daniel 12:1–2 proclaims an unambiguous resurrection. Frequently cited, Job 19:26 is ambiguous and well-known. In Ezekiel 37, the dry bones represent the resurrection of the nation of Israel; see verse 11. Against this background, Isaiah 25 proclaims that the day is coming when God will destroy death forever, swallowing it up. Belief in resurrection will become normative for most traditions of Judaism, including that of Jesus, for Christians, as well as for Muslims.

Psalm 118 is a festival hymn in the form of a temple liturgy. It is part of the Great *Hallel* (Praise) recited during the major festivals: Passover, Pentecost (*Shavuoth*), and Booths (*Sukkot*). Many understand the Hallel to be the "hymn" that Jesus and the disciples sang after the Last Supper, particularly when it is formed as a Passover meal (though likely not a seder). In these readings, Psalm 118 echoes the theme of salvation in Isaiah 25. In verse 17, the line "I shall not die but live" likely refers to deliverance from death rather than resurrection. Together these collected readings present a God who delivers on both sides of death. While the psalm emphasizes deliverance from death, 2 Timothy offers an ancient hymn for the believer confident in resurrection after death.

It's hard to know what to make of Jesus calling the disciples foolish in Luke 24:25. It sounds like a rebuke but may have been said in humor with a twinkle, the way a text, tweet, or e-mail may sound harsher than intended.

The road to Emmaus stories are Easter evening stories. The traveling disciples have had all day to grapple with incomprehensible claims of resurrection from sister disciples. Notably, they don't doubt the women; rather, they find the whole saga— trial, crucifixion, and resurrection claims—simply astounding. This is an important reminder that the terrible images of the crucifixion and the trauma it generated don't simply vanish with proclamation of the good news. The disciples are traumatized and on an emotional rollercoaster.

Jesus, the Bread of Life, confected in the womb of the Blessed Virgin, makes himself known in the breaking of bread. Jesus, who is bread, offers bread, and Jesus, who is the Word, interprets the word. When Jesus interprets the scriptures—in

Luke 24:27, Torah and Prophets, and in Luke 24:44, Torah, Prophets, and Psalms—the text does not say he shows where the scriptures "predict" him. Reducing the relationship of Jesus with the Hebrew Bible to prediction and fulfillment presents a skewed view of prophecy, scripture more broadly, and Jesus. Rather, I understand him to teach the scriptures that are foundational to him, his identity, his teaching and ministry, after which he patterned himself, which scriptures Christians read through subsequently read through Jesus.

One of the travelers is male; the other is not described. Grammatically, they could have been a woman and man or two men. There were women, children, and men in the village where they stopped absent from the text, as are their hosts. The only women's voices are the echoing proclamations that Christ is risen from the dead.

MONDAY IN EASTER WEEK

1 Peter 1:3–9; Psalm 16:8–11; John 20:19–23

Note: Easter Week services do not traditionally include a Hebrew Bible Reading. In the traditional pattern, the first lesson is a New Testament lesson followed by the psalm and Gospel.

1 Peter 1:3 Blessed be the God and Father of our Redeemer Jesus Christ who in great mercy has engendered a new birth for us into a living hope, through the resurrection of Jesus Christ from the dead, [4] into an inheritance that is incorruptible, undefiled, and unfading, kept in the heavens for you all, [5] who in the power of God are kept through faith for a salvation ready to be revealed in the end time. [6] In this you rejoice even when necessary for you to suffer various trials, [7] in order that the examination of your faith, more precious than gold, which though perishable is tested by fire, may be found yielding praise and glory and honor when Jesus Christ is revealed. [8] You have not seen him, yet you love him. You do not see him now, yet you believe in him and rejoice with a joy glorious and beyond words. [9] You are receiving the completion of your faith, the salvation of your souls.

Psalm 16:8–11

[8] I keep the FAITHFUL ONE before me always;
because she is at my right hand, I shall not be moved.
[9] Therefore my heart rejoices, and my inner being delights;
even my body resides in safety.
[10] For you will not abandon my soul to Sheol,
or let your faithful one see the Pit.
[11] You show me the way of life.
There is fullness of joy in your presence;
delights fill your right hand forevermore.

John 20:19 When it was evening on that day, the first of the week, and the doors of the house where the disciples were closed for fear of the Judeans, Jesus came and stood in their midst and said to them, "Peace be with you all." [20] And having said this, Jesus showed them his hands and his side, then the disciples rejoiced when they saw the Messiah. [21] Jesus said to them again, "Peace be with you all, just as the God of Peace has sent me, so I send you all." [22] When Jesus had said this, he breathed on them and said to them, "Receive the Holy Spirit; [23] if you forgive the sins of any, they are forgiven them; if you retain the sins of any, they are retained."

PROCLAMATION

Text Notes

The reading from 1 Peter has rather long, unwieldy sentences that make for challenging reading, particularly aloud.

In Psalm 16, Sheol, the abode of the dead in the Israelite worldview, was variously described as a place of great gloom, deep below the surface of the (flat) earth. It is an equitable destination for great and small, righteous and wicked. Presumed to be inescapable except by the rarest of miracles, deliverance from Sheol refers to escape from death and its clutches *before* death. The "Pit" is an occasional synonym for Sheol and the grave.

In the Gospel of John, the disciples in the house are as Jewish as their fellow residents of Judea, as Jewish as Jesus. It would be centuries before there was clear separation between Jews and Christians. Scriptural language pitting Jesus, his disciples, and the early Christians against "the Jews" is one of the more challenging aspects of our faith.

Preaching Prompts

These Easter Week first Lesson readings explore some of the Church's earliest reflections on resurrection. All of the psalms focus on God's deliverance from death, and its abode in the Israelite worldview, Sheol. The Gospel readings center the stories from immediately after the resurrection.

The Epistle addresses believers who, like us, have not seen Jesus yet believe. The active voice in the Epistle emphasizes that the readers and hearers, and we, are being kept by God and that they and we are receiving the salvation of our souls.

Rather than a fixed point at which we "were" saved, we live into our salvation in faith.

The second-person addresses of the Epistle and psalm—the first to the reader, the second to God—do not include gendered language. There are, of course, women among the believers to whom the Epistle is written and women who would have prayed, and perhaps composed, the psalmist's prayer. We are left to imagine them.

The women are necessarily absent from the Gospel, having proclaimed the good news of Jesus's resurrection to male disciples who still don't quite get it, let alone its implications for a fearless life. They, Mary Magdalene and other women, suggested by the "we" in John 20:2, are arguably still telling the news. What to make of the gift of the Holy Spirit breathed onto those disciples hiding in the house? It matters that the power and authority to forgive and retain sins is connected to the receipt of the Holy Spirit, grammatically and theologically. The text appears to be organizing if not setting up a hierarchy in the community. This early statement of the nascent community's priorities shows them continuing Jesus's radical work, declaring the forgiveness of sins.

TUESDAY IN EASTER WEEK

1 Corinthians 15:3–7; Psalm 18:1–6; Luke 24:36–43

1 Corinthians 15:3 For I handed on to you all as primary what I in turn had received, that Christ died for our sins in accordance with the scriptures. ⁴ And that he was buried, and that he was raised on the third day in accordance with the scriptures. ⁵ And that he was seen by Cephas, then the twelve. ⁶ Then he was seen by more than five hundred sisters and brothers together, many of whom remain, though some have died. ⁷ Then he was seen by James, then all the apostles.

Psalm 18:1–6

¹ I love you, MIGHTY ONE, my strength.
² The ROCK WHO GAVE US BIRTH is my rock,
   and my fortress, and my deliverer,
   my God, my rock in whom I take refuge,
   my shield, and the horn of my salvation, my stronghold.
³ I call upon the HOLY ONE, may she be praised,
   and from my enemies I shall be saved.
⁴ The snares of death encompassed me;
   the rivers of wickedness assailed me.
⁵ The snares of Sheol encircled me;
   the snares of death confronted me.
⁶ In my distress I called upon SHE WHO HEARS;
   to my God I cried for help.
   From her temple she heard my voice,
   and my cry came before her, to her ears.

Luke 24:36 While they [two of Jesus's disciples] were talking about this [his resurrection], he himself stood between them and said to them, "Peace be with you." ³⁷ Now they were frightened and became terrified, and thought they were seeing a spirit. [38] Jesus said to them, "Why are you troubled, because of thoughts rising in your hearts? [39] Look at my hands and my feet; that it is I. Touch me and see; for a spirit does not have flesh and bones as you see I have." [40] And saying this, Jesus showed them his hands and his feet. [41] Yet still disbelieving and in their joy and wondering, he said to them, "Have you any food here?" [42] They gave him a piece of broiled fish, [43] and he took it in their presence and ate.

PROCLAMATION

Text Notes

One of the ways in which the translation of the scriptures is often anti-Judaistic is the intentional changing of Jewish names in the New Testament to Gentile forms. "James" in 1 Corinthians 15:7 is a case in point. His name is Jacob, *Iakob* in Greek, yet translators use "Jacob" for the Hebrew Bible patriarch occurring in the New Testament while treating the Hebrew names of people in the Jesus story differently. Changing *Mariam* (Greek Miriam) to Mary is another example of what is a standard practice. These changes obscure and, in some cases, erase the primary Jewish identity of the family and followers of Jesus.

The occasion of Psalm 18 is David's escape from Saul; that introduction takes up the first verse in Hebrew. The psalm proper begins with "He said," often included with the introductory verse. David's "love" in what is now verse 1, as Christian translations number the psalms, is *racham*, mother-love, love that is rooted in the womb, *rechem*, and otherwise used only by God to express her love. From David, we should perhaps read it as gesturing toward a reciprocal love that originates deep within.

Verse 3 of the psalm has the passive "be praised" without supporting grammar. Other translators have added "*worthy to* be praised." Some translations render verse 3 in the future (see NRSV and KJV). However, the introduction makes clear David is reflecting on his past deliverance. The imperfect here is more present, i.e., because of God's faithfulness, whenever I call on God as before, I shall be saved.

The Gospel uses the same word for "spirit" (as in the Holy Spirit) for spirit of the dead, or what we might hear as "ghost" in Luke 24:37 and in verse 39.

Preaching Prompts

Given that the Epistles predate the Gospels, the brief telling of the good news of Jesus's resurrection triumph over the grave is one of the first recorded articulations of the Gospel. It lacks all of the narrative detail and the women evangelists collectively or by name. Not only is Mary Magdalene missing, but there is no mention of Mary the mother of Jesus or the beloved disciple. It lacks the angels and reports only Peter (called Cephas) and the twelve as initial witnesses. The text does go on to position Paul as in the chain of apostles.

The mention of James receiving his own postresurrection appearance is significant. Long understood to be the brother of Jesus, the appearance has been interpreted as confirming James as leader of the emerging church. While the Epistle is invested in hierarchy (hence the lack of women) and continuity, Jesus also takes time to appear to family in the person of his beloved brother. The appearances to the more than five hundred in the plural form that can be inclusive, mixed—with only one male required, or all-male suggest Jesus going to his beloveds to comfort and assure them after his death.

Jesus's evening journey with the pair, or perhaps couple, of disciples on the road to Emmaus reads like an expansion of the note in 1 Corinthians 15 about Jesus's appearances to so many. Even with the scolding of beloved teacher and friend, the account reads as comforting and affectionate. As with the five hundred, only one of these disciples must be male grammatically; I chose to read the other as female, likely a spouse.

WEDNESDAY IN EASTER WEEK

1 Corinthians 15:12–20; Psalm 30:1–5; Luke 24:44–53

1 Corinthians 15:12 Now if Christ is preached as raised from the dead, how can some of you say there is no resurrection of the dead? [13] For if there is no resurrection of the dead, then Christ has not been raised; [14] and if Christ has not been raised, then our preaching has been in vain along with your faith. [15] Then we are even found to be false witnesses of God, because we bore witness of God that God raised Christ—whom God did not raise if the dead are not raised. [16] For if the dead are not raised, then Christ has not been raised. [17] And if Christ has not been raised, your faith is useless and you are yet in your sins. [18] And therefore those who have died in Christ have been destroyed. [19] If for this life we have only hoped in Christ, we are of all people most pitiable. [20] But now indeed Christ has been raised from the dead, the first fruits of those who have died.

Psalm 30:1–5

[1] I will exalt you, ARK OF SAFETY, because you have pulled me up
     and have not let my enemies rejoice over me.
[2] HEALING ONE, my God, I cried to you for help,
     and you healed me.
[3] EVER-LIVING GOD, you brought my soul up from Sheol;
     you preserved my life from descent to the Pit.
[4] Sing praises to the FAITHFUL GOD, you her faithful;
     give thanks remembering her holiness.
[5] For her fury is a moment, her favor a lifetime.
     Weeping may pass the night, yet in the morning, joy.

Luke 24:44 Jesus said to [the two disciples], "These are my words that I spoke to you while I was still with you all, because everything must be fulfilled in the teaching of Moses, the prophets, and the psalms written about me." [45] Then he opened their minds to understand the scriptures. [46] Then he said to them, "So it is written, the Messiah is to suffer and to rise from the dead the third day, [47] and repentance and forgiveness of sins is to be preached in his name to all nations, beginning from Jerusalem. [48] You are witnesses of these things. [49] Now look! I am sending you the promise of my Father. You all stay in the city until you have been clothed with power from on high."

[50] Then Jesus led them out as far as Bethany, and lifting his hands, he blessed them. [51] While he was blessing them, Jesus retreated from them and was carried up into heaven. [52] And they worshiped him, and returned to Jerusalem with great joy; [53] and they were in the temple every day blessing God.

PROCLAMATION

Text Notes

Both of the readings from 1 Corinthians 15 and Luke 24 continue from the previous day, even though not contiguous.

Preaching Prompts

People have grappled with the Jesus story from the very beginning. Even in a world in which miracles were accepted uncritically, some of the claims about Jesus were astounding—a word that occurs often in the Gospels. As now, there were those for whom a literal resurrection was difficult to believe. Paul's rebuttal draws a straight line from the resurrection to the forgiveness of our sins and our salvation.

The wonder and incredulity of the disciples on the Emmaus road contrasts with doctrinal disputers in Corinth. The disciples are overjoyed and accept the miracle, though they do not seem to understand it. Jesus calls them back to the Jewish scriptures, somewhat fewer than would eventually be canonized: Torah, Prophets, and only psalms from the third traditional division, Writings. (In the Hebrew Bible the Prophets include Joshua, Judges, Samuel, Kings, Isaiah, Jeremiah, Ezekiel, and the Minor Prophets. The Writings include everything else not in the Torah; Daniel is not a prophet in Jewish tradition.) In other passages, the scriptures consist of the Torah (Law) and Prophets suggesting the Writings were still in formation (see Matt. 22:40; Luke 16:16; Acts 13:15; Rom. 3:21).

Physical salvation is the theme of the psalm as it is all of Easter Week. Deliverance, salvation, and resurrection are available to all without regard for gender or its performance. However, the scriptures and their writers will try to make these stories make sense in the world they knew with all of its hierarchies in place for the most part.

THURSDAY IN EASTER WEEK

1 Corinthians 15:35–44; Psalm 49:5–15; John 21:4–14

1 Corinthians 15:35 Now then, someone will ask, "How are the dead raised? In what kind of body do they come?" [36] Fool! What you plant is not brought to life unless it dies. [37] Now about what you plant, you do not plant the body that will be, but a bare seed, for example, wheat or of some other grain. [38] Yet God gives it a body as God wills, and to each kind of seed its own body. [39] Not all flesh is the same flesh, rather there is one flesh for human beings, another for animals, another for birds, and another for fish. [40] Yet there are heavenly bodies and earthly bodies, while the glory of the heavenly is one kind, and that of the earthly is another. [41] There is one glory of the sun and another glory of the moon, yet another glory of the stars, each star even differs in glory.

[42] So it is with the resurrection of the dead. What is planted is perishable; what is raised is imperishable. [43] It is planted in dishonor; it is raised in glory. It is sown in weakness; it is raised in power. [44] It is planted a physical body; it is raised a spiritual body. If there is a physical body; there is also a spiritual body.

Psalm 49:5–15

5 Why should I fear in evil days,
   when iniquity at my heels surrounds me?
6 Those who trust in their wealth
   and praise of the abundance of their riches?
7 Certainly, it cannot redeem a person,
   or can one give [it] to God as their ransom.
8 For the redemption-price of a soul is costly,
   they come to an end, forever.
9 Shall one should live eternally
   and never see the Pit?
10 For when one sees the wise, they die;
   the foolish and ignorant perish together
   and leave to others their wealth.
11 Their graves are their homes for all time,
   their dwelling places from generation to generation,
   though they put their name on lands.
12 Humanity will not recline in grandeur;
   rather they are like the animals that perish.
13 This is the way of the foolish,
   those pleased with their own words. *Selah*
14 Like sheep they are set for Sheol;
   Death shall be their shepherd.

The upright shall rule over them until the morning,
and their form shall waste away;
Sheol shall be their abode.

15 But God will ransom my soul,
for from the grasp of Sheol she will take me. *Selah*

John 21:4 Now when morning came, Jesus stood on the beach; but the disciples did not know that it was Jesus. 5 Jesus said to them, "Children, do you have any fish prepared?" They answered him, "No." 6 Then he said to them, "Cast the net to the right side of the boat, and you will find some." So, they cast it, and they were not able to drag it in because of the abundance of fish. 7 That disciple whom Jesus loved said to Peter, "It is the Messiah!" When Simon Peter heard that it was the Messiah, he put on some clothes, for he was naked, and threw himself into the sea. 8 But the other disciples came in the boat, dragging the net full of fish, for they were not far from the land, only two hundred cubits [about a hundred yards] off.

9 As soon as they turned back to land, they saw a fire there, with fish laid over it, and bread. 10 Jesus said to them, "Bring some of the fish that you have just caught." 11 So Simon Peter went up and dragged the net to land, full of large fish—one hundred fifty-three—and with so many the net was not torn. 12 Jesus said to them, "Come and eat." Now none of the disciples dared to ask him, "Who are you?" because they knew it was the Messiah. 13 Jesus came and took the bread and gave it to them, and did the same with the fish. 14 Now this was the third time that Jesus appeared to the disciples after he was raised from the dead.

PROCLAMATION

Text Notes

There are a couple of phrases in the psalm, in verses 7 and 13, that are difficult to translate. I have drawn from the translations of the Jewish Publication Society and Robert Alter, *The Hebrew Bible: A Translation with Commentary.*

Preaching Prompts

Resurrection is the foundation of the Gospel Easter story and even when proclaimed as a certainty, holds a full share of mystery. It seems unreasonable to expect folk to have no questions or to mock them, or call them names (i.e., "fool" in 1 Cor. 15:36), for asking. The Gospel story, resurrection included, is strong enough to bear the weight of our questions, and God, unlike the apostle, is eternally patient with them.

The psalmist trusts in God for her deliverance, recognizing that wealth is of no avail and there is no price that can be placed on a human life.

John 21 offers a potential narrative response to the questioners mocked in the Epistle. What kind of body do the resurrected have? In this story, one that is solid and tangible, capable of mundane tasks like cooking. One that was recognizable to those who had known the formerly dead. While not putting an end to questions about the resurrection, John 21 demonstrates that the resurrected Jesus has the same demeanor and shows the same care for his disciples that he did in his previous life.

While some forms of fishing were likely performed by women or men, the dragnet fishing indicated by the text, along with Peter's casual nudity, suggests only male disciples were present. This is in keeping with the theme that the male disciples needed to be convinced.

FRIDAY IN EASTER WEEK

Romans 6:5–11; Psalm 86:8–13; Mark 16:9–15, 19–20

Romans 6:5 For if we have been united in a death like Christ's, we will certainly be so within the resurrection. ⁶ This we know, that our old self was crucified with him so that the body of sin might be destroyed, and we might no longer be enslaved to sin. ⁷ The woman or man who has died is freed from sin. ⁸ But if we have died with Christ, we believe that we shall also live with him. ⁹ We know that Christ, being raised from the dead, will never die; death no longer has dominion over him. ¹⁰ For dying, he died once to sin, in living, he lives to God. ¹¹ So also should you consider yourselves dead to sin and alive to God in Christ Jesus.

Psalm 86:8–13

⁸ There is none like you among the gods, MOST HIGH,
   and there are no works like yours.
⁹ All the nations that you made shall come,
   and they shall bow down before you Sovereign One,
   and they shall glorify your name.
¹⁰ For you are great and work wonders;
   you are God, you alone.
¹¹ Teach me, HOLY ONE, your way,
   that I may walk in your truth;
   let my heart be undivided to revere your name.
¹² I give thanks to you, Sovereign One my God, with my whole heart,
   and I shall glorify your name forever.
¹³ For great is your faithful love toward me;
   you have delivered my soul from the depths of Sheol.

Mark 16:9 Now after he rose early on the first day of the week, Jesus appeared first to Mary Magdalene from whom he had cast out seven demons. ¹⁰ She went out and she told the ones mourning and weeping who had been with him. ¹¹ But when they heard that he lives and was seen by her, they did not believe. ¹² After this Jesus was made known in another form to two of [the disciples] as they were walking into the countryside. ¹³ And they went back and told the rest, but they did not believe them. [14] Now later on, while they were sitting at table, Jesus appeared to the eleven themselves and he rebuked their lack of faith and stubbornness, because they did not believe those [the women] who saw Jesus after he had risen. [15] Then Jesus said to them, "Go into all the world and proclaim the good news to all creation."

[19] And then Jesus the Messiah, after he had spoken to them, was taken up into heaven and sat down at the right hand of God. [20] And they went out proclaiming the good news everywhere, the Messiah worked with them and confirmed the message by the signs that followed.

PROCLAMATION

Text Notes

Mark's Gospel has a variety of endings that shock many Bible readers who think the scriptures were unchanged from inception. They are missing from the oldest most reliable manuscripts, Sinaticus and Vaticanus, and from more than a hundred Syriac, Coptic, and Armenian manuscripts; in many of the manuscripts in which they are found, they are set off with notations equivalent to an asterisk denoting lack of originality. There is near-universal acceptance that verses 1–8 are original. Some scholars further subdivide the remaining verses. The Church (across denominations) treats them as authoritative to varying degrees, and they do appear in an abridged form in the lectionary of the Episcopal Church.

In Mark 16:12, the description of Jesus appearing in "another form" to two disciples "walking in the countryside" closely resembles the Emmaus Road story in Luke 24. In verse 14, Jesus "reprimands" or "rebukes" the (presumably male) disciples for not believing "those" who proclaimed his resurrection. I have specified "the women" here; they were "those" who were not believed, Mary Magdalene, another Mary, and Salome in Mark 16:1.

Preaching Prompts

Whether in spite of or because of being part of the addendum to Mark, 16:14 includes a strong rebuke by Jesus for those who did not believe the gospel of his resurrection from the dead preached by women, perhaps because it was preached by women. It still speaks to those who discount the words and ministries of women. The disciples are sent to preach to all creation, and Jesus won't let them be treated like the women: he will work with them, verse 20, providing signs to confirm the message. For the women and the few male disciples, his appearances were the sign. And for some, women and men, surely the women's witness was sufficient. It would have been enough for children. The signs and ascension in verse 19 point to a new reality: Jesus will not continue to appear as he had. And at some point, the signs will come to an end as well. All that will remain will be the proclamation of the gospel by women and men and the faith of those who choose to believe.

SATURDAY IN EASTER WEEK

Acts 13:29–38; Psalm 116:1–9; Matthew 28:8–10, 16–20

Acts 13:29 Now when they had finished doing everything written about him, they took him down from the tree and laid him in a tomb. ³⁰ But God raised him from the dead. ³¹ He appeared for many days to those [women and men] who traveled with him from Galilee to Jerusalem, and they are now his witnesses to the people. ³² And we proclaim the good news to you that what God promised to our mothers and fathers ³³ God has fulfilled for us, their children, by raising Jesus; as also it is written in the second psalm,

> 'You are my Son; today I have begotten you.'

³⁴ Because God raised him from the dead, never to return to corruption, God spoke thusly,

> 'I will give you the holy promises of David.'

³⁵ Therefore David has also said in another psalm,

> 'You will not let your holy one experience corruption.'

³⁶ For indeed David, after he had served the purpose of God in his own generation, died, and was placed beside his mothers and fathers, and experienced corruption; ³⁷ yet the one whom God raised up saw no corruption. ³⁸ Let it be known to you, therefore, my sisters and brothers, that through this man forgiveness of sins is proclaimed to you.

Psalm 116:1–9

¹ I love the GOD WHO HEARS,
   for God has heard my voice and my supplications.
² For she opens her ear to me,
   whatever day I call.
³ The snares of death encompassed me;
   the torments of Sheol took hold of me,
   I found distress and sorrow.
⁴ Then I called on the name of the HOLY ONE OF OLD:
   "HOLY ONE, please, save my life!"
⁵ Gracious is the FOUNT OF JUSTICE, and righteous;
   our God loves [like a mother].
⁶ The FAITHFUL ONE protects the simple;
   I was brought low and she saved me.
⁷ Return, O my soul, to your rest,
   for the GRACIOUS ONE has dealt generously with you.
⁸ For you have delivered my soul from death,
   my eyes from tears,

my feet from stumbling.
⁹ I shall walk before the AUTHOR OF LIFE
in the lands of the living.

Matthew 28:8 So the women left the tomb quickly with fear and great joy and ran to tell his disciples the news. ⁹ Then all of a sudden Jesus met them and said, "Shalom!" And they came to him, took hold of his feet, and bowed down worshiping him. ¹⁰ Then Jesus said to them, "Fear not; go and tell my sisters and brothers to go to Galilee; there they will see me."

¹⁶ Now the eleven disciples went to Galilee, to the mountain to which Jesus sent them. ¹⁷ And when they saw him, they bowed down worshiping him; but some doubted. ¹⁸ Then Jesus came and said to them, saying, "All authority in heaven and on earth has been given to me. ¹⁹ Go therefore and make disciples of all nations, baptizing them in the name of the Father and of the Son and of the Holy Spirit, ²⁰ and teaching them to obey everything that I have commanded you. Now look, I am with you always, to the end of the age."

PROCLAMATION

Text Notes

In Acts 13:33–35, Paul cites Psalm 2:7, Isaiah 55:3, and Psalm 16:10 from the LXX (note the psalms are known to be numbered while chapter and verse numbers would not be added for centuries). Paul is in synagogue addressing "Men of Israel, and others who fear God." Women were not excluded from synagogue and would have also been present. "God-fearers" was often language for Gentile worshipers. Paul's language, "men" and "brothers," excludes women and renders them invisible in this passage. Are women to understand themselves included, or is Paul specifically addressing men exclusively, figuring they'll pass the good news on to the women in their lives? I read his language as customarily androcentric and patriarchal, as is the bulk of scripture, and make women visible as appropriate.

In Matthew 28:8, the word translated as "authority" also means "power." In verse 10, Jesus tells the women to tell his "siblings" to go to meet him in Galilee. That certainly includes the eleven male disciples but is not necessarily limited to them. At some point, the eleven receive other more specific instructions to go to a particular mountain indicated by verse 16.

Preaching Prompts

In Acts 13, Paul tells the Gospel story, adding his own proof-texting exegesis of the Hebrew Scriptures to "prove" that Jesus, who was nothing like the warrior messiah many expected and some scriptures predicted, was nevertheless the fulfillment of the scriptures. Paul is demonstrating the flexibility of the scriptures for reinterpretation in every age; rereading them in light of Jesus yields tantalizing and suggestive readings, which now, with full knowledge of the Jesus story, seem specifically predictive. These are particularly Christian ways of reading the Hebrew Bible. It is important to remember that Jewish readings, even of passages considered messianic, do not always focus on a single individual. Sometimes the entire nation is the messianic figure, sometimes an individual or specific ruler, sometimes an unknown individual.

In Psalm 116:5, God's love is articulated with the word whose root is "womb," often unhelpfully translated as "merciful" or "compassion."

The Gospel reading combines the resurrection appearances to the women, Mary Magdalene and the "other" Mary, and to the eleven remaining disciples. The women believe immediately and run with joy to tell the news. They are also afraid, perhaps of what this might mean, potentially more violence. The male disciples also bowed down before Jesus, but they do not yet believe. The story of the church will soon become their story as they proclaim the resurrection they first doubted. It might be worthwhile to imagine the evangelism of the women, how the women and men they proclaimed the good news to also became part of the new and expanding Church.

SECOND SUNDAY OF EASTER

Acts 1:3–5, 12–14 (or Proverbs 9:1–6); Psalm 104:1–4, 10–15, 27–30; 2 Corinthians 9:6–10; John 14:1–7

The Sundays of Easter traditionally have a choice of readings from the Hebrew Bible and Acts for the first lesson. Those wishing to preach on Saint Thomas may find those texts in Years W and A.

Acts 1:3 Jesus presented himself to them, living, after his suffering through many convincing proofs, by appearing to them forty days and speaking about the reign of God. [4] And staying with them, Jesus commanded them not to leave Jerusalem, rather to wait there for the promise of the Faithful One, "what you heard from me. [5] For John baptized with water, but you will be baptized with the Holy Spirit not many days from this one."

[12] Then they returned to Jerusalem from the mount called Olivet, which is near Jerusalem, a sabbath day's journey away. [13] And when they entered the city, they went upstairs to the room where they were staying, Peter, and John, and James, and Andrew, Philip and Thomas, Bartholomew and Matthew, James son of Alphaeus, and Simon the Zealot, and Judas son of James. [14] All these were persevering in prayer together with women, including Mary the mother of Jesus, as well as his [sisters and] brothers.

Proverbs 9:1 Wisdom has built her house,

she has sculpted her seven pillars.

[2] She has slaughtered her meat; she has mixed her wine,

indeed she has set her table.

3 She has sent out her girls, she calls
   from the highest ascent in the city:
4 "You that are naive, turn in here!"
   To those without sense she says,
5 "Come, eat of my bread
   and drink of the wine I have mixed.
6 Lay aside naïveté and live,
   and walk in the way of understanding."

Psalm 104:1–4, 10–15, 27–30

1 Bless the FOUNT OF LIFE, O my soul.
   MOTHER OF ALL, my God, you are very great.
   You don honor and majesty,
2 Wrapped in light as a garment,
   you stretch out the heavens like a tent-curtain.
3 She who lays on the waters the beams of her upper chambers,
   she who makes the clouds her chariot,
   she is the one who rides on the wings of the wind.
4 She is the one who makes the winds her celestial messengers,
   fire and flame her ministers.
10 She is the one who makes springs gush forth in the torrents;
   they flow between the hills.
11 They give drink to every wild animal;
   the wild donkeys slake their thirst.
12 By the torrents the birds of the heavens dwell;
   among the branches they give voice.
13 She is the one who waters the mountains from her high chambers;
   the earth is satisfied with the fruit of your work.
14 She is the one who makes grass to grow for the cattle,
   and vegetation for human labor,
   to bring forth food from the earth,
15 and wine to make the human heart rejoice,
   with oil to make the face shine,
   and bread to sustain the human heart.
27 All of these hope in you
   to provide their food in due season.
28 You give it to them, they glean it;
   you open your hand, they are well satisfied.
29 You hide your face, they are dismayed;
   when you collect their breath, they die

and to their dust they return.

³⁰ You send forth your spirit, they are created;
and you renew the face of the earth.

2 Corinthians 9:6 Now hear this: The one who sows sparingly, sparingly will also reap, and the one who sows in abundance, in abundance will also reap. ⁷ Each one must give as decided in your heart, not out of reluctance or under pressure, for "God loves a cheerful giver." ⁸ And the power of God is able to grant you all every gift abundantly, so that always having enough of everything, you all may abound in every good work. ⁹ As it is written,

"God scatters generously, and gives to the poor;
God's righteousness endures forever."

¹⁰ The one who supplies seed to the sower and bread for food will supply and multiply your seed and increase the harvest of your righteousness.

John 14:1 "Let not your hearts be troubled. Believe in God then also believe in me. ² In my Abba's house there are many homes. If it were not so, would I have told you all that I go to prepare a place for you? ³ And if I go and prepare a place for you all, I will come again and will take you all to myself, in order that where I am, there you may be also. ⁴ Thus I am going. You all know the way." ⁵ Thomas said to him, "Rabbi, we do not know where you are going. How would we be able to know the way?" ⁶ Jesus said to him, "I am the way, and the truth, and the life. No one comes to the Creator except through me. ⁷ If you know me, you will know my Abba also. From now on you do know and have seen my Abba."

PROCLAMATION

Text Notes

Psalm 104 switches between second and third person, as is common in the genre. Verses 14–15 use the word that means both "bread" and "food in general" in both senses.

In Acts 1:12, "a sabbath's day journey" indicates the amount of walking one could do on Sabbath; across time, the distance has ranged from one-third to two-thirds of a mile with variables such as whether one is pasturing animals and whether one is still in a city (determined by how far apart are the houses). It is certainly possible that the sisters of Jesus were present with his male siblings in verse 14; the grammar allows for inclusion.

Second Corinthians 9:7 quotes part of the Greek text of Proverbs 22:8, which differs significantly from the Hebrew: *God blesses a cheerful and generous man.* With the exception of "bless/love," it is an exact quote. Verse 9 cites Psalm 112:9, also from the LXX.

Preaching Prompts

"Home" and "table" can represent some of the most comforting images. They provide the vocabulary for the followers of Jesus joining the community of God on the other side of eternity. It is in the intimate spaces of home that Jesus continues to come to show his resurrected body to women and children and men. The home was a "democratic" space, ensuring full access to Jesus across gender and age lines. That is also the image of eternal life with God, home, and homes. In the psalm, God is the one who causes families in their homes to flourish, and not only humans but also provides for the animals and all creation. In the alternate First Lesson, Wisdom in Proverbs sets a table that feeds more than our bellies. Proclaiming abundance as a characteristic of the divine points to the social economic status of those for whom that image was most satisfying. Agricultural abundance is heaven for those dependent on the mysterious fusion of sun and soil. It is aspirational for those on the knife's edge of survival.

These lessons also offer an opportunity to reflect on homes that are not flourishing, nourishing, protective of, or even safe. Wisdom's table is open to all, modeling a wide welcome. The table is in a home, but the guests are from different families forming a new family.

THIRD SUNDAY OF EASTER

Acts 5:12–16 (or Isaiah 43:1–3a, 5–7); Psalm 50:1–6;
Ephesians 1:7–14; John 5:25–29

Acts 5:12 Now, many signs and wonders were done among the people through the apostles; they were all together in the Portico of Solomon. [13] None of the others dared to join them, but the people extolled them. [14] Yet more believers were added to Christ, a multitude of both women and men. [15] So much so that they even carried the sick into the streets, and laid them on cots and mats, so that Peter's shadow might overshadow some of them as he passed. [16] Multitudes would also gather from the towns around Jerusalem, bringing the sick and those tormented by unclean spirits, and they were all made well.

Isaiah 43:1 And now, thus says the MAKER OF ALL,

the one who created you, Jacob [Rebekah's seed],
the one who formed you, Israel [of Sarah's line]:
Do not fear, for I have redeemed you;
I have called you by name, you are mine.
[2] For when you pass through the waters, I will be with you;
and through the rivers, they shall not overwhelm you;
even when you walk through fire you shall not be burned,

and the flame shall not scorch you.

³ For I am the INCOMPARABLE ONE your God,
the Holy One of Israel, your Savior.

⁵ Fear not, for with you am I;
from the east will I bring your seed,
and from the west will I gather you.

⁶ I will say to the north, "Release them!"
and to the south, "Do not keep [them];
bring my sons from far away
and my daughters from the end of the earth."

⁷ Everyone who is called by my name,
whom I created for my glory,
whom I formed and made.

Psalm 50:1–6

¹ God, the LORD God,
speaks and summons the world
from the rising of the sun to its setting.

² From Zion, perfect in beauty,
God appears in radiance.

³ Our God comes and is not silent,
fire precedes her, devouring,
and around her, a whirling wind, storming.

⁴ She calls to the heavens above
and to the earth to judge her people:

⁵ "Gather to me my faithful ones,
who made a covenant with me over sacrifice!"

⁶ The heavens declare her righteousness,
for God is the one who judges. She alone. *Selah*

Ephesians 1:7 In Christ we have redemption through his blood, the forgiveness of our trespasses, according to the riches of God's grace. ⁸ Grace which God has abundantly poured upon us along with all wisdom and understanding. ⁹ God has made known to us the mystery of God's will according to God's good pleasure that God set forth in Christ. ¹⁰ A plan in the fullness of time to gather up all things in Christ, things in the heavens and things on earth, all into Christ. ¹¹ In Christ there is also an inheritance from before time according to the purpose of the one who does all things according to God's counsel and will. ¹² This so that we might live for the praise of God's glory, we who first trusted in Christ. ¹³ In Christ you also heard the word of truth, the gospel of your salvation and believed, and were marked with the seal of the promised Holy Spirit. ¹⁴ She is the deposit of our inheritance toward redemption as God's own possession to the praise of God's glory.

John 5:25 "Truly, truly, I tell you all, the hour is coming, and is now here, when the dead will hear the voice of the Son of God, and those who hear will live. [26] For just as the Living God has life internally, just so God has granted the Son to have life internally. [27] And God has given the Son authority to render justice, because he is the Son of Woman. [28] Do not be astonished at this; for the hour is coming when all who are in their graves will hear his voice [29] and will come out—those who have done good, to the resurrection of life, and those who have done evil, to the resurrection of judgment."

PROCLAMATION

Text Notes

In Acts 5:13, the "others" in the temple complex would have been other Jews and perhaps Gentiles devoted to the God of Israel. The temple Jerusalem should be thought of as a campus and not a building; there were multiple interconnected structures on the site. Worship occurred outdoors where the main sacrificial altar was. The primary temple building was entered only by select priests.

In Isaiah 43:1, "Rebekah's seed" and "of Sarah's line" are offered in brackets to modify "Jacob" and "Israel."

In John 5:27, the work of justice is more than passing a sentence; rather, "judging" or "executing judgment" or "rendering a verdict" are but one dimension of justice work.

Preaching Prompts

These Eastertide lessons tie together the themes of salvation, redemption, and judgment where salvation includes physical well-being and is not a checkmark for believing the right things about Jesus. Empowered by Jesus, the apostles continued his healing ministry, saving people from the illnesses and ailments that imperiled their lives and impacted their ability to live an abundant and flourishing life.

It is worthwhile to ask if any of Jesus's female disciples received the ability to heal. It is hard to imagine the Holy Spirit limiting gifts according to societal biases. It is easier to imagine the male biases of authors and editors and canon shapers crafting narratives that reflect their own worldview. What gifts might the Blessed Mother have had? Would not people have flocked to her, healing gifts or no? Would not the women who knew Jesus, touched Jesus—including preparing his body and embracing his freshly resurrected flesh—have been seen as receptacles of power?

The power gifted to the apostles in the Acts reading is held in conversation with the awesome power of God in the alternate first lesson, Isaiah, used to gather in her children from the four corners of the earth and to protect them in such a way as to violate the laws of nature to ensure their safety. The miraculous doesn't fall far from the tree. The power granted to the apostles is the power of Jesus, by virtue of being the Holy Child of God who is all powerful. In the psalm, God appears in a dramatic theophany to render judgment upon her faithful ones whom she has gathered, as in the Isaiah lesson. In the Epistle, God gathers all things for redemption, not just humanity, and the text begins to look forward to Pentecost with the Holy Spirit as the "deposit" or down payment on an inheritance to be received in full later. Building upon the resurrection of Jesus, the Gospel reading looks forward to the final resurrection at which all will be judged. When read in conversation with the day's lessons, the final judgment is not a threat but the culmination of redemption and the act of a loving faithful God who does not target her children or her creation for destruction. It is important to address the terms and concepts that have been used to marginalize, other, and wreak theological harm in the name of the Church.

FOURTH SUNDAY OF EASTER

Acts 6:1–7 (or Jeremiah 7:1–7); Psalm 68:4–11;
1 Timothy 5:1–4, 8; John 14:18–24

Acts 6:1 Now during those days the disciples, women and men, were multiplying and the Greek [followers] grumbled against the Hebrew [followers] because their widows were being neglected in the daily ministry [to the poor]. ² And the twelve called together the whole multitude of the disciples and said, "It is not right that we should neglect the word of God in order to do table work. ³ Select therefore [sisters and] brothers from among yourselves seven men of whom there is good testimony, full of the Spirit and of wisdom, whom we can put in charge of this duty. ⁴ Now we, in prayer and the ministry of the word, will continue." ⁵ And their statement pleased the whole multitude and they selected Stephen, a man full of faith and the Holy Spirit, together with Philip, Prochorus, Nicanor, Timon, Parmenas, and Nicolaus, a convert to Judaism from Antioch. ⁶ These stood before the apostles and they prayed and laid their hands on them. ⁷ And the word of God spread and the number of the disciples, women and men, multiplied greatly in Jerusalem, and a great crowd of the priests became obedient to the faith.

Jeremiah 7:1 The word that was [revealed] to Jeremiah from the HOLY ONE OF OLD said: ² Stand in the gate of the HOLY ONE's house and proclaim there this word, and say, 'Hear the word of the HOLY ONE, all you of Judah, you that enter these gates to worship the HOLY ONE. ³ Thus says the SOVEREIGN of heaven's vanguard, the God of Israel: Reform your ways and your doings and I shall dwell with you all in this place. ⁴ Do not trust in them, these deceptive words: "This is the temple of the HOLY ONE, the temple of the HOLY ONE, the temple of the HOLY ONE."

⁵ For if you all truly reform your ways and your doings, if you all truly do what is just between one person and another, ⁶ if you all do not oppress the immigrant, the orphan, and the widow, or pour out innocent blood in this place, and if after other gods you all do not go

to your own harm, [7] then I will dwell with you all in this place, in the land that I gave to your mothers and fathers from forever and to eternity.

Psalm 68:4–11

[4] Sing to God, sing praises to her Name;
exalt her who rides upon the clouds;
Holy is her Name, rejoice before her!

[5] Mother of orphans and defender of widows,
is God in her holy habitation!

[6] God settles the solitary in a home bringing prisoners into prosperity;
while the rebellious shall live in a wasteland.

[7] God, when you marched before your people,
when you moved out through the wilderness,

[8] the earth shook, even the heavens poured down,
at the presence of God, the ONE OF SINAI,
at the presence of God, the GOD OF ISRAEL.

[9] Rain in abundance, God, you showered abroad;
when your heritage grew weary you prepared rest.

[10] Your creatures found a dwelling in her;
God, you provided in your goodness for the oppressed.

[11] The AUTHOR OF LIFE gave the word;
the women who proclaim the good news are a great army.

1 Timothy 5:1 Do not rebuke an elder man, but speak to them as to a father, to those younger, as brothers, [2] to elder women as mothers, to younger women as sisters, in absolute purity. [3] Honor widows who are really widows. [4] If a widow has children or grandchildren, let them learn first to show devotion to their own family and make repayment to their parents; for this is pleasing in God's sight.

[8] And whoever does not provide for their own, and especially for family members, has denied the faith and is worse than an unbeliever.

John 14:18 [Jesus said,] "I shall not leave you orphaned; I am coming to you all. [19] Yet, in a little while the world will no longer see me, but you will see me; because I live you all also shall live. [20] On that day you all will know that I am in my Abba, and you all in me, and I in you all. [21] The one who has my commandments and keep them is the one who loves me and the one who loves me will be loved by my Abba; I shall love that person and reveal myself to them." [22] Judas (not Iscariot) said to Jesus, "Rabbi, how is it that you will reveal yourself to us and not to the world?" [23] Jesus answered him, "The one who loves me will keep my word and my Abba will love that person and we will come to them and make our home with them. [24] Whoever does not love me does not keep my words, and the word that you hear is not mine rather, it is from the Creator who sent me."

PROCLAMATION

Text Notes

There are echoes of the exodus story, particularly Numbers, with the repeated use of "multitude" and "grumbling" in the Acts reading. In Acts 6:1, "Greeks" and "Hebrews" appear as nouns without further explication; thus, I have added "followers" in brackets. "Greeks" and "Greek [followers]" can also be understood as "Gentile," i.e., Greek-speaking but not necessarily of Greek ancestry. "Table work" in verse 2 captures the ambiguity between working at tables as a financial enterprise, i.e., managing the funds to feed all of the widows or working at tables to serve them. I hold out the slim and likely unlikely possibility that women participated in the selection of the first deacons even though they were not numbered among them (yet) in verse 3. The reader can make their own decision there.

In the world of 1 Timothy 5, "widow" signifies more than being bereaved of a husband; it is also a ministerial office in the early church. The term is used both ways in the Epistles (see Annette Bourland Huizenga's discussion in the 1–2 Timothy and Titus volume of the *Wisdom Commentary* and Joanna Dewey's discussion of the passage in the *Women's Bible Commentary*). The ministerial widow could also be a virgin or otherwise unmarried.

In John 14:18–20, Jesus addresses his disciples collectively using the plural; in the verses that follow, he specifies the individual who loves in the singular.

Preaching Prompts

The Acts lesson portrays the early institutionalization of the Jesus movement. It is a movement whose story draws and compels women and men to follow and believe. It is also a movement entrenched in the prevailing gender norms. That bondage remains even with changing gender norms and expanded understandings of gender. There is also the charge of disparate treatment based on ethnic identity with the minoritized group suffering disproportionately. The response of the apostles is instructive; they delegate a team to ensure equity, understanding it is their responsibility to ensure the Church acts justly. The alternate lesson in Jeremiah assures God's presence with God's people and warns against tying God's presence to the temple. This will become critical when the newly institutionalized Church, led and populated by Jewish Christians, faces the unimaginable horror of the destruction of the temple by the Romans in 70 CE. The psalm proclaims that God is the God of the vulnerable, widows, orphans, the impoverished, and imprisoned. The same people who made up the early Church and for whom the apostles provided in their need and who remain among us in the Church today. Care for the vulnerable, particularly widows, remains an issue in the Epistle. Notably, as in the first lesson, the issue is how best to provide, not whether to provide for the vulnerable among us.

And the Gospel reminds us that God claims us all; that there are no orphans in her embrace.

Reflecting on the origins of our Church can be more than holy nostalgia. It can be the impetus for continuing to build the infrastructure and institution of the Church more justly with authority and decision-making disentangled from the male gender.

FIFTH SUNDAY OF EASTER

Acts 8:1–12 (or Isaiah 52:7–10); Psalm 71:15–23;
Romans 10:9–15; John 4:24 –29

Acts 8:1 Now Saul approved of the mob killing Stephen. There began that day a great per-secution in the church in Jerusalem, now and everyone was scattered throughout the coun-tryside of Judea and Samaria except the apostles. [2] Devout men buried Stephen and made loud lamentation over him. [3] And Saul was ravaging the church one house at a time, drag-ging off both women and men, and he handed them over to prison.

[4] Now the women and men who were scattered traveled proclaiming the word. [5] Philip went down to a Samarian city and preached the Messiah to them. [6] The crowds of women and men listened eagerly with one accord to what was said by Philip with hearing and seeing the signs that he did. [7] For many had unclean spirits crying out with loud voices; they came out of many, and many others who were paralyzed or lame were cured. [8] So there was great joy in that city.

[9] Now there was a man named Simon who had previously practiced magic in the city and amazed the people of Samaria; he said that he was someone great. [10] They all paid attention to him, from the least to the greatest, saying, "This man is the one known as the Great Power of God." [11] Now they paid attention to him because, for a long time, he had amazed them with his magic. [12] But when they believed Philip, who was proclaiming the good news about the realm of God and the name of Jesus Christ, they were baptized, both women and men.

Isaiah 52:7 How beautiful upon the mountains

are the feet of one who brings good news,

proclaiming peace,

bringing good news,

proclaiming salvation,

who says to Zion, "Your God reigns, daughter."

[8] Daughter, the sound of your sentinels, lifting their voice!

As one they sing for joy;

for from one eye to another they see

the return of the HOLY ONE OF SINAI to Zion.

⁹ Revel! Raise a song together,
   you ruins of Jerusalem.
   For the Holy One of Old has comforted God's people,
   God has redeemed Jerusalem.
¹⁰ The Mighty God has bared a holy arm
   before the eyes of all the nations;
   and all the ends of the earth shall see
   the salvation of our God.

Psalm 71:15–23

¹⁵ My mouth will recount your righteousness,
   all day long [recount] your salvation,
   though I cannot know their counting.
¹⁶ I come with the mighty deeds of the Sovereign God,
   I recall your righteousness, yours alone.
¹⁷ God, you have taught me from my youth,
   and even now I yet proclaim your wonders.
¹⁸ And yes, even to old age and gray hair;
   God, do not forsake me until I proclaim your might
   to the generation to come and your power.
¹⁹ Your righteousness, God, is as the highest.
   You who have done great things, God, who is like you?
²⁰ You who have let me see many troubles and adversities
   will restore me, bringing me to life;
   from the depths of the earth
   you will restore me bringing up.
²¹ You will magnify my greatness,
   and turn and comfort me.
²² I, even I, will praise you with the harp
   for your faithfulness, my God;
   I will sing praise to you with the lyre,
   Holy One of Israel.
²³ My lips will shout for joy as I sing praise to you;
   even my soul which you have redeemed.

Romans 10:9 Now then, if you confess with your lips, "Jesus is Sovereign," and believe in your heart that God raised him from the dead, you will be saved. ¹⁰ For with the heart one believes [leading] to righteousness, and with the mouth one confesses [leading] to salvation. ¹¹ The scripture says, "*No one who believes in that one will be put to shame.*" ¹² For there is no distinction between Jew and Greek; the same Sovereign is Sovereign of all and is richly generous to all who call on the Sovereign. ¹³ For, "Everyone who calls on the name of the Sovereign shall be saved."

[14] How then are they to call on one in whom they have not believed? And how are they to believe in one of whom they have never heard? And how are they to hear without one who preaches? [15] And how are they to preach without being sent? As it is written: *How beautiful are the feet of those who proclaim the good news!*

John 4:24 [Jesus said to the woman at the well,] "God is spirit, and those who worship God must worship in spirit and truth." [25] The woman said to him, "I know that Messiah is coming, the one who is called Christ. When he comes, he will proclaim all things to us." [26] Jesus said to her, "I AM, the one who is speaking to you."

[27] Now just then his disciples came and were astonished that he was speaking with a woman, but no one said, "What do you want?" or "Why are you speaking with her?" [28] Then the woman left her water jar and went back to the city and said to the people, [29] "Come and see a man who told me all I have ever done! Is this not the Messiah?"

PROCLAMATION

Text Notes

In Acts 8:3 the language used for Saul handing over women and men to prison is the same as that for Judas handing over Jesus to be crucified (Matt. 20:18; 26:2; Mark 10:33; Luke 18:32; 24:7). In verse 4, all of the verbs are masculine plural, functioning as inclusive, common plurals. Just as it was not only men who were scattered after the persecution raids, there is no reason to believe that only men proclaimed the gospel of the risen Christ. Therefore, I have translated both verbs in the same way as pertaining to both women and men; notably, the expression "both women and men" appears in Greek (in inverse order) in verses 3 and 12. In verse 6, I expand "crowd" to the women and men listening intently; there may have been children present but not listening with the same attentiveness. The awkward syntax of verse 10 yields, "This man is the power of God [who or that] is called Great." Joseph Fitzmyer argues that the phrase is a self-imposed title, e.g., "I am the great power of God," see verse 9 (Anchor Bible Commentary, *Acts*, p. 404).

The verb is missing from the second line of Psalm 71:15; I have repeated the first verb for clarity.

In the Epistle reading from Romans, Paul combines verses without regard for their original context. Just prior to this portion, he takes material from Deuteronomy 30:12–13, where Moses says that "the commandment," meaning everything God has commanded to and through him, is not unobtainable or too low. This commandment is "the word" in verse 14; however, Paul represents "the word" as Jesus in Romans 10:9, just before this reading. In Romans 10:11, Paul quotes Isaiah 28:16; in verse 13, he cites Joel 2:32; and in verse 15, he adds Isaiah 52:7 to this freewheeling exegesis.

In John 4:26, Jesus's reply evokes God's self-articulation as "I Am" in Exodus 3:14. The question form of her identification of Jesus as the Messiah is rhetorical, similar to Deborah's command of Barak to execute her orders also in question form in Judges 4:6. The CEB preserves the question in both cases; however, NRSV renders them as statements.

Preaching Prompts

All these readings contain accounts of telling the good news of God. In Acts, the church grows in spite of persecution, including by Paul in his former life, because women and men tell the gospel story. In the alternate first reading quoted by Paul in the Epistle, the messenger in Isaiah proclaims the good news of God's liberating salvation to Daughter Zion. The psalmist commits to proclaiming the name, fame, and glory of God until they reach the age of gray hair and beyond. In the Epistle, Paul calls new believers to proclaim faith in Jesus through a confessing word, then calls for preachers to proclaim the word that others might believe. In the Gospel, a woman at a well proclaims her understanding of the Messiah to Jesus. He proclaims to her that he IS, and she runs to proclaim him to her city.

In one option, the complexity of Saul's/Paul's identity invites a trans (embodied or reading alongside in companionship) reading, but not an overly simplistic one, i.e., Shaul, Saul is not a dead name. Saul is the Jewish name of a man who understands himself to be and remain a Jew. Paul is a Roman name. His two names signify his existence in two different worlds that are sometimes at violent odds with each other. He lives in both of those worlds while helping to create a new world that will fuse elements of both of his home worlds. Queerkin know what it is to fuse a new identify out of elements of an old one while building a new home that transcends the imaginations and understandings of those around them, including those with whom they previously shared a home, a world, and an identity. Transkin know this, perhaps better than most.

SIXTH SUNDAY OF EASTER

Acts 9:36–42 (or Isaiah 26:16–19); Psalm 36:5–10; Romans 8:11–17; John 6:35–40

Acts 9:36 Now in Joppa there was a disciple whose name was Tabitha—which translated into Greek is Dorcas; she was abundant in good works and benevolent giving. [37] And it happened at that time she became ill and died and they washed her and laid her in a room upstairs. [38] Now Lydda was near Joppa so the disciples who heard that Peter was there, sent two people to him urging, "Without delay, come to us." [39] Then Peter got up and went with them; when he arrived, they took him to the room upstairs. And standing beside him were all the widows, weeping and displaying the tunics and other clothing that Dorcas made while she was with them. [40] Then Peter put all of them outside, and got on his knees and prayed, and he turned to the body and said, "Tabitha, arise." And she opened her eyes, and seeing Peter, she sat up. [41] Then he gave her his hand and raised her up and calling the saints and widows, he presented her alive. [42] Now this became known throughout Joppa, and many believed in the Messiah.

Isaiah 26:16 HOLY ONE, in distress they sought you,

they pressed out a whispered prayer
when your chastening was on them.

[17] Just as an expectant mother
writhes-in-labor and cries out in her pangs
when her birthing time is near;
thus were we because of you, HOLY ONE.

[18] We too were expectant, we writhed-in-labor,
but it was as though we birthed only wind.
No victories have we won on earth,
neither do the inhabitants of the world fall.

[19] Your dead shall live; their corpses shall rise.
Awake and sing for joy you who dwell in the dust!
For your dew is a radiant dew,
and the earth shall release those long dead.

Psalm 36:5–10

[5] HOLY ONE, throughout the very heavens is your faithful love,
your faithfulness beyond the clouds.

[6] Your righteousness is like the eternal mountains,
your judgments are like the mighty deep;
you save humankind and animalkind alike, FAITHFUL ONE.

[7] How precious is your faithful love, O God!
All the woman-born take shelter in the shadow of your wings.

[8] They feast on the abundance of your house,
and you give them drink from the river of your delights.

[9] For with you is the fountain of life;
in your light we see light.

[10] Extend your faithful love to those who know you,
and your justice to the upright of heart!

Romans 8:11 Now if the Spirit of the one who raised Jesus from the dead dwells in you, the one who raised Christ from the dead will give life, including your mortal bodies, through the Spirit of the one who that dwells in you all. [12] So then, sisters and brothers [or friends

and kin], we are debtors, not to the flesh, according to the flesh to live [that way]. ¹³ For
if according to the flesh you live, you shall soon die; but if by the Spirit you put to death
the deeds of the body, you all shall live. ¹⁴ Now as many as are led by the Spirit of God are
daughters and sons of God. ¹⁵ For you all did not receive a spirit of slavery to fall again into
fear, but you have received a spirit of adoption through which we cry, "Abba! Father!" ¹⁶ It
is that same Spirit who bears witness with our spirit that we are daughters and sons of God.
¹⁷ And if daughters and sons, then heirs, heirs of God and heirs with Christ, if it is true that
we suffer with Christ so that we may also be glorified with Christ.

John 6:35 Jesus said to them, "I am the bread of life. The person who comes to me will
never be hungry and the one who believes in me will never be thirsty. ³⁶ Rather I said to you
all that you have seen me and yet you all do not believe. ³⁷ Everything that the Creator gives
me will come to me and anyone who comes to me I will never drive away. ³⁸ That is why I
have come down from the heavens, for this reason, not to do my own will, but the will of the
one who sent me. ³⁹ And this is the will of the one who sent me, that out of all that God has
given me I should lose nothing, rather, raise it up on the last day. ⁴⁰ This is indeed the will of
my Abba, that all who see the Son and believe in him may have eternal life, and I will raise
them up on the last day."

PROCLAMATION

Text Notes

In Acts, Peter also performs a resurrection closely patterned after Jesus raising a little girl in Mark 5:35–43. Jesus says, "*Talitha qumi*," very similar to *Tabitha qumi*
in his native Aramaic and as it is found in the Peshitta and contemporary Hebrew
translations. Some manuscripts drop the "i," marking the feminine imperative.

In Romans 8:13, *mello* means both, "to take place at some point in the future"
and "to be about to" do something.

Preaching Prompts

These texts demonstrate God's partiality to life and power over life and death across
the canon. In Acts, the life-giving and sustaining power of God that transforms
death into life is at work in at least one of the disciples of Jesus. This is an important
witness that the power of God is not limited to Jesus himself and that the Spirit is
present and active in the followers of Jesus even though he himself has ascended.
In the alternate first lesson from the "little apocalypse" in Isaiah, Isaiah or another
writing in his name articulates one of the few clear expectations of life beyond death
in the Hebrew Bible. The psalmist celebrates the one who lavishes life and love on
her creation. The Epistle is concerned with how we steward the life that God has
granted us and the new life which we received through the love and grace of God

expressed through the accompaniment and guidance of the Holy Spirit. And in the Gospel, Jesus proclaims that the rationale for his woman-born presence among us is to bring us into eternal life, losing no one and no thing.

Meditations on life and love are very much at odds with the world in which they are being bound together into this set of Sunday readings. In a world in which churchgoers in Nigeria, including babies and grandparents and elementary school students and grocery shoppers, were slaughtered—and we can expect more of the same—life and love can feel like a hard sell. Yet these very few weeks after the resurrection were the same very few weeks after the crucifixion, and weeks in which crucifixions continue to occur and the occupation of Rome was no less brutal. These are the times in which we need the sure promise of life and love and the presence of the Holy Spirit with and within us.

Lastly, it is easy to focus on the resurrection miracle that Peter performs and lament that we do not have that power in this world that needs it. The life-giving generosity of Tabitha is an act of love that is not beyond our reach. We can supply the material needs of those whose lives are precarious. There is one final act of love that is most often overlooked: the loving preparation of Tabitha's body for burial, the Jewish practice of *tahara*, by the women who loved her. To this day, women and men (separately) in circles of friendship covenant to wash each other's bodies when the time comes.

FEAST OF THE ASCENSION

Acts 1:1–11; Psalm 24; Revelation 3:20–22; Luke 24:46–53

Acts 1:1 In the first writing, I worked on, Theophilus, everything Jesus did and taught from the beginning [2] until the day he instructed the apostles whom he had chosen through the Holy Spirit and was taken up to heaven. [3] Jesus presented himself to them, living, after his suffering through many convincing proofs, by appearing to them forty days and speaking about the reign of God. [4] And staying with them, Jesus commanded them not to leave Jerusalem, rather to wait there for the promise of the Faithful God, "what you heard from me." [5] For John baptized with water, but you will be baptized with the Holy Spirit not many days from this one.

[6] When they [the disciples] came together, they asked Jesus, "Rabbi, is this the time when you will restore sovereignty to Israel?" [7] He replied, "It is not for you to know the times or seasons that the Sovereign God has set through divine authority. [8] But you will receive power when the Holy Spirit comes upon you, and you will be my witnesses in Jerusalem, in all Judea and Samaria, and to the end of the earth."

[9] And saying this as they were watching, Jesus was taken up, and a cloud took him out of their sight. [10] While they were gazing up toward heaven as Jesus was going, suddenly, two

in white robes stood by them. ¹¹ They said, "Galileans, why are you standing looking up into heaven? This Jesus, who has been taken up from you into heaven, will come in the way as you saw him go into heaven."

Psalm 24

¹ To the CREATOR OF ALL belongs the earth and all that fills her,
  the world, and those who dwell in her.
² For God upon the seas has founded her,
  and on the rivers has established her.
³ Who shall ascend the hill of the HOLY ONE?
  And who shall stand in God's holy place?
⁴ The woman or man who has clean hands and pure hearts,
  who does not lift up their [hands] to what is false,
  and does not swear deceitfully on their souls.
⁵ [Instead] they will lift up a blessing from the FAITHFUL GOD,
  and what is right from the God of their salvation.
⁶ Such is the generation of those who seek God,
  who seek the face of the God of Rebekah. *Selah*
⁷ Lift up your heads, you gates!
  and be lifted up, you everlasting doors!
  that the One of glory may come in.
⁸ Who is the One of glory?
  The FIRE OF SINAI, strong and mighty,
  the GOD WHO IS MAJESTY, mighty in battle.
⁹ Lift up your heads, you gates!
  and be lifted up, you everlasting doors!
  that the One of glory may come in.
¹⁰ Who is this One of glory?
  The COMMANDER of heaven's legions,
  God is the One of glory. *Selah*

Revelation 3:20 "Look! I stand at the door and knock. If you hear my voice and open the door, I will come in to you and dine with you, and you with me. ²¹ To the one who conquers, I will give a place with me on my throne, just as I myself conquered and sat down with my Abba on God's throne. ²² Let anyone who has an ear listen to what the Spirit is saying to the churches."

Luke 24:46 Then Jesus said to them, "So it is written, the Messiah is to suffer and to rise from the dead on the third day, ⁴⁷ and repentance and forgiveness of sins is to be preached in his name to all nations, beginning from Jerusalem. ⁴⁸ You are witnesses of these things. ⁴⁹ Now look! I am sending you the promise of my Abba. You all stay in the city until you have been clothed with power from on high." ⁵⁰ Then Jesus led them out as far as Bethany, and lifting his hands, he blessed them. ⁵¹ While he was blessing them, Jesus retreated from them and was carried up into heaven. ⁵² And they bowed down and worshiped him, and returned to Jerusalem with great joy; ⁵³ and they were in the temple every day blessing God.

PROCLAMATION

Text Notes

The divine beings in Acts 1:10 are described as "men" using the human term. Curiously, there are no female divine beings, messengers, angels, etc., in the canon. It is not clear whether women are present at the Ascension, obscured by masculine grammar. If they are not present, it is worth asking why not when women have been the birthing wombs, companion witnesses, participants in, and preachers of the entire Christ story. It is tempting to say the women were out in the world proclaiming the gospel while the men still needed one more sign. Yet, there were women with these very men (who are identified as the remaining apostles by name in Acts 1:13). If they were not with them at the Ascension, how did they learn of the meeting place? Since they seemed to have arrived at the same time, they could not have been very far. The texts and the cultures of the biblical world collude to minimize and erase women.

In Psalm 24:1–2, I have retained the feminine grammatical gender of the earth since it fits well with the contemporary notion of earth as mother. In verse 6, "the God of Rebekah" replaces "the God of Jacob."

Preaching Prompts

Chronologically, the Gospel for the Feast of the Ascension goes before the first reading from Acts. It may be useful to reread the Acts account of the Ascension *after* the Gospel, perhaps at the beginning of the sermon (if tacking it on to the Gospel seems like liturgical heresy). The Gospel points to the Ascension in Acts 1, and Acts 1 points to Pentecost, coming soon in the next chapter.

In the Ascension, the glory of the Resurrection ratchets up another level. The risen Christ appears to followers—addressed as "men" but possibly inclusive—and prepares the burgeoning church for the baptism of the Holy Spirit. The psalm makes clear that God is the One of glory, and only the pure-hearted can stand in her presence. The multiple Ascension accounts highlight the divinity of the post-Ascension Christ. Revelation 3 reminds us that the divine, risen, and ascended Christ is not so far away that he cannot come to us. He can and will still meet us at the table, for the Church that meeting is primarily in the Eucharist. Christ also comes to us in communion with one another. That communion, whether at the Eucharist or beyond, is communal, not hierarchal, though the scriptures and their authors will continue to assert ancient hierarchies, particularly along class and gender lines.

SEVENTH SUNDAY OF EASTER

Acts 8:26–39 (or Deuteronomy 25:5–9); Psalm 45:6–10, 12–15;
1 Corinthians 7:32–40; Mark 12:18–27

Acts 8:26 Now a messenger of the Holy One spoke to Philip, saying, "Get up and go toward the south on the road that goes down from Jerusalem to Gaza." This is desert. [27] So he got up and went. And look at that! There was an Ethiopian man, a eunuch high official of the Kandake, the queen of the Nubians, who was over the whole of her treasury. He had come to worship in Jerusalem. [28] Thus, he was returning home and was seated in his chariot and he was reading the prophet Isaiah. [29] Then the Spirit said to Philip, "Go to and join this chariot." [30] So Philip ran and heard him reading Isaiah the prophet. He asked, "Do you really understand what you are reading?" [31] He replied, "How would I be able without that someone guides me?" And he invited Philip to climb in and sit beside him. [32] Now the passage of scripture that he was reading was this:

> *Like a sheep to the slaughter he was led,*
> *and like a lamb silent before its shearer,*
> *thus he does not open his mouth.*
> [33] *In his humiliation justice was denied him.*
> *His generation, who can describe?*
> *For his life is taken away from the earth.*

[34] Now the eunuch asked Philip, saying, "About whom does the prophet say this, about himself or about someone else?" [35] Then Philip opened his mouth, and from that scripture, proclaimed to him the good news about Jesus. [36] And as they were going along the road, they came upon some water and the eunuch said, "Look, water! What prevents me from being baptized?" [38] He commanded the chariot to stop, and both of them, Philip and the eunuch, went down into the water, and Philip baptized him. [39] When they came up out of the water, the Spirit of the Holy One snatched Philip away; the eunuch saw him no more and went on his way rejoicing.

Deuteronomy 25:5 When brothers dwell together, and one of them dies and he has no son, the wife of the deceased shall not go outside [the family] to a stranger. Her husband's brother shall come upon her, taking her for himself and performing the duty of a husband's brother. [6] And it shall be that the firstborn son whom she births shall carry on the name of the deceased brother, so that his name not be erased from Israel. [7] Now if the man has no desire to take his brother's wife, then his brother's wife shall go up to the elders at the gate and she shall say, "My husband's brother refuses to carry on the name of his brother in Israel; he is not willing to perform the duty of a husband's brother to me." [8] Then the elders of his town shall call him and speak to him, and if he stands unmoved and says, "I do not desire to take her," [9] then his brother's wife shall go up to him in the sight of the elders, pull his sandal off his foot, spit in his face and respond, saying, "This is what is done to the man who does not build up his brother's house."

Psalm 45:6–10

6 Your God-given throne is everlasting;
a scepter of integrity is your royal scepter.
7 You love righteousness and hate wickedness;
therefore God, your God, has anointed you
with the oil of gladness more than your companions.
8 Myrrh and aloes and cassia scent all your garments;
from ivory palaces stringed instruments bring you joy.
9 Royal daughters are your treasures;
the consort stands at your right hand in gold of Ophir.
10 Hear daughter, consider and incline your ear;
forget your people and the house of your [mother and] father.
12 Daughter of Tyre, with gifts shall they seek your favor,
the wealthiest of the people.
13 With all kinds of wealth is the princess ensconced;
her garments are woven with gold.
14 In embroidery is she led to the king;
behind her the maidens, her companions, follow.
15 They are brought with joy and gladness
into the palace of the king.

1 Corinthians 7:32 I want you all to be free from concerns. The unmarried man is concerned for the Holy One, how to please the Holy One. 33 But the married man is concerned about the affairs of the world, how to please his woman. 34 And so, he is spread out. Similarly, the unmarried woman and the virgin are concerned for the Holy One, so that they may be holy in body and spirit whereas the married woman is concerned for the world, how to please her man. 35 I say this for your own benefit, not to put any restraint upon any of you rather, [that you be] presentable and consistent to the Holy One without distraction.

36 If anyone thinks someone is not behaving properly toward their betrothed, if passions are strong and [child-bearing] age is a concern, thus it has to be as he wishes; it is no sin. Let them marry. 37 But if someone's heart is firmly set and not under any constraint, having their own desire under control, and adjudges in their own heart to keep the virgin as their betrothed, that one will do well. 38 So then, the one who marries their betrothed does well, and the one who refrains from marriage will do better.

39 A woman is bound during the lifetime of her husband. Now if the husband falls asleep [in death], she is free to marry who she wishes, only in Christ. 40 But blessed is she, in my opinion, if she remains as she is. And I think I too have the Spirit of God.

Mark 12:18 Now Sadducees came to him, the ones who say there is no resurrection, and they asked him a question, saying, [19] "Teacher, Moses wrote for us that if a man's brother dies and leaves a wife but no children, the brother should take the woman [as a wife] and raise up children for his brother [20] There were seven brothers and the first took a woman [as a wife] and he died, leaving no children. [21] And the second took her [as a wife] and died, leaving no children and the third, likewise. [22] And of the seven, none left children. Last of all, the woman died. [23] In the resurrection whose wife will she be? For the seven had her as a wife."

[24] Jesus said to them, "Is not this the reason you go astray, that you know neither the scriptures nor the power of God? [25] For when they rise from the dead, women and men neither marry nor are given in marriage, but are like angels in heaven. [26] Now about the dead being raised, have you not read in the book of Moses, in the story about the bush, how God said to him, 'I am the God of Abraham, the God of Isaac, and the God of Jacob?' [27] God is God not of the dead, but of the living; you have wandered quite far astray."

PROCLAMATION

Text Notes

Hebrew and Greek each have one word, which means both "messenger" and "angel"; functionally, both are messengers. The author of Acts uses a number of Hebraisms, including the figure of the "angel of the Lord" and the "snatching away" of verse 39. In the Hebrew Bible, the messenger of the Holy One is often God Themselves in human drag, evident as the character often switches between speaking in third person on God's behalf and in first person as God. Many scholars understand this disguise to be so that God can be among her people without her holiness harming them.

In Acts 8:26, *mesembria* means both "south" and "noon" and is variably translated. The eunuch was generally a castrated man who served as a harem attendant or as a bureaucratic official. In some cases, the title is used for an intact man who is as trustworthy as a eunuch; e.g., in the Joseph story in Genesis 40, the term is used for the married Potiphar and Pharoah's other officials. Eunuchs could and did form intimate and sexual relationships, as is well documented in Chinese royal history and its literature, and among the *castrati*, European boy singers who were castrated to preserve their vocal range. In verse 27, the eunuch is also called a "man." His descriptor, *dunastes* (dynast), is also used for monarchs and God. The Kandake is the royal title of the Nubian queendom, often misconstrued as a name, "Candace." Verse 37, which includes a Christic confession, is missing from most reliable manuscripts and not included in most translations.

Psalm 45 is the rare hymn of praise for a human person rather than God: "you are the most handsome of men" in verse 2. Verse 6 looks like a turn to God: see NRSV, KJV, and NETS, "your throne, O God." However, "throne" and "God" are in a construct chain, the same structure as "house of God." Here "throne of God" means "God-given"; see "divine throne" in JPS and CEB. The royal wife is called a "consort," *shegal*, not queen, *malkah*, in verse 9, which term was not used by Israel for its royal women. (*Gevirah*, queen-mother, was exclusive to the mother of the Judean king, see my *Womanist Midrash: A Reintroduction to the Women of the Torah and of the Throne* for more on royal women is Israel and Judah.) As a verb, *shagal* indicates sexual violence (see Deut. 28:30; Isa. 13:16; and Zech. 14:2); it may be that the consort was a royal hostage to secure a peace.

Psalm 45 is a royal wedding psalm; the human monarch in Psalm 45 is most likely Ahab, given the reference to the Tyrian princess in verse 12. Inexplicably, NRSV substitutes "people" for "daughter"; CEB uses "city"—while "daughter" can indicate a suburb or "daughter city," the bride is clearly the subject; see JPS, Alter, LXX, and KJV (though the latter adds language to make the bride the supplicant).

Though the onus of decision-making is ultimately presented as the man's, the reading from 1 Corinthians 7 uses ambiguous language regarding the gender of the persons with repeated use of "a certain one" and "virgin," which can be male or female. However, in verse 36, the possessive (accusative) makes it clear that the virgin is "his." In the next phrase, the adjective *hyperakmos*, a *hapax legomenon,* meaning a word occurring one time, has distinct meanings depending on whether the subject is female or male with regard to age: if a woman, she is at peak or past childbearing age and if a man, at the peak of virility and thus horny. The muddled rendering of the verse would have meant that a person would have heard both of these options thus, I have included them. Jouette M. Bassler (*Women's Bible Commentary*, pp. 560–61), and Joseph Fitzmeyer (Anchor Bible Commentary, *1 Corinthians*, pp. 322–25) offer a fuller range of options. "Betrothed" replaces "virgin" throughout the passage.

The Sadducees' question is very loosely based on Deuteronomy 25:5–6 but missing the key context that the brothers were still living with their father and had not established their own households because the land had not yet been divided between them. In Deuteronomy, the deceased brother never had the opportunity to try and start a family or even try and fail. In Mark 12:24 and verse 27, the verb *planao* means "err, wander, go, and lead astray" and "deceive," thus, Jesus was saying they were much more than "wrong" as in NRSV.

Preaching Prompts

These readings present a series of gender expectations and the coexisting plural realities. While some parts of the tradition are fixated on men and their perpetuation, there are other folk and paradigms in the community and in the knowledge and love of God. Traditionally understood as the origin story of the African Church, the text presents its founding parent as a black genderqueer person. Philip's Christocentric reading of Isaiah presents an opportunity to address contextual readings of the Hebrew Bible that preserve earlier and subsequent Jewish readings.

The story in Acts 8 takes place on the side of the road in the wilderness, and at a crossroads at the intersection of race, ethnicity, and gender. The gentilic Greek man, Philip, crosses paths with the black Jewish eunuch/man bureaucrat serving an African queendom. Eunuchs have long been identified as queer figures in biblical studies. Nameless, the eunuch is reduced to (presumably) absent body parts as an identity evoking the inappropriate fixation on the genitalia of transkin. The mention of his maleness lends itself to a reading in which folk can be marginalized while enjoying the benefits of male privilege.

The alternate reading from Deuteronomy offers the Torah teaching on what has come to be called levirate marriage that is misrepresented by the Sadducees in the Gospel reading, thus Jesus's characterization that they have "wandered afar" from the Torah in the very framing of their question.

In spite of the set-up of the question, Jesus uses the opportunity to teach about the enduring nature of the human soul, eternal life, and the transience of our deepest held constructions like marriage—and, one might say, gender, as the "marriage-lessness" of angels points to them being beyond the gender binary.

Paul, likely based on his understanding of his own sexuality, expresses a preference for celibacy, providing an opportunity to talk about the ways in which those with power and authority have normalized and generalized their own sexual expression and expected others to reproduce it. Meanwhile, the psalm offers an unexpected glimpse at the royal wedding of Jezebel and Ahab in their relative youth and innocence.

This somewhat odd clutch of passages has within it diverse understandings of the ways in which persons lived in their bodies with regard to the potential of intimate connection with another person gesturing toward the increasingly diverse ways in which we now understand gender and intimacy. This diversity joins the ethnic and cultural diversity on display in the following Pentecost readings, illustrating the expansive inclusivity of the church.

PENTECOST VIGIL (OR EARLY SERVICE)

Joel 2:27–32 (or Exodus 19:1–19); Psalm 139:7–14;
Acts 2:1–18; John 4:7–26

Joel 2:27 You all shall know that I am in the midst of Israel,

and that I, the HOLY ONE OF SINAI, am your God and there is no other.
And my people shall not be put to shame ever again.
²⁸ And it shall be after that,
I will pour out my Spirit on all flesh;
and your daughters and your sons shall prophesy,

your elders shall dream dreams,
and your youths shall see visions.

29 Even on the enslaved women and men,
in those days, will I pour out my Spirit.

30 I will place portents in the heavens and on the earth, blood and fire and pillars of smoke. 31 The sun shall be turned to darkness, and the moon to blood, before the great and terrible day of the DREAD GOD comes. 32 Then it shall be that everyone who calls on the name of the FAITHFUL GOD shall be saved; for in Mount Zion and in Jerusalem there shall be those who escape, as the HOLY ONE OF OLD has said, and among the survivors, those whom the GOD WHO SAVES calls.

Exodus 19:1 On the third new moon after the women, children, and men of Israel had gone out of the land of Egypt, on that day, they entered the wilderness of Sinai. 2 They had journeyed from Rephidim, entered the wilderness of Sinai, and camped in the wilderness; Israel camped there in front of the mountain. 3 Then Moses went up to God and the HOLY ONE OF OLD called to him from the mountain, saying, "Thus you shall say to the house of Jacob, and tell the women, children, and men of Israel: 4 You all have seen what I did to the Egyptians, that I raised you all up on the wings of eagles and brought you all to myself. 5 Now, if you all obey my voice and keep my covenant, you all shall be my treasure from among all peoples, for the whole earth is mine. 6 And you all shall be for me a sovereignty of priests and a holy nation. These are the words that you shall speak to the women, children, and men of Israel."

7 So Moses came and called the elders of the people and placed before them all these words that the HOLY ONE had commanded him. 8 Then the people, women and men, all answered together: "Everything that the HOLY ONE has spoken we will do." And Moses conveyed the words of the people to the HOLY ONE OF SINAI. 9 Then the HOLY ONE said to Moses, "I will come to you in an impenetrable cloud, so that the people can hear when I speak with you and also trust you always." When Moses had told the words of the people to the HOLY ONE, 10 the HOLY GOD said to Moses:

"Go to the people and have them consecrate themselves today and tomorrow. Have them wash their clothes, 11 and be prepared for the third day, because on the third day the MOST HIGH will come down upon Mount Sinai in the sight of all the people. 12 You shall set a boundary around the people, saying, 'Take heed not to go up the mountain or to touch the edge of it yourselves; anyone who touches the mountain shall surely be put to death. 13 No hand shall touch them, rather they shall be stoned or shot with arrows; whether animal or human, they shall not live.' When the ram's horn sounds a long blast, they may go up on the mountain." 14 So Moses went down from the mountain to the people. He consecrated the people, and they washed their clothes. 15 And Moses said to the people, "Prepare for the third day; do not go near a woman."

16 And it was on the third day as morning came there was thunder and lightning, as well as a cloud heavy upon the mountain, and a blast of a trumpet so loud that all the people who were

in the camp trembled. [17] Then Moses brought the people out of the camp to meet God. They stationed themselves at the base of the mountain. [18] Now Mount Sinai was in smoke, because the HOLY ONE OF OLD had descended upon it in fire; the smoke ascended like the smoke of a kiln, while the whole mountain shook violently. [19] And it was that as the sound of the trumpet grew stronger and stronger, Moses would speak and God would answer him in thunder.

Psalm 139:7–14

[7] Where can I go from your spirit?
Or where from your presence can I flee?

[8] If I ascend to the heavens, there you are;
if I recline in Sheol, see, it is you!

[9] If I take up dawn's wings
if I settle at the farthest reaches of the sea,

[10] even there your hand shall lead me,
and your right hand shall hold me fast.

[11] If I say, "Surely darkness shall cover me,
and night will become light behind me,"

[12] even darkness is not dark to you;
night is as daylight,
for dark is the same as light.

[13] For it was you who crafted my inward parts;
you wove me together in my mother's womb.

[14] I praise you, for I am awesomely and marvelously made.
Wonderous are your works;
that my soul knows full well.

Acts 2:1 When the day of Pentecost had come, they were all together in the same place. [2] And there came suddenly from heaven a sound like the sweeping of a mighty wind, and it filled the entire house where they were sitting. [3] Then there appeared among them divided tongues, as of fire, and one rested on each of them. [4] And all of them were filled with the Holy Spirit and they began to speak in other tongues just as the Spirit gave them to speak.

[5] Now there were dwelling in Jerusalem devout Jews from every nation under heaven. [6] Now at this sound the crowd gathered and was confused because each heard them speaking in the native language of each. [7] Amazed and astounded, they asked, "Are not all these who are speaking Galileans? [8] And how do we hear, each in our own native language? [9] Parthians and Medes and Elamites, and those who live in Mesopotamia, Judea and Cappadocia, Pontus and Asia, [10] Phrygia and Pamphylia, Egypt and the parts of Libya adjacent to Cyrene, and visitors from Rome, both Jews and proselytes, [11] Cretans and Arabs, we hear them speaking in our own tongues about God's deeds of power." [12] All were amazed and questioning to one another, saying, "What does this mean?" [13] But others mocking said, "They are filled with new wine."

¹⁴ But Peter, standing with the eleven, raised his voice and addressed them, "Judeans and all who live in Jerusalem, let this be known to you all, and attend to my speech. ¹⁵ For these persons are not drunk as you suppose, it is only the third hour [nine o'clock] in the morning. ¹⁶ No, this is what was spoken through the prophet Joel:

¹⁷ *'In the last days it will be, God declares,*
that I will pour out my Spirit upon all flesh,
and your daughters and your sons shall prophesy,
and your young men shall see visions,
and your elders shall dream dreams.
¹⁸ *Even upon my slaves, both women and men,*
in those days I will pour out my Spirit;
and they shall prophesy.'"

John 4:7 A Samaritan woman came to draw water. Jesus said to her, "Give me a drink." ⁸ Now his disciples had gone to the city to buy food. ⁹ The Samaritan woman said to him, "How are you, a Judean, asking a drink of me, a woman of Samaria?" (Judeans do not share things in common with Samaritans.) ¹⁰ Jesus answered and said to her, "If you knew the gift of God and who is the one telling to you, 'Give me a drink,' you would have asked him, and he would have given you living water." ¹¹ The woman said to him, "Sir, you have no bucket, and the well is deep. From where do you get that living water? ¹² Are you greater than our ancestor Jacob, the one who gave us the well, and with his daughters and sons and his flocks drank from it?" ¹³ Jesus answered and said to her, "Everyone who drinks of this water will thirst again. ¹⁴ But the one who drinks of the water that I will give will never thirst. The water that I will give will become in them a fount of water springing up into eternal life." ¹⁵ The woman said to him, "Sir, give me this water, that I may never thirst or keep coming here to draw water."

¹⁶ Jesus said to her, "Go, call your husband, and come [back] to this place." ¹⁷ The woman answered and said to him, "I have no husband." Jesus said to her, "You said rightly, 'I have no husband.' ¹⁸ For five husbands have you had, and now the one you have is not your husband. What you have said is true!" ¹⁹ The woman said to him, "Sir, I see that you are a prophet. ²⁰ Our mothers and fathers worshiped on this mountain, yet you say in Jerusalem is the place where people must worship." ²¹ Jesus said to her, "Believe me, woman, the hour is coming when neither on this mountain nor in Jerusalem will you worship the Sovereign God. ²² You all worship what you do not know; we worship what we know, for salvation is from the Judeans. ²³ But the hour is coming, and now is, when the true worshipers will worship the Sovereign God in spirit and truth, for these are the worshipers the Sovereign God seeks. ²⁴ God is spirit, and those who worship God must worship in spirit and truth." ²⁵ The woman said to Jesus, "I know that Messiah is coming" (the one who is called Christ). "When he comes, he will proclaim all things to us." ²⁶ Jesus said to her, "I am, the one who is speaking to you."

PROCLAMATION

Text Notes

Verse numbers in Christian Bibles diverge from those (now) in Hebrew and Jewish Bibles. What is Joel 2:28 in Christian texts is 3:1 in Jewish texts such as the JPS *Tanakh* and Hebrew Masoretic Text, as well as other ancient texts including the LXX and Peshitta. "Elders" in verse 28 is an inclusive plural that grammatically includes women; it can represent chronological age or status. The "elders of Israel" served as an administrative layer (Num. 16:25; Deut. 27:1, 31:9; Josh. 7:6, 8:10; 1 Sam. 4:3). They are only spoken of as a group so it is unclear if there were any women among them. In Joel "elders" is paired with "youth," indicating it should be read chronologically, and therefore I argue, inclusively.

In Exodus 19:10 and 14, "consecrate" or "sanctify" has a reflexive sense; one does it to oneself, primarily through water: bathing and washing one's clothing. Scholars from the rabbinic period (Rashi, Ramban, Ibn Ezra, and Nahmanides) understood Moses's sanctification of the people to be a charge to them to sanctify themselves, hence "warn them to stay pure" in the JPS.

The use of the masculine pronoun "him" for both a person who transgresses the boundary of the mountain and the mountain itself means that in verse 13, the referent of "no hand shall touch him/it" is unclear.

In Psalm 139:14, "marvelous" and wondrous" are the same word. I alternate them for alliteration to give a sense of the poetry.

The author limits the multinational Jews in Jerusalem to "devout men" in Acts 1:5 as though there were no women or none of the women were devout. The androcentric language discounts women who were living in the city and women who did make the journey. Yet Deuteronomy 16:11 specifies celebrating the festival with daughters and sons and women and men who are enslaved in the household (no mention of wives). Similarly, Peter addresses "men of Judea" but also "all who live in Jerusalem" in 1:14; I treat both as inclusive.

In John 4:26, Jesus says, *ego eimi*, "I am," echoing God's self-identification in Exodus 3:14 or, in some other translations, "I am [he]"—the masculine pronoun is missing.

Preaching Prompts

Pentecost, the fiftieth day, marks the end of the Festival of Weeks, *Shavuoth* (from the Hebrew for "weeks"), originally named the festival of "Harvest," see Exodus 23:16; Leviticus 23:15–16. The seven weeks follow from Passover, and the festivals are entwined. By the time of the New Testament, it was also understood as the anniversary of the revelation of the Torah on Mount Sinai in Exodus 19. These traditions underlie the outpouring of the Holy Spirit on that same day. The Christian observance is inexorably linked to its ancestral Jewish heritage.

Because of its citation in Acts 2, the primary Pentecost narrative, Joel 2 is regarded as fulfilled in the event in Christian interpretation. In Joel, repeated in Acts, "everyone who calls upon the name of the Holy One shall be saved" (or "rescued") means two very different things in each of those contexts. In the Hebrew Bible, salvation, rescue, and deliverance are normally corporate (with few exceptions) and relate to physical safety from threats of violence, war, occupation, and even natural and ecological disasters (as is the case in Joel). In the New Testament, the Church has replaced the nation as the frame of reference; to call upon the name, now of Jesus, is to profess faith in him. It is important to tell the Christian story without erasing or rewriting the story of God's faithfulness to Jewish people or their Israelite ancestors.

Exodus 19 is the story of God's covenant with Israel ratified on Sinai with God present in veiled majesty. The language is, by turns, inclusive and exclusive, inviting reflection on who we understand to be part of and to represent the people of God. The traditional language for Israel, "the sons" or "children of Israel," is both androcentric and inclusive. In verse 8, the people "all" answer, meaning women and men; children would not be subject to a legal agreement like the covenant. ("Children" in the commandments refers to adult children in relation to their parents.) "People" is inclusive and yet is sometimes used as though men are the only ones who count; in verse 15, Moses tells the "people" not to approach women, presumably for sex. In this construction, women are not "people." Perhaps more disturbing, Moses *adds* this line to God's instructions and receives no rebuke. (Compare God's directive in verses 10–13 with those of Moses.) The attempts of Moses and his writers notwithstanding, God appears to all the women, children, and men of Israel. Though earlier in Exodus, the people see God regularly in the alternating pillars of cloud and fire, God's appearance in verse 16 is perhaps closer than the front of their vanguard and much more dramatic with the addition of thunder and lightning and the sound of God's voice.

Who experiences the touch of the Holy Spirit in Acts 2? Who are the "they"? If they are the upper room community, then they are Mary, the mother of Jesus, and other unnamed women along with the eleven remaining apostles (Acts 1:13–14), plus a newly elected apostle (who will immediately disappear), verses 23–26. "They" may also refer to the larger group of one hundred and twenty in the following verse. An intriguing possibility reads the two together: Mary and an undisclosed number of women together with the twelve apostles constituted the one hundred and twenty. This might explain why Peter chooses Joel to explain the phenomenon because of its explicit inclusivity.

The *Samarians* were the inhabitants of the northern monarchy of Israel who ultimately fell to Assyria and were largely deported. The land was repopulated with other conquered peoples, and their descendants became known as *Samaritans* (see 2 Kings 17:24–34). Judeans held them in low esteem because of their mixed heritage, to which they attributed the differences between their worship traditions. Notably, the Samaritan Pentateuch is the entirety of their Bible; nothing else is canonical, which remains the case for Samaritan Jews in the present. (*Ioudaiois* should be understood as "Judean" in opposition to Samaritan, as both communities are Jewish.) The dispute about the mountain in John 4:20–22 is rooted in one of the many differences between the Samaritan and Judean Torahs: Whether the mountain in Deuteronomy 27:4 on which Joshua (8:30) later built an altar is Ebal (Judeans) or Gerizim (Samaritans). As a result, the Samaritan temple was built on Mt. Gerizim, the "this mountain" of John 4:22. Palestinian Samaritan Jews continued to worship on the mountain, the temple long destroyed by the Romans in 70 CE.

In John 4:12, the woman mentions Jacob and his children (or sons), which I have made explicitly inclusive given that Jacob had an unknown number of daughters, including one named Dinah, among his thirty-three children (see Gen. 37:35, 46:15).

PENTECOST PRINCIPAL SERVICE

Acts 2:1–18 (or Isaiah 44:1–8); Psalm 104:1–4, 10–15, 27–30; Romans 8:14–27; John 14:8–17

Acts 2:1 When the day of Pentecost had come, they were all together in the same place. [2] And there came suddenly from heaven a sound like the sweeping of a mighty wind, and it filled the entire house where they were sitting. [3] Then there appeared among them divided tongues, as of fire, and one rested on each of them. [4] And all of them were filled with the Holy Spirit and they began to speak in other tongues just as the Spirit gave them to speak.

[5] Now there were dwelling in Jerusalem devout Jews from every nation under heaven. [6] Now at this sound the crowd gathered and was confused because each heard them speaking in the native language of each. [7] Amazed and astounded, they asked, "Are not all these who are speaking Galileans? [8] And how do we hear, each in our own native language? [9] Parthians and Medes and Elamites, and those who live in Mesopotamia, Judea and Cappadocia, Pontus and Asia, [10] Phrygia and Pamphylia, Egypt and the parts of Libya adjacent to Cyrene, and visitors from Rome, both Jews and proselytes, [11] Cretans and Arabs, we hear them speaking in our own tongues about God's deeds of power." [12] All were amazed and questioning to one another, saying, "What does this mean?" [13] But others mocking said, "They are filled with new wine."

[14] But Peter, standing with the eleven, raised his voice and addressed them, "Judeans and all who live in Jerusalem, let this be known to you all, and attend to my speech: [15] For these persons are not drunk as you suppose, it is only the third hour [nine o'clock] in the morning. [16] No, this is what was spoken through the prophet Joel:

¹⁷ *'In the last days it will be, God declares,*
   that I will pour out my Spirit upon all flesh,
   and your daughters and your sons shall prophesy,
   and your young men shall see visions,
   and your elders shall dream dreams.
¹⁸ *Even upon my slaves, both women and men,*
   in those days I will pour out my Spirit;
   and they shall prophesy.'"

Isaiah 44:1 Hear now, Jacob [Rebekah's child], my slave,

Israel whom I have chosen!
² Thus says the WELLSPRING OF LIFE who made you,
   who shaped you in the womb and will help you:
   Fear not, Jacob [Rebekah's son], my slave,
   Jeshurun whom I have chosen.
³ For I will pour water upon thirsty soil,
   and streams upon the dry ground;
   I will pour my spirit upon your descendants,
   and my blessing on your offspring.
⁴ They shall spring up in green [places],
   like willows by flowing waters.
⁵ This one will say, "I am GOD's,"
   that one will name the name of Jacob,
   another will write on their hand, "This belongs to GOD,"
   and adopt the name of Israel.
⁶ Thus says the AGELESS GOD, the Sovereign of Israel,
   and Israel's Redeemer, the COMMANDER of heaven's legions:
   I am the first and I am the last;
   apart from me there is no god.
⁷ Who is like me? Let them proclaim it,
   let them declare it and set it out before me.
   Who like me from old has laid out things which are coming?
   Let them declare to us what will come.
⁸ Fear not and be not afraid;
   have I not from old told you and declared it?
   You all are my witnesses!
   Is there any god besides me?
   There is no rock; I know not one.

Psalm 104:1–4, 10–15, 27–30

1 Bless the FOUNT OF LIFE, O my soul.
  MOTHER OF ALL, my God, you are very great.
  You don honor and majesty,

2 Wrapped in light as a garment,
  you stretch out the heavens like a tent-curtain.

3 She who lays on the waters the beams of her upper chambers,
  she who makes the clouds her chariot,
  she is the one who rides on the wings of the wind.

4 She is the one who makes the winds her celestial messengers,
  fire and flame her ministers.

10 She is the one who makes springs gush forth in the torrents;
  they flow between the hills.

11 They give drink to every wild animal;
  the wild donkeys slake their thirst.

12 By the torrents the birds of the heavens dwell;
  among the branches they give voice.

13 She is the one who waters the mountains from her high chambers;
  the earth is satisfied with the fruit of your work.

14 She is the one who makes grass to grow for the cattle,
  and vegetation for human labor,
  to bring forth food from the earth,

15 and wine to make the human heart rejoice,
  with oil to make the face shine,
  and bread to sustain the human heart.

27 All of these hope in you
  to provide their food in due season.

28 You give it to them, they glean it;
  you open your hand, they are well satisfied.

29 You hide your face, they are dismayed;
  when you collect their breath, they die
  and to their dust they return.

30 You send forth your spirit, they are created;
  and you renew the face of the earth.

Romans 8:14 Now as many as are led by the Spirit of God are daughters and sons of God. ¹⁵ For you all did not receive a spirit of slavery to fall again into fear, but you have received a spirit of adoption through which we cry, "Abba! Father!" ¹⁶ It is that same Spirit who bears witness with our spirit that we are daughters and sons of God. ¹⁷ And if daughters and sons, then heirs, heirs of God and heirs with Christ, if it is true that we suffer with Christ so that we may also be glorified with Christ.

¹⁸ I consider that the sufferings of this present time are not worth comparing with the glory about to be revealed to us. ¹⁹ For the creation waits with eager longing for the revealing of the daughters and sons of God; ²⁰ for the creation was subjected to futility, not of its own will but by the will of the one who subjected it, in hope ²¹ that the creation itself will be set free from its bondage to decay and will obtain the freedom of the glory of the daughters and sons of God. ²² We know that the whole creation has been groaning in labor pains until now; ²³ and not only the creation, but we ourselves, who have the first fruits of the Spirit, groan inwardly while we wait for adoption, the redemption of our bodies. ²⁴ For in hope we were saved. Now hope that is seen is not hope. For who hopes for what is seen? ²⁵ But if we hope for what we do not see, we wait for it with patience.

²⁶ Likewise the Spirit helps us in our weakness; for we do not know how to pray as is necessary, but that very Spirit intercedes with sighs too deep for words. ²⁷ And God, who searches the heart, knows what is the mindset of the Spirit, because the Spirit intercedes for the saints according to the will of God.

John 14:8 Philip said to Jesus, "Rabbi, show us the Father, and we will be content." ⁹ Jesus said to him, "Have I been with all of you all this time, Philip, and you still do not know me? The one who has seen me has seen the Father. How can you say, 'Show us the Father'? ¹⁰ Do you not believe that I am in the Father and the Father is in me? The words that I speak to you I do not speak on my own; but the Father who dwells in me does the works of God. ¹¹ Believe me that I am in the Father and the Father is in me; but if not, then believe because of the works themselves. ¹² Very truly, I tell you all, the one who believes in me will also do the works I do and even will do greater works than these, because I am going to the Father. ¹³ And whatever you all ask in my name I will do, so that the Father may be glorified in the Son. ¹⁴ If you all ask me anything in my name, I will do it.

¹⁵ "If you love me, you will keep my commandments. ¹⁶ And I will ask the Father, and God will give you another Advocate, to be with you forever. ¹⁷ This is the Spirit of truth, whom the world cannot receive, because it neither sees nor knows the Spirit. You know her, because she abides with you, and she will be in you."

PROCLAMATION

Text Notes

See the discussion of the Acts 2 text in the readings for the Pentecost Vigil/Early Service.

Jeshurun, in Isaiah 44:2, is something of a pet name for Israel from Deuteronomy (see verses 32:15; 33:5, 26). In verse 4, there is a missing noun to describe the site of flourishing; I have supplied "places."

Psalm 104 switches between second and third person, as is common in the genre. Verses 14–15 use the word that means both bread and food in general in both senses.

In the Hebrew Bible, the Spirit of God (and more broadly) is grammatically feminine. This is not easily visible when reading in English. Translators have historically avoided grammatical constructions that would require a pronoun for the Spirit in the First Testament. Rather, they repeat "the spirit" as the perpetual subject. I have adopted that practice for the translation of John 14:17.

In Greek, in the Septuagint, and in Christian scriptures, the word for "spirit" is neuter, meaning that in the breadth of the scriptures, the spirit is anything and everything but masculine. The deliberate choice to render the spirit in masculine terms in Latin texts such as the Vulgate reflects theological commitments apart from the grammar of the texts. If we were to hear Jesus speak John 14:17 in Aramaic, we would most likely hear the feminine pronouns represented by the translation above.

Preaching Prompts

The outpouring of the Holy Spirit on Pentecost marks the dawn of the Church, but it is not the dawn of the Holy Spirit; she births creation, hovering over her newly hatched brood in Genesis and breathes through the scriptures, celebrated in the final verse of the psalm. Here in Isaiah 44, she is God's promise for coming generations. The God of wind and flame in Psalm 104:4 is the same God, the same Spirit who is the wind and breath of the Pentecostal fire.

Isaiah 44 is significant for its strident monotheism in a largely henotheistic tradition. Henotheism is the worship of one god above others while not denying the existence of the others, i.e., "God of gods," and "choose this day whom you will serve," etc. But in Isaiah 44:8 God says she has never even heard of another god in the rhetoric of her poet-prophet. This is a bold, audacious claim, for the author is not ignorant of the world around her, nor is the God for whom she speaks. Rather, it is both creation and affirmation of a worldview, as is the Pentecost moment.

The psalm is rich with the majesty of creation. And in Romans 8:20 and 22, that same creation waits, longing for us, humanity, to live into the fullness of our glory as the children and God. That same mighty fire-swirling spirit pays for us to live up to and into our full potential like the rest of creation, even when we do not know the words to pray. Indeed, language as we understand it is insufficient; the spirit intercedes, and advocates through sounds and sighs, beyond our capacity to interpret. The Gospel promises that Advocate, Comforter, and Intercessor who will be with us forever.

TRINITY SUNDAY

Hosea 11:1–4; Psalm 130:5–8; 131:1–3;
2 Peter 1:16–18; Matthew 28:16–20

Hosea 11:1 When Israel was a child, I loved them,

and out of Egypt I called my child.

2 They, the Baals, called to them,

they went out to the Baals;

they sacrificed and to idols,

they offered incense.

3 Yet it was I who walked toddling Ephraim,

taking them by their arms;

yet they did not know that I healed them.

4 I led them with human ties,

with bonds of love.

I was to them like those

who lift babies to their cheeks.

I bent down to them and fed them.

Psalm 130:5–8; 131:1–3

5 I wait for the WOMB OF CREATION, my soul waits,

and in her word I hope.

6 My soul keeps watch for the Creator,

more than those who watch for the morning,

more than those who watch for the morning.

7 Israel, hope in the MOTHER OF CREATION!

For with the CREATOR OF ALL there is faithful love,

and with her is abundant redemption.

8 It is she who will redeem Israel

from all their iniquities.

131:1 WOMB OF LIFE, my heart is not lifted up,

nor my eyes exalted;

I do not keep company with things

great and too wondrous for me.

2 Rather, I have soothed and quieted my soul,

like a weaned child with her mother;

my soul is like a weaned child within me.

3 Israel, hope in the WELLSPRING OF LIFE

from now until forever.

2 Peter 1:16 For we did not follow sophisticated mythologies when we made known to you all the power and coming of our Redeemer Jesus Christ, rather we had been eyewitnesses of his majesty. [17] For Christ from God the Sovereign received honor and glory, a voice came to him from the Majestic Glory, saying, "This is my Son, my Beloved, with whom I am well pleased." [18] And we ourselves heard this voice that came from heaven, while we were with him on the holy mountain.

Matthew 28:16 Now the eleven disciples went to Galilee, to the mountain to which Jesus sent them. [17] And when they saw him, they bowed down worshiping him; but some doubted. [18] Then Jesus came and said to them, "All authority in heaven and on earth has been given to me. [19] Go therefore and make disciples of all nations, baptizing them in the name of the Father and of the Son and of the Holy Spirit, [20] and teaching them to obey everything that I have commanded you. Now look, I am with you always, to the end of the age."

PROCLAMATION

Text Notes

In the first line of Hosea 11, "boy," a very ambiguous term, ranges from prepubescent to young adult and can also represent minor or junior status among adults. The passage moves between conceptions of Israel as a singular collective "boy," to a notion of individuals, "them," in the first two verses. In verse 3, "toddling" renders a verb made out of the word for foot, consistent with the child learning to walk and still being nursed, verse 4. Human "ties" in verse 4 is a pun on ropes and cords and the bonds of human relationships.

In Psalm 130:8, Israel is a singular entity, and their sin is also collective and singular here.

Preaching Prompts

The three-fold way in which God has been traditionally named is male in form (Father and Son) and function (the postbiblical construction of the Holy Spirit as male). This rubric, which seeks to articulate the essential nature and identity of God to be used in worship and prayer, liturgy, and preaching, allows men and boys to hear themselves and their pronouns identified with God along with the exclusion and invisibility of women and girls and nonbinary persons. This exclusion is formative for men and boys in casting gender hierarchy from which they benefit in divine terms. For those who do not hear their pronouns invoke their creation as *imago dei* in the language of the Church, trinitarian language, and the observance of the Trinity, remain a sanctified proclamation of male divinity. For this reason, this project offers more ways to name God, drawn from the scriptures.

While the overwhelming majority of God-language is masculine, there remains a significant collection of feminine imagery for and descriptions of God. The description of the soul as a weaned child in Psalm 131:2 invokes an image of God as the mother upon whose breast it rests.

The Epistle writer uses rare language for God, Majestic Glory, in 2 Peter 1:17. (The author of Hebrews uses "the Majesty on high" in 1:3 and "the Majesty in heaven" in Hebrews 8:1.) The Epistle also comes with a healthy caution for those caught up in the Church's often heated, occasionally violent debates over the Trinity, its Persons, and their relationships, hierarchy, and origins. In disputes about "sophisticated" myths or mythologies—and, I add, theologies, philosophies, and church doctrines—the writer turns to their witness of the faith, what they saw and heard. In turn, they pass their testimony down to us.

Matthew 28:19 is the place where what has become the primary Trinitarian formula occurs. (Galatians 4:6 has the same elements but presented discursively: "And because you are children, God has sent the Spirit of God's Son into our hearts, crying, 'Abba! Father!'") While the traditional language will always have a place in the liturgical lexicon, Trinity Sunday offers an opportunity to craft language that draws more widely on the biblical texts and traditions.

Some of mine include:

Sovereign, Savior, and Shelter;
Author, Word, and Translator;
Parent, Partner, and Friend;
Majesty, Mercy, and Mystery;
Creator, Christ, and Compassion;
Potter, Vessel, and Holy Fire;
Life, Liberation, and Love.

SEASON AFTER PENTECOST (29)

The Season after Pentecost runs nearly thirty weeks and the rather short Gospel of Mark races toward Holy Week in ten chapters punctuated by the feasts, festivals, and observances of the liturgical year. In this extended season in Year B, the Lectionary returns to the beginning of the Gospel and passes through it again, building up to the expectation of the return of Christ.

PROPER 1 (CLOSEST TO MAY 11)

Genesis 1:1–5; Psalm 31:1–5, 15, 18–19; Romans 5:1–5; Mark 1:9–13

Genesis 1:1 When beginning he, God, created the heavens and the earth, [2] the earth was shapeless and formless and bleakness covered the face of the deep, while the Spirit of God, she, fluttered over the face of the waters. [3] Then God said, "Let there be light"; and there was light. [4] And God saw that the light was good; so God separated the light from the bleakness. [5] Then God called the light Day, and the bleakness God called Night. And there was evening and there was morning, day one.

Psalm 31:1–5, 15, 18–19

[1] In you, WOMB OF LIFE, I take refuge;
   let me not ever be put to shame;
   in your righteousness rescue me.

[2] Incline your ear to me;
   quickly deliver me.
   Be for me a rock of refuge,
   a stronghold to save me.

[3] For you are my rock and my stronghold;
   for your name's sake lead me and guide me.

[4] Free me from the net that is hidden for me,
   for you are my refuge.

[5] Into your hand I commit my spirit;
   you have redeemed me, ARK OF SAFETY, God of truth.

[15] My times are in your hand;
   deliver me from the hand of my enemies and those who hound me.

[18] Let lying lips be stilled
   the ones that speak against the righteous,
   arrogant with pride and contempt.

[19] How great is your goodness
   that you have secured for those who fear you,
   and that you do for those who take refuge in you,
   before all the woman-born.

Romans 5:1 Now, since we are made righteous through faithfulness, we have peace with God through our Savior Jesus Christ. [2] Through Christ we have obtained access to this grace in which we stand and we rejoice in our hope of God's glory. [3] And not only that, for we also rejoice in our sufferings, knowing that suffering produces endurance, [4] and endurance character, and character hope, [5] and hope does not disappoint, because God's love has been poured into our hearts through the Holy Spirit, She, who has been given to us.

Mark 1:9 And it was in those days that Jesus came from Nazareth of Galilee and was baptized by John in the Jordan. [10] And just as he was rising up out of the water, he saw the heavens torn apart and the Spirit [she was] descending like a dove on him. [11] And a voice came from the heavens, "You are my beloved Son; with you am I well pleased." [12] Then the Spirit suddenly drove Jesus out into the wilderness. [13] He was in the wilderness forty days, tempted by Satan, and he was with the wild beasts, and the angels waited on him.

PROCLAMATION

Text Notes

In Genesis 1:1, God and God's verb, "create," are grammatically masculine. In Genesis 1:2, the Spirit of God and her verb are grammatically feminine. While this project generally eschews masculine God language with few exceptions, I preserve it here with the feminine language erased by virtually every translation to note God's introduction in the scriptures transcends the singular masculine gender to which God is often reduced.

Given "the Spirit" was feminine in Hebrew and Aramaic, the languages in which Jesus spoke and prayed, I have provided the gendering with which he would've been familiar as an option in verse 10. Traditions vary as to whether Jesus should be understood as "my son, the Beloved" or "My beloved son" in Mark 1:11. "You are my son" is a quote of Psalm 2:7; in the song it is royal adoption language common between gods and monarchs (of both genders) in the Afro-Asiatic world.

In verse 4 of the psalm, "free me" is the "let my people go" verb of the exodus.

In Romans 5:1 (and Hab. 2:4), "justified by faith/fulness" is notoriously difficult to translate. "Faith" as a belief in someone or something, i.e., God, is not a Hebrew biblical concept. The word *'-m-n*, root of "amen," means "faithful," and "faithfulness," and "trust," and "trustworthy. Its Greek equivalent, *pistis*, initially had the same semantic range; however, it was adapted to refer primarily to faith *in* Jesus as the Child of God, his resurrection, etc. Nevertheless, the word maintains its full semantic range. Theologically speaking, there is no small difference between the claim that a believer is made righteous by her own act of faith or belief and that God makes a believer righteous through her own divine faithfulness.

The ubiquity of masculine grammar in each passage contributes to the difficulty. Whose faith or faithfulness is being invoked? In Habakkuk, is the righteous person justified by her own faithfulness to God or by God's faithfulness to her? Similarly, in Romans, is the righteous person justified by her faith or belief in Jesus as the Messiah or is she justified by God's faithfulness to her? (And is Paul even preserving the sense of the earlier reading?) The grammar and semantic ranges allow for all of these. My choice of "faithfulness" here leaves open these possibilities to be explored by the preacher while maintaining fidelity to both textual traditions.

The Spirit is grammatically feminine in Hebrew and Aramaic, the primary languages of Paul's (and Jesus's) culture and scriptures, as in the Genesis reading. The corresponding Greek pronoun is neuter. I offer the feminine pronoun as a contextually appropriate option for readers, preachers, and lectors in Romans 5:5.

In the Israelite cultural and literary context, "angels," as in Mark 1:11, are really "messengers." The word is used for both human and divine beings; both senses endured into the New Testament. However, in both Psalm 91 and the wilderness sojourn of Jesus in Mark 1, divine beings are clearly meant, and there is a particular sentimental attachment to angels in both of these passages.

Preaching Prompts

While the Gospel of Mark marches furiously toward Jerusalem, where nearly one-third of the book will take place, it presents Jesus as the son of God who is known in power and majesty through the Hebrew Bible and who is present in the form of her spirit that same spirit with which Jesus is endowed in Mark. The multiple gendering of God's Spirit, feminine in Hebrew, neuter in Greek, Latin, and much of the successive tradition, provide space to talk about the complexity of gender and the inability to pin it down in a simple binary. We who are created in God's image share that complexity, as does Jesus, with the human mother who birthed and raised him, the feminine (or neuter) Spirit whose overshadowing resulted in his conception, his human father by marriage and choice, and his Abba, his Father.

The Holy Spirit ties all of these lessons together, from the dawn of creation to the dawning of the public ministry of Jesus. The spirit is with us in the difficulties that accompany us on our life journey as the psalmist testifies. And the Holy Spirit is the perpetual dispenser of the love of God as we walk in the way of Jesus.

PROPER 2 (CLOSEST TO MAY 18)

Proverbs 4:1–10; Psalm 111; 1 Corinthians 1:26–31; Matthew 11:7–19

Proverbs 4:1 Listen, children, to a parent's instruction,

and attend that you may know understanding.

² For I give to you all good training:

forsake not my teaching.

³ When I was a child with my father,

tender, and my mother's only [child],

⁴ I was taught, and it was said unto me,

"Let your heart hold fast my words;

keep my commandments and you shall live.

⁵ Get Wisdom; get understanding: do not forget,

nor turn away from the words of my mouth.
6 Do not forsake her, and she will keep you;
love her, and she will guard you.
7 The beginning of wisdom is this:
Get Wisdom,
and in all you get, get insight.
8 Value her highly and she will exalt you;
she will honor you if you embrace her.
9 She will set on your head a graceful garland;
she will place on you a beautiful crown."
10 Hear, my child, and accept my words,
that the years of your life may be many.

Psalm 111

1 Praise the LIVING GOD!
I will give thanks to the ONE GOD with my whole heart,
in the assembly of the upright, in the congregation.
2 Great are the works of GOD,
contemplated by all who delight in them.
3 Splendor and majesty are her work,
and her righteousness stands forever.
4 She has gained renown for her wonderful deeds;
the WOMB OF LIFE is gracious and abounds in mother-love.
5 She provides fresh meat for those who revere her;
she remembers her covenant perpetually.
6 She has declared the strength of her works to her people,
giving them the heritage of the nations.
7 The works of her hands are truth and justice;
trustworthy are all her precepts.
8 They stand fast forever and ever,
Executed in truth and uprightness.
9 She sent redemption to her people;
she has ordained her covenant forever.
Holy and awesome is her name.
10 Awe of the AGELESS GOD is the beginning of wisdom;
all those who do have good understanding.
Her praise endures forever.

1 Corinthians 1:26 Now look to your own call, sisters and brothers [or friends and kin]: not many of you were wise by mortal standards, not many were powerful, not many were highborn. 27 Rather, God chose what is foolish in the world to shame the wise and God chose what is weak in the world to shame the strong. ²⁸ And what is insignificant in the world and what is despised God chose, to eradicate what is, ²⁹ so that no mortal can boast in the presence of God. ³⁰ God is the source of your life in Christ Jesus, who became for us Wisdom from God, and righteousness and sanctification and redemption, ³¹ in order that, as it is written, "Let she or he who boasts, boast in the Messiah."

Matthew 11:7 As John's disciples went away, Jesus began to speak to the crowds about John: "What did you go out into the wilderness to see? A reed shaken by the wind? ⁸ But what did you go out to see? A person dressed in luxurious robes? Look, those who wear luxurious robes are in royal houses. ⁹ What then did you go out to see? A prophet? Yes, I tell you, and more than a prophet. ¹⁰ He is the one about whom it is written,

> *'Look, I am sending my messenger ahead of you,*
> *who will prepare your way before you.'*

¹¹ Truly I tell you, no one has arisen among those born of women greater than John the Baptizer; yet the least in the realm of the heavens is greater than he. ¹² From the days of John the Baptizer until now the realm of the heavens endures violence, and the violent seize it. ¹³ For all the prophets and the law prophesied until John came; ¹⁴ and if you are willing to receive it, he is Elijah who is to come. ¹⁵ Let those with ears hear!

¹⁶ "Now to what shall I liken this generation? It is like girls and boys sitting in the marketplaces and calling to one another saying,

> ¹⁷ *'We played the flute for you, and you did not dance;*
> *we sang a lament, and you did not mourn.'*

¹⁸ For John came neither eating nor drinking, and they say, 'He has a demon'; ¹⁹ the Son of Woman came eating and drinking, and they say, 'Look, a glutton and a drunk, a friend of tax collectors and sinners!' Yet Wisdom is vindicated by her deeds."

PROCLAMATION

Text Notes

In Proverbs 4 (and throughout the book, deuterocanonical writings, and rabbinic interpretation), Wisdom occurs as both a desired human characteristic that facilitates knowledge of God and as a distinct eminence. In both cases, the requisite grammar is feminine, demonstrated by the feminine pronouns in verses 6, 8–9 in the KJV, NRSV, and CEB translations.

I have rendered Proverbs 4:4 in the passive voice to illuminate the pronoun.

In Psalm 111:3, I replaced the nouns "honor and majesty" with "splendor and majesty" for smoother English grammar, following JPS in part. God's *tzedakah* primarily means "righteousness" but also has the sense of "beneficence," including generosity to the poor, as in JPS. In verse 4, God's love is articulated with *racham,* which has the womb, *rechem,* as its grammatical root, informing the choice of MOTHER OF ALL as the divine name. The "meat" God provides is literally "prey"; God is apparently quite the huntress. In verses 5 and 10, the verb *y-r-'* is translated "revere," well within the semantic range and preferable to "fear."

In 1 Corinthians 1:25, Paul uses *anthroupou,* "human," to emphasize the limitations of mortal human wisdom and strength; verses 26 and 29 use *sarx,* "flesh," in the same manner. In each case, "mortal" conveys the sense. In verse 31, he refers to, but does not directly quote, Jeremiah 9:24: "Let those who boast, boast in this, that they understand and know me, that I am the HOLY ONE."

In Matthew 11:8, John's robe is described with a word that can mean "soft," "fancy," or with regard to men, one who sexually penetrated. (I avoid "homosexual" contra to the dominant Greek lexicon, BDAG; that is a contemporary understanding of sexual orientation not applicable to the ancient world.) Verse 10 quotes Malachi 3:1; the word "messenger" here is *aggelos,* otherwise translated as "angel," though "messenger" is its primary meaning and covers both human and divine messengers. In verse 19, Wisdom is vindicated or justified by her deeds; in other manuscripts, she is justified by her children (hence "children" here in the Vulgate, KJV, and early English translations); the reading "children" endures in Luke 7:35.

Preaching Prompts

This week's readings focus on Wisdom, regularly personified in the Hebrew and Greek Scriptures (e.g., Proverbs 7 and its midrash in Wisdom), and variably understood as an expression or extension of God—or even as a separate entity and cocreator (Prov. 3:19), in a sense very much like the Trinity. Jesus will come to be identified as both the male Word (*logos*) and the feminine Wisdom (*chokmah/sophia*).

Proverbs 4 represents the Hebrew wisdom tradition in which wisdom as a characteristic is taught by both parents in the household and is not, as in the Greek tradition, an exclusively male scholarly pursuit. This passage provides an opportunity to celebrate folk wisdom and motherwit, the lessons passed on by elders, grandmothers, and aunties. The psalm offers the traditional path to Wisdom, awe, or fear of the living God. The Epistle contrasts human and divine wisdom and culminates with a proclamation that Jesus has become Wisdom for us. The dual nature of Christ, Wisdom, and Word is gender fluid and available to be read as nonbinary queer. As Jesus reflects on John as the greatest among those women born, the proof in which he grounds his discourse is his vindication by Wisdom. Reading the Gospel in conversation with the Hebrew Bible, John the baptizer is raised in the way of wisdom at home by mother and father, Elizabeth and Zachariah, and Jesus is himself the Wisdom of God but also a child of Wisdom. Wisdom in Matthew 11:19 is both God language and a nod to the mother of Jesus, Mary of Nazareth.

PROPER 3 (CLOSEST TO MAY 25)

2 Kings 4:1–7; Psalm 94:1–15; James 2:5-13; Matthew 5:21-26

2 Kings 4:1 Now the woman of a member of the company of prophets cried to Elisha, "Your servant my husband is dead and you know that your servant revered the HOLY ONE, even so, a creditor has come to take my two children as slaves." ² So Elisha said to her, "What shall I do for you? Tell me, what have you in the house?" And she answered, "Your slave-woman has nothing at all in the house, except a jar of oil." ³ Then he said to her, "Go ask from outside, vessels from all your neighbors, empty vessels and not a few. ⁴ Then go in and shut the door behind you and your children and pour into all these vessels and when full, you shall put each aside." ⁵ Thus she departed from him and shut the door behind her and her children; they continued bringing vessels to her and she continued pouring. ⁶ And it happened as the vessels were filled she said to her child, "Bring me another vessel." And her child said to her, "There is no other vessel." And the oil ceased. ⁷ Then she came and told it to the man of God, and he said, "Go, sell the oil and pay your debts and you and your children can live on the remainder."

Psalm 94:1–15

¹ God of vengeance, DREAD GOD,
  God of vengeance, shine forth!
² Rise up, Judge of the earth;
  repay recompense on the proud!
³ How long shall the wicked, JUST ONE,
  how long shall the wicked exult?
⁴ They gush, they speak arrogance;
  all the workers of iniquity boast.
⁵ Your people, they crush, FAITHFUL ONE,
  and your heritage, they abuse.
⁶ Widow and immigrant they slay,
  and orphans they murder.
⁷ And they say, "The HOLY ONE, she does not see,
  the God of Rebekah's line does not understand."
⁸ Understand, you ignorant among the people;
  fools, when will you become wise?
⁹ The one who planted the ear, does she not hear?
  The one who formed the eye, does she not see?
¹⁰ The one who disciplines the nations,
  the one who teaches knowledge to the woman-born,
  does she not chastise?
¹¹ The ALL-KNOWING GOD knows the thoughts of the woman-born,
  that they are but breath.

12 Blessed is the one who you admonish, Just One,
    whom you instruct from your teaching,
13 To grant them respite from evil days,
    until a pit is dug for the wicked.
14 For the Faithful One will not forsake her people;
    her heritage she will not abandon.
15 For to the righteous justice will return,
    and after it go all the upright in heart.

James 2:5 Listen, my beloved sisters and brothers [or friends and kin]. Has not God chosen the poor in the world to be rich in faith and to be heirs of the majesty promised to those who love God? [6] But you all have dishonored the poor. Is it not the rich who oppress you? Is it not they who drag you all into court? [7] Is it not they who blaspheme the worthy name that was invoked over you? [8] You all will do well if you actually fulfill the majestic law according to the scripture, *"You shall love your neighbor as yourself."* [9] But if you show favoritism, you commit sin and are convicted by the law as transgressors. [10] For whoever keeps the whole law but fails in one point becomes accountable the whole. [11] For the one who said, *"You shall not commit adultery,"* also said, *"You shall not murder."* Now if you do not commit adultery but if you murder, you have become a transgressor of the law. [12] So speak and so act as those who are to be judged by the law of liberty. [13] For judgment will be merciless to anyone who has shown no mercy; mercy shouts victory over judgment.

Matthew 5:21 Jesus said, "You have heard that it was said to those of old, '*You shall not murder,*' and 'whoever murders shall be subject to judgment.' [22] But I say to you all that if you are angry with a sister or brother, you will be liable to judgment, and if you call a sister or brother an idiot, you will be subject to the council; and if you say, 'You fool,' you will be subject to the hell of fire. [23] Therefore, if you are offering your gift at the altar and you remember that your sister or brother has something against you, [24] leave your gift there before the altar and go; first be reconciled to your sister or brother, and then come and offer your gift. [25] Come to favorable terms quickly with your accuser while you are on the way with them or your accuser may hand you over to the judge, and the judge to the court officer, and you will be thrown into prison. [26] Truly I tell you, you will never get out until you have paid the last penny.

PROCLAMATION

Text Notes

In 2 Kings 4:1, the woman may be a prophet herself. The most literal translation of the verse is *A woman from the women of the community of prophets.* She is certainly a wife, and since there are women prophets and this community of prophets includes wives and mothers, there is no reason that there could not be women prophets among them.

In verse 6 of the psalm, *anah*—"abuse"—includes "oppression," "humiliation," and physical and sexual violence; in the same verse, "orphan" is a fatherless child, hence the frequent pairing of "widow" and "orphan." "Yah," a short form of the divine Name, occurs in verse 7. Though traditionally taking masculine verbs, its grammatical form is feminine, and in some feminist and egalitarian Jewish contexts is used with feminine verbs in prayer and liturgy. Also in verse 7, "the God of Rebekah's line" is "the God of Jacob." In verse 11, *chevel* can mean "breath" or "futility."

James 2 quotes Leviticus 19:18 in verse 8 and the Decalogue in verse 11 (Exod. 20:13–14/Deut. 5:17–18). In verse 13, *katakauchatai* represents more than the "triumph" of the NRSV; it is the shout of a victorious gladiator (BDAG).

The second quote in verse 21 about being liable to judgment is extra-biblical. In some sense, Jesus is extending the understanding of insulting a rabbinic teacher as being criminal to the whole (see Talmud *b. Ber.* 19a and *b. B. Metz.* 58b). The Aramaic word *raka* in Matthew 5:22 means "empty-headed." "Gehenna/Hell of fire" acknowledges that the Gehenna they could all see, the Geh Hinnom Valley just south of Jerusalem, was not literally hell.

Preaching Prompts

These lessons present an opportunity to discuss the way legal and financial systems disproportionately affect women and children, and the poor who are often in the same category. In the world of the text, as in the world that reads the text, financial extremists could lead to legal difficulties. Debt, and thus poverty, was often criminalized. There are opportunities here to discuss medical and student debt and their impact on the ability to secure housing contemporarily.

In the first lesson, unlike other widows in the scriptures, this woman remains with the community in which she lived with her husband when he was alive. She has people. Elisha not only pays off her debt but leaves her so financially secure that she will not need to marry again. He understands that debt relief by itself is not enough to secure the physical and social stability of the vulnerable.

In the psalm, God is the just one whose judgments are trustworthy and held in opposition to the often corrupt judgments of human justice and legal systems. God is the final recourse of the desperate and disenfranchised.

The reading from the Epistle of James begins with God's "preferential option for the poor," a concept originated in South American liberation theology that became a mainstay of mujerista, femiminista, and other liberationist theologies. James, presumptively the brother of Jesus, also addresses the enduring bias of legal systems toward the wealthy. James equates such favoritism with the transgressions often considered to be more serious (i.e., murder and adultery) corresponding with the teaching of Jesus in Matthew 5.

In the Gospel, Jesus compares insulting friends and kin to committing murder, similar to James 2. The intent of his rhetoric and that of James is to communicate the seriousness of practices people may not consider transgressions to folks who see themselves as without sin because they are not murderers and adulterous. Their respective communities understood this, and there was no attempt to establish criminal or lethal consequences for any of this conduct. A secondary point is the beloved community should do all in its ability to avoid entanglements with the easily corruptible justice system.

PROPER 4 (CLOSEST TO JUNE 1)

Isaiah 51:1–6; Psalm 92:1–5, 12–15; 1 Corinthians 3:1–9; Mark 4:30–34

Isaiah 51:1 Listen to me, all you that pursue righteousness,
>
> all you that seek the AUTHOR OF LIFE.
> Look to the rock from which you were hewn,
> and to the quarry from which you were dug.

2 Look to Abraham your father,
>
> and to Sarah who writhed-in-labor for you all;
> he was just one when I called him,
> but I blessed him and made him many.

3 For the GOD WHO SAVES has comforted Zion;
>
> she has comforted all her waste places.
> And she shall make her wilderness like Eden,
> her desert like the garden of the CREATOR OF ALL;
> joy and gladness will be found in her,
> thanksgiving and the sound of song.
> [Sorrow and mourning will flee away.]

4 Listen to me, my people,
>
> and my nation, to me give heed;
> for a teaching shall from me go forth,
> and my justice for a light to the peoples.
> I will do so suddenly.

5 My deliverance is near,
>
> my salvation has gone forth
> and my arms will govern the peoples;
> for me the coastlands wait,
> and upon my arm they await.

6 Lift up your eyes to the heavens,
>
> and look to the earth below.

For the heavens like smoke will vanish,
the earth like a garment will wear out,
and those who live on it will die like gnats;
yet my salvation will be forever,
and my deliverance will never be broken.

Psalm 92:1–5, 12–15

1 It is good to give thanks to the AGELESS GOD,
to sing praises to your name Most High;
2 to declare your faithful love in the morning,
and your trustworthiness by night,
3 upon the ten strings and the harp,
upon the murmurings of the lyre.
4 For you have made me glad,
WELLSPRING OF LIFE, by your work;
at the works of your hands I sing for joy.
5 How great are your works, WOMB OF CREATION!
Your designs are so very profound.
12 A righteous woman or man flourishes like a palm tree,
and grows like a cedar in Lebanon.
13 They are planted in the house of SHE WHO IS HOLY;
in the courts of our God, they flourish.
14 Still producing fruit in their elder years;
fat with sap and ever green.
15 They declare that the MIGHTY GOD is upright;
she is my rock, and there is no unrighteousness in her.

1 Corinthians 3:1 Now sisters and brothers [or friends and kin], I could not speak to you all as spiritual, but rather as carnal, as infants in Christ. 2 I fed you all with milk, not solid food, for you were not yet ready for solid food. Even now you are still not ready, 3 for you all are still carnal. Given there is still jealousy and discord among you, are you not carnal, and going around as merely human? 4 For when one says, "I am Paul's," and another, "I am Apollos," are you not merely human?

5 What then is Apollos? What is Paul? Ministers through whom you came to believe, as the Messiah granted to each person. 6 I planted, Apollos watered, but God produces growth. 7 Therefore neither the one who plants nor the one who waters is anything, rather it is God who produces growth. 8 The one who plants and the one who waters are alike, and each will receive wages according to their labor. 9 For we are God's coworkers, working together; you are God's cultivation, God's construction.

Mark 4:30 Jesus also said [to the women and men around him], "With what can we represent the realm of God, or in what parable shall we put it? 31 It is like a mustard seed, which, when sown upon the earth, is smaller than all the other seeds on earth. [32] Yet when it is sown it grows up and becomes bigger than all other shrubs, and produces large branches, so that the birds of the heavens can nest in its shade." [33] Now with many such parables he spoke the word to them, as they were able to hear. [34] And Jesus did not speak to them except in parables; however, privately, he explained everything to his disciples.

PROCLAMATION

Text Notes

Sarah's labor in Isaiah 51:2 is described with a verb that means "writhe" and "twist" in birthing, and in some cases, dancing, as in Psalm 150:4. In verse 3, God has already begun to comfort Zion (see JPS); the future tense translation of NRSV and KJV neglect the immediate nature of God's response. The tense changes in the third verse, emphasizing the ongoing work of God (JPS keeps the passage in the past tense). The last line of verse 3 comes from the Great Isaiah Scroll of the Dead Sea collection, 1QIsaᵃ; the reader may choose to omit it. While some unnecessarily move the last verb constituting the final line of verse 4 to verse 5 (NRSV, CEB, Alter), it is entirely comprehensible in its place.

I use "murmuring" in Psalm 92:3 to render *higgion*; the wider semantic range includes melodic speech, song, the sound of instruments, murmuring and, left untranslated (see Ps. 9:16 [v 17 in Heb.]; 19:14; 92:3; Lam. 3:62). "Elder years" in verse 14 is *sevah*, "gray hair."

The "they" and "them" of the Gospel reading is either the disciples, a larger, gender-inclusive group that surrounded Jesus, or the twelve male apostles. In Mark 4:10, there are "the people around Jesus" and the twelve. There is no clarifying intervening language. I have chosen the more inclusive option, "women and men," representing the inner circle, including but not limited to the twelve.

Preaching Prompts

The garden is an enduring metaphor in the biblical world in which food could be scarce because of the scarcity of arable land and paucity of sufficient water needed to ensure food production. Thus, paradise looks like a garden full of fruit-producing trees riven with healing waters. Portraits of God as Creator, Planter, and Sustainer (not intentionally Trinitarian language here) bear witness to the power of God to create life and life-sustaining resources, a cultivatable earth and the harvest of her foodstuffs and sea and sky full of potentially edible fish and birds.

Each lesson draws on the ancient agricultural metaphor. There is a reenactment of creation in Isaiah 51 in which the wilderness becomes a life-sustaining garden. In the psalm and Epistle, human beings are the planting of God. In the Gospel, the reign and realm of God are also the planting of God started with the smallest of seeds, the mustard seed.

Note that the theology in 1 Corinthians 3:3–4 unhelpfully pits the flesh against the spirit, identifying humanity with the flesh as carnal. This seems very much at odds with the Incarnation. The spirit/flesh dichotomy is fueled by Greek philosophy and will become a gendered hierarchy for some church fathers, with women being identified with the flesh.

Among the ministers who could have been referenced in 1 Corinthians 3:5–6 is the long list of women who served with Paul enumerated in Romans 16, more particularly Priscilla (Prisca), who is named before her husband, signifying leadership, and who corrected Apollos's theology, see Acts 18:18, 26. Verse 9 uses the same language of coworker to describe the relationship between these ministers and God that Paul uses in Romans 16:3 for his female colaborers and elsewhere for men like Timothy.

When read together, these lessons illustrate the majesty of God as a place of abundance and fecundity, a space where none will hunger, a banquet of luscious and succulent fruit and the life-saving water, and God is gardener and keeper of our souls and this good earth, her good creation.

PROPER 5 (CLOSEST TO JUNE 8)

1 Samuel 28:5–17; Psalm 95:1–7; 1 John 4:1 –6; Mark 5:1–20

1 Samuel 28:5 Now Saul saw the army of the Philistines and he was frightened and his heart trembled greatly. [6] When Saul [whose name means asked and answered] asked of the HOLY ONE OF OLD, the INSCRUTABLE GOD did not answer him through dreams, or even through Urim, and not even through prophets, women or men. [7] So Saul said to his slaves, "Seek for me a woman who is a ghost-master, so that I may go to her and inquire through her." His slaves said to him, "Look! There is a woman who is a ghost-master at En-Dor."

[8] So Saul disguised himself and put on other clothes and he went there along with two men and they came to the woman by night. Then he said, "Please, divine for me through a ghost and bring up for me who I say to you." [9] The woman said to him, "You—you must know what Saul has done, how he has cut off the ghost-workers and the necromancers from the land. So why are you setting a snare for my life to kill me?" [10] And Saul swore to her by the FAITHFUL ONE, "As the EVER-LIVING GOD lives, no [charge of] iniquity shall befall you for this thing." [11] Then the woman said, "Who shall I bring up for you?" And he said, "Bring up Samuel for me." [12] And the woman saw Samuel and she cried out with a loud voice and the woman spoke to Saul, saying, "Why have you deceived me? You are Saul!" [13] The king said to her, "Fear not. What do you see?" And the woman said to Saul, "I see divine beings coming up out of the ground." [14] Then he said to her, "What is his appearance?" And

she said, "An old man is coming up and he is wrapped in a robe." So Saul knew that it was Samuel and he bowed with his face to the ground and gave him homage.

¹⁵ Then Samuel said to Saul, "Why have you disturbed me to the point of bringing me up?" And Saul answered, "I am greatly troubled, for the Philistines are attacking me and God has turned away from me and does not answer me at all, through female or male prophets or even through dreams and so I have called you to tell me what I should do."

¹⁶ Then Samuel said, "So why do you ask me, since the HOLY ONE OF OLD has turned from you and become your enemy? ¹⁷ Thus the HOLY ONE has done to you just as God spoke through me, so the JUDGE OF ALL THE EARTH has torn the monarchy out of your hand, and given it to your neighbor, to David."

Psalm 95:1–7

¹ Come, let us sing joyfully to the ROCK WHO BIRTHED US;
let us shout to the rock of our salvation!
² Let us come into her presence with thanksgiving;
with songs of praise let us shout to her!
³ For the EVER-LIVING GOD is a great God,
and a great Majesty above all gods.
⁴ For in her hand are the depths of the earth;
the heights of the mountains are hers also.
⁵ For hers is the sea, for she made it,
and the dry land, which her hands have crafted.
⁶ Come, let us worship and bow down,
let us kneel before the AGELESS GOD, our Maker!
⁷ For she is our God,
and we are the people of her pasture,
and the sheep of her hand.
If only you would listen to her voice today!

1 John 4:1 Beloved, do not believe every spirit, rather test the spirits to see whether they are from God; for many false prophets, women and men, have gone out into the world. ² By this you all shall know the Spirit of God: every spirit that confesses that in the flesh Jesus the Messiah has come, is from God. ³ And every spirit that does not confess Jesus is not from God. And this is the spirit of the antichrist, of which you have heard that it is coming; and now it is already in the world. ⁴ You are of God little children, and you have conquered them; for greater is the one who is in all of you than the one who is in the world. ⁵ They are of the world; therefore, they speak according to the world, and the world listens to them. ⁶ We are of God. Whoever knows God listens to us and whoever is not of God does not listen to us. From this we know the spirit of truth and the spirit of error.

Mark 5:1 [Now Jesus and the women and men with him] came to the far side of the sea, to the region of the Gerasenes. ² And when he got out of the boat, just then a man out of the tombs with an unclean spirit met him. ³ He lived among the tombs and not even with a chain could anyone bind him. ⁴ For he had often been bound with shackles and chains, but the chains he tore off of him and the shackles he smashed, and no one had the strength to subdue him. ⁵ So the whole of the night and every day he was among the tombs and on the mountains howling and cutting himself with stones. ⁶ Then he saw Jesus from a distance; he ran and bent down before him (on the ground). ⁷ And he shouted with a loud voice, saying, "What have you to do with me, Jesus, Son of the Most High God? I charge you to swear by God, not to torture me." ⁸ For Jesus had said to him, "You unclean spirit, come out of the man!" ⁹ Then Jesus asked him, "What is your name?" He replied, "Legion is my name; for we are many." ¹⁰ He begged Jesus repeatedly that he not send them out of the region. ¹¹ Now there on the hillside a large herd of pigs was feeding. ¹² And they [the unclean spirits] begged Jesus, saying, "Send us into the pigs that we may enter them." ¹³ So he gave them permission, thus the unclean spirits came out and entered the pigs and the herd—about two thousand— rushed down the steep decline into the sea and were drowned in the sea.

¹⁴ Now the pigherders fled and told the news in the city and in the farm country and people came to see what it was that happened. ¹⁵ Women, children, and men came to Jesus and saw the man in whom the demons had been sitting there, clothed and in his right mind, the very man who had had the legion; and they were afraid. ¹⁶ And they explained it, they who had seen what had happened to the man with the demons and to the pigs. ¹⁷ And then they began to beg Jesus to leave their neighborhood. ¹⁸ Then as he was getting into the boat, the man who had been possessed by demons begged Jesus that he might be with him. ¹⁹ And Jesus did not permit him, rather saying to him, "Go to your home, to your [people] and tell them the news of what the Holy One has done for you, and what mercy God has shown you." ²⁰ And he went away and began to proclaim in the Decapolis (the ten cities) how much Jesus had done for him and everyone was amazed.

PROCLAMATION

Text Notes

I have made explicit the pun of Saul's name in 1 Samuel 28:6. "Answer" is not technically part of the name; however, it is implied; asking, answering, and not being answered are the pivots on which this story turns. In keeping with the aims of this project and the demonstrable presence of women prophets throughout the canon, I specify the inclusion of women prophets in the grammatical form, which includes but obscures them in verse 6. The woman's title is comprised of two words, *ba'al*, an alternate form of "lord" that became the familiar name of the Canaanite deity, Ba'al Haddu, and the word for "ghost." The latter word is used for ghosts (Deut. 18:11; Isa. 8:19; 19:3; 29:4), those who commune with them (Lev. 19:31; 20:6), and indeterminate usage (2 Kings 21:6, 23:24; 1 Chron. 10:13; 2 Chron. 33:6). 'Ov, ghost, is used both ways in this passage. She is often presented as a medium in other translations, one who is possessed by ghosts; however, the first part of the description indicates mastery, i.e., she was a ghost master. In verse 9, "ghost" is shorthand for ghost master. The plural verb indicates multiple beings arise from the ground in verse 13. Saul is focused on only one in verse 14, hence its singular grammar. The word for Samuel's robe is the same as the one used for the robes his mother, Hannah made for him when he was a little boy in the care of Eli (1 Sam. 2:19; 15:27).

The language for God in Psalm 95:1 comes from Deuteronomy 32:18, where God is: "The Rock who gave birth to you . . . the God who gave you birth."

Throughout Mark, Jesus travels with a group often reduced to "they." The group includes the first twelve disciples at a minimum and likely a secondary group often described as being with or around Jesus, as in Mark 4:10. There is no reason to exclude female followers from the secondary group. In verse 7, *horkizo* means to "beg," "compel," or "make swear," usually by a deity. I have chosen the strongest reading given the events. In verse 15, "women, children, and men" replaces "they" because everyone would have come to see if this extraordinary claim was true. Jesus tells the man to go home to "yours." It is similar to the contemporary expression "me and mine."

Preaching Prompts

At first glance, one might think these readings would be better placed on the Sunday closest to All Hallows Eve, which has come to be called the Vigil of All Saints. Though they deal with otherworldly beings, these lessons are not horror stories. They are an opportunity to think about the world we know, surrounded by and permeated with worlds we may not know (or believe in). Whether one believes in ghosts or spirits or communing with ancestors or not, there are people who do now, just as peoples in the world of the scriptures also believed. Just as then, there are folks who speak to and hear from the holy dead, saints, and ancestors. Many of those practices occur among African, Afro-Caribbean, Asian, and other indigenous peoples, and were virulently persecuted by white missionaries, and are still frowned upon by parts of the western Church. Yet the communion of the saints is a foundational tenant of the church, and praying to (or through for those for whom that language matters) the saints has been acceptable even when other indigenous practices are not. As in the first lesson, people seek answers and spiritual comfort from a much broader spiritual palette than the church.

The psalm acknowledges belief in a multitude of gods with the sovereignty of One overall. This is not monotheism; it is henotheism. There is, of course, a broad monotheistic tradition in the Hebrew Scriptures; it is simply not the only tradition. Vanity has not always lived well with our religious neighbors. One of the gifts of henotheism is that it permits devotion to one's God without denying the existence of someone else's. (It does not require subjugating the deities of other religious traditions to one's own.)

The author of 1 John offers a strategy for dealing with the spiritual plurality in their world, using Jesus as the measuring stick for validation. While that can be useful in addressing some conflicts within the church, it can very easily be used to label any nondominant cultural or spiritual practice as "the spirit of the antichrist." As central as Jesus is, the full revelation of God extends beyond his holy person and holy example as he himself taught.

The Legion story exists in a world where there are angels, demons, God, and Satan. The Jewish literary tradition beginning within the canon of scripture has transformed the gods of other nations into divine beings, sometimes into angels. Though rarely mentioned in the Hebrew Bible (see Deut. 32:17; Ps. 106: 37), stories about demons multiply in the post-Hebrew Bible world and continue into, through, and beyond the early rabbinic period. The story is often read as a way of talking about what we now understand to be mental illness or atypical neurological functioning. In conversation with the other readings, this passage offers an opportunity to talk about what we believe about the spirit/ual world and what beliefs and practices are resident in our communities. One may often also address the way diverse and divergent practices and practitioners are labeled, particularly women.

PROPER 6 (CLOSEST TO JUNE 15)

Numbers 11:4–15; Psalm 147:7–14; 1 Timothy 6:6–16; Mark 6:30–44

Numbers 11:4 The rabble among them craved a craving, and the women and men of Israel also wept again, and they said, "Who will give us meat? [5] We remember the fish we ate in Egypt for nothing, the cucumbers, the melons, the leeks, the onions, and the garlic. [6] And now our souls are parched, and there is nothing at all but this manna before our eyes."

[7] Now the manna was like coriander seed, and it was dark and gummy like plant resin. [8] The people—women, children, and men—went around and gleaned it; they ground it in a mill or beat it in a mortar, and they boiled it in a pot and made cakes of it. The taste of it was like the taste of cakes with oil. [9] While the dew was falling on the camp at night, the manna fell upon it.

[10] Moses heard the people weeping, each clan apart, each person at the entrance of their tents. Then the HOLY ONE's rage burned extremely hot, and it was wrong in the sight of Moses. [11] So Moses said to the HOLY ONE, "Why have you done your servant wrong? And why have I not found favor in your sight, that you put the burden of this whole people on me? [12] Was it I, did I conceive this whole people? Did I give birth to them myself that you said to me, 'Carry them in your bosom, like a nurse carries a nursing child,' to the land that

you promised on oath to their ancestors? [13] From where am I to get meat to give to this whole people when they weep on me and say, 'Give us meat to eat!'? [14] I am not able to carry this whole people by myself, for it is too heavy for me. [15] [Mother God] If this is what you are going to do to me, kill me now—if I have found favor in your sight—and let me not see my wrongdoing."

Psalm 147:7–14

[7] Sing to the GLORIOUS ONE with thanksgiving;
   make melody to our God on the lyre.
[8] She covers the heavens with clouds,
   she provides rain for the earth,
   she makes grass grow on the hills.
[9] She gives to the animals their food,
   and to the raven chicks when they cry.
[10] Not in the strength of the horse is her delight,
   nor is her pleasure in human thighs.
[11] The HOLY ONE OF OLD takes pleasure in those who revere her,
   in those who hope in her faithful love.
[12] Praise the EVER-LIVING GOD, O Jerusalem!
   Praise your God, O Zion!
[13] For she strengthens the bars of your gates;
   she blesses your children within you.
[14] She sets peace at your border;
   she satisfies you with the finest of wheat.

1 Timothy 6:6 Of course, there is great gain in godliness with contentment. [7] For nothing did we bring into the world, so there is nothing we can take out of it. [8] But if we have food and clothing, with these we will be content. [9] Now those who want to be rich fall into temptation and a trap. And many foolish and harmful passions plunge women and men into ruin and destruction. [10] For the root of all evil is the love of money, and some desiring [it] have wandered away from the faith and pierced themselves with many pains.

[11] But as for you, child of God, shun all this; pursue righteousness, godliness, faith, love, endurance, gentleness. [12] Fight the good fight of the faith; take hold of the eternal life, to which you were called and to which you professed the good profession in the presence of many witnesses. [13] I charge you in the presence of God, who enlivens all things, and of Christ Jesus, who in his testimony before Pontius Pilate made the good profession, [14] to keep the commandment without spot or blame until the appearing of our Redeemer Jesus Christ, [15] who God will reveal in God's own time—God who is the blessed and only Sovereign, the Power beyond all powers and Majesty of majesties. [16] It is God alone who has immortality and dwells in light unapproachable, whom no human has seen or can see; to God be honor and everlasting might. Amen.

Mark 6:30 [One day] the apostles gathered near Jesus and told him all that they had done and taught. [31] And Jesus said to them, "Come on! Let's get away, just ourselves, to a desert place so you all can be refreshed for a while." For many women, men and children were coming and going and they had no leisure even to eat. [32] So they went by boat to a deserted place by themselves. [33] Now many women and men saw them going and recognized them and by foot they ran there together from all the towns before them. [34] And Jesus came seeing a numerous crowd; so he had compassion for them, because they were *like sheep without a shepherd*; and he began to teach them many things. [35] And when many hours passed his disciples came to him and said, "This is a desert place and many hours have passed. [36] You send them away so that they may go into the surrounding countryside and villages and buy themselves something to eat." [37] But he answered them, "You all give them something to eat." And they said to him, "Are we to go and buy two hundred denarii [more than half a year's pay] worth of bread, and give it to them to eat?" [38] Then Jesus said to them, "How many loaves do you have? Go and see." And they had learned it and said, "Five, and two fish." [39] Then Jesus ordered them to sit everyone down in parties on the green grass. [40] And they sat down cluster by cluster in hundreds and in fifties. [41] Then taking the five loaves and the two fish Jesus looked up to the heavens and blessed and broke the loaves and gave them to his disciples to set before everyone, and he divided the two fish among them all. [42] So all ate and were filled. [43] And they took up twelve baskets full of fragments, and of the fish. [44] Now there were five thousand men who had eaten the loaves.

PROCLAMATION

Text Notes

Manna, *man*, means something like "whatsit." In making the women visible in Numbers 11:4, I exclude children from the Israelites who complain, understanding the text holds accountable those who are of an age to be judged for their actions. In verse 7, the "eye," sight, or appearance of the manna is like "bdellium," a dark gummy resin from plants that are burned as incense. The "people" gathered manna in verse 8; all were hungry. "They" prepared and cooked it; that is traditional women's work.

Moses's displeasure is expressed with a word that also means "evil" in verse 10; the verb form follows in verse 11. In verse 15, the text uses the form of the feminine second person pronoun for God; some read it as masculine anyway. I read it as intentionally feminine, corresponding with the maternal portrait of God in the text.

Jerusalem and Zion are both feminine; all of the discourse to them in Psalm 147 is in second person feminine, as one would speak to an individual woman in biblical or modern Hebrew. In verse 10 of the psalm, "human thighs" is a more literal rendering of "the thighs of men" than the "runner" of NRSV and CEB.

In 1 Timothy 6:10, *odynais* can be either "pains" or "sorrows." While the Epistle is purportedly written to Timothy by Paul (it is among the disputed Epistles), it was also written to the ancient church and received as speaking to us. Therefore, I have changed "man of God," specific to Timothy in verse 11, to "child of God," applicable to him and all future readers.

The identity of the "selves" meant by the third person pronoun *autois* in Mark 6:31 is unclear. Some read it as "yourselves" with the earlier pronoun, *humeis*, second person plural, after the exclamation (not a verb), "come on." Since Jesus is going with them, I render it as "ourselves."

The notion of "sheep without a shepherd" is deeply rooted in the literature and cultural context of the Hebrew Scriptures (see Num. 27:17; 1 Kings 22:17; 2 Chron. 18:16; Ps. 49:14; Ezek. 34:8; Zech. 10:2; 11:7; Jth. 11:19). It begins with Moses asking God to appoint a leader and receiving Joshua. It comes to signify the failure of the monarchs of Israel and Judah to be faithful to God and to faithfully tend her flock.

The use of "parties" in verse 39 replicates its literal sense, a group of diners.

Preaching Prompts

Women are woven into this Gospel lesson and weeded out. It is, in some ways, representative of the "search" for women in the scriptures and in the early church. At one level, this is likely a version of the feeding story in Mark 8, perhaps the earlier version, with the language indicating only men were fed, removed from the later version. When read as is:

- women are excluded from the male apostles (plus Jesus) in verses 30–32,
- women are surely present in the local crowd from the villages in verses 33–43, where their presence must be inferred from obscure in terms like "many," "crowd," "groups/parties," and "they/them" and the third person common grammatical forms;
- only men are identified as eating with a gender-specific term in verse 44.

Wrestling with this Gospel reading's use of gender illustrates the wrestling and contortions that many women, nonbinary, and trans folk have to do when reading scripture or praying the liturgies of our churches, leaving folk hungry even when the lessons are about the abundance with which God feeds her flock.

In the Numbers passage, God is the divine mother whose ill-equipped nanny has just quit. Moses asks a series of rhetorical questions to which the answer is you Mother God. These are her children; she conceived and birthed them, then passed them off to a nanny who cannot feed them because he, unlike God, has no breasts. In the psalm, God is more than up to the task of feeding her children, her creation, and her cosmos. In the Epistle, one of Paul's admirers and imitators warns about being too consumed with physical things, including the needs of our physical bodies and contentment with what we have.

There is more than one kind of hunger represented in these texts, yet all of them are the responsibility of the church in its role of shepherding and stewarding the people of God.

PROPER 7 (CLOSEST TO JUNE 22)

1 Kings 19:19–21; Psalm 23; 1 Peter 2:21–25; Mark 8:27–38

1 Kings 19:19 Now Elijah set out from the wilderness and found Elisha son of Shaphat and he was plowing; there were twelve yoke of oxen ahead of him and he was with the twelfth. And Elijah passed by Elisha and threw his mantle over him. ²⁰ And Elisha left the oxen and ran after Elijah, and said, "Let me kiss my mother and my father and then I will follow you." Then Elijah said to him, "Go back, for what have I done to you?" ²¹ And Elisha turned back from following after Elijah and took the yoke of oxen and slaughtered them. Then with the equipment from the oxen Elisha boiled their flesh and gave it to the women, children, and men [around him], and they ate. And then Elisha set out and followed Elijah, and ministered to him.

Psalm 23

¹ She Who Birthed the Earth is my shepherd,
   I shall not want.
² In green pastures she makes me lie down;
   beside still waters she leads me.
³ My soul she restores;
   she leads me in right paths for her Name's sake.
⁴ Yea, even though I walk through Shadow-Valley Death,
   I do not fear evil, for you are with me;
   your rod and your staff, they comfort me.
⁵ You prepare before me a table
   in the presence of my enemies;
   you anoint my head with oil,
   my cup overflows.
⁶ Only goodness and lovingkindness shall follow me
   all the days of my life,
   and I shall dwell in the house of She Who is Faithful
   for days without end.

1 Peter 2:21 For unto this were you all called, because the Messiah also suffered for you, leaving behind an example for you, so that you all would follow in his steps:

²² He committed no sin,

nor was deceit found in his mouth.

²³ He, when reviled, did not revile in turn;

when he suffered, he did not threaten.

But he entrusted himself to the one who judges justly:

²⁴ *He himself bore our sins*

in his body on the tree.

This, so that we, taking no part in sins, might live for righteousness—*by his wounds you have been healed.* ²⁵ For, *you were like sheep going astray,* but now *you have returned* to the shepherd and guardian of your souls.

Mark 8:27 Now Jesus went with his disciples to the villages of Caesarea Philippi and on the way he asked his disciples, "Who do people say that I am?" ²⁸ And they answered, saying, "John the Baptizer and others, Elijah; and still others, one of the prophets." ²⁹ He asked them, "But who do you all say that I am?" Peter answered him, "You are the Messiah." ³⁰ And he warned them so they would tell no one about him. ³¹ Then Jesus began to teach them that the Son of Woman must undergo great suffering, and be rejected by the elders, the chief priests, and the scholars, and be killed, and after three days rise again. ³² And he boldly said this thing. Then Peter took him aside and began to rebuke him. ³³ But turning and looking at his disciples, Jesus rebuked Peter and he said, "Get behind me, Satan!—because the mind is not on that which is God's, rather on that which is mortal."

³⁴ And Jesus called the crowd along with his disciples, and said to those women and men, "If any want to follow after me, let them deny themselves and take up their cross and follow me. ³⁵ For the one who wants to save their life will lose it, and the one who loses their life for my sake, and for the sake of the gospel, will save it. ³⁶ For what will it profit a person to gain the whole world and lose their life? ³⁷ What then can a human being give in return for their life? ³⁸ Indeed, the one who is ashamed of me and of my words in this unfaithful and sinful generation, the Son of Woman will also be ashamed of that one when he comes in the glory of his Father with the holy angels."

PROCLAMATION

Text Notes

In 1 Kings 19:21, Elisha feeds "the people." I have expanded them to make visible the women and children who would have been included.

"Shadow" and "valley" are a single compound word in Psalm 23:4. The concluding phrase of verse 6 is "a length of days."

The Petrine author strings together bits of scripture into their own poetic composition. Verse 22 includes a misremembered or intentionally paraphrased line from Isaiah 53:9. The first line of verse 22 corresponds neither to the MT, which has that he committed no "violence," nor to the LXX, which has he committed no "lawlessness." The second phrase accurately represents a phrase from Isaiah 53:9 (italics signify quotations from the Hebrew Bible). 1 Peter 2:24 includes a shortened form of Isaiah 53:5. Verse 25 includes a quote from Isaiah 53:6. In 1 Peter 2:24, Jesus dies on a "tree" rather than the cross, as in NRSV and CEB.

In Mark 8:32, *logos* can be either "this thing" or "this word." In verse 33, when Jesus rebukes Satan, he does not tell Peter that *his* mind is on the wrong thing. Rather, Jesus makes a general statement without pronouns specific to Peter or any other character or entity; the statement applies to all without regard to number or gender. In verse 34, Jesus addresses the crowd and speaks to "them," expanded to make visible women and children. Son of Woman represents historical and theological claims about the maternity of Jesus and the broad inclusivity of the underlying Greek expression rooted in the word for anthropology, *huios tou anthropou*, representing all human persons. It could easily be translated "Mortal One," "Child of Earth," or "the Human One."

Preaching Prompts

Each of these lessons portrays what it is to follow a calling, to follow God, and be followed in turn by God's goodness. In the first lesson, Elijah calls Elisha to follow him, to apprentice with him, and to succeed him abruptly, without preparation. Elijah wants not to set his affairs in order, but to simply kiss his parents goodbye. Elijah leaves him in the middle of his plowing, standing in the field. Elijah's own calling was urgent, and he could not wait for Elijah to figure this out. Eventually, Elisha leaves to pursue and accept his calling. There is a deep resonance between the story of Elijah and Elisha and John and Jesus. The scene in Luke 9:58–62 where Jesus calls a person to follow him who asked to bury his mother and father first and to whom Jesus says, "No one who puts a hand to the plow and looks back is fit for the majesty of God," may draw on this passage. The notion of paired prophets and sages, one of whom succeeds the other, is a staple in rabbinic literature.

In the beloved Twenty-Third Psalm, the psalmist, in the literary guise of a sheep, follows God in her own way as a sheep follows her shepherd and, in return, is followed by the goodness and loving kindness of God. Ironically, the sheep metaphor comes to an unpleasant end as the function of sheep in the temple was to be sacrificed.

The larger narrative of the Gospel has gotten to the point where it is difficult to follow Jesus. Death is at hand. Making a commitment to follow Jesus means risking one's life. This conversation in Mark 9 takes place between Jesus and his disciples, not just his apostles. Discipleship and the commitment to follow Jesus even to the point of death were not limited to his male apostles.

PROPER 8 (CLOSEST TO JUNE 29)

Genesis 2:4b–7; Psalm 139:1, 7–14; Ephesians 1:3–10; Mark 9:33–37, 42

Genesis 2:4b In the day that the AGELESS ONE, God, made the earth and the heavens: ⁵ Before any plant of the field was in the earth and before any herb of the field had sprung up—for the AUTHOR OF LIFE, God, had not caused it to rain upon the earth, and there was no human to till the humus—⁶ Yet a stream rose from the earth and watered the entire surface of the humus. ⁷ Then the MAKER OF ALL, God, crafted the human from the dust of the humus and breathed into its nostrils the breath of life and the human became a living being.

Psalm 139:1, 7–14

¹ SOURCE OF LIFE, you have searched me and known me.
⁷ Where can I go from your spirit?
Or where from your presence can I flee?
⁸ If I ascend to the heavens, there you are;
if I recline in Sheol, see, it is you!
⁹ If I take up dawn's wings
if I settle at the farthest reaches of the sea,
¹⁰ even there your hand shall lead me,
and your right hand shall hold me fast.
¹¹ If I say, "Surely darkness shall cover me,
and night will become light behind me,"
¹² even darkness is not dark to you;
night is as daylight,
for dark is the same as light.
¹³ For it was you who crafted my inward parts;
you wove me together in my mother's womb.
¹⁴ I praise you, for I am awesomely and marvelously made.
Wonderous are your works;
that my soul knows full well.

Ephesians 1:3 Blessed be the God and Abba of our Redeemer Jesus the Messiah, who has blessed us with every spiritual blessing in the heavens in the Messiah. ⁴ Just as in choosing us in the Messiah before the foundation of the world to be holy and blameless before God in love, ⁵ God destined us for adoption as their children through Jesus Christ, according to the good pleasure of God's will, ⁶ to the praise of God's glorious grace freely bestowed on us in the Beloved. ⁷ In Christ we have redemption through his blood, the forgiveness of our trespasses, according to the riches of God's grace. ⁸ Grace which God has abundantly poured upon us along with all wisdom and understanding. ⁹ God has made known to us the mystery of God's will according to God's good pleasure that God set forth in Christ. ¹⁰ A plan in the fullness of time to gather up all things in Christ, things in the heavens and things on earth, all into Christ.

Mark 9:33 Now they [the disciples of Jesus] came to Capernaum. And when he was in the house he asked them, "What were you all arguing about on the way?" [34] But they were silent, for they had argued with one another on the way who was the greatest. [35] So Jesus sat down, called the twelve, and said to them, "Whoever wants to be first must be last of all and servant of all." [36] Then Jesus took a little child and put them among the disciples, and taking them in his arms, Jesus spoke to the disciples: [37] "Whoever welcomes one such child in my name welcomes me, and whoever welcomes me welcomes not me but the One who sent me."

[42] [Later Jesus said] "If any one puts a stumbling block before one of these little ones who believes in me, it would be better if a great millstone were hung around their neck and they were thrown into the sea."

PROCLAMATION

Text Notes

God's creation of the human in Genesis 2:7 uses a verb for crafting pottery. "The human," *ha'adam*, is a specific distinct creation; later, *adam*—without the definite article—will refer to humanity as a whole and serve as the name of the first male human. The earth from which this first earthling was crafted is *ha'adamah*. Earth, *adamah*, and *adam*, humanity (or person), share the same root. We are earth-crafted earthlings, humus-sourced humans. To preserve the wordplay, I have used human/humus (earthling/earth works as well): humus, pronounced "HUE-muss," is dark, richly fertile, life-giving soil, thus, the matrix of human creation (hummus is something else). I use the pronoun "it," lacking in Hebrew, for the first human that has within it what will be called woman, *isshah*, and man, *ish*.

In Psalm 139:14, "marvelous" and "wondrous" are the same word. I alternate them for alliteration to give a sense of the poetry.

Throughout the Ephesians reading, I have endeavored to sort out the masculine singular pronouns with regard to their antecedents, God or Jesus, and here, the Messiah. In verse 5, I use the nonbinary pronoun "their" for God, pointing to the complex portrait of divinity here that may gesture toward an articulation of one of the principles of the trinity, preexistence expressions of God. In keeping with the commitments of this volume, the most expansive language possible is used when and where possible for the Divine.

Paide (child) is neuter and, therefore, nonbinary in Greek. Other translations use "it." I want to preserve the nonbinary language in the Gospel reading because there are so few places where it occurs naturally.

Preaching Prompts

These lessons allow us to reflect on the human creation as fully beloved by God while acknowledging the ways in which human gender transcends binary understanding in a month when many will participate in or host Pride celebrations. In the first reading, the first human is "gender-full" and pluripotent, containing within itself the full plurality of human gender crafted by the divine hand. Though the binary nature of the Hebrew language limits those genders to two (they begin to expand toward the eight or more genders identified in rabbinic literature with the construction of social roles and parameters for eunuchs), when read as a merism, female and male represent the poles on a gender continuum with all genders contained within them and represented by them. It is important to note the Hebrew Bible does not acknowledge gender diversity apart from these two large categories into which its writers literarily construct all of humanity, even when aware of the visual diversity of human bodies and genitalia that have always been present.

The psalmist contemplates their creation as an act of weaving; a craft performed nearly exclusively by women. (Similarly, the verb "to craft" in the Genesis reading is also used for crafting pottery, predominantly a women's activity). When read with the first lesson, the psalmist in the fullness of their gender is handcrafted by God in the holy darkness of the womb in which light and dark are not antitheses.

The "all-ness" of the Epistle is a testimony to the fulsomeness of God's inclusive redeeming love expressed in and through Christ Jesus.

Subverting traditional understandings of hierarchy, Jesus places a child (grammatically gender neutral) before his embarrassed apostles. While the discussion about the greatest included disciples (without gender-based exclusion) and apostles, it was the male apostles Jesus determined needed ego-checking instruction. This nonbinary child (in the grammar of the text) and those like them are the ones the apostles and disciples are called to serve if they would be "great." More than that, using strong rhetoric, Jesus declares that harm to one of these "little ones" will be met with severe penalties. He decrees not just a death sentence but a torturous death.

In our world, the world that reads and hears the text, this nonbinary child represents nonbinary children and adults, gender-atypical children and adults, trans children and adults, and anyone who does not fit easily into the dominant constructed genders. In each instance, the person is an intentional, beloved act of creation. As for the penalty for harming such a person, such a child, in our world, it is useful to read the text not as a prescription, but as a warning severe enough to never be tested.

PROPER 9 (CLOSEST TO JULY 6)

1 Samuel 8:1, 4–18; Psalm 72:1–4, 12–14, 18–19;
1 Timothy 2:1–6; John 6:14–20

1 Samuel 8:1 Now it was that when Samuel was old that he made his sons judges over Israel.

⁴ Then all the elders of Israel gathered themselves together and came to Samuel at Ramah. ⁵ They said to him, "Look here! You—you are old, and your sons do not walk in your ways; now then, set up for us a ruler to judge us, like all the heathen nations." ⁶ But the thing was evil in Samuel's sight when they said, "Give us a ruler to judge us." Then Samuel prayed to the HOLY ONE OF OLD.

⁷ And the HOLY ONE said to Samuel, "Hearken to the voice of the people in all that they say to you; for it is not you they have rejected, but it is me they have rejected from ruling over them. ⁸ Like everything else they have done to me, from the day I brought them up out of Egypt to this very day, forsaking me and serving other gods; they are doing the same to you. ⁹ Now then, hearken to their voice; but—you shall testify against them, and show them the judgment of the ruler who shall rule over them."

¹⁰ So Samuel relayed all the words of the HOLY ONE to the people who were asking him for a ruler. ¹¹ Samuel said, "This will be the judgment of the ruler who will rule over you all: your sons he will take and set them aside for himself in his chariots and in his cavalry, and to run before his chariots. ¹² And he will set aside for himself commanders of thousands and commanders of fifties, and some to plow his plowing and to reap his reaping, and to make his furnishings of war and the furnishings of his chariots. ¹³ Your daughters he will take to be apothecaries and cooks and bakers. ¹⁴ He will take the best of your fields and vineyards and olive orchards; he will take and give to those who serve him. ¹⁵ One-tenth of your grain and of your vineyards he will take and give to his eunuchs and those he enslaves. ¹⁶ Your male slaves and your female slaves, and the best of your cattle and donkeys, he will take and put them to his work. ¹⁷ Your flocks he will tithe . . . and you all, you shall be his slaves. ¹⁸ And you all will cry out on that day in the face of your sovereign, whom you have chosen for yourselves; and GOD WHOSE NAME IS HOLY will not answer you all on that day."

Psalm 72:1–4, 12–14, 18–19

¹ God, give the ruler your justice,
  and your righteousness to a ruler's son.
² May the [next] ruler judge your people with righteousness,
  and your afflicted ones with justice.
³ May the mountains raise up well-being for the people,
  and the hills, righteousness.
⁴ May the ruler do justice for the poor of the people,
  grant deliverance to those born in need
  and crush the oppressor.

12 For the ruler delivers the needy when they call,
   the oppressed and those who have no helper.
13 The ruler has pity on the poor and the needy,
   and saves the lives of the needy.
14 From oppression and violence the ruler redeems their life;
   and precious is their blood in the sight of their ruler.
18 Blessed be the FOUNT OF JUSTICE, the God of Israel,
   who alone does wondrous things.
19 Blessed be her glorious name forever;
   may her glory fill the whole earth.
   Amen and Amen.

1 Timothy 2:1 I urge firstly that supplications, prayers, intercessions, and thanksgivings be made for all persons: 2 for monarchs and all who are in authority, so that we might live a quiet and peaceable life in all godliness and dignity. 3 This is right and acceptable before God our Savior, 4 who desires every person to be saved and come to the knowledge of the truth.

5 For God is one;
   and there is one mediator between God and the woman-born,
   the woman-born Messiah, Jesus,
6 the one who gave himself a ransom for all;
   this testimony came at the right time.

John 6:14 When the people saw the sign that Jesus had done [multiplying the loaves and fish], they said, "This is indeed the prophet who is to come into the world." 15 When Jesus realized that they were about to kidnap him in order to make him king, he withdrew again to the mountain by himself.

16 And when it was evening, his disciples went down to the sea. 17 And they boarded a boat and headed across the sea to Capernaum. It was now dark and Jesus had not yet come to them. 18 The sea surged; a strong wind was blowing. 19 When they had rowed about twenty-five stadia [three or four miles], they saw Jesus walking upon the sea and coming near the boat and they were terrified. 20 But he said to them, "It is I; be not afraid."

PROCLAMATION

Text Notes

The people ask Samuel in verse 5 for the same kind of governance he provided, one based in the grammatical root for judges and judging, but they want a monarch rather than another judge. The Hebrew vocabulary for "monarchy" uses the same root word for noun and verb, i.e., "rulers rule," a common feature of the language. In addition, the word is the same for both genders, which does not work for "king," "queen," and "reign." (Think: prophets and prophetesses prophesy prophecy.)

"Female and male rulers rule in a realm" may be as close as we can get to preserving both form and function.

Samuel tells the people that a monarch will take their daughters to be "mixers of ointments" in verse 13. In Sirach 38:8, the mixer is an apothecary working with a physician. In other texts the mixer makes scented ointment and incense for use in worship; in yet others the mixer makes perfume (see Exod. 30:25, 35; 37:29; Eccles. 10:1; 1 Chron. 9:30; Sir. 49:1). I chose "apothecary" to denote their skill, which could be channeled for either purpose.

Throughout Psalm 72, I use "the ruler" for the monarch and his son and the many masculine pronouns for clarity and for the broader utility of this psalm beyond male monarchs. In verses 2 and 12, the people are afflicted (or oppressed) through a poverty that is imposed on them through unjust means, hence punishment of "the oppressor" in verse 4; Hebrew's lexicon of poverty has different words for different contexts. "Those born in need" replaces "children/sons of the needy" in the same verse. Hebrew uses "soul" for both the essence of a person's life, what we in the West tend to call a "soul," and a person's life. The language of saving and redeeming in Psalm 72:13–14 refers properly to lives; a leader's economic policies are matters of life and death.

Preaching Prompts

These lessons offer disparate models of monarchy. There is the human monarch whom Samuel predicts will plunder the people and their resources; scholars understand this passage to be a critique of Solomon. Imaginatively, Psalm 72 is a response to that critique in the form of a prayer that Solomon might receive divine guidance to avoid the pitfalls of Samuel's prophecy. In the Epistle, Jesus is presented as a claimant to the throne in order to portray his followers as enemies of the state. In the Gospel, Jesus goes to extreme measures to avoid having an earthly crown forced upon him; he literally (or literarily) walks on water to escape his would-be subjects. Is there any better critique of monarchy? Yet we continue to perpetuate that language and imagery for God.

At this time of year, American users of this lectionary will be marking the American independence day in their civil lives and some in congregational life. Monarchal texts always offer an opportunity to reflect on the kind of leadership scriptures endorse and how and why it is that most nations have moved away from dynastic monarchy and theocratic government.

PROPER 10 (CLOSEST TO JULY 13)

Esther 1:1–11; Psalm 49:5–15; James 5:1–6; Mark 10:17–31

Esther 1:1 Now it was in the days of Ahasuerus, he, Ahasuerus, ruled from India to Nubia, one hundred twenty-seven provinces—[2] And it was in those days when King Ahasuerus inhabited his royal throne in the Susa fortress—[3] in the third year of his reign, he gave a banquet for all his officials and servants; the army of Persia and Media and the nobles and governors of the provinces came before him. [4] When he displayed the glorious riches of his kingdom and the exquisite beauty of his majesty, it was many days, one hundred eighty days.

[5] And when these days were completed, the king gave for all the people who could be found in the fortress, Susa, great and small, a banquet lasting for seven days in the court of the garden of the palace of the king. [6] And there were white linen and royal blue [hangings] held up with cords of fine linen and purple on silver rings and alabaster columns; there were reclining-couches of gold and silver on a pavement of porphyry, alabaster, mother-of-pearl, and colored stones. [7] And there were drinks in golden vessels, vessels upon vessels of different kinds, and there was abundant royal wine at the direction of the king. [8] And the rule for the drinking was, "No restraint!"; for thus it was established by the king for all the officials of his palace to do as each one desired. [9] In addition, Queen Vashti gave a banquet for the women in the palace of King Ahasuerus.

[10] On the seventh day, when the heart of the king was merry with wine, he commanded Mehuman, Biztha, Harbona, Bigtha and Abagtha, Zethar and Carkas, the seven eunuchs who served in his presence: [11] They were to bring Queen Vashti before the king wearing the royal crown in order to show the peoples and the officials her beauty; for she was beautiful to behold.

Psalm 49:5–15

5 Why should I fear in evil days,
   when iniquity at my heels surrounds me?
6 Those who trust in their wealth
   and praise of the abundance of their riches?
7 Certainly, it cannot redeem a person,
   or can one give [it] to God as their ransom.
8 For the redemption-price of a soul is costly,
   they come to an end, forever.
9 Shall one should live eternally
   and never see the Pit?
10 For when one sees the wise, they die;
   the foolish and ignorant perish together
   and leave to others their wealth.
11 Their graves are their homes for all time,

their dwelling places from generation to generation,
though they put their name on lands.
12 Humanity will not recline in grandeur;
rather they are like the animals that perish.
13 This is the way of the foolish,
those pleased with their own words. *Selah*
14 Like sheep they are set for Sheol;
Death shall be their shepherd.
The upright shall rule over them until the morning,
and their form shall waste away;
Sheol shall be their abode.
15 But God will ransom my soul,
for from the grasp of Sheol she will take me. *Selah*

James 5:1 Come now, wealthy people, weep, wail for the miseries that are coming to you all. ² Your riches are rotting and your clothes are moth-eaten. ³ Your gold and silver have decayed and their decay shall be a witness against you, and it shall eat your flesh like fire. You all have laid up treasure for the last days. ⁴ Listen! The wages of the workers who reaped your fields—which you all defrauded them out of—cry out and the cries of the farm workers have reached the ears of the Commander of heaven's legions. ⁵ You all have lived on the earth in self-indulgence and in luxury; you all have gorged your hearts in a day of slaughter. ⁶ You all have condemned, murdered, the righteous one. Does not God resist you?

Mark 10:17 As Jesus went out the road a person ran to him and knelt before him and asked him, "Good Teacher, what must I do in order to inherit eternal life?" ¹⁸ And Jesus said to the person, "Why do you call me good? No one is good but God alone. ¹⁹ The commandments you know:

> *You shall not murder;*
> *You shall not commit adultery;*
> *You shall not steal;*
> *You shall not bear false witness;*
> *You shall not defraud;*
> *Honor your mother and your father."*

²⁰ Then the person said to him, "Teacher, all these have I kept from my youth." ²¹ And then Jesus, looking at the person, loving them, said, "One thing you lack; go, sell what you have, and give to the poor and you will have treasure in heaven and come, follow me." ²² Now the person was shocked at this word and went away grieving, for the person had many possessions.

²³ Then looking around Jesus said to his disciples, "How hard it will be for those who have wealth to enter the majesty of God!" ²⁴ And the disciples were astounded at these

words. So Jesus spoke to them again, "Children, how hard it is to enter the majesty of God! [25] It is easier for a camel to go through the eye of a needle than for a rich person to enter the majesty of God." [26] And they were amazed all the more and said among themselves, "Who then can be saved?" [27] Jesus looked at them and said, "For the woman-born it is impossible, but not for God; all things are possible for God."

[28] Peter began to speak to him, "Look! We have left everything and followed you." [29] Jesus said, "Truly I tell all of you, there is no one who has left house or sisters or brothers or mother or father or children or fields, for my sake and for the sake of the gospel, [30] who will not receive a hundredfold now in this age: houses, sisters and brothers [or friends and kin], mothers and children, and fields with persecutions and, in the age to come, eternal life. [31] But many who are first will be last, and the last will be first."

PROCLAMATION

Text Notes

The same word means both "to sit" and "to dwell." In Esther 1:2, the king's "sitting" is synonymous with his rule; thus, he "inhabits" his throne. The notion that Queen Vashti was to be exhibited in the nude, wearing only her crown, is neither supported nor contradicted by the text.

The Epistle attributed to James peppers snippets of Hebrew Scripture throughout today's reading. The phrase "in the ears of Lord of Hosts," translated in verse 4 as "the ears of the Commander of heaven's legions," can be found in Isaiah 5:9. "In the day of slaughter" from verse 5 occurs in Jeremiah 12:3.

James 5:2 uses "rust" to describe the tarnishing of gold and silver; "decay" fits better without ascribing rust to metals that do not in fact rust. (There is a similar issue in Matt. 6:19 where a separate noun describes the process of consumption by rust or blight or eating food.) I follow the translation of Luke Timothy Johnson for the question form of that latter phrase of verse 6 (see his *Anchor Bible Commentary* on James). The subject, "God," is elicited from the masculine singular verb and the presence of God earlier in the passage.

Jesus quotes from the commandments in Exodus 20:12–16 and Deuteronomy 5:16–20 and presents an interpretation of the commandment against covetousness, not to defraud (out of covetousness). The same term in Sirach refers to defrauding the poor, Sirach 4:1; 29:6–7; 34:25–26.

In this volume, "majesty" is used predominantly to represent the space where God dwells rather than a feudal system of bureaucracy or colonization, i.e., monarchy. In verse 29 of the Gospel, the text presents brothers before sisters, inverted for this translation, and surprisingly, mothers before fathers in the original wording. In the following verse, the fathers drop out.

Preaching Prompts

The critique of wealth in the scriptures is grounded in their origins as the literatures of oppressed peoples. Wealth and its beloved, power, were responsible for virtually every act of ill fortune that befell Israel and Judah and their successor entities. In Esther, wealth, power, and a seven-day drunk fest combine to propose using a woman for some sort of spectacle entertainment.

The psalmist's critique is of the wealthy who trust in their riches (v. 6), not wealth itself (and not those wealthy folk who trust in God, although it does not appear she knows any such folk). The end of those pleased with themselves, their riches, and their own words (v. 13) is the repose of the dead, in Israelite cosmology: Sheol, also referred to as the Pit. The psalmist's eminent rescue from the Pit in verse 16 may mark a rare nod to resurrection in the First Testament. One may wish to take a particular note of the anti-imperial critique in verse 11 against those who "put their name on lands."

James delivers a harsh critique of the wealthy and sets the corruptly wealthy in opposition to "the righteous one," Jesus, setting them in opposition to God; thus, the murder of Jesus is laid at the feet of the powerful across religious and ethnic lines.

The critique of wealth and of the wealthy can be particularly unwelcome in churches as well-resourced as mainline lectionary-using denominations and congregations. The biblical writers, particularly the New Testament writers, did not often see wealth as a resource for ministry, a tool for achieving the aims of the gospel. Frequently it was a temptation, if not an impediment to salvation. Yet Jesus assures that not even the wealthy are beyond the grace of God while at the same time making clear it is only the grace of God that leads to the salvation of the wealthy.

Conversations about poverty must address its effects on women and children and other vulnerable segments of society, the unhoused, the undocumented, the underpaid, and those lacking health insurance.

PROPER 11 (CLOSEST TO JULY 20)

Ruth 1:1–14; Psalm 80:1–7; 1 Thessalonians 5:12–24; Mark 12:41–44

Ruth 1:1 In the days when the judges judged, it happened that there was a famine in the land, and a man of Bethlehem in Judah went to sojourn in the country of Moab, he and his wife and their two sons. ² And the name of the man was Elimelech and the name of his wife Naomi, and the names of his two sons were Mahlon and Chilion; they were Ephrathites from Bethlehem in Judah. They went into the country of Moab and remained there. ³ Then Elimelech, the husband of Naomi, died, and she was left, she and her two sons. ⁴ They abducted Moabite women for themselves; the name of the one was Orpah and the name of the second, Ruth. And they lived there about ten years. ⁵ They also died, both of them, Mahlon and Chilion, and the woman was left without her two sons and without her husband.

⁶ Then she got up, she and her daughters-in-law and she returned from the country of Moab, for she had heard in the country of Moab that the FAITHFUL ONE had considered God's people and given them food. ⁷ So she set out from the place where she was while there, with her two daughters-in-law, and they journeyed on the road to return to the land of Judah. ⁸ Then Naomi said to her two daughters-in-law, "Go, return, each to your mother's house. May the HOLY ONE deal kindly with you, as you have done with the dead and with me. ⁹ The SAVING GOD grant that you may find security, each in the house of your own husband." Then she kissed them, and they wept aloud. ¹⁰ They said to her, "We will return with you to your people." ¹¹ Then Naomi said, "Turn back, my daughters, why will you go with me? Are there yet sons in my belly that may become your husbands? ¹² Turn back, my daughters, go your way, for I am too old to be with a man. Let me say I have hope and even was with a man tonight and give birth to sons. ¹³ Would you then wait and hope until they were grown? Would you then refrain from marrying? No, my daughters, it has been far more bitter for me than for you, because the hand of the SAVING GOD has turned against me." ¹⁴ Then they wept aloud again. Orpah kissed her mother-in-law, but Ruth clung to her.

Psalm 80:1–7

¹ Shepherd of Israel, pray, hearken,
  you who lead the line of Rebekah like a flock.
  You, enthroned upon the cherubim, pray, shine forth.
² Before Ephraim and Benjamin and Manasseh,
  stir up your might and come to save us!
³ God restore us and let your face shine,
  that we may be saved.
⁴ SOVEREIGN of heaven's vanguard,
  how long will you fume at the prayers of your people?
⁵ You have fed them tears for bread,
  and you have given them tears to drink thrice over.
⁶ You make us the scorn of our neighbors;
  our enemies laugh among themselves.
⁷ God of heaven's vanguard restore us and let your face shine,
  that we may be saved.

1 Thessalonians 5:12 We appeal to you all, sisters and brothers [or friends and kin], to acknowledge those who labor with you all, and lead you all in Christ, and admonish you all. ¹³ Esteem them more than before in love because of their work. Be at peace among yourselves. ¹⁴ Now we urge you, kindred, to admonish the undisciplined, encourage the discouraged, support the weak, be patient with all. ¹⁵ See that none of you repays evil for evil, rather always seek to do good to one another and to all. [16] Rejoice always. [17] Pray without ceasing. [18] In all things give thanks, for this is the will of God in Christ Jesus for you all. [19] Quench not the Spirit. [20] Do not despise the words of women or men who prophesy, [21] rather examine everything. To what is good, hold fast. [22] Avoid every appearance of evil.

[23] May the very God of peace sanctify you all wholly, and may your spirit and soul and body be kept blameless at the coming of our Redeemer Jesus Christ. [24] The one who calls you is faithful and will do this.

Mark 12:41 Now Jesus sat down opposite the treasury and watched the crowd putting money into the treasury. Many rich people put in much. [42] One poor widow came and put in two small Greek copper coins, which together are worth the smallest Roman coin. [43] Then Jesus called his disciples and said to them, "Truly I tell you all, this poor widow has put in more than all those giving to the treasury. [44] For all of them out of their abundance have given but she out of her lack has put in everything she had, her whole livelihood."

PROCLAMATION

Text Notes

The judges (Ruth 1:1) were rulers or governors in addition to resolving disputes and settling claims. They were the de facto leaders of the people. Verse 2 identifies the children as "his," Elimelech's, not "theirs," though Naomi's maternity will be established later in verse 4. As Hebrew does not have specific words for "wife" and "husband," Naomi is Elimelech's "woman" in verse 3 and he is her "man" in verse 4.

Normally, "to take" a wife indicates a consensual union through the verb *l-q-ch*. In Ruth 1:4, the verb is *n-s-'*, which primarily means "lift up"; it indicates abduction here and in other places such as the abduction of the Shiloh virgins in Judges 21:23. "Marriage" and "marry" reflect the Western world rather than the language of the text. There is a word that signifies marriage, *b-'-l*, which also means to master (the root is the same as Baal and as a noun means "lord" and "master"). It is rarely used, and not at all in Ruth.

In the psalm, "the line of Rebekah" replaces "Joseph" in verse 1. The root of "thrice over" in verse 5 shares its form with the number three, see Alter's "triple measure" following the Targum and "three times over" in the CEB.

"Women and men who prophesy" expands "prophet" in 1 Thessalonians 5:20, reflecting the activity of prophets of both genders in both testaments, i.e., Miriam, Deborah, Huldah, Noadiah, Anna, the four virgin daughters of Philip in Acts 21:9, and the Corinthian women prophets in 1 Corinthians 11:5. (For more on these and others, see my *Daughters of Miriam: Women Prophets in Ancient Israel*.)

The widow put in two *lepta*: the CEB notes observe that a *lepta* was "the smallest Greek copper coin, each worth 1/128 of a single day's pay," and that a *kodrantes* was "the smallest Roman coin, equal in value to two *lepta*."

Preaching Prompts

The theme of faithfulness binds these readings. While Naomi's family has suffered wave after wave of hardships, she has heard a report of God's faithfulness and changed the course of her life trusting in that faithfulness. Similarly, the psalmist trusts in the faithfulness of God. The Epistle and Gospel portray human faithfulness in service to the God who is faithful, those who labor and lead in the early church, and the widow who gives all she has to live on.

A close reading of Ruth reveals many surprises and challenges to the romantic readings common to many; in this way Ruth's story is a fit predecessor to David's story. Ruth and Orpah were trafficked and may not have been well received upon their return home. Interestingly, Orpah and Ruth come from matrilineal, if not matriarchal, households indicated by "mother's house" in 1:8. (Israelite households include both mother's houses and father's houses.)

The vulnerability of Naomi and Ruth, and to a lesser degree of Orpah, set the stage for the monarchal epic that marks the golden age of ancient Israel. They are part of a mobile population crossing international conflict-ridden borders in search of bare sustenance, as Moab and Israel were often at war.

Psalm 80 could well be the prayer of someone trying to eke out a life in the borderlands as well as Naomi's prayer for sustenance. Food insecurity was a regular condition for the vast bulk of Israelites; part of the promise of Canaan was that it "flowed milk and honey," making it a paradise of sorts.

Part of the labor of the church in 1 Thessalonians and beyond was relief of the food insecure and otherwise impoverished, like the widow in the Gospel. The poor are yet with us as Jesus said they would be. Women and children account for the majority of those living without adequate housing and food; gay and trans teens are particularly vulnerable to sexual exploitation, violence, and suicide. Contrasting God's faithfulness, these lessons also disclose the reality (and potential for) sexual transactions as a survival mechanism. Extending God's faithfulness, these lessons also reveal the role of the Church and community in meeting the need of our most vulnerable members.

FEAST OF MARY MAGDALENE, JULY 22

Genesis 16:10–13; Psalm 68:4–11; Romans 16:1–16; John 20:1–2, 11–18

Genesis 16:10 The messenger of the WELLSPRING OF LIFE said to Hagar, "Greatly will I multiply your seed, so they cannot be counted for multitude." [11] Then the messenger of the FOUNT OF LIFE said to her,

"Look! You are pregnant and shall give birth to a son,
and you shall call him Ishmael (meaning God hears),

for the FAITHFUL ONE has heard of your abuse.

¹² He shall be a wild ass of a man,
with his hand against everyone,
and everyone's hand against him;
and he shall live in the sight of all his kin."

¹³ So Hagar named the LIVING GOD who spoke to her: "You are El-ro'i"; for she said, "Have I really seen God and remained alive after seeing God?"

Psalm 68:4–11

⁴ Sing to God, sing praises to her Name;
exalt her who rides upon the clouds;
HOLY is her Name, rejoice before her!

⁵ Mother of orphans and defender of widows,
is God in her holy habitation!

⁶ God settles the solitary in a home, bringing prisoners into prosperity;
while the rebellious shall live in a wasteland.

⁷ God, when you marched before your people,
when you moved out through the wilderness,

⁸ the earth shook, even the heavens poured down,
at the presence of God, the One of Sinai,
at the presence of God, the God of Israel.

⁹ Rain in abundance, God, you showered abroad;
when your heritage grew weary you prepared rest.

¹⁰ Your creatures found a dwelling in her;
God, you provided in your goodness for the oppressed.

¹¹ The AUTHOR OF LIFE gave the word;
the women who proclaim the good news are a great army.

Romans 16:1 I commend to you all our sister Phoebe, a deacon of the church in Cenchreae, ² so that you all may receive her in Christ as is worthy of the saints, and stand by her in whatever thing she may need of you, for she has been a benefactress of many, and of myself as well.

³ Greet Prisca and Aquila, my coworkers in Christ Jesus, ⁴ and who for my life risked their necks, to whom not only I give thanks, but also all the churches of the Gentiles, ⁵ and the church in their house. Greet Epaenetus my beloved, who was the first fruit in Asia for Christ. ⁶ Greet Mary, who has worked much among you all. ⁷ Greet Andronicus and Junia, my kin and my fellow prisoners; they are eminent among the apostles, and they were in Christ before I was. ⁸ Greet Ampliatus, my beloved in Christ. ⁹ Greet Urbanus, our coworker in Christ, and Stachys my beloved. ¹⁰ Greet Apelles, who is proven in Christ. Greet those who belong to Aristobulus. ¹¹ Greet Herodion, my kinsman. Greet those who

belong of Narcissus in Christ. [12] Greet Tryphaena and Tryphosa who toil in Christ. Greet the beloved Persis who has worked much in Christ. [13] Greet Rufus, chosen in Christ, and greet his mother who is also mine. [14] Greet Asyncritus, Phlegon, Hermes, Patrobas, Hermas, and the sisters and brothers [or friends and kin] who are with them. [15] Greet Philologus and Julia, Nereus and his sister, and Olympas, and all the saints with them. [16] Greet one another with a holy kiss. All the churches of Christ greet you.

John 20:1 Now it was the first day of the week. Mary Magdalene came, early on while it was still dark, to the tomb and saw the stone removed from the tomb. [2] So she ran and went to Simon Peter and to the other disciple, the one whom Jesus loved, and said to them, "They have taken the Messiah out of the tomb, and we do not know where they have laid him."

[11] Now Mary stood outside, facing the tomb, weeping. As she wept, she bent down to see in the tomb. [12] Then she saw two angels in white sitting, one at the head and the other at the feet, where the body of Jesus had been lying. [13] They said to her, "Woman, why do you weep?" She said to them, "Because they have taken my Savior, and I do not know where they have laid him." [14] Having said this, she turned around and saw Jesus standing, but she did not know that it was Jesus. [15] Jesus said to her, "Woman, why do you weep? For whom do you look?" Thinking that he was the gardener, she said to him, "Sir, if you have carried him away, tell me where you have laid him, and I will take him away." [16] Jesus said to her, "Mary." She turned and said to him in Aramaic, "Rabbouni!" (which means Teacher). [17] Jesus said to her, "Do not hold me, because I have not yet ascended to the Father. Rather, go to my brothers and say to them, 'I am ascending to my Abba and your Abba, to my God and your God.'" [18] Mary Magdalene went and announced to the disciples, "I have seen the Savior"; and she told them that he had said these things to her.

PROCLAMATION

Text Notes

The language of Hagar's annunciation parallels the promise to Abraham in Genesis 13:16 closely; each is promised that their "seed" (or offspring) will be numerous beyond counting. Hagar is the first woman in scripture granted an annunciation, the unnamed mother of Samson follows in Judges 13:3–7, followed in turn by Mary the mother of Jesus. Hagar and Rebekah (Genesis 24:60) are the only women in the canon credited with their own seed/offspring; the language is usually reserved for men. (Rebekah's seed is blessed by her matrilineal family; her father Bethuel ben Milcah bore his mother's name, not his father's.) Notably, God speaks to Abraham *about* Sarah in Genesis 17:15–16, as do the divine messengers in Genesis 18:9–10, even when she is within hearing; none speak to her.

Hagar's abuse or affliction, more rightly, Sarah's abuse of Hagar in verse 11, is articulated with a verb that encodes both physical and sexual violence; the verb is also used of the abuse the Israelites suffered at the hands of the Egyptians. Some translate Ishmael's fate as living "in opposition," i.e., conflict, with his kin rather than "opposite," i.e., in their sight or presence; the verb has both senses.

The "we" in John 20:2 likely refers to other women with Mary Magdalene at the tomb. Other resurrection accounts include Mary the mother of James and Salome from Mark 16:1 and Joanna (with Mary Magdalene and James's mother) in Luke 24:10. Yet other possibilities include Jesus's aunt—the unnamed sister of Mary—with Mary the wife of Clopas, present at his crucifixion in John 19:25, and Susanna, who with other women supported Jesus financially, from Luke 8:3.

Mary Magdalene "messages," *aggellō*, the gospel of Christ's resurrection. The verb shares the root of messenger, one who announces, *aggelos*, commonly rendered "angel," though the term is not restricted to divine beings. Both she and the divine messengers she encountered are angels. See the use of "angel" as church leader in Revelation 2:1, 8, 12, 18; 3:1.

Preaching Prompts

For this feast of the disciple Orthodox Christians call the Apostle to the Apostles, the readings focus on women's proclamations to and about God, including their work in shaping the early church that speaks for them. Hagar is the only person in the scriptures to name God. She is a matron saint for this project in which I too name God, using God's characteristics revealed in the texts and in the experiences of its readers and hearers to render the unpronounceable name.

Hagar tells God who She is in her, Hagar's, experience and perception. In Psalm 68:11 at the command of God, an army of women proclaim the good news of God's care for her people. The language for that good news, *basarah* in Hebrew, *euaggelia* in Greek, becomes "gospel" in English, the gospel of the risen Christ that Mary Magdalene proclaimed to the absent male disciples and apostles. The women church leaders acknowledged by Paul spread that good news through Asia, though their words are lost to us.

The Magdalene texts are extensive: Matthew 27:55–61; 28:1–10; Mark 15:40–41, 47; 16:1–8 [9–11]; Luke 8:1–3; 23:55–56; 24:1–10; John 19:25; 20:1–2, 11–18. The fifty-seven verses tell a story of discipleship and faith that is virtually without peer among male disciples yet is not unique to this one woman, for there were other women at the cross and tomb who followed Jesus in life, attended him in death, and proclaimed him in resurrection. Yet she is distinguished by the preservation of her name and frequency of appearance. Mary the mother of Jesus and Mary Magdalene are the only women represented in all four Gospels, even considering the difficult to separate and identify Marys, even with multiple traditions about which Mary anointed Jesus.

Peeling back the traditions accreted around her, some of which—like the red egg—may be useful, she remains a disciple, functionally an apostle, preacher, eyewitness of the Passion, conversant with angels, benefactrix, burial attendant, healed/transformed/exorcised, messenger (angel) of the gospel.

PROPER 12 (CLOSEST TO JULY 27)

Isaiah 61:1–4, 8–10; Psalm 133; 2 Corinthians 2:14–16; Mark 14:3–9

Isaiah 61:1 The Spirit of the Sovereign GOD is upon me,

because the HOLY GOD has anointed me.
God has sent me to declare good news to the oppressed,
to bind up the brokenhearted,
to proclaim liberation to the captives,
and freedom to the prisoners;
2   to proclaim a year of the MOST HIGH God's favor,
and the day of vengeance of our God;
to comfort all children, women, and men who mourn;
3   to provide for those women, children, and men who mourn in Zion;
to give them glory instead of ashes,
the oil of gladness instead of mourning,
the mantle of praise instead of a faint spirit.
They will be called oaks of righteousness,
the planting of the MOST HIGH,
for God to display God's own glory.
4   They shall build up the ancient ruins,
they shall raise up the former devastations;
they shall restore the ruined cities,
devastations across generations.
8   For I, the ETERNAL GOD, am the One who loves justice,
and the One who hates robbery sacrificed as a burnt offering;
I will faithfully give them their recompense,
and I will make an everlasting covenant with them.
9   Their descendants shall be known among the nations,
and their offspring among the peoples;
all who see them shall recognize
that they are a people whom the HOLY ONE has blessed.
10   I will greatly rejoice in the MOST HIGH God,
my soul shall exult in my God;
for God has clothed me in garments of salvation,

God has covered me with a robe of righteousness,
as a bridegroom vests himself with a garland,
and as a bride adorns herself with her jewels.

Psalm 133

1 Look! How precious and how lovely
when [friends and] kin live together as one!
2 Like the precious oil on the head,
running down upon the beard,
on the beard of Aaron,
running down over the collar of his robes.
3 Like the dew of Hermon,
That falls on the mountains of Zion.
For there the WOMB OF CREATION commanded her blessing,
life eternal.

2 Corinthians 2:14 Thanks be to God, who parades us in triumph in Christ, and through us makes known in every place the scent that comes from knowing Christ. 15 For we are the fragrant aroma of Christ to God among those who are being saved and among those who are perishing. 16 To the one, a scent from death to death, to the other a scent from life to life. Who indeed is sufficient for these things?

Mark 14:3 Now Jesus was at Bethany in the house of Simon who had a skin disease; as he reclined at table, a woman came with an alabaster vessel of pure nard ointment—very expensive—she broke open the alabaster and poured it on his head. 4 But some being angry said among themselves, "For what was the nard wasted? 5 For this ointment could have been sold for more than three hundred denarii, [three hundred days' wages] and given to the poor." And they were indignant with her. 6 But Jesus said, "Leave her alone! Why do you trouble her? A good work has she done for me. 7 For always shall you have the poor with you and whenever you wish you can do good by them; but me, you shall not always have. 8 What she had it to do, she did; she has anointed my body beforehand for its burial. 9 Truly I tell you all, wherever the gospel is proclaimed in the whole world, what she has done will be told in remembrance of her."

PROCLAMATION

Text Notes

In Isaiah 61:1, "vests" has a liturgical sense. The actual verb is a form of the word for priest; the bridegroom dresses himself just as a priest puts on his ornaments.

In the first two verses of the psalm, the basic and utilitarian adjective "good" serves to describe both the feeling of community and the quality of the anointing oil. "Precious" fits both contexts.

The verb signifying "parading" and "triumph" in 2 Corinthians 2:14 is unclear here but can include a celebratory parade and one in which the conquered are put on display.

In the ancient world, the term "leprosy" was used to refer to a host of diseases (and in the Hebrew Bible to some infestations affecting objects).

Preaching Prompts

Oil had profound cultural value and was indispensable in the ancient Afro-Asiatic world. It had mundane (grooming), lifecycle (birth, death), medicinal, and religious uses. The good stuff also had financial value, likely due to rare or valuable spices and other aromatics (Exod. 25:6 mentions "spices" to be used in the anointing oil for the dedication of the wilderness, sanctuary, and ordination of Israel's first priests, including Aaron.) Athalyah would have been anointed upon her ascension, but not many other women, if any.

The head was a site of honor for crowns and wreaths and garlands, as at the end of the Isaiah 61 reading; the horns of animals often signify glory and honor. Oiling the head and hair, "greasing the scalp," are enduring social and cultural practices in the African diaspora. It is also somewhat common in some Black American Christianities to refer to persons with spiritual anointings like the subject of Isaiah 61 as "oily," like Aaron at his ordination (Exod. 29:7; he was further sprinkled with blood and blood mixed with oil, verses 20–21, and rubbed with fat from a fresh slaughter).

Reading Isaiah 61 in its own context yields a reminder that God does not just call Jesus to the work of liberation. The poet-prophet says, "The Spirit is upon *me*" for this same work centuries before Jesus. The work is contextual and concrete. The physical and financial costs of Israelite subjugation will be reversed; liberation is all encompassing, physical as well as spiritual. Indeed, the work of liberation is dangerous because of its very contextualization. The powers of empire that seek to subjugate, degrade, and exploit are lethal, as the anonymous woman who bestows her touch on Jesus in Mark makes visible with her fragrant, precious offering. The fragrant offering of the early followers of Jesus in the Epistle is their willingness to die like Jesus, and pending the uncertain grammar, the lead in a mocking procession which for them would be a triumphal procession.

PROPER 13 (CLOSEST TO AUGUST 3)

Ruth 1:15–22; Psalm 44:1–4, 8, 17, 23–26; Acts 6:1–6; Luke 18:1–8

Ruth 1:15 Naomi said, "Look, your sister-in-law has gone back to her people and to her gods; go back after your sister-in-law." [16] But Ruth said,

"Do not press me to forsake you
or to turn back from following you.
Where you go, I will go,
where you abide, I will abide;
your people shall be my people,
and your God my God.
¹⁷ Where you die, I will die,
there will I be buried.
May the HOLY ONE OF OLD do thus and more to me,
if even death parts me from you."

¹⁸ When Naomi saw that Ruth had strengthened herself to go with her, she ceased speaking to her. ¹⁹ So the two of them traveled until coming to Bethlehem. When they came to Bethlehem, the whole town was buzzing over them; and the women said, "Is this Naomi?" ²⁰ Naomi said to the women,

"Call me not Naomi [Pleasant One],
call me Mara [Bitter One]
for Shaddai [the Breasted One] has greatly embittered me.
²¹ I went away full,
but the HOLY ONE OF SINAI brought me back empty.
Why call me Naomi?
The HOLY ONE has spoken against me,
and Shaddai [the Breasted One] has brought evil upon me."

²² So Naomi returned with Ruth the Moabite woman, her daughter-in-law, with her; she was the one who came back from the country of Moab. They came to Bethlehem at the beginning of the barley harvest.

Psalm 44:1–4, 8, 17, 23–26

¹ God, with our ears have we heard,
  our mothers and fathers have told us,
  the deeds you did in their days,
  in the days of old:
² You with your own hand displaced nations,
  and you planted them;
  you afflicted peoples,
  and you set free them.
³ For not by their own sword did they inherit the land,
  nor did their own arm save them;
  for it was your right hand, and your arm,
  and the light of your countenance,

for you delighted in them.
⁴ You are my Sovereign and my God;
  you command deliverance repeatedly for the line of Rebekah.
⁸ In God we glory all the day,
  and give thanks to your Name for all time. *Selah*
¹⁷ All this has come upon us,
  yet we have not forgotten you,
  or been false to your covenant.
²³ Rouse yourself! Why do you sleep, my ruler?
  Awaken yourself! Do not cast us off forever!
²⁴ Why do you hide your face,
  forgetting our affliction and our oppression?
²⁵ For our necks lay upon the dust;
  our bellies cling to the ground.
²⁶ Raise yourself as our help;
  redeem us for the sake of your faithful love.

Acts 6:1 Now in those days as the number of disciples was multiplying, the Hellenists grumbled against the Hebrews because their widows were being neglected in the daily food distribution ministry. ² And the twelve called together the multitude of the disciples and said, "It is not right that we should forsake the word of God in order to minister upon tables. ³ Appoint then kindred, seven of whom there is good testimony from among yourselves, full of the Spirit and of wisdom, whom we may task to this need. ⁴ But we will devote ourselves to prayer and to ministering the word." ⁵ What they said pleased the whole multitude [of disciples], and they chose Stephen, full of faith and the Holy Spirit, together with Philip, Prochorus, Nicanor, Timon, Parmenas, and Nicolaus, a convert [to Judaism] from Antioch. ⁶ They had them stand before the apostles, who prayed and laid their hands on them.

Luke 18:1 Jesus told the disciples a parable about the need to pray continually and not be discouraged. ² He said, "There was a judge in a certain city who neither feared God nor respected people. ³ There was a widow in that city and she came to him continually and saying, 'Grant me justice against my accuser.' ⁴ And he was not willing for some time; but later he said to himself, 'Though I do not fear God nor respect anyone else, ⁵ yet because this widow persists in troubling me, I will grant her justice, so that she may not ultimately come to violence against me.'" ⁶ And the Messiah said, "Listen to what the unjust judge says. ⁷ And will not God grant justice to the elect of God who cry to God day and night? Will God forbear in helping them? ⁸ I tell you all, God will quickly grant justice to them. And yet, when the Son of Woman comes, will he find faith on the earth?"

PROCLAMATION

Text Notes

In Ruth 1:20 and 21, God is called *Shaddai*, translated as "Almighty" in most mainline translations; yet the root of the word is not "might" or "strength" but arguably "breast," *shad*. Another argument is that Shaddai is related to Akkadian "mountain," or a class of Arabian deities. Feminist scholars have remarked upon the desire of traditionally trained, primarily male, scholars to find an etymology outside of the obvious cognate, breast. What is not disputed is that Shaddai is invoked in contexts where God is promising or providing fertility, such as Genesis 28:3 and 35:11. Genesis 49:25 offers a blessing from "the God of your father, who shall help you; and by Shaddai, who shall bless you with blessings of the heavens above, blessings of the deep that lies below, blessings of breasts (*shadim*) and womb." (*Shadim* is the plural of *shad*.) There is a possibility that the Akkadian cognate "mountain" is also breast imagery with the mountains as breasts (and snow cap as nipple) that nourish the world through their lifegiving water in the desert realm. Bearing these considerations in mind, I translate Shaddai as "Breasted One."

In Psalm 44:4, "the line of Rebekah" stands for "Jacob." In the same verse, "salvation" or "deliverance" is plural, hence "repeatedly." "Ruler" in verse 23 replaces "lord," *adonai*—not the Tetragrammaton. Though *nephesh* generally means "soul" or perhaps better, "life-breath," signifying "life" broadly, it occasionally means "neck" or "throat," the passage through which the life-breath escapes. Here combined with "bellies" it indicates a prostrate person, as in Alter.

Diakonia, "service" and "ministry," includes the care of and provision for widows as a religious duty and the practical mechanics of the task (Acts 6:1–2) and likewise, the ministry of the word (as in v. 4), preaching, and evangelism. In verse 3, *adelphos*, "kindred," can refer to a gender-inclusive or all-male group. They are to select seven men, *andras*, not persons or women.

The "justice" the widow seeks in verse 4 of the Gospel, *ekdikēson*, includes the notion of vengeance; her adversary—one possible translation of *antidikou*—can also be understood as a plaintiff or accuser who has brought legal charges against her. In Luke 18:5, the corrupt judge uses a bit of dramatic hyperbole with the verb *hypōpiazō*, meaning "to blacken the eye." While most translations treat the expression as euphemistic for "wearing [him] out," the BDAG *Greek-English Lexicon of the New Testament and Other Early Christian Literature* lists as its first meaning: "to blacken an eye, give a black eye, strike in the face . . . of a woman who is driven to desperation and who the judge in the story thinks might in the end express herself physically. . . . Hyperbole is stock-in-trade of popular storytelling. Some prefer to understand [*hypōpiazō*] in this pass[age] in [this] sense." In 1 Corinthians 9:27, Paul describes "punishing" (or "pummeling") his body using the same verb.

Preaching Prompts

In the lessons from Ruth, Acts, and Luke, community members meet the needs of those in want of food, shelter, and justice. The psalmist seeks an unresponsive God. One could imagine Naomi's lament in Ruth 1:20–21 as a response to praying something like Psalm 44, calling on God to rouse herself and meet her needs, reminding her of her previous faithfulness to her people. Ultimately, she finds the help she needs with her home-folk, her kinfolk. Widowhood in Ruth, Acts, and Luke also connects these passages.

While the passage in Acts 6 is ostensibly about a disparity in the treatment of widows in the nascent Jesus-following community based on ethnicity, it presents a perceived disparity in the value of different sorts of ministries, perhaps pitting the food pantry against the pulpit. It is also possible all of the widows are Jewish and the distinction is between Greek-speaking and therefore Hellenized Jewish widows and Aramaic-speaking widows, remembering that Hebrew and Aramaic were not generally distinguished. In his *Yale Anchor Bible* commentary on Luke, Joseph Fitzmyer highlights Paul's use of "Hebrew," *Hebraioi*, as a cultural marker for himself, though he is an apparently prolific Greek speaker. Used this way, the term seems to evoke a sense of keeping to traditional rather than colonized culture and values.

Whether serving food or serving at the eucharistic table is unclear; linguistically, both are possible. In the *Women's Commentary*, Margaret Aymer notes that the "tables" may be a euphemistic reference to banking, considering the concerns of the larger narrative; "tables" were used to manage and administer funds, including the charitable work of the newly formed community, and would have evoked banking to early readers and hearers. Further, widows are more than bereaved wives in the early Christian community; they are official functionaries and yet another reading might be that the disparity was in who gave acts of charity rather than who received. See Bonnie Thurston's *The Widows: A Women's Ministry in the Early Church*.

The decision makers in Acts 6:3 are most likely men, "brothers" who are to choose among themselves, "men" to address the perceived inequity. In so doing, they enshrine another. Acts 9:36 explicitly names Tabitha a disciple; it is unreasonable to imagine she is the only woman disciple known to the author of Luke-Acts. Where are the other women disciples and what do they have to say about the treatment of their sisters? Notably the women who followed Jesus are virtually missing from Acts with the exception of "certain women" in 1:14. This is in sharp distinction to the number of women in Luke who follow, accompany, and support Jesus and serve as eyewitnesses to his death and resurrection. Their rare and precious firsthand testimony seems to have no value to the community that claims to follow Jesus.

Though the scriptures regularly present widows as vulnerable, victims, and potential victims, the widow in Luke 18 demonstrates the persistence and resourcefulness of women to, in womanist parlance, "make a way out of no way" and survive until they can thrive. For an analysis of the stereotypical use of widows and widowhood in Luke-Acts, see Febbie Dickerson's *Luke, Widows, Judges, and Stereotypes.*

PROPER 14 (CLOSEST TO AUGUST 10)

Ruth 2:1–16; Psalm 112; 2 Corinthians 8:1–5; Luke 12:13–21

Ruth 2:1 Now Naomi had a relative through her husband, a warrior-hearted man of worth, from the family of Elimelech, and his name was Boaz. [2] And Ruth the Moabite said to Naomi, "Let me go to the field and glean among the ears of grain, behind someone in whose eyes I may find favor." Naomi said to her, "Go, my daughter." [3] And she went, and came and gleaned in the field behind the reapers. As it happened, she happened upon the part of the field that belonged to Boaz, who was from Elimelech's family. [4] Then suddenly, Boaz came from Bethlehem. He said to the reapers, "GOD be with you." They answered, "GOD bless you." [5] Then Boaz said to his boy stationed over the reapers, "To whom does this girl belong?" [6] The boy stationed over the reapers answered, "She is the Moabite, the one who returned with Naomi from the country of Moab. [7] She said, 'Please, let me glean and gather among the sheaves behind the reapers.' So, she came, and she has been standing from the morning until now, only resting in the shelter a little."

[8] Then Boaz said to Ruth, "Have you not heard my daughter? Go not to glean in another field neither leave this one, thus you will cling to my girls. [9] Keep your eyes on the field that is being reaped, and follow after them [the girls]. Have I not commanded the boys not to touch you? When you thirst, go to the vessels and drink from what the boys have drawn." [10] Then she fell on her face and bowed down to the ground, and said to him, "Why have I found favor in your sight, that you would distinguish me, as I am a foreigner?" [11] And Boaz answered and said to her, "It has been told to me, all that you have done for your mother-in-law after the death of your husband, that you have forsaken your mother and father and your native land and came to a people that you did not know before yesterday. [12] May the HOLY ONE OF OLD reward your works, and may you have a full recompense from the HOLY ONE, the God of Israel, under whose wings you have come for refuge." [13] Then Ruth said, "May I continue to find favor in your eyes, my lord, for you have comforted me and have spoken to the heart to your slave woman, and I, I am not one of your slave women."

[14] Boaz said to her when it was time to eat, "Draw near, and eat from this bread, and dip your piece in the vinegar." And she sat beside the reapers, and he handed her some roasted grain; and she ate and was satisfied, and she had some left over. [15] When Ruth got up to glean, Boaz commanded his boys, saying, "She may even glean between the sheaves, and do not humiliate her. [16] You must also pull out some for her from the bundles, and leave them for her to glean, and do not rebuke her."

Psalm 112

¹ Hallelujah!
Happy is the woman or man who revers the FAITHFUL ONE,
in whose commandments they deeply delight.
² Mighty in the land will be their descendants;
the generation of the upright will be blessed.
³ Wealth and riches are in their houses,
and their righteousness endures forever.
⁴ They rise in the darkness as a light for the upright;
gracious, loving as would a mother, and righteous.
⁵ It is well with the woman or man who is gracious and lends;
they conduct their concerns with justice.
⁶ For the righteous will never be shaken [this is true] forever;
they will be remembered forever.
⁷ Of evil tidings they have no fear;
their hearts are firm, trusting in the WORTHY ONE.
⁸ Their hearts made steady; they will not fear;
in the end they will look upon their foes.
⁹ They disperse [their resources]; they give to the poor;
their righteousness endures forever;
their horn is exalted in honor.
¹⁰ The wicked see and are angry;
they gnash their teeth and melt;
the desire of the wicked will be destroyed.

2 Corinthians 8:1 We are making known to you all, sisters and brothers [or friends and kin], the grace of God granted to the churches of Macedonia. ² For in a manifold test of affliction, their abundant joy and the depth of their poverty have overflowed in the wealth of their generosity. ³ Indeed, according to their means—on my word—and even beyond their means, [it was] of their own accord. ⁴ With much pleading they begged us earnestly for the grace of participation in this ministry to the saints. ⁵ And not just as we expected, rather, they gave themselves first to the Savior and to us by the will of God.

Luke 12:13 Someone in the crowd said to Jesus, "Teacher, tell my sibling to divide the inheritance with me." ¹⁴ But Jesus said to him, "Friend, who appointed me a judge or arbitrator over you?" ¹⁵ Then Jesus said to the crowd, "Beware! Be on guard against all kinds of greed; for one's life is not one's abundance of possessions." ¹⁶ Then Jesus relayed a parable to them, saying: "A certain rich person produced land crops abundantly. ¹⁷ And the person pondered internally, 'What should I do, for I have no place to store my crops?' ¹⁸ Then that person said, 'This will I do: I will pull down my barns and build larger ones and I will store there all my grain and my goods. ¹⁹ And I will say to my soul, 'Soul, you have many goods laid up for many years; relax, eat, drink, be merry.' [20] But God said to the rich person, 'Fool! This very night your soul will be demanded back from you. And the things you have prepared, whose will they be?' [21] So it is with those who store up treasures for themselves but are not rich toward God."

PROCLAMATION

Text Notes

Used for Boaz in Ruth 2:1, *gibor* indicates a man of status, often a warrior; the term is compounded with *chayil,* meaning both warrior and one who holds the values of a warrior, including wealth acquired through military exploits. Boaz will address Ruth as a woman of *chayil* in 3:11. In Proverbs 31, the Queen Mother instructs her son not to give his *chayil* to unworthy women and instructs him on value of a woman of *chayil*; *chayil* is explicitly martial and refers to armies, e.g., Pharaoh's army throughout Exodus. "Warrior-hearted" encompasses the full range and does not dilute the meaning for women as do many translations such as "worthy woman/ wife," "noble," or the infamous, "Who can find a virtuous woman."

In verse 5 and following, the text uses diminutive language, "youth/girl/boy" for Boaz's servants and for Ruth. This is the same language Jeremiah uses when he says, "I am only a boy," in response to God's call in Jeremiah 1:6. There is a pun in verse 8. Boaz tells Ruth to cling to his girls the way she clung to Naomi, using the same verb. In verse 9 Boaz tells Ruth the follow "them," which in this case is feminine plural and refers to the girls and not the boys. God's wings in Ruth 2:12 suggest a mother bird.

In the acrostic psalm 112, in verse 4 the verb *racham* expresses a feeling rooted in the womb, its grammatical root, *rechem*. Generations of male translators render it "to have compassion" or "be merciful," stripping root and referent. Its most iconic uses are for the sex worker confronted with the possibility of her child being sawn in half surrendering him "because her mother-love burned within her" in 1 Kings 3:25 and the "can a woman forget her nursing child or show no mother-love to the child of her body" in Isaiah 49:15. Verse 6 includes "forever" on each line, though the first is often omitted; the addition of "true" permits its retention and comprehension. Verse 8 ends with model subject "look[ing] upon their foes," with no further description, frustrating translators. I have left it so following the MT, LXX, and Peshitta. Others supply a variety of solutions: NRSV, "in triumph"; JPS "the fall of"; CEB "their enemies' defeat"; Alter "defeat of their enemies." Similarly, in verse 9, what is "dispersed" or "scattered" (like grain) to the poor is unnamed; I supply the generic "resources" for clarity.

Preaching Prompts

These lessons are bound together by themes of wealth and generosity. Boaz uses his largesse to meet Ruth's material needs. In the psalm, wealth is a sign of blessing, as is often (but not always) the case in the scriptures; the one so blessed is deeply generous as a sign of their righteousness and just deeds.

There is a lot going on in Boaz's field in terms of gender, class, and identity. It is being worked by women and men who due to their social status relative to Boaz are called girls and boys, very much in the way some used to refer to grown men as house boys, also evoking the racist practice of black women and men being called "gal" and "boy" in (and not just in) the South. In verse 9, the boys draw water, a caution against stringent notions of women's and men's work. Curiously neither the narrator nor Boaz use the language of slavery; Boaz's boy and girls may be paid workers. Ruth, who does not know their arrangements, calls herself and the women slave-women in 2:13. In 2:9, Boaz tells his boys not to touch Ruth—he says nothing about his girls. A charitable reading says his girls were already off-limits, but Ruth was a foreign woman, whom the Israelites tended to view as promiscuous and enticing; she was also hungry, poor, and vulnerable. She may well have been prey without his intervention, which he knew, begging the question if there were other vulnerable women who were not off-limits.

In 2 Corinthians 8, Paul proffers a different model of wealth and of dealing with wealth, generosity. He describes a wealth of generosity in distributing material wealth to meet the needs of the community.

Jesus's parable in Luke 12 might well be an excursus on the psalm in reverse; his wealthy exemplar is far from righteous, hoarding his resources and expending capital only in order to horde on a larger scale.

While there are a few wealthy women in the scriptures, those who fund Jesus and the early church, there are even fewer independently wealthy women like the widow Judith. Women described as owning their homes (indicated by "her house") should be considered if not wealthy, then secure in an uncertain world. Examples would include Rahab and Delilah, the former's security achieved through sex work, the latter unexplained. The woman whose son Elisha raises in 2 Kings 4 is married, yet when she flees famine at his word it is "her household," no mention of her husband, and when the famine ends, the king restores "all that was hers, together with all the revenue of the fields from the day that she left the land until now" in 2 Kings 8:6. However, the generic wealthy person in wisdom literature and didactic texts is always male.

These readings provide the necessary if unwelcome opportunity to talk about wealth, class, and gender in our world and in the world of the text and examine our beliefs, budgets, and priorities.

FEAST OF THE EVER-BLESSED VIRGIN MARY, AUGUST 15

Judith 13:18–20; Canticle 15, the Magnificat (Luke 1:46–55);
Revelation 21:1–7; Luke 1:26–38

Judith 13:18 Uzziah said to Judith, "O daughter, you are blessed by the Most High God above all other women on earth, and blessed be the Holy God, who created the heavens and the earth, who has guided you to cut off the head of the leader of our enemies. [19] Praise of you will never depart from the hearts of women and men who remember the power of God. [20] May God do these things for you as an eternal exaltation, and may God visit you with blessings, because you did not withhold your life when our nation was humiliated, rather you rallied against our demise, walking straight before our God." And all the people said, "Amen. Amen."

Canticle 15, the Magnificat, Luke 1:46–55

[46] "My soul magnifies the Holy One,
[47] and my spirit rejoices in God my Savior,
[48] for God has looked with favor on the lowliness of God's own womb-slave.
Surely, from now on all generations will call me blessed;
[49] for the Mighty One has done great things for me,
and holy is God's name.
[50] God's loving-kindness is for those who fear God
from generation to generation.
[51] God has shown the strength of God's own arm;
God has scattered the arrogant in the intent of their hearts.
[52] God has brought down the powerful from their thrones,
and lifted up the lowly;
[53] God has filled the hungry with good things,
and sent the rich away empty.
[54] God has helped God's own child, Israel,
a memorial to God's mercy,
[55] just as God said to our mothers and fathers,
to [Hagar and] and Sarah and Abraham, to their descendants forever."

Revelation 21:1 I saw a new heaven and a new earth, for the first heaven and the first earth had passed away, and the sea was no more. [2] And I saw the holy city, the new Jerusalem, descending heaven from God, prepared as a bride adorned for her beloved. [3] And I heard a loud voice from the throne saying,

"Look! The home of God is among the woman-born.
God will dwell with them as their God;

they will be God's peoples,
and selfsame God will be with them.

^{4} God will wipe every tear from their eyes.
Death will be no more;
grief and weeping and pain will be no more,
for the first things have passed away."

^{5} And the One who seated upon the throne said, "Look! I am making all things new." The One also said, "Write, for these words are trustworthy and true." ^{6} Then the One said to me, "It is done! I am the Alpha and the Omega, the beginning and the end. I will give to the thirsty from the spring of the water of life freely. ^{7} Those who overcome will inherit these things, and I will be their God and they will be my daughters and sons."

Luke 1:26 In the sixth month the angel Gabriel was sent by God to a town of Galilee, Nazareth, ^{27} to a virgin betrothed to a man whose name was Joseph, of the house of David. And the name of the virgin was Mary. ^{28} And the angel came to Mary and said, "Rejoice, favored one! The Most High God is with you." ^{29} Now, she was troubled by the angel's words and pondered what sort of greeting this was. ^{30} Then the angel said to her, "Fear not Mary, for you have found favor with God. ^{31} And now, you will conceive in your womb and give birth to a son, and you will name him Jesus. ^{32} He will be great and will be called the Son of the Most High, and the Sovereign God will give him the throne of his ancestor David. ^{33} He will reign over the house of Jacob forever, and of his sovereignty there will be no end." ^{34} Then Mary said to the angel, "How can this be, since I have not known a man intimately?" ^{35} The angel said to her, "The Holy Spirit, She will come upon you, and the power of the Most High will overshadow you; therefore the one born will be holy. He will be called Son of God. ^{36} And now, Elizabeth your kinswoman has even conceived a son in her old age, and this is the sixth month for she who was called barren. ^{37} For nothing will be impossible with God." ^{38} Then Mary said, "Here am I, the woman-slave of God; let it be with me according to your word." Then the angel left her.

PROCLAMATION

Text Notes

In Judith 13:20, Judith's actions are described awkwardly as "rallying against" the "corpse" (understood as the eminent demise) of her people, i.e., taking action to oppose that which would end in their deaths.

Revelation 21 deploys a marriage metaphor that does not require a rigid gender binary or heteronormativity to be effective, so I have translated *aner*, "man," meaning "husband" in verse 2, as "beloved." *Nike* in verse 7 means to "overcome obstacles" or "prevail." To "be victorious" and "conquer" are also within the semantic range; however the latter two choices do not clearly indicate struggle, and "conquer" (as in NRSV) seems unnecessarily martial here.

In Mary's languages, Hebrew for prayer and religious texts and Aramaic for daily life, the Holy Spirit is feminine. The Greek scriptures use the neuter pronoun corresponding to "it." It is not until the production of the Vulgate and other Latin texts that the masculine pronoun is inserted. While the literary language is Greek, the translation choice reflects the underlying Semitic linguistic cultural context. In verse 48 of the Magnificat, Mary uses the same slave language that Hannah does, "woman-slave of God," a common expression across the canon. When used with reference to reproduction, as here, I use womb-slave; the language of slavery pervades the scriptures and forms the rhetoric of the most familiar stories, often without examination. In verse 55 of the Magnificat, I have added Hagar as a witness to God's fidelity proclaimed in the verse.

Preaching Prompts

Like Judith, whose name can be translated "Jewish woman," Miriam rendered "Mary" in English (along with other Hebraic names in the Second Testament to sound less Jewish) was a Jewish woman. Where Judith is an older widowed woman when she puts her body on the line to save her people, Mary, named for the prophet Miriam like all of the "Marys," was young and on the cusp of marriage. Each woman has her bona fides established in a lengthy genealogy. Judith's is the longest of any woman in the canon, stretching from the time of Nebuchadnezzar to Simeon, Leah's son by Jacob (Jth. 8:1; 9:2); though some argue against her historicity. While Judith's husband is folded into *her* genealogy, "Her husband Manasseh, who belonged to her tribe and family," Mary's genealogy is *Joseph's* genealogy.

The patriarchal genealogy fails to tell the story of Mary and Jesus as descendants of Bathsheba and David, though it does so for Joseph (Matt. 1:1–17, see verses 6 and 16, and Luke 2:4), even while naming Tamar (I), Ruth, and describing Bathsheba as the wife of Uriah but without her name (Matt. 1:3, 5–6). Mary is *presumed* to be from Joseph's tribe, Judah, following the most common marital pattern and likely from a more closely related clan within the tribe. Mary is likely not Joseph's sister, though she could be his cousin; somewhere between Solomon in verse 7 and Mattan, Joseph's grandfather, in verse 15 Mary's genealogy is obscured.

Both Judith and Mary have their virtue attested—Judith's piety as a widow (Jth. 8:4–6) and Mary's virginity (Luke 1:26ff)—and both will use their bodies in scandalous ways to effect salvation. Judith entices an enemy general who seeks to seduce her—but with a maid present to testify to her virtue—and beheads the man with his own sword (Jth. 13:4–10). Mary agrees to the divine pregnancy, risking being ostracized and perhaps stoned for the appearance of breaking faith with Joseph. For some readers there will always be a question of the degree to which Mary was free to refuse. That she affirmatively consents is clear: "Let it be with me according to your word." But could she refuse? Before she consents, Gabriel says: "You will. . . ." The timing is crucial, helping readers and hearers grapple with consent issues in the text and the gulfs between ancient and contemporary ethical standards.

Mary and Judith are also linked in the words of blessing "among" and "above other" women in Judith 13:18 and Luke 1:42. Elizabeth, Mary's relative, could have chosen the blessing by drawing from her scriptures, from Judith, and from the words of Deborah's blessing on Jael in Judges 5:24: "Most blessed of women . . . of tent-dwelling women most blessed." (Judith was included in the Greek Jewish Bible and influential where not later canonical.) Like her textual sisters, Jael's story is framed by scandal, assassinating an enemy general after welcoming him to hide there; a man who was so well known as a rapist his mother imagines his delay is caused by his proclivities (Judg. 4:17–24; 5:24–30). His position at his death, between (not "at" per NRSV) Jael's legs, would seem confirmation.

The blessings of Jael and Judith with their histories of violence worry the innocence of the annunciation with the reminder of the violence to which Mary is at risk now and the violence she will live to see enacted on the body of her son. In the words of another holy person, "a sword will pierce her soul" (Luke 2:35).

John (1:1) says, "The Word became flesh and dwelled, *eskēnōsen*, among us." If Jesus is the heir of Bathsheba and David according to the flesh; it is through Mary's flesh, the matrix of the Incarnation, that God comes to dwell with us. That verb, *skēnoō*, "to dwell" is also used in the second reading chosen for today: "God will dwell with them as their God." The Feast of the Ever-Blessed Virgin Mary affords an opportunity to reflect on the ways in which God dwells with us and a model of hospitality.

PROPER 15 (CLOSEST TO AUGUST 17)

Ruth 3:1–18; Psalm 65:1–13; 2 Corinthians 9:6–13; Luke 8:1–3

Ruth 3:1 Naomi, Ruth's mother-in-law, said to her, "My daughter, am I not seeking respite for you, that will be good for you? [2] Now is not Boaz our kin, with whose girls you have been? Look! He is winnowing barley on the threshing floor tonight. [3] Now bathe and anoint yourself and put on your [best] clothes and go down to the threshing floor; do not make yourself known to the man until he has finished eating and drinking. [4] When he lies down, note the place where he lies, and go and uncover his thighs and lie down, and he will tell you what you should do." [5] Ruth said to Naomi, "All that you tell me I will do."

[6] Then Ruth went down to the threshing floor and did just as her mother-in-law commanded her. [7] Now Boaz had eaten and drunk and his heart was content, and he went to lie down at the end of the heap [of grain]. Then Ruth came in secret and uncovered his thighs and lay down. [8] At midnight the man trembled and turned and right there a woman was

lying at his thighs! ⁹ Then Boaz said, "Who are you?" And she said, "I am Ruth, your slave-woman; spread your cloak over your slave-woman, for you are a kin redeemer." ¹⁰ And he said, "May you be blessed by the MOST HIGH, my daughter; your most recent act of fidelity is greater than the first; you have not gone after young men, whether poor or rich. ¹¹ And now, my daughter, fear not; all that you have spoken, I will do for you, for all the assembly of my people know you are a warrior-hearted woman. ¹² And now, it is true that I am a kin redeemer, there is a kin redeemer closer than I. ¹³ Spend the night tonight and when morning comes, if he will redeem you as kin, good; let him redeem you. If he does not want to redeem you as kin, then, as the AGELESS GOD lives, I will redeem you as kin myself. Lie down until the morning."

¹⁴ So Ruth lay at his thighs until morning, but got up before one person could recognize a neighbor for Boaz said [to himself], "Let it not be known that the woman came to the threshing floor." ¹⁵ Then he said, "Bring the cloak you are wearing and hold it out." So she held it and Boaz measured out six helpings of barley, and put it on her back; then he went into the city. ¹⁶ And Ruth came to her mother-in-law and Naomi asked, "Who are you, my daughter?" And she told her all that the man had done for her. ¹⁷ Ruth explained, "He gave these six helpings of barley to me, for he said, 'Do not go back to your mother-in-law empty-handed.'" ¹⁸ She replied, "Wait, my daughter, until you learn how the matter will shake out, for the man will not rest, but will conclude the matter today."

Psalm 65:1–13

¹ To you silence is praise, God in Zion;
    and to you vows shall be performed,
² You who answer prayer!
    To you shall all flesh come.
³ When deeds of iniquity overwhelm us,
    you forgive our transgressions.
⁴ Happy are those whom you choose and bring near
    to dwell in your courts.
    We shall be satisfied with the goodness of your house,
    your holy temple.
⁵ Through wondrous deeds you answer us with deliverance,
    O God of our salvation,
    hope of all the ends of the earth
    and of the farthest seas.
⁶ You established the mountains through your might;
    you are girded with strength.
⁷ The one who silences the roaring of the seas,
    the roaring of their waves,
    the rumble of the peoples.

8 They who live at the farthest reaches are awed by your signs;
   you make the dawnings of morning and evening sing for joy.
9 You attend the earth and water her,
   you enrich her greatly;
   the river of God is full of water;
   you provide the people with grain,
   thus you have established it.
10 Irrigating earth's furrows,
   smoothing her ridges,
   softening her with showers,
   and blessing her growth.
11 You crown the year with your goodness;
   your paths overflow with fatness.
12 The pastures of the wilderness overflow,
   and with joy the hills gird themselves.
13 The meadows are clothed with flocks,
   the valleys arrayed in grain,
   indeed they, shout for joy.

2 Corinthians 9:6 Now hear this: The one who sows sparingly, sparingly will also reap, and the one who sows in abundance, in abundance will also reap. 7 Each one must give as decided in your heart, not out of reluctance or under pressure, for "God loves a cheerful giver." 8 And the power of God is able to grant you all every gift abundantly, so that always having enough of everything, you all may abound in every good work. 9 As it is written,

"God scatters generously, and gives to the poor;
God's righteousness endures forever."

10 The one who supplies seed to the sower and bread for food will supply and multiply your seed and increase the harvest of your righteousness. 11 Enriched in every way for every kind of generosity which will yield through us thanksgiving to God, 12 for the offering of this ministry does not only supply the needs of the saints but also overflows with many thanksgivings to God. 13 Through the character of this ministry you all glorify God by your obedience to the confession of the gospel of Christ and by the generosity of your companionship with them and with all others.

Luke 8:1 Now after [a woman anointed his feet] Jesus went on through cities and villages, proclaiming and bringing the good news of the reign of God. The twelve were with him. 2 There were also some women who had been cured of evil spirits and infirmities: Mary, called Magdalene, from whom seven demons had gone out, 3 and Joanna, the wife of Herod's steward Chuza, and Susanna, and many others, who provided for them out of their resources.

PROCLAMATION

Text Notes

The text of Ruth uses questions as a narrative device throughout that are often converted to sentences in other translations; KJV tends to preserve the question form (see Judg. 4:6 and Ruth 2:8–10). The same expression in Ruth 2:1 means "good for" as well as "good to" you. The word used for the lower extremities in Ruth 3:4 refers to the whole leg and particularly the thighs and genitalia as in childbirth (Deut. 28:57); in Isaiah 7:20 "hair of the feet" refers to pubic hair shaved with other body hair in a ritual of humiliation. All of the slave language in Ruth is Ruth's; the narrator, Boaz, and Naomi all refer to Boaz's agricultural workers as his "girls" and "boys." Ruth refers to them and herself as enslaved (see Ruth 2:3 and 3:9), which is difficult to observe in translations that use "servant" throughout. Perhaps that communicates something about the harshness and desperation of her character's worldview.

The "kin redeemer," *go'el*, is the nearest adult male who bears responsibility for redeeming, or buying back, their hard-up kin from debt slavery and avenging their blood (Lev. 25:25–26, 48–49; Num. 35:12; Deut. 19:6, 12). That language is also used for God redeeming Israel and applied to Jesus in the Christian Testament. Ruth's fidelity in 3:10 is what is usually described as "lovingkindness" or "faithful love" when applied to God. Boaz describes Ruth as a "warrior-hearted" woman using the same description that the narrator uses for him in 2:1 (see discussion on Proper 14). In verse 16, Naomi asked Ruth the same question Boaz asked in verse 9, "who are you?" i.e., are you betrothed? Most translations opt for the nonliteral "how is it with you" for the latter. Verses 15 and 17 lack a unit of measure and say simply "six barleys." Similarly, verse 17 lacks "handed," saying merely "empty."

Second Corinthians 9:7 quotes part of the Greek text of Proverbs 22:8, which differs significantly from the Hebrew: "God blesses a cheerful and generous man."

With the exception of "bless/love," it is an exact quote. Verse 9 cites Psalm 112:9, also from the LXX.

Preaching Prompts

These texts portray divine and godly human providence; necessary providence because hunger and lack were regularly the lived experience of the framers of the stories and sometimes of their preservers. God provides for Boaz, Boaz provides for Ruth and through her, Naomi; in the psalm God provides for widows, orphans, and all the creatures of earth. The Epistle calls for the very generosity that Boaz demonstrates. And in the Gospel, Mary Magdalene, Johanna, and Susanna model the generosity that the Epistle commends.

In today's Ruth reading, Naomi has Ruth offer herself to Boaz, nominally under the levirate provision where a brother would marry his brother's widow to raise children in his name. Boaz is a more distant relative who will only become eligible when a nearer kinsman passes on the opportunity. One might well wonder what would happen if no relative accepted the responsibility; Ruth and Naomi would likely be indigent and perhaps turn to sex work with no other options.

Romantic readings of Ruth often ignore Naomi's grooming of her to sexually service Boaz—make herself attractive, wait until he is drunk, uncover his thighs, and do what he tells her—as a survival strategy for them both. Note that once they determine another man has the legal right to wed her, Boaz tells her to lie back down, knowing he has no legal access to her, and tells her to sneak out in the morning when she would have been more visible. It is likely that there was sexual contact between them, which, given Ruth's vulnerable status, is problematic for contemporary readers. The story of Ruth can easily be read as a story of survival sex and draws our attention to the plight of vulnerable, hungry, desperate migrant women.

The God of the psalmist is the God who provides, for humankind and animal kind, for the entire world as far as it is known. One might contemplate hearing the psalm from the perspectives of both those who have unshakable faith and trust in such a God and those who have no such trust, whose prayers for provision have not been answered.

In 2 Corinthians 9, the Christian community does the work of God in sharing what they have received abundantly, following the example set by the women who follow Jesus and supported his work. Both the Epistle and the Gospel illustrate that the way of Jesus drew a diversity of followers from different class strata, and they were expected to share their resources.

A final note on the Gospel: the text says the women provided for "them." The women did not just ensure that Jesus was housed and fed and clothed; they bankrolled the entire movement, likely supporting some number of the male disciples. These lessons present women as both beneficiaries and benefactresses and from either pole, members of communities that support one another, financially when necessary. However, it should not be neglected that behind these texts and in the world that receives and reads them, there are many, many individuals and families whose needs are not met by community or kin.

PROPER 16 (CLOSEST TO AUGUST 24)

Ruth 4:9–17; Psalm 107:1–9, 19–22; 1 Corinthians 12:14–26; Matthew 5:43–48

Ruth 4:9 Then Boaz said to the elders and all the people, "Today you are witnesses that I am acquiring all that belonged to Elimelech and all that belonged to Chilion and Mahlon from the hand of Naomi. [10] Also, Ruth the Moabite, the wife of Mahlon am I acquiring for myself as a wife to maintain the dead man's name on his inheritance, to reestablish the name of the deceased on his heritable property, that it may not be cut off from his kin and from the gate of his native place; today you are witnesses."

¹¹ All the women and men who were at the gate, along with the elders, said, "We are witnesses. May the FAITHFUL GOD grant that the woman who is coming into your house be like Rachel and Leah; the two of them built up the house of Israel. May you prosper in Ephrathah and establish a lineage in Bethlehem; ¹² and may your house, through the children that the FOUNT OF LIFE will give you by this young woman, be like the house of Perez, whom Tamar gave birth to for Judah."¹³ So Boaz took Ruth as his own for a wife. He came to her and the SOURCE OF LIFE granted her a pregnancy, and she gave birth to a son. ¹⁴ Then the women said to Naomi, "Blessed be the FAITHFUL GOD, who has not deprived you this day of next-of-kin; and may the child's name be renowned in Israel! ¹⁵ He shall be to you a restorer of life and a provider in your latter years; for your daughter-in-law has given birth to him, she who loves you, she who is more to you than seven sons." ¹⁶ Then Naomi took the child and laid him in her bosom, and she fostered him. ¹⁷ The neighbor-women gave him a name, saying, "A son has been born to Naomi." They named him Obed; he became the father of Jesse, the father of David."

Psalm 107:1–9, 19–22

¹ Give thanks to SHE WHO IS MAJESTY, for she is good,
   and her faithful love endures forever.

² Let the redeemed of SHE WHO SAVES proclaim
   that she redeemed them from the hand of the foe.

³ And she has gathered them from [all] the lands;
   from the east and from the west, from the north and from the south.

⁴ They wandered in the wilderness, in the desert;
   no path to a city fit for settling did they find.

⁵ They were hungry and thirsty;
   their souls fainted within them.

⁶ Then they cried to SHE WHO HEARS in their trouble,
   and from their distress she delivered them.

⁷ And she led them on a straight path
   to a city fit for settling.

⁸ Let them give thanks to WOMB OF LIFE for her faithful love
   and her wonderful works for the woman-born.

⁹ For she satisfies the thirsty soul
   and the hungry souls she fills with goodness.

¹⁹ They cried to the MOTHER OF ALL in their trouble,
   and she delivered them from their distress.

²⁰ She sent forth her word and healed them

and saved them from their pits.

²¹ Let them give thanks to the WOMB OF LIFE for her faithful love
and wonderful works for the woman-born.

²² Let them sacrifice sacrifices of thanksgiving
and tell of her acts with shouts of joy.

1 Corinthians 12:14 Now look, the body is not a single part but rather, many. ¹⁵ If the foot says, "Because I am not a hand, I am not part of the body," is it then, not of the body? ¹⁶ And if the ear says, "Because I am not an eye, I am not part of the body, is it then, not of the body? ¹⁷ If the whole body were an eye, where would be the hearing? If the whole body were hearing, where would be the smelling? ¹⁸ Thus it is that God has designated the parts of the body, each of them, according to the will of God. ¹⁹ If all were a single part, where would be the body? ²⁰ Thus it is that there are many parts, yet one body. ²¹ The eye cannot say to the hand, "I have no use for you," nor again the head to the feet, "I have no use for you." ²² Rather, on the contrary, the parts of the body that seem to be weaker are indispensable. ²³ And those parts of the body that we think dishonorable we clothe with more honor, and our unpresentable parts are treated with more decorum. ²⁴ However our more respectable parts do not need such. Yet God has so composed the body, giving the more honor to the lesser part, ²⁵ that there may be no division within the body, rather that the parts may have the same concern for one another. ²⁶ And if one part suffers, all suffer together with it; if one part is honored, all rejoice together with it.

Matthew 5:43 "You all have heard that it was said, '*You shall love your neighbor* and hate your enemy.' ⁴⁴ Yet I say to you all: Love your enemies and pray for those who persecute you, ⁴⁵ so that you may be children of the One in heaven who begot you; for the sun—which belongs to God—rises on the evil and on the good, and God rains on the righteous and on the unrighteous woman or man. ⁴⁶ For if you all love those who love you, what reward do you have? Do not even the tax collectors do the same? ⁴⁷ And if you greet only your sisters and brothers, what more are you doing than others? Do not the Gentiles do the same? ⁴⁸ Be perfect, therefore, as your heavenly Sovereign is perfect."

PROCLAMATION

Text Notes

In Psalm 107:8 and 2, "woman-born" renders the euphemism for humanity, "human children/children (or sons) of men." Son of Woman for the comparable Greek expression communicates the humanness called for in Matthew 8:20.

The choice of "unpresentable parts" in 1 Corinthians 12:23 for *aschēmona* excludes some of its translation options to avoid proclaiming as scripture that any parts of our bodies are "shameful" or "unworthy." The choice of "compose" in verse 24 is an English word play on the "parts" of the body, which parts can also be parts of a musical composition in Greek; the underlying verb means to "mix," "join," or "unite." Also in verse 24, NRSV's choice of "dissension" gives the false impression that the text speaks against disagreement; "division" better captures *schisma*, schism, see CEB and KJV.

Preaching Prompts

The story of Ruth functions as an introduction to the story of David; it is also a story of community, relationship, and cultural values: God's relationship with Israel results in the provisioning of Bethlehem and is extolled in the psalm. Naomi returns to her community in her time of need. Ruth's relationship with Naomi grows closer while Orpah seeks the comfort of her community. And it is as a member of the same community that Boaz enters into a new relationship with Ruth that will see her and Naomi provided for. In the Epistle, the God of creation also creates community, and the God who provides for creation expects this beloved community to provide and care for one another. As is often the case, Jesus expands our circles of care and concern beyond our own community and those we love to those we do not like and do not want to love.

Jesus quotes the common wisdom which is a combination of the command to love your neighbor (from Lev. 19:18) and its interpretive corollary, hate your enemies, cited together as an equally authoritative text. This is a useful reminder that interpretations can be as authoritative as primary texts, often holding the weight of scripture. As is the case for Jesus in Matthew before his transforming encounter with the Canaanite mother, his language here about the Gentiles presents them as negative examples in stereotypical terms, an opportunity to discuss the ways in which human biases are present in the text. The call to love enemies is also a call to love those from whom we are separated by societal and cultural structures like race, class, and gender; "enemies" are just the most extreme example of the radical limitlessness of our love.

PROPER 17 (CLOSEST TO AUGUST 31)

2 Chronicles 28:1, 5, 8–15; Psalm 106:1–6, 40–47;
Ephesians 4:1– 8; John 4:7 –26

2 Chronicles 28:1 Ahaz was twenty years old at his reign; he reigned sixteen years in Jerusalem. He did not do what was right in the sight of the GOD WHOSE NAME IS HOLY like David his ancestor.

⁵ So the HOLY ONE his God gave him into the hand of the king of Aram, who smote him and captured from him a great number of captives and brought them to Damascus. He was also given into the hand of the king of Israel, who smote him a great smiting.

⁸ Thus the Israelites captured two hundred thousand of their [Judean] kinfolk—women, and their daughters and sons—and they also plundered from them much booty and brought the booty to Samaria. ⁹ Yet there was a prophet of the LIVING GOD, Oded was his name and he went out in the face of the army coming to Samaria, and said to them, "Look, it was out of fury over Judah that the HOLY ONE OF OLD, the God of your mothers and fathers, gave them into your hands, but you all have killed them in a rage that has struck the heavens.

¹⁰ And now, the daughters and sons of Judah and Jerusalem, you all speak of subjugating: as slave-women, as enslaved men, for yourselves! So then, what do any of you have except offenses against the RIGHTEOUS ONE your God? ¹¹ Now hear me and send back the captives whom you have captured from your kinfolk, for the raging fury of the GOD WHO THUNDERS is upon you."

¹² Then men from among the leaders of the Ephraimites, Azariah ben Johanan, Berechiah ben Meshillemoth, Jehizkiah ben Shallum, and Amasa ben Hadlai, stood up against those who were coming from the war. ¹³ And they said to them, "You shall not bring the captive women, children, and men here, for these are offenses against the HOLY GOD you propose to bring on us in addition to our own sins and offenses. For our offense is already great, and there is raging fury against Israel." ¹⁴ So the troops abandoned the captives and the plunder before the officials and the whole assembly. ¹⁵ Then the men who were mentioned by name got up and took custody of the captive women, children, and men, and with the booty they clothed all that were naked among them. They clothed them, they gave them sandals, they fed them, they gave them drink, and they anointed them. And carrying all those who staggered on donkeys, they led them, and they brought them to their kinfolk at Jericho, the City of Palms. Then they returned to Samaria.

Psalm 106:1–6, 40–47

¹ Hallelujah! Give thanks to the ANCIENT OF DAYS, for she is good;
  for her faithful love endures forever.
² Who can utter the mighty acts of the MAJESTY OF THE AGES,
  or disclose all her praise?
³ Happy are those who preserve justice,
  doing righteousness at all times.
⁴ Remember me, FAITHFUL ONE,
  when showing favor to your people;
  visit me in your saving work.
⁵ that I may see goodness attend your chosen ones,
  that I may rejoice in the joy of your nation,
  that I may proclaim praise along with your possession.
⁶ We have sinned along with our mothers and fathers;
  we have committed iniquity, we have done wickedly.

40 Then the anger of the DREAD GOD ignited against her people,
and she abhorred her possession.

41 She gave them into the hand of the nations;
they who ruled over them were they who hated them.

42 Their enemies oppressed them,
and they were humbled under their hand.

43 Many times she delivered them,
yet they rebelled through their own design,
and were brought low through their iniquity.

44 And she saw them through their distress
when she heard their cry.

45 For their sake God remembered her covenant,
and showed compassion
according to the abundance of her faithful love.

46 She caused them to be viewed tenderly
by all who held them captive.

47 Save us, HOLY SHEPHERD, our God,
and gather us from among the nations,
that we may give thanks to your holy name
and rejoice in your praise.

Ephesians 4:1 I exhort you all, I, prisoner for the Savior, to walk worthy of the calling to which you have been called: ² With all humility and gentleness, with patience, bearing with one another in love, ³ doing your best to keep the unity of the Spirit in the bond of peace. ⁴ There is one body and one Spirit, just as you were called to the one hope of your calling, ⁵ one Redeemer, one faith, one baptism, ⁶ one God and Parent of all, who is above all and through all and in all. ⁷ Yet each of us was given grace according to the measure of the gift of the Messiah. ⁸ Therefore it is said,

> When God ascended on high she took captivity captive;
> she gave gifts to her people.

John 4:7 A Samaritan woman came to draw water. Jesus said to her, "Give me a drink." ⁸ Now his disciples had gone to the city to buy food. ⁹ The Samaritan woman said to him, "How are you, a Judean, asking a drink of me, a woman of Samaria?" (Judeans do not share things in common with Samaritans.) ¹⁰ Jesus answered and said to her, "If you knew the gift of God and who is the one telling to you, 'Give me a drink,' you would have asked him, and he would have given you living water." ¹¹ The woman said to him, "Sir, you have no bucket, and the well is deep. From where do you get that living water? ¹² Are you greater than our ancestor Jacob, the one who gave us the well, and with his daughters and sons and his flocks drank from it?" ¹³ Jesus answered and said to her, "Everyone who drinks of this water will thirst again. [14] But the one who drinks of the water that I will give will never thirst. The water that I will give will become in them a fount of water springing up into eternal life." [15] The woman said to him, "Sir, give me this water, that I may never thirst or keep coming here to draw water."

[16] Jesus said to her, "Go, call your husband, and come [back] to this place." [17] The woman answered and said to him, "I have no husband." Jesus said to her, "You said rightly, 'I have no husband.' [18] For five husbands have you had, and now the one you have is not your husband. What you have said is true!" [19] The woman said to him, "Sir, I see that you are a prophet. [20] Our mothers and fathers worshiped on this mountain, yet you say in Jerusalem is the place where people must worship." [21] Jesus said to her, "Believe me, woman, the hour is coming when neither on this mountain nor in Jerusalem will you worship the Sovereign God. [22] You all worship what you do not know; we worship what we know, for salvation is from the Judeans. [23] But the hour is coming, and now is, when the true worshipers will worship the Sovereign God in spirit and truth, for these are the worshipers the Sovereign God seeks. [24] God is spirit, and those who worship God must worship in spirit and truth." [25] The woman said to Jesus, "I know that Messiah is coming" (the one who is called Christ). "When he comes, he will proclaim all things to us." [26] Jesus said to her, "I am, the one who is speaking to you."

PROCLAMATION

Text Notes

In Psalm 106:46, "view tenderly" renders "view with/through mother-love" from the verb whose root is the womb. "Save us" in the following verse is the Hebrew expression that will become "Hosanna."

"Prisoner for the Savior" in Ephesians 4:1 translates "prisoner in the Lord." Verse 8 quotes Psalm 68:18 where God is personified as the divine warrior scaling heights, up into the heavens, descending to the field of battle and waging war. Like human monarchs, she takes captives but unlike them, she takes them to freedom and destroys captivity in the same moment.

In John 4:12, the woman mentions Jacob and his children (or sons) which I have made explicitly inclusive given that Jacob had an unknown number of daughters, including one named Dinah, among his thirty-three children (see Gen. 37:55, 46:15).

The *Samarians* were the inhabitants of the northern monarchy of Israel who ultimately fell to Assyria and were largely deported. The land was repopulated with other conquered peoples and their descendants became known as *Samaritans*. Judeans held them in low esteem because of their mixed heritage to which they attributed the differences between their worship traditions. Notably, the Samaritan Pentateuch is the entirety of their Bible; nothing else is canonical, which remains the case for Samaritan Jews in the present. The dispute about the mountain in John 4:20–22 is rooted in one of the many differences between the Samaritan and Judean Torahs: Whether the mountain in Deuteronomy 27:4 on which Joshua (8:30) later built an altar is Ebal (Judeans) or Gerizim (Samaritans). As a result, the Samaritan temple was built on Mt. Gerizim, the "this mountain" of John 4:20–21. Palestinian Samaritan Jews continued to worship on the mountain, the temple long destroyed by the Romans in 70 CE. *Ioudaois* should be understood as "Judean" in opposition to Samaritan in verse 24, as both communities are Jewish.

Preaching Prompts

This Sunday's readings and those of the following one explore the ancient conflict between Judeans and Samaritans that frames Jesus's encounter with the Samaritan woman, also spread over these two Sundays. She is an evangelist, proclaiming Jesus as Messiah at the beginning of his ministry and brought others to Jesus. She has not been given enough credit for what the Gospel calls her "testimony," as confessing Christ, following Christ, or proclaiming Christ. In today's first lesson, the southern Judean monarchy is at war with the northern monarchy, Israel, whose capital is Samaria, and at war with a neighboring state, Aram, in what is now Syria. The war is characterized as God's punishment for disobedience and idolatry. It will be useful to remind congregants that this is a standard theology in some parts of the canon while other passages offer differing theology. The text shows a level of animus between these two nations that are one people, albeit divided. The Israelites who win this round take their Judean kin captive and prepare to enslave them but for the intervention of a little known prophet. When they repent and prepare to release them, clothing them and providing shoes, the reader/hearer learns that the captives have been stripped naked publicly for their disposition as enslaved persons, evoking the slave markets of this country. While this incident is unknown to many readers and hearers of the text, it would have been known to Jesus and his disciples and the Samaritan woman. This story is set before the Israelite people of Samaria became transformed into an essentially distinct people, the Samaritans (see the first lesson of the following Sunday); these tensions go all the way back to the division of the monarchy.

When read together, these texts portray the deep and enduring divisions that remain between nations and peoples and proclaim a God who delivers for people time and time again and even softens the hearts of those with whom they are in conflict, their captors according to the psalm. Even in a framework in which God is held responsible for the depredations of hostile nations, the power of God to save is never doubted. In the repurposed psalm, God takes the field of battle herself and takes captivity itself captive, putting an end to imperial conquest and subjugation in a vision not yet fully realized. Jesus points us to that day when national and cultural and religious distinctions will not divide us, but we will all worship the one God.

It is important to note that Jesus is not calling for colonizing evangelism. "Spirit and truth" are not doctrinal categories; they are broad enough to include peoples with profound differences as illustrated by Jesus's conversations and visits with the Samaritan woman and her people.

PROPER 18 (CLOSEST TO SEPTEMBER 7)

2 Kings 17:21–28, 41; Psalm 34:1–14; 1 Peter 5:6–11; John 4:27–29, 39–42

2 Kings 17:21 When God tore Israel from the house of David, they [the people] made Jeroboam son of Nebat king and Jeroboam drove Israel from following the HOLY ONE OF OLD and made them commit great sin. ²² Thus the women and men of Israel walked in all the sins that Jeroboam did and they did not turn from them. ²³ That is until the HOLY ONE turned Israel away from God's presence as God had foretold through all God's bond-servants, the women and men who were prophets, and Israel was exiled from their own land to Assyria until this day.

²⁴ Then the king of Assyria brought from Babylon, Cuthah, Avva, Hamath, and Sepharvaim, and placed them in the cities of Samaria in place of the women and men of Israel, and they took possession of Samaria, and settled in its cities. ²⁵ And it was in the beginning of their settling there that they did not revere GOD WHOSE NAME IS HOLY, so the DREAD GOD sent lions among them, and there were killings among them. ²⁶ Then they spoke to the king of Assyria, saying, "The nations you exiled and settled in the cities of Samaria do not know the way of the god of the land so therefore it has sent among them lions and they are putting them to death because they do not know the way of the god of the land." ²⁷ Then the king of Assyria issued a command, saying, "Send there one of the priests whom you sent into exile from there and they shall go back [he and his wife and his children] and they shall live there, and he shall teach them the way of the god of the land." ²⁸ So one of the priests whom they had carried away from Samaria came and settled in Bethel and he was teaching them how they should revere the HOLY ONE OF OLD.

⁴¹ And it was that these nations revered the HOLY ONE, and their idols they also worshiped and to this day their children and their children's children continue to do as their ancestors did.

Psalm 34:1–14

¹ I will bless SHE WHO IS GOD at all times;
   her praise shall ever be in my mouth.
² I will glory in SHE WHO IS STRENGTH;
   let the humble hear and rejoice.
³ Proclaim with me the greatness of SHE WHO IS EXALTED
   and let us exalt her Name together.

⁴ I sought SHE WHO SAVES, and she answered me
and delivered me out of all my terror.

⁵ Look upon her and be radiant,
and let not your faces be ashamed.

⁶ I called in my affliction and SHE WHO HEARS heard me
and saved me from all my troubles.

⁷ The messenger of SHE WHO SAVES encompasses those who revere her,
and she will deliver them.

⁸ Taste and see that SHE WHO IS DELIGHT is good;
happy are they who trust in her!

⁹ Revere SHE WHO IS GOD, you that are her saints,
for those who revere her lack nothing.

¹⁰ The young lions suffer want for food and starve,
but those who seek SHE WHO PROVIDES lack no good thing.

¹¹ Come, children, listen to me;
I will teach you the reverence of SHE WHO IS MAJESTY.

¹² Who is the woman or man that desires life,
and would love long days to enjoy good?

¹³ Keep your tongue from evil,
and your lips from speaking deceit.

¹⁴ Turn from evil, and do good;
seek peace, and pursue it.

1 Peter 5:6 Humble yourselves so under the mighty hand of God, that God may exalt you all in due time. ⁷ All your anxiety, cast on God, because God cares for you all. ⁸ Be sober, keep alert: Like a roaring lion your adversary the devil, goes around seeking someone to devour. ⁹ Resist it, firm in your faith, for you all know the same sufferings that are throughout the world your sisters and brothers are experiencing. ¹⁰ And the God of all grace, who has called you to God's eternal glory in Christ, will Godself, after you all have suffered for a little while, restore, support, strengthen, and establish you all. ¹¹ To God be the power forever and ever. Amen.

John 4:27 Now at that moment [after Jesus said to the Samaritan woman, "I am, the one who is speaking to you,"] his disciples came and marveled that with a woman Jesus was speaking; but no one said, "What do you want?" or "Why are you speaking with her?" ²⁸ Then the woman left her water jar and went back to the city and she said to the people, ²⁹ "Come right now and see a person who told me all, everything I ever did. Is this not the Messiah?"

³⁹ Thus many Samaritans from that city believed in Jesus because of the woman's testimony, "He told me all I had ever done." ⁴⁰ Therefore, when the Samaritan women and men came to Jesus, they asked him to stay with them and he stayed there two days. ⁴¹ And many more believed because of his word. ⁴² So they said to the woman, "It is no longer because of

what you said that we believe, for we ourselves have heard and we know that this is truly the Savior of the world."

PROCLAMATION

Text Notes

In 2 Kings 17:23, the text uses the term "slaves" for the prophets of God, employing the same language as the bondage of their ancestors in Egyptian enslavement. Slavery is normative all throughout the scriptures and is used for "positive" and negative examples, e.g., "the slave of Christ" in 1 Corinthians 7:22 and "enslaved to sin" in Romans 6:6, as well as mundane descriptions of ordinary life.

In verse 24, language for "people," who/what was brought from this wide array of nations and city states from Syria to Mesopotamia is lacking. When an unknown speaker in verse 26 describes the situation in which "the god of the land" is unknown, I use the pronoun "it," reflecting the speaker's lack of knowledge as well. (Similarly, I use the neuter pronoun for the devil in the Epistle, as the Greek pronoun can be translated as masculine, feminine, or neuter, and as the devil is a character out of this world, I choose not to ascribe either of the world's most common genders to it.)

The MT uses the common plural for the return and settling of the priest and the masculine singular for his teaching of God's ways. Most translations amend to "him." Reading that his family returned and resettled accounts for the plural and for his singular teaching subsequently. The "way of God" in 26–27 is the singular *mishpat* of God, normally "judgment" or "precept."

Biblical Hebrew does not have a word that means simply "divine winged being," what many conceive when they read or hear the word "angel." Instead, Hebrew uses a word, *mal'akh,* that means "messenger," whether the one bearing the message is human or divine. Further, these messengers are distinct from cherubim and seraphim—consider them different species; they are never interchanged—and as in the story of Jacob's ladder, do not have wings. Greek *aggelos* has the same sense of human or divine messenger, and none of the angels of the New Testament are described with wings. There is one distinct angel among the host of heaven, the angel of God (or the Lord) in other translations, here in Psalm 34:7, the Messenger of She Who Saves. Many scholars understand this angel to be God in disguise so that she can be among her people without her holiness harming them, a kind of divine drag.

The call for sobriety in 1 Peter 5:8 is not a call for total abstinence, just as the call to "keep alert" is not a call to insomnia. This one piece of rhetoric has been abused apart from the other. Together they are a call to clearheaded mindfulness and situational awareness, careful consideration of what one consumes in one's faith, i.e., teaching, preaching, philosophy, etc.

Preaching Prompts

There is a tension between proclaiming Christ to and for the world and respecting the traditions of our neighbors. The name of Christ has been badly damaged by conquest in his name ostensibly to spread the gospel. Conquest is as old as humanity. Conquest in the name of God is as old as the scriptures Jews and Christians share uneasily; the story of the Promised Land is one of conquest and one the Europeans seized upon in the name of Jesus. The "creation" of the Samaritans and the enduring animus between them and Judean Jews is the result of the Assyrian conquest in part. However, animus between the two communities goes back to the division of the monarchy and likely before, the uneasy yoking of the disparate tribes into a confederation, as many scholars understand rather than ever a truly united monarchy.

In sharp relief to the previous presentation is the gospel of the Samaritan woman "come see a man . . ." from the previous Sunday. Her witness, her testimony has borne fruit. Her people have come to Christ and bid him come to them and the number of these early Samaritan believers multiplies.

Prowling through the Samaritan story in biblical and postbiblical tradition are lions; because the multiethnic Samaritans did not turn to Israel's God until they were set upon by lions, their worship was regarded as insincere.

The teaching priest in the first lesson, like Jesus, is an occupied person. They share the story and tradition of God with their conversation partners without threat of violence. Either could've used Psalm 34 to teach "the way of God." In the psalm God is the caretaker of the earth, her people, and her creatures including fearsome, young, hungry lions.

In the Epistle, the believing community is in peril from an enemy that is modeled on the rapacious lions prevalent in the first testament and the writings that came after it. The lion which has been associated with the ancient gods of the land like Asherah and the Israelite God becomes a metaphor for animate, if not embodied, evil, providing an opportunity to address how people see and name evil. The Epistle written to a people under occupation makes the same affirmations as does the psalm: God is present in and through suffering and hardship. Both call their readers to ethical behavior, avoiding evil, and both see a promise of a change to come.

PROPER 19 (CLOSEST TO SEPTEMBER 14)

1 Samuel 1:1–6, 9–18; Psalm 113; 1 Thessalonians 2:9–12; John 16:16–22

1 Samuel 1:1 Now there was a certain man of Ramathaim, a Zuphite from the hill country of Ephraim, whose name was Elkanah son of Jeroham son of Elihu son of Tohu son of Zuph, an Ephraimite. ² He had two wives; the name of the one was Hannah, and the name of the second, Peninnah. Peninnah had children, but Hannah had no children.

³ Now this man went up year by year from his town to worship and to sacrifice to the SOVEREIGN of heaven's vanguard at Shiloh; there the two sons of Eli, Hophni, and Phinehas, were priests of the HOLY ONE OF OLD. ⁴ And it was, on the day Elkanah sacrificed, he would give to his wife Peninnah and to all her daughters and her sons portions [of the sacrifice]. ⁵ But to Hannah he gave a double portion, because he loved her, though the WOMB OF LIFE had closed her womb. ⁶ Her rival used to provoke her severely, to irritate her, because the WELLSPRING OF LIFE had closed her womb.

⁹ After they had eaten and drunk at Shiloh, Hannah rose and presented herself before the HOLY ONE OF OLD. Now Eli the priest was sitting on the seat beside the doorposts of the temple of the HOLY ONE. ¹⁰ Hannah's soul was embittered, and she prayed to the SOURCE OF LIFE, and she wept profusely. ¹¹ And she vowed a vow and said, "HOLY ONE of heaven's legions, if only you would truly look on the affliction of your slave-woman, and remember me, and not forget your slave-woman, but will give to your slave-woman man-seed, then I will place him before you as a nazirite all the days of his life. He shall not drink wine or strong drink, and a razor shall not go upon his head."

¹² And it was as she increased praying before the FAITHFUL ONE, Eli was observing her mouth. ¹³ Now Hannah, she was speaking in her heart, only her lips moved; her voice was not heard. So, Eli took her for a drunkard. ¹⁴ And Eli said to her, "How long will you remain drunk? Put your wine away woman—away from you!" ¹⁵ Then Hannah responded and said, "No, my lord, I am a woman whose spirit has hardened; I have not drunk either wine or strong drink; I have been pouring out my soul before the GOD WHO HEARS. ¹⁶ Do not regard your slave as a worthless woman, for I have been speaking from my great grief and vexation all this time." ¹⁷ Then Eli answered and said, "Go in peace; the God of Israel grant the petition you have made to God." ¹⁸ And Hannah said, "May your slave-woman find favor in your eyes." Then the woman went on her way to her quarters, ate and drank with her husband, and her countenance was sad no longer.

Psalm 113

¹ Hallelujah! Give praise, you slaves of the MOST HIGH;
   praise the Name of the WISDOM OF THE AGES.
² Let the Name of the HOLY ONE OF OLD be blessed,
   from this time forth forevermore.
³ From the rising of the sun to its going down
   the Name of the AUTHOR OF LIFE is praised.
⁴ SHE WHO IS WISDOM is high above all nations,
   and her glory above the heavens.
⁵ Who is like the MOTHER OF ALL, our God, who sits enthroned on high?
⁶ Yet bends down to behold the heavens and the earth?
⁷ She takes up the weak out of the dust
   and lifts up the poor from the ashes.

⁸ She sets them with the rulers,
  with the rulers of her people.
⁹ She makes the woman of a childless house
  to be a joyful mother of children.

1 Thessalonians 2:9 You all remember, sisters and brothers, our labor and our toil; night and day we worked, so that we might not be a financial burden to any of you while we proclaimed to you the gospel of God. ¹⁰ You all are witnesses, with God, how holy, just, and blameless was our conduct toward you believers. ¹¹ As you all know, we dealt with each one of you like a parent with children, ¹² urging and encouraging you and pleading that you lead a life worthy of God, who calls you into God's own realm and glory.

John 16:16 [Jesus said,] "A little while, and you all will not see me, and another little while, and you all will see me." ¹⁷ Then some of his disciples said to one another, "What does this mean that he is saying to us, 'A little while, and you all will no longer see me, and again a little while, and you will see me'; and 'Because I am going to the Creator'?" ¹⁸ They said, "What does he mean by this 'a little while'? We do not know what he is talking about." ¹⁹ Jesus knew that they wanted to ask him, so he said to them, "Are you all discussing among yourselves what I meant when I said, 'A little while, and you all will no longer see me, and again a little while, and you all will see me'? ²⁰ Very truly, I tell you all that you will weep and mourn, but the world will rejoice; you all will have pain, but your pain will turn into joy. ²¹ When a woman is giving birth, she has pain because her time has come. But when her child is born, she no longer remembers the tribulation because of the joy of having brought a human being into the world. ²² So you all have pain now; but I will see you all again, and your hearts will rejoice, and no one will take your joy from you."

PROCLAMATION

Text Notes

In verse 5 in Hebrew, Hannah's portion is a "nose" portion with "double" being construed from context. The alternate equally common meaning for *apayim*, "anger," is not helpful here.

The Dead Sea Scrolls (DSS) versions of 1–2 Samuel offer a significant number of corrections to the text, most of which occur in the NRSV—look for the letter Q in the translation notes at the bottom of the text, present in every NRSV Bible. (Indeed, the NRSV is the first scholarly post–DSS discovery Bible and includes some 100 corrections.) The DSS are authoritative because they are the oldest, most complete manuscripts of the scriptures that have ever been found.

I follow the DSS, including "nazirite," "all the days of his life," and "he shall not drink wine or strong drink" in 1:11 from scroll 4QSam^a. In verse 11, Hannah asks for the gender-specific "seed of men," here "man-seed," elsewhere "man-child."

I also include "she presented herself to the Holy One" in verse 9 and "she went to her quarters, ate and drank with her husband" from the LXX, which shares content with the DSS here.

In John 16:21, I have replaced "hour" with "time" for smoothness. In the same verse, I selected "tribulation" from among the semantic range options in conversation with people who had given birth; that choice reflects the majority opinion.

Preaching Prompts

The first lesson proffers Hannah and her desperate plea for a child. The many biblical accounts of miraculous pregnancies that do not conform to the lived experience of most people can be difficult for women with unwelcome infertility. Peninnah is often demonized in the text and interpretive tradition. It's worth thinking about the hurt Penninah felt as a woman who had fulfilled society's expectation, yet was unloved and unfavored. Note: In the ancient Israelite sacrificial system, most offerings (except whole burnt offerings) were split between God and the giver. Select parts could only be offered to God with designated portions for the giver and his or her family; women and men made these offerings.

Psalm 113 shares with Hannah's hymn and Mary's Magnificat the language of reversal, lifting the poor and weak/needy (Ps. 113:7–8; 1 Sam. 2:7–8; Luke 1:52–53). One of the Magnificat's reversals seems to speak more to Hannah than to Mary: a mother of many who is forlorn like Penninah and a previously barren woman who gives birth like Hannah. The psalm affirms that God provides infertile women with children, equated to a proper "home," and some suggest that it was prayed or recited by women living with infertility. There is no broad consensus as to whether the psalm pre- or postdates Samuel. It will be important to affirm God's gift of the child without demeaning child-free homes and families. To this end, the Epistle models the Christian community as a family of choice in which the relationships between leaders and new believers are modeled on the family. The nurture and care of the new believer correspond largely with the role of mothers to impart wisdom and shape character in partnership with fathers in the Hebrew Scriptures, particularly in Wisdom Literature. In the Gospel, Jesus pushes us to look at the expanse of time in which we live our lives, build our families, and in some cases, labor to give birth from a cosmic perspective. In that light, our lives and our struggles are fleeting—though not meaningless—and Jesus is looking forward to the time in which we are all together on the other side of our lives and struggles. While we await his return, we are in the imagery of the Gospel: all expectant, all pregnant, all experiencing the pain of labor, and all soon to experience the joy that endures.

PROPER 20 (CLOSEST TO SEPTEMBER 21)

1 Samuel 1:19–28; Canticle of Hannah (1 Samuel 2:1–10);
1 Corinthians 3:1–9; Matthew 10:34–39

1 Samuel 1:19 Hannah and Elkanah rose early in the morning and bowed down and worshiped before the HOLY ONE OF OLD; then they turned back and went to their house at Ramah. Elkanah knew his wife Hannah, and the HOLY ONE remembered her. [20] And it was with the turning of the days that Hannah conceived and gave birth to a son. She called his name Samuel (God hears), for she said, "From the GOD WHO HEARS have I asked him."

[21] Now the man Elkanah went up along with his whole household to offer to the HOLY ONE the yearly sacrifice, and on account of a vow. [22] Yet Hannah did not go up, for she said to her husband, "[Not] until the child is weaned, then will I bring him, that he may be seen in the presence of the MOST HIGH and remain there perpetually. I will present him as a nazirite in perpetuity, for all the days of his life." [23] Her husband Elkanah said to her, "Do what is best in your eyes, stay until you have weaned him. May the FAITHFUL GOD establish the words of your mouth." So, the woman remained and nursed her son until she weaned him. [24] And she took him up with her after she had weaned him along with a three-year-old bull, an ephah of flour, and a jug of wine. Hannah brought him to the house of the EVER-LIVING GOD at Shiloh and the boy was just a little boy. [25] Then they slaughtered the bull, and they brought the boy to Eli. [26] And Hannah said, "My lord! As you live, my lord, I am the woman, the one who was standing beside you in this [place] to pray to the GOD WHO HEARS. [27] For this boy I prayed; and the FAITHFUL GOD gave me my asking, what I asked from God. [28] Therefore have I bequeathed him to the GRACIOUS GOD; all his days will he be a bequest to the GOD WHOSE NAME IS HOLY."

So she left him there and she bowed down and worshiped the FAITHFUL GOD.

Canticle of Hannah (1 Samuel 2:1–10)

[1] Hannah prayed and she said,
"My heart exults in the HOLY ONE OF OLD;
my horn is lifted up in my God.
My mouth [opens] wide against my enemies,
for I will rejoice in my victory.

[2] "There is none holy like the MOST HIGH,
none besides you;
there is no rock like our God.

[3] Speak proudly no more, multiplying pride,
nor let arrogance come from your mouth;
for the AGELESS GOD is a God of knowledge,
and by God deeds are accounted.

4 The bows of the mighty are broken,
   yet the feeble gird on warrior-strength.
5 Those who were full have hired themselves out for bread,
   yet those who were hungry are fat.
   She who was barren has birthed seven children,
   yet she who has many children languishes.
6 The CREATOR OF ALL kills and gives life;
   brings down to Sheol and raises up.
7 The GRACIOUS ONE makes poor and makes rich;
   brings low and also lifts up.
8 God raises the poor from the dust,
   and lifts the needy from heaps of human waste,
   to seat them with nobles and inherit a seat of honor.
   For to the CREATOR belong the pillars of the earth,
   and on them God has set the world.
9 God will guard the feet of the faithful who belong to God,
   while the wicked perish in shadow;
   for it is not by might that one prevails.
10 The HOLY ONE OF SINAI!
   Those who strive against God shall be shattered;
   God thunders against them from heaven.
   The FOUNT OF JUSTICE will judge the ends of the earth;
   God will give strength to God's ruler,
   and exalt the power of the anointed of God."

1 Corinthians 3:1 Now sisters and brothers, I could not speak to you all as spiritual, but rather as carnal, as infants in Christ. [2] I fed you all with milk, not solid food, for you were not yet ready for solid food. Even now you are still not ready, [3] for you all are still carnal. Given there is still jealousy and discord among you, are you not carnal, and going around as merely human? [4] For when one says, "I am Paul's," and another, "I am Apollos," are you not merely human?

[5] What then is Apollos? What is Paul? Ministers through whom you came to believe, as the Messiah granted to each person. [6] I planted, Apollos watered, but God produces growth. [7] Therefore, neither the one who plants nor the one who waters is anything, rather it is God who produces growth. [8] The one who plants and the one who waters are alike, and each will receive wages according to their labor. [9] For we are God's coworkers, working together; you are God's cultivation, God's construction.

Matthew 10:34 [Jesus said,] "Do not think that I have come to bring peace upon the earth; I have not come to bring peace rather, a sword.

[35] For I have come to set

> *a man against his father,*
> *and a daughter against her mother,*
> *and a daughter-in-law against her mother-in-law;*
>
> ³⁶ and *a person's enemies will be members of their household.*

³⁷ The woman or man who loves mother or father more than me is not worthy of me, and the woman or man who loves daughter or son more than me is not worthy of me. ³⁸ And whoever does not bear the cross and follow me is not worthy of me. ³⁹ The ones who find their life will lose it, and the ones who lose their life for my sake will find it.

PROCLAMATION

Text Notes

I chose "GOD WHO HEARS" to render the divine Name in 1 Samuel 1:20 to reiterate the etymology of Samuel's name. Some scholars argue that the etymology belongs more properly to Saul, whose name stems from the verb for "to ask"; the "bequest" of verse 28 is the same spelling and pronunciation of Saul, *Shaul.* Hannah's last line in verse 22, "I will present him . . ." comes from the Qumran scroll 4QSamᵃ and is not present elsewhere. According to the older reading supported by the LXX, in verse 23, Elkanah prays that God would establish the words of *Hannah's* mouth; the Masoretic Text has "the words of God's mouth." The same scroll corrects "three bulls" in verse 24 to "three year-old bull." The end of verse 24 is simply the word for "boy" or "youth" repeated twice; the meaning must be reconstructed and construed from context. I use "bequeath/bequest" in verse 28 to mirror the continuing verb "ask" now in a causative form that indicates fulfilling a request. The very last line occurs in two forms: *They bowed down and worshiped God there* from the MT and *she left him there and worshiped* from Qumran. The Dead Seas scrolls are the oldest, most complete manuscripts of the Hebrew Scriptures and generated nearly ninety corrections to the Hebrew Bible, the bulk in Samuel.

Verse 4 of the Canticle uses *chayil,* denoting warrior strength, a warrior's heart, or an army; it is used of Boaz and Ruth and the desirable wife in Proverbs 31 (whose attributes are selected by another woman) and Pharaoh's army. I use "shadow" in verse 9 for "darkness," given the way "dark" has been conflated negatively with "black" and black people in interpretation for harm. "Shattered" in verse 10 also has the sense of being terrified.

In Matthew 10:35, Jesus offers a literal translation of Micah 7:6 from the MT that varies from the LXX in all of the principal vocabulary, but not in meaning.

Preaching Prompts

These readings reflect the cultural needs of the world in which they were set, the production of children, as many as possible, and an evaluation system in which some children, due to gender or status, were more valued. The need for children, rather than the desire for children some experience contemporarily, was rooted in the vulnerability and lethality of pregnancy, childbirth, infancy, and childhood. Additionally, the bias toward sons reflected paternal understandings of peoplehood so that without sons to make more sons, a people could disappear, particularly with the intentional use of rape as a tool of war with the aim of eradication, genocide. Hannah's desperation for a son is comprehensible against that background. According to Targum Onqelos, Hannah worships on her own in 1 Samuel 1:19 without her husband. She names her child in accordance with the broader practice in ancient Israel; the episodes where God or a father name a child should be viewed as exceptions. Hannah's participation in the slaughter of her offering is signaled by the "they" in verse 25; the exact nature of that participation is unclear.

The theology in 1 Corinthians 3:3–4 unhelpfully pits the flesh against the spirit, identifying humanity with the flesh as carnal. This seems very much at odds with the Incarnation. The spirit/flesh dichotomy is fueled by Greek philosophy and will become a gendered hierarchy for some church fathers, with women being identified with the flesh. Yet, in its self-understanding as a people, the church chooses the metaphor of birthing and nursing to produce and nurture new Christians while spiritualizing this evangelical motherhood such that it pertains primarily to men.

At the same time, among the ministers who could have been referenced in 1 Corinthians 3:5–6 are the long list of women who served with Paul enumerated in Romans 16, more particularly Priscilla (Prisca), who is named before her husband, signifying leadership, and who corrected Apollos's theology, see Acts 18:18, 26. Verse 9 uses the same language of coworker to describe the relationship between these ministers and God that Paul uses in Romans 16:3 for his female colaborers and elsewhere for men like Timothy.

When reading from the perspective of Hannah and her culture, one largely shared by Jesus, his appropriation and reinterpretation of Micah's prophecy is shocking as intended. No matter how dear the bonds of family and kinship nor how hard it was to produce the blessed child who will carry the family forward, all of those bonds, indeed the very fabric of society, are dispensable. True life is found not in the propagation that comes from pregnancy but in bearing an instrument of death to its inevitable conclusion.

PROPER 21 (CLOSEST TO SEPTEMBER 28)

1 Samuel 2:18–21, 26; Psalm 144:3–4, 12–15;
1 Peter 2:4–10; Mark 9:14–29

1 Samuel 2:18 Now Samuel was ministering in the presence of the HOLY ONE OF OLD, a boy dressed in a linen ephod. [19] A little robe his mother would make for him and bring up to him year by year, when she went up with her husband to offer the yearly sacrifice. [20] And Eli would bless Elkanah and his wife, and say, "May the HOLY ONE repay you (Elkanah) with seed from this woman in place of the bequest she made to the FOUNT OF LIFE"; and then they would return to their home.

[21] And the FAITHFUL ONE attended Hannah and she conceived and gave birth to two daughters and three sons. And the boy Samuel grew up there in the presence of the LIVING GOD.

[26] Now the boy Samuel went on and grew in goodness with the MOST HIGH and with humanity.

Psalm 144:3–4, 12–15

[3] WOMB OF LIFE, what is humanity that you even know them,
  or the woman-born that you think of them?
[4] Humanity is like a breath;
  whose days are like a passing shadow.
[12] Our sons in their youth
  are like plants full grown,
  our daughters are like cornerstones,
  cut for the building of a palace.
[13] Our barns are full,
  from produce of every kind;
  our sheep have increased by thousands,
  many thousands in our surroundings.
[14] Our cattle are heavy,
  there is no breach in the walls, no exile,
  and no cry of distress in our surroundings.
[15] Happy are the people to whom such blessings fall;
  happy are the people whose God is the WOMB OF LIFE.

1 Peter 2:4 Come to Jesus, a living stone, although rejected by humanity yet chosen and precious to God. [5] And are yourselves, like living stones, being built into a spiritual house to be a holy priesthood, to offer spiritual sacrifices acceptable to God through Jesus Christ. [6] Thus scripture contains [the following]:

> *"See, I am laying in Zion a stone,*
> *a cornerstone chosen, precious;*
> *and whoever believes in that stone will not be put to shame."*

[7] To you all who believe then, a precious honor; but for those who do not believe,

> *"The stone that the builders rejected*
> *has become the chief cornerstone,"*

[8] and

> *"A stumbling stone,*
> *and a rock of offense."*

They stumble over the word "disobeying, disobedient" by design. [9] Yet you all are a chosen race, a royal priesthood, a holy nation, God's own possession, in order that you may proclaim the mighty acts of God who called you out of shadow into God's marvelous light.

> [10] Once not a people,
> but now God's people;
> once bereft of mercy,
> but now rich in mercy.

Mark 9:14 Now when they [Jesus, John and Peter] came to the disciples [after the Transfiguration], they saw a great crowd around them, and some scholars arguing with them. [15] And the whole crowd of women, children, and men saw Jesus; they were immediately overcome with awe and they ran forward to greet him.

[16] Then Jesus asked them, "What are you all arguing about with them?" [17] Someone from the crowd answered him, "Teacher, I brought my child to you who has a spirit of speechlessness. [18] And whenever it overtakes my child, it throws them down and they foam and grind their teeth and my child becomes paralyzed, and I asked your disciples to cast it out and your disciples were not able." [19] Then Jesus answered them, saying, "O faithless generation! How much longer must I be among you all? How much longer must I bear with you all? Bring the child to me." [20] And they brought the child to Jesus. When the spirit saw the child, immediately it threw the child into convulsions who then fell on the ground rolling and foaming. [21] Then Jesus asked the parent, "How long has this been happening?" And the parent said, "From childhood. [22] Often has it cast the child into fire and into water, to destroy the child; yet if you are able to do anything to help us, have pity on us." [23] Jesus said to the parent, "If you are able! All things can be done for the one who believes." [24] Immediately the child's parent cried out [with tears], "I believe; help my unbelief!" [25] Now when Jesus saw that a crowd of women, children, and men came running together, he rebuked the unclean spirit, saying to it, "You spirit of speechlessness and deafness, I command you, come out of the child, and never enter the child, again!" [26] After crying out and throwing the child into more convulsions it came out and the child was like the dead, so much so that

many said, "He is dead." ²⁷ Yet Jesus took the child by the hand and lifted the child up, and the child was able to stand. ²⁸ When Jesus had entered the house, his disciples asked him privately, "Why were we not able cast it out?" ²⁹ He said to them, "This kind can come by nothing but prayer [and fasting]."

PROCLAMATION

Text Notes

In 1 Samuel 2:19, all of the action verbs are feminine; they are Hannah's, even when her husband is with her. This is a common feature of biblical Hebrew, a singular verb (any gender) followed by a plural subject, indicating that the first person led in the action and the other followed. On the other hand, the blessing of Elkanah in verse 20 is spoken to him alone: may God repay "you," masculine singular. "Repay" comes from the DSS text supported by the LXX. Without the corrections from Qumran, the MT says that Samuel "grew up with God" in verse 21.

In Psalm 144:3, "woman-born" replaces "children of man."

1 Peter 2 is a mélange of texts, including a quote from Isaiah 28:16 in verse 6 that closely corresponds to the Greek LXX, but not exactly, yet is closer to the LXX than the Hebrew Masoretic Text. Verse 7 cites Psalm 118:22 and verse 8 loosely incorporates Isaiah 8:14. In the MT, the stone is "tested," as in "tried and true" and "precious." In the LXX, the two-fold description becomes three-fold, "expensive, chosen (or elect)," and "precious." The NT text preserves "elect and precious." The root of "precious" is used in noun form applied to believers, hence "precious honor." Here, NRSV's "he is precious" is without foundation.

The latter phrase reveals more variability; in the MT, it is "the one who trusts will not fear/panic," where the NT following the LXX has "the one who believes/ trusts will not be put to shame." It should be noted that the practical meaning of *pistis* changes significantly between the testaments. As a result of the Jesus story, the broad sense of trust, as in "trusting God," becomes "believe in Jesus as the Son of God." However, where both ancient texts fail to specify in whom or in what the trusting person trusts, the NT generates a potentially masculine subject, "the one who trusts in him," as both Jesus and the stone in Greek are both grammatically masculine. (It should be noted that in Greek, this same pronoun can be neuter, masculine, and feminine.) In contrast, in Hebrew, the stone is grammatically feminine; here one could translate "the one who trusts her will never be put to shame." I use "that stone" in my translation to preserve the ambiguity of the early traditions and wordplay of the Epistle.

The Targum (which includes translation and interpretation intertwined) also reads Isaiah 28:16 as pertaining to a male person: "Behold I am appointing in Zion a king, a mighty king, a warrior and a terrifying one . . . and the righteous who believe in these things, when the distress comes, they will not be shaken."

1 Peter 2:8 cites Isaiah 8:14 with similar alteration. In Isaiah, God will become "a stone one strikes against and a rock causing stumbling" in the MT. The LXX diverges significantly: "If you trust in God . . . you will not meet God as a stumbling caused by a stone nor as a fall [in death] caused by a rock." That "fall" is deadly; *ptōmati* means "corpse." The NT text has "rock of offense," using *skandalou* in place of rock that leads one to fall (making the "fall" into sin as explained by verse 9). In verse 8, *apeithountes* means "disobey" and "disbelieve," so I include both options.

Verse 9 draws upon the "priestly kingdom and holy nation" of Exodus 19:6. Here, I render "darkness" as "shadow," avoiding the light/dark binary with its racial implication in its history of interpretation. And verse 10 quotes Hosea 2:23, where the lack of mercy is a lack of the maternal love of God, *rachum*, rooted in the womb, *rechem*, its grammatical root.

It is difficult to identify the reference for the pronouns in Mark. I have identified the most likely possibilities based on the preceding verses. In keeping with the intent of the project to mitigate the effects of hearing male pronouns nearly exclusively in the parables and miracles, nonbinary language for the parent and child, both of whom are male in Greek. In verses 24 and 29, I include the common readings from the minority manuscripts that the parent cried out "with tears" and that this kind of spirit could only be exercised by "prayer and fasting."

Preaching Prompts

This week's readings are about family, building families, families as the building blocks of nations, and the early church's self-articulation as people and nation using that same language. In these lessons, the provision of children is one of the ways in which God blesses a person, family, and nation. The tender love for children and raising of them to perpetuate the family and nation is equally mother's work and father's work. While the specifics of Hannah's story are not imitable, her willingness to sacrifice raising her own child during that precious childhood period is a partial model of the kind of parental love that will be demonstrated by God in the New Testament in placing Jesus with Joseph and Mary. An imperiled child, particularly a son, is a threat to the future survival of a family.

The psalmist is blessed with manifold prosperity, including children and cattle. These gifts, like humanity itself, are as in verse 4 of this psalm, as fleeting as shadows. The Epistle sees God building a people out of the building blocks of persons without regard to their families of origin or whether they themselves parent children. In this vision of community, people are more than their potential to reproduce. Peoplehood is no longer biological.

In the Gospel, parents desperate for their child's healing brings them first to the disciples of Jesus, who fail to provide any relief, and then encounter Jesus. The child's ailments are personified as spirits that are resistant to the efforts of the disciples. Their attempted exorcism is not described. This child, like the young Samuel, embodies the hope of their parents for their future and the future of their people. It will be important to discuss difference, divergence, and disease as perceived in the ancient world and in the world that reads ancient words.

The role of the community in nurturing children and providing for its own continuation apart from reproduction is not highlighted in the readings but can be teased out. Reading between the lines, Hannah does not have a supportive community either in her home life, represented by her sister-wife or in her religious life, represented by the initial hostility of Eli. The parent in the Gospel has community, including access to the disciples and the hope of healing. The disciples represent the most recent attempt at healing; surely there were other attempts with other healers and practitioners. There is also the question of the missing second parent from the Gospel, the mother.

Jesus is the last and ultimate hope for healing. His final words in this passage, that the healing, deliverance, or exorcism could not be accomplished without prayer and fasting, remain as an invitation to deeper mysteries and as a somewhat unsatisfactory response to those situations in which healing has not occurred. These words are easy to twist into blame that one has not been sufficiently faithful in prayer or fasting if there is unhealed disease or disorder in a person's life.

PROPER 22 (CLOSEST TO OCTOBER 5)

1 Samuel 4:19–22; Psalm 74:1–12; Revelation 21:10, 22–27; Mark 13:1–8

1 Samuel 4:19 Now Eli's daughter-in-law, the wife of Phineas, was pregnant at the point of birthing and she heard the news-being-heard that the ark of God was taken and her father-in-law and her husband were dead. Then she squatted and gave birth, for they—her wrenching pangs—were upon her. [20] And at the moment of her dying the women who stood with her said to her, "Fear not, for you have given birth to a son." But she did not answer nor incline her heart. [21] She named the boy *I-Kavod*, meaning, "Exiled is the Glory, the Kavod, from Israel," because the ark of God had been taken and because of her father-in-law and her husband. [22] She said, "Exiled is the Glory from Israel, for the ark of God has been taken!"

Psalm 74:1–12

1 Why God, do you reject for all time;
   your rage smoke against the sheep of your pasture?
2 Remember your congregation you acquired before time,
   that you redeemed to be the tribe of your heritage;
   Mount Zion, where you came to dwell upon it.
3 Lift up your steps to the perpetual ruins;
   every kind of evil has the enemy done in the sanctuary.

⁴ Your foes have roared within your meeting-place;
  they set their emblems there.
⁵ It was perceived like when they go up
  upon a tangle of trees with axes.
⁶ And then its carved work altogether,
  with hatchets and hammers, they smote it.
⁷ They set your sanctuary on fire;
  they brought it to the ground,
  defiling the dwelling place of your Name.
⁸ They said within their hearts, "We will crush them";
  they burned all the meeting places of God in the land.
⁹ Our emblems we no longer see;
  there is no longer any prophet [woman or man],
  and there is no one among us who knows how long.
¹⁰ How long, God, is the adversary to taunt?
  Is the enemy to defame your name for all time?
¹¹ Why do you hold back your hand;
  your right hand, unavailable, in your bosom?
¹² Yet God my Sovereign is from before time,
  working salvation in the midst of the earth.

Revelation 21:10 Now the angel carried me away in the spirit to a great, high mountain and showed me the holy city Jerusalem coming down from the heavens, from God. ²² I saw no temple in the city, for the Sovereign God, the Almighty with the Lamb is its temple. ²³ And the city has no use of sun or moon to shine in it, for the glory of God is its light, and its lamp is the Lamb. ²⁴ And the nations will walk by its light and the queens and kings of the earth will bring their glory into it. ²⁵ And its gates will not be shut by day and there will be no night there. ²⁶ Women, children, and men will bring into it the glory and the honor of the nations. ²⁷ Now there shall not enter it anything unclean or anyone who does what is detestable or untrue, but only those who are written in the Lamb's book of life.

Mark 13:1 Now as Jesus came out of the temple, one of his disciples said to him, "Teacher! Look! Such stones and such buildings!" ² Then Jesus said to his disciple, "Do you see these great buildings? Not a single stone will be left here upon another that will not be demolished." ³ So when Jesus was sitting on the Mount of Olives opposite the temple, Peter, James, John, and Andrew asked him privately, ⁴ "Tell us when all this will be, and what will be the sign these things are about to come to pass?" ⁵ Thus Jesus began to say to them, "See to it no one leads you all astray. ⁶ Many will come in my name and say, 'I am he!' and they will deceive many. ⁷ So when you all hear of wars and rumors of wars do not be alarmed; this must be however, the end is not yet. ⁸ For nation will rise against nation, and monarchy against monarchy; there will be earthquakes in particular places; there will be famines. This is the beginning of the birthpangs."

PROCLAMATION

Text Notes

There is wordplay in 1 Samuel 4:19, "hearing" and what is being heard, the "news" or "report" in standard translation.

God's "rage" in Psalm 74:1 is the divine "nose" complete with snorting smoke. The image of God as a bull runs deep among the peoples of ancient Israel and their surrounding nations. There is some perplexing grammar in the psalm. In verse 3, God is directed to "exalt" her steps. In verse 5, "Being made known like/as going" was rendered as "it was perceived as when going. . . ." Similarly, God's right hand is "finished" or "completed," leading to a translation of "unavailable."

In Revelation 21:26, those who bring glory are unidentified; the subject is included in the verb, inclusive plural. When cities or nations offered tribute in hospitality or conquest, representatives from each section of the populace often participated. The choice of "women, children, and men" rather than the "people" of the NRSV or "they" in the CEB make the population of heaven visible.

Preaching Prompts

Jesus's declaration that the temple's extraordinary Herodian stonework would be demolished is comparable to an announcement that Pearl Harbor or September 11 would occur again. Jesus is speaking about more than another destruction of the temple, though Rome will indeed destroy it again after his death and resurrection; he is talking about a social and political upheaval on such a scale that all social, political, cultural, and religious institutions will be destroyed. The upheaval is also signified by his use of birthing language associated with harbingers of death, war, and famine.

Mark 13 is set against the enduring anguish caused by the Babylonian destruction of the temple and its subsequent rebuilding and Herod's major renovation of it to a previously unimaginable scale. Psalm 74 presents a near-immediate lament in response to what was an unimaginable catastrophe because of the prevailing theology that God, in the form of her glory, resided in the temple and could not be defeated or dislodged. Similarly, in the first lesson, a heavily pregnant woman, upon seeing the glory of God captured by the enemies of Israel, immediately goes into labor, expels her child, and dies lamenting the loss of the Glory as her last words. Revelation 21 offers a vision of an indestructible temple, the indestructible God and the Lamb of God. The glory of God is there, radiating from the lamb, Jesus. At one level, this vision aims to heal the lingering hurts from the repeated loss of the temple and the ark of the covenant and a home and throne for the glory of God.

It would be useful to have teaching or discussion about the role of the temple in Israelite religion and Second Temple Judaism and its losses and memorialization and the ongoing grief embedded in liturgy and practice along with the forced evolution of Judaism in response to that devastating loss.

The Markan apocalypse and Apocalypse of John both envision a cosmic change in which systems that oppress or can be perverted will be swept away through a cataclysm of violence, making room for a new cosmos and world. One can only hope that unmentioned systems such as hierarchy, patriarchy, biases, and prejudices will also be swept away. The challenge of apocalyptic visions is that all of the work to change the world is laid on God for some future time. Yet there is no reason that we, mere mortals, cannot undertake the work of repair and renewal that falls within our grasp.

PROPER 23 (CLOSEST TO OCTOBER 12)

1 Samuel 15:1–3, 8, 10–17, 24–25; Psalm 25:1–11;
Ephesians 4:25–32; Mark 11:12–14, 20–25

1 Samuel 15:1 Samuel said to Saul, "I was sent by the DREAD GOD to anoint you ruler over God's people, over Israel; now then, hearken to the call of the words of the INSCRUTABLE GOD: [2] Thus says the SOVEREIGN of heaven's vanguard, 'I will punish Amalek for what they did to Israel, setting against them in their ascent from Egypt. [3] Now go and smite Amalek, and put to holy destruction all they have; do not spare them and put them to death from woman to man and from infant to nursing baby and from ox to sheep, from camel to donkey.'"

[8] Saul seized Agag, ruler of the Amalekites, alive and put to holy destruction all the people at the edge of the sword.

[10] The word of the SOVEREIGN GOD to Samuel was: [11] "I regret that I crowned Saul as ruler, for he has turned away from me, and my commands he has not instituted." Then Samuel was angry, and he cried out to the GOD WHO HEARS, all night. [12] And Samuel rose early in the morning to meet Saul, and it was told to Samuel: "Saul went to Carmel, where he erected a monument for himself, then turned around and passed by, going down to Gilgal." [13] Now, Samuel came to him and Saul said to him, "Blessed are you by the HOLY ONE OF OLD; I have instituted the command of the HOLY ONE OF SINAI." [14] Then Samuel said, "What is this sound of sheep in my ears, and the sound of cattle I am hearing?" [15] And Saul said, "They brought them from the Amalekites, for the people spared the best of the sheep and the cattle to sacrifice to the HOLY ONE your God; but the rest we have put to holy destruction." [16] Then Samuel said to Saul, "Stop! Let me tell you what the ANCIENT ONE said to me last night." Saul replied, "Speak."[17] Samuel said, "Though you are small in your own eyes, are you not the head of the tribes of Israel? The HOLY ONE anointed you ruler over Israel."

[24] Saul said to Samuel, "I have sinned; for I have transgressed the utterance of the DREAD GOD and your words, because I feared the people and obeyed their voice. [25] Now then, I pray, pardon my sin, and return with me, so that I may worship the HOLY ONE OF OLD."

Psalm 25:1–11

¹ To you, RIGHTEOUS ONE, I lift up my soul.

² My God, in you I trust;
  let me not be put to shame,
  let not my enemies exult over me.

³ Even more, let not those who hope in you be put to shame;
  let them be ashamed who are treacherous [and] empty.

⁴ Make known to me your ways, AGELESS GOD;
  teach me your paths.

⁵ Guide me in your truth, and teach me,
  for you are the God of my salvation;
  for you I wait all day long.

⁶ Remember your maternal love, O WOMB OF LIFE,
  and your faithful love,
  for they have been from of old.

⁷ The sins of my youth and my transgressions remember not;
  according to your faithful love remember me,
  for the sake of your goodness, GRACIOUS ONE.

⁸ Good and upright is the FOUNT OF WISDOM,
  therefore she instructs sinners in the way.

⁹ She guides the humble in what is just,
  and teaches the humble her way.

¹⁰ All the paths of the WISDOM OF THE AGES are faithful and true
  for those who keep her covenant and her decrees.

¹¹ For your Name's sake, LOVING GOD,
  pardon my guilt, for it is great.

Ephesians 4:25 Therefore putting away lying, *speak the truth, each to their neighbors*, for we are parts of one another. ²⁶ *Be angry but do not sin*; do not let the sun go down on your anger. ²⁷ Make no opportunity for the devil. ²⁸ Thieves must no longer thieve but rather, labor and work with their own hands, honestly, in order to have something to share with the needy. ²⁹ All foul speech—let none come out of your mouths, rather only what is good for building up as there is need in order that grace be given to those who hear. ³⁰ And do not grieve the Holy Spirit of God in whom you were sealed for the day of redemption. ³¹ All bitterness and wrath and anger and shouting and slander shall be taken away from you, together with all malice. ³² Now, be to one another: kind, tenderhearted, forgiving one another, as God in Christ has forgiven you all [or us].

Mark 11:12 On the following day [after the precession into Jerusalem], when they [Jesus and his disciples] came from Bethany, Jesus was hungry. ¹³ And seeing a fig tree from afar bearing leaves, Jesus went, perhaps to find anything on it, and when he came to it nothing did he find but leaves for it was not the time for figs. [14] And he spoke to it, saying, "Never again will anyone eat fruit from you." And his disciples heard it.

[20] Now they passed by in the morning and saw the fig tree dried up to its roots. [21] And Peter remembering said to Jesus, "Rabbi, look! The fig tree that you cursed has withered." [22] Then Jesus answering told them, "Have faith in God. [23] Truly I tell you all, if anyone says to this mountain, 'Be taken up and thrown into the sea,' and does not doubt in their heart but believes that they will come to pass, it will be done for you. [24] Because of this I tell you all, all of whatever you all pray and ask, believe that you have received it, and it will be yours. [25] And whenever you all stand praying, forgive, if someone has anything against anyone, so that your Reconciler in heaven may also forgive you all your trespasses."

PROCLAMATION

Text Notes

I choose language to render the divine name that communicates the horror of Samuel's claim that God called for annihilation "from woman to man and from infant to nursing baby," dread and inscrutable. In 1 Samuel 15:1, the "call" of the words of God is the "sound" or "voice." In the prosecution of holy war called for by God, utter annihilation is sanctified as the ultimate offering to God. People, animals, and sometime the land itself is "put under the ban"—banned from existence, the living beings slaughtered, the land torn up and often salted to prevent planting. The verb, *haram*, means "ban," "devote" (to God), and "destroy." There is no respite, rescue, or redemption from holy destruction (Lev. 27:28–29); failure to complete this genocidal action is punishable, they can be shown no mercy or pity (Deut. 7:2.)

God expresses regret—not quite repentance—for enthroning Saul in the same terms that Job expresses regret and not repentance for demanding an account of God in Job 42:6.

To "wait" in Psalm 25:4 also includes hoping; the psalmist waits with expectation. God's maternal love in verse 6 emanates from her womb, which provides the grammatical root for this love.

Ephesians 4:25 quotes the LXX of Zechariah 8:16. Verse 26 quotes Psalm 4:4, also from the LXX (rather than "be not angry" the MT has "been not excited/anxious"). Verse 28 uses a Semitic formulation in which the subject and verb share the same lexical root like "teachers teach" and "preachers preach." Verse 31 employs a passive verb signifying the undesired characteristics will be "taken away" and not an active verb calling for persons to rid themselves of these behaviors. There is a dual manuscript tradition with regard to the end of verse 32; one collection says "as God in Christ has forgiven you all" and the other, "as God in Christ has forgiven us." As there is good support for each on textual and theological grounds, I preserve the dichotomy so the worshiping community and congregational leaders and readers may determine for themselves.

Mark 11:1 provides the context for the passage, who "they" are, and the previous sequence of events. A minority collection of manuscripts preserves a 26th verse, *But if you do not forgive, neither will your Father in heaven forgive your trespasses.*

Preaching Prompts

Themes of prayer, repentance, and anger unite these passages. First, there is the nearly inexplicable anger of God and Samuel against Saul. The literary presentation makes it seem almost divinely orchestrated that he should fall and make room for David. Beyond moving the story of Israel's monarchy along, the fall of Saul offers a hard study on repentance and forgiveness, and Saul's unanswered plea for pardon illustrates the difficulty in teasing out the human and divine in the scriptures. The psalmist's presentation of God as good and upright echoes throughout the canon and contributes to the dissonance of hearing God call for the slaughter of innocents, including babies at the breast in 1 Samuel (and elsewhere).

Needless to say, these claims and their underlying theology require frank discussion and thoughtful engagement, not least for what they signify about God. An important caveat is that these texts are retrospective and the bulk of them are ahistoric. A rare moment of grace in this story is that even though it marks God's rejection of Saul, Samuel seems not to have given up on him. More significantly, he gets angry (at God?) and pours out his heart all night long. Yet we should remain troubled by Saul's fate and the purported fate of the Amalekites, and the claims made in God's name by God's prophet.

The psalmist presents a familiar and perhaps aspirational portrait of prayer. Yet in verse 2 reality sets in. There are those who wish harm and harm that befalls us no matter our fidelity to God or God's fidelity to us.

The Epistle presents a picture of a properly penitent life. One in which one's repentance is lived out and demonstrated by a transformed life, particularly cessation of previous transgressive activities.

The Gospel offers, perhaps, the most shocking presentation of prayer. Jesus curses a fig tree that has not failed to produce figs because it is not yet the time for figs, and therefore possible for it to produce fruit. Cursing is as much praying as it is blessing. There is a parallel to be drawn between the fig tree and Saul. He is pruned from the throne in a circumstance over which he has little control. He and the tree are on the wrong side of someone's prayer.

There are women missing from all of these passages. Missing from the telling of Saul's fall from grace is his primary wife, Ahinoam, the daughter of Ahimaaz (1 Sam. 14:50), and two daughters, Merab and Michal (1 Sam. 14:49). He also has a low-status wife, Rizpah. His rise and fall affected them all, not least because it brought David into their orbit, leading to the engagement of both daughters, marriage (and abandonment) of one, and ultimately the death of Merab's children and those of Rizpah, at the word of David (2 Sam. 21:8–9). The anonymity of the psalm allows us to hear a woman praying it, though it is presented as a composition to (on behalf of) or for David; the traditional rendering, "A psalm of David," is a common mistranslation. Women are surely present in the undifferentiated community of disciples around Jesus. But they are neither heard from nor seen.

Together these texts offer an opportunity to talk about the ways in which women and other underrepresented and excluded communities are often chastised for their anger at the systems that subjugate them. It is also an opportunity to talk about the power of prayer as a healing, transforming, and even coping mechanism and to explore the mechanics and mysteries of prayer and its efficacy and unanswered prayer.

PROPER 24 (CLOSEST TO OCTOBER 19)

1 Samuel 14:49–51; 18:17–21, 29; Psalm 3:1–8; Romans 5:6–11; Mark 4:21–25

1 Samuel 14:49 Now the sons of Saul were Jonathan, Ishvi, and Malchishua, and the names of his two daughters, the name of the firstborn was Merab, and the name of the younger, Michal. [50] The name of Saul's wife was Ahinoam, daughter of Ahimaaz, and the name of the commander of his army was Abner, son of Ner, Saul's uncle. [51] Kish was the father of Saul, and Ner, the father of Abner, was the son of Abiel.

[18:17] Then Saul said to David, "Look, here is my older daughter Merab. I will give her to you as a wife; only be my valiant warrior and fight the battles of the HOLY ONE." For Saul said [to himself], "Let me not raise a hand against him, rather let the hand of the Philistines do it." [18] Then David said to Saul, "Who am I and what is my lineage, my ancestral house in Israel, that I should be son-in-law to the ruler [of Israel]?" [19] But at the time for giving Merab the daughter of Saul to David, it happened that she was given to Adriel the Meholathite as a wife.

[20] Now [at the same time] Saul's daughter Michal loved David. Saul was told, and the matter was all right in his eyes. [21] So Saul said [to himself], "Let me give Michal to David that she may be a snare for him and that the hand of the Philistines may be against him." So, Saul said to David a second time, "Through the second shall you be my son-in-law this day."

[29] And Saul came to fear David more and Saul became the enemy of David every day from then.

Psalm 3:1–8

[1] HOLY ONE, how many are my enemies!
Many are rising against me.

2 Many are saying to me,
   "There is no help for her in God." *Selah*
3 Yet you, SAVING ONE, are a shield behind me,
   my glory, and the lifter of my head.
4 I cry aloud to the FAITHFUL ONE,
   and she answers me from her holy hill. *Selah*
5 I lay myself down and I sleep;
   then I wake for the WELLSPRING OF LIFE upholds me.
6 I do not fear ten thousand people,
   all around, set against me.
7 Rise up, MIGHTY GOD!
   Save me, my God!
   For you smite all my enemies on the cheek;
   you break the teeth of the wicked.
8 To the HOLY ONE OF OLD belongs salvation;
   upon your people be your blessing! *Selah*

Romans 5:6 Now while we were helpless, at the designated time, for the ungodly the Messiah died. 7 Rarely indeed will anyone for a righteous person die; though for a good person perhaps someone might dare to die. 8 Yet God proves God's love for us in that while we still were sinners the Messiah died for us. 9 Much more then, now that we have been justified by the blood of the Messiah, will we be saved through him from the wrath [to come]. 10 For if while enemies we were reconciled to God through the death of God's Child, much more, having been reconciled, we will be saved by the life of God's Child. 11 And even more than that, we boast in God through our Savior Jesus the Messiah, through whom we have now received reconciliation.

Mark 4:21 Jesus said to [the crowd of women, men, and children], "A lamp is not brought in to be put under the grain basket, under the bed and not on the lampstand is it? 22 For there is nothing hidden, except in order that it may be revealed; nor is anything concealed, except to be made known. 23 Let the one who has ears to hear, heed!" 24 Then Jesus said to them, "Watch what you hear; by the measure you all measure shall it be measured unto you, and still more will be given you. 25 For to the one who has, more will be given to them, and from the one who does not have, even what they have will be taken away from them."

PROCLAMATION

Text Notes

In 1 Samuel 14:49, Merab is Saul's firstborn, though her brothers are listed previously. "Father's family" is translated "ancestral house" in 18:18 and "my life" as "my lineage."

Both Hebrew and Greek manuscripts have "many are saying to him" in Psalm 3:2 where NRSV and others change to "you." God is a shield "behind" the psalmist in verse 3, i.e., protection from sneak attacks. In verse 7, "save me" is *hoshiani,* which will become "hosanna."

Romans 5:9 ends with "the wrath." Some translations make that the wrath of God. I have chosen to leave it as ambiguous as it is in the text.

In the Gospel reading, I have supplied the crowd based on the contextual information given in verse 10, "those who were around him." Verse 23 uses the same verb, "to hear" twice at the end and could be translated, *Let the one who has ears to hear, hear!*

Preaching Prompts

These passages look at brokenness in human relationships and the brokenness between God and humanity. In his conflict with David, Saul uses his daughters as tools to gain leverage. In the Epistle, our enmity with God is healed through the death of Jesus. In conversation with these readings, the Gospel's call to be light that can be seen as a call to be agents of reconciliation. And the Gospel warns us that what we give, do, "measure out" will be returned to us.

In the first lesson, Saul, like monarchs across time, uses his daughters to secure allies and loyalty. In most of the contexts in which these lessons will be read, fathers do not hold absolute sway over their daughter's lives, marriages, and ultimately, sexuality. But there are multiple social, political, cultural, and religious contexts where women, nonbinary folk, trans folk, and gender-nonconforming folk are not free to make choices about their lives, bodies, and relationships.

While love and loyalty are often intertwined in covenants between monarchs in treaties and between God and humanity articulated in covenantal terms, interpersonal human love occurs with some limitations. In most cases, men love and women are loved (passively) in terms of romantic love. Michal's unrequited love for David is the sole exception. For example, Isaac loved Rebekah (Gen. 24:67); Jacob loves Rachel more than Leah (Gen. 29:18); Samson loved Delilah (Judg. 16:4); Elkanah loved Hannah (1 Sam. 1:5); the king loved Esther (Esther 2:17). Two rapists express love for their victims in Genesis 34:3 and 2 Samuel 13:1. Mothers love their children—sons (Gen. 25:28) as do fathers (Gen. 37:3), but no one loves their daughter in the text, though Nathan evokes that love in his parable about an ewe loved as a daughter in 2 Samuel 12:3. Jerusalem/Zion is God's daughter often subject to harsh discipline; God's love for her is presumed but unspoken (Isa. 62:11; Jer. 6:2, 23; Lam. 1:6).

Covenant love is expressed between God and humanity broadly, and God and Israel in particular. God also enters into covenant with individual men but not women, not even when granting theophanies and annunciations. This is likely rooted in an Iron Age understanding of legal competence.

As an expression of God's covenant love with us, reconciliation comes with no requirements or preconditions. In contrast, reconciliation between human beings requires contrition, repentance, where possible, restoration, and when restoration is not possible, reparation. Too often Christians use calls for near-immediate reconciliation to avoid doing the necessary work. This can be seen in the way in which dominant culture churches engage communities which they have harmed, from black and indigenous peoples to women and gender and sexual minorities.

These readings offer an opportunity to explore the relationships the larger church has with its constituencies, and for individual congregations, the relationships between internal constituencies and the communities with which they engage and especially those who hold enmity for the church because of its past—and sometimes current—actions.

PROPER 25 (CLOSEST TO OCTOBER 26)

1 Samuel 25:14–19, 23–25, 32–34, 42–43; Psalm 37:1–2, 7–11, 16, 35–40;
2 Corinthians 8:1–9; Matthew 5:38–42

1 Samuel 25:14 To Abigail, wife of Nabal, one of the boys reported: "Look! David sent messengers out of the wilderness to greet our lord; and he screamed at them. [15] Yet the men were very good to us, and we were not put to shame, and we never missed anything all the days we were with them when we were in the field. [16] They were a wall to us even by night and also every day; we were with them, keeping the sheep. [17] Now know this and see what you can do; for evil against our master and against all his house has been resolved; he is worthless, no one can speak to him."

[18] Then Abigail hurried and she took two hundred loaves, two skins of wine, five prepared sheep, five measures of parched grain, one hundred clusters of raisins, and two hundred fig cakes and she loaded them on donkeys. [19] And Abigail said to her boys, "Go on before me; I am coming after you." And her husband Nabal she did not tell.

[23] And Abigail saw David and she hurried and got down from the donkey, fell before David on her face, bowing to the ground. [24] She fell at his feet and said, "Upon me my lord, the iniquity; please let your slave-woman speak in your ears and hear the words of your slave. [25] Please my lord, do not set your thought on this worthless man Nabal, for as his name, thus is he; Nabal [meaning Disgrace] is his name, and he is a disgrace; now I, your slave, did not see my lord's boys whom you sent."

[32] Then David said to Abigail, "Blessed be the HOLY ONE, the God of Israel, who sent you to meet me today! [33] Blessed be your discernment, and blessed be you, who have kept me today from coming for blood and saving me from my own hand. [34] Surely as the HOLY ONE the God of Israel lives, who has restrained me from hurting you [Abigail], unless you had hurried and come to meet me, truly by the light of daybreak there would not have been left to Nabal anyone urinating against a wall."

⁴² [Later after Nabal's death,] Abigail hurried and got up and mounted a donkey with five of her girls at her heels; she went after the messengers of David and she became his wife. ⁴³ David also married Ahinoam of Jezreel; both of them became his wives.

Psalm 37:1–2, 7–11, 16, 35–40

¹ Be not angry on account of the wicked,
   be not envious of wrongdoers;
² for they will soon wither like the wild grass,
   and fade like the planted grass.
⁷ Be still before the MOST HIGH, and wait patiently for her;
   be not angry on account of those who prosper on their path,
   or the one who carries out plots.
⁸ Let go of anger and forsake wrath;
   be not angry; it leads only to evil.
⁹ For the wicked shall be cut off,
   but those who hope in the FOUNT OF JUSTICE shall inherit the land.
¹⁰ And a little more time and the wicked will be no more;
   you will reflect upon their place and they will not be there.
¹¹ But the humble poor shall inherit the land,
   and delight themselves in abundant well-being.
¹⁶ Better is a little that the righteous person has
   than the abundance of many wicked.
³⁵ I have seen the wicked oppressing,
   and spreading themselves out like a native green tree.
³⁶ They passed on, and suddenly! They were no more;
   though I sought them, they could not be found.
³⁷ Regard the blameless and behold the upright,
   for there will be a future for the peaceable.
³⁸ But transgressors shall be utterly destroyed together;
   the future of the wicked shall be cut off.
³⁹ The salvation of the righteous is from the EVER-PRESENT GOD;
   she is their stronghold in the time of trouble.
⁴⁰ The REDEEMING GOD helps them and delivers them;
   she delivers them from the wicked, and saves them,
   because they take refuge in her.

2 Corinthians 8:1 Now we want you all to know, sisters and brothers, about the grace of God given to the churches of Macedonia: ² For in a great trial of affliction, their abundant joy and their extreme poverty have overflowed in a wealth of generosity on their part. ³ For, according to their means, as I can testify, and even beyond their ability, voluntarily, ⁴ with much exhortation begging us earnestly for the grace of participation in this ministry to the saints. [5] And not simply as we expected; rather they gave themselves first to the Savior, and to us by the will of God. [6] Thus we exhorted Titus that just as he had begun, so he should also complete this [work of] grace among you all. [7] So then, as in everything you excel—in faith, in speech, in knowledge, in zeal, and in love, ours for you [yours for us]—so we want you to excel also in this [act of] grace.

[8] Not as a command do I say this rather against the zeal of others am I proving the genuineness of your love. [9] For you all know the grace of our Redeemer Jesus the Messiah, that for you all he became poor though he was rich, so that you through his poverty might become rich.

Matthew 5:38 [Jesus said,] "You all have heard that it was said, 'An eye for an eye' and 'a tooth for a tooth.' [39] But I say to you: Do not set yourself against the wicked. But when someone strikes you on the right cheek, turn the other to them also. [40] And when someone wants you to be judged and take your coat, let your other clothing go as well. [41] And when someone forces you to go one mile, go the second mile too. [42] Give to those who ask from you, and those who want to borrow from you, do not refuse."

PROCLAMATION

Text Notes

In the Samuel text, "bless" is used to signify a greeting, indicating common forms of greeting such as, "May God bless you" (see Ruth 2:4). In verse 16, "even by night and also every day" translates "even night and even days." My translation of this verse is indebted to Everett Fox's translation in The Schocken Bible, vol. 2, *The Early Prophets*. Nabal is *ben belial*, "the son of worthlessness." In verse 25, Abigail begs David not to "set his heart to[ward]" Nabal. His name encodes all sorts of bad behavior, from impiety to sacrilege, to disorderly conduct and sexual assault. David's threat includes Abigail specifically in verse 34 through the use of the feminine singular form of the second person pronoun "you." Some understand the "wall pisser" of verse 34 to be a euphemism for soldier like "jarhead" or "leatherneck."

The language of Psalm 37:1 is somewhat stronger than the traditional "fret not" found in KJV and NRSV. Rather, it is the verb for burning anger that often discloses divine wrath. Verse 2 uses two different words for grass, with the latter sometimes having the sense of cultivated grass. To be "still" in verse 7 is also to be "silent," as in Aaron's silence in Leviticus 10:3 (elsewhere, Jer. 47:6; 48:2; Ezek. 24:17; Amos 5:13; Ps. 4:4; 30:12; 31:17). The word used for "hope" in verse 9 can also mean "wait"; some translators (KJV, NRSV) use "wait" here while others (CEB, Alter) use "hope" to distinguish it from "wait" in verse 7, a separate word (where JPS uses "look to"). The traditional translation "meek" in verse 11 obscures the impoverished estate of the referent. Further, "meekness" is a personality and behavioral characteristic, whereas the term here denotes those who have been made humble by their impoverished circumstances, often in the biblical text, through the unethical actions of others. In the same verse, "well-being," *shalom*, includes but is not limited to "prosperity," as in the NRSV. The humble poor and those who wait for and hope in God in verses 9 and 11 will inherit the "land," previously translated "earth." Both translations are tenable. However, the land itself is the treasure, heritage, and promise of God. The verse is not speaking of dominion over the world as it was known. The Hebrew of verse 35 is awkward but not untenable. There is no need to replace the MT with the LXX as do the NRSV and CEB.

2 Corinthians 8 uses "grace" to mean "privilege, benefits, gift," and "work." In each case, I have kept grace, the primary lexeme, at the center of translation and modified around it. Inclusive plural *adelphoi* refers to both mixed gender groups and all male groups. This project uses "sisters and brothers," inverting the traditional patriarchal sequencing. In verse 7, there are two manuscript traditions; the minority tradition, "your love for us" makes more sense than "our love for you." I have supplied both options for the reader.

The "eye for an eye" teaching occurs in Exodus 21:24, Leviticus 24:20, and Deuteronomy 19:21. "The wicked" in Matthew 5:39 can be translated as "evil (itself)" or a "wicked/evil person," or "a person who does evil/wickedness." The verb in verse 39 can also mean do not "oppose" or "resist."

Preaching Prompts

While some biblical passages equate wealth with blessing uncritically, these lessons look more deeply at what one does with one's wealth as a measure of character. Nabal was stingy and mean-spirited when he could have shown hospitality. Of people like him, the psalmist counsels that they and their riches will not last, but those who have been reduced to humble circumstances through the ill-gotten gain of others will inherit the earth.

At this phase of his life, David is a thug, robbing and extorting people for cash crops and currency on the hoof. Nabal is a vile person, a nasty drunk, a difficult, if not abusive, husband, but that does not entitle David to his goods; he is not yet king. Nabal had a cultural obligation to provide hospitality but that should not merit a death sentence. Yet David vowed that he would have killed them all if Abigail had not brought him the goods. He and Abigail ride off into the sunset after the death of her husband. He then pulls over somewhere and picks up another woman. One purpose of this story in its original context was to emphasize David's youth, strength, and virility. He will have seven wives when he has Bathsheba abducted and will continue collecting them. One wonders what Paul would have made of David and his sexual conduct. For all that David is idolized and idealized in and out of the text, he is a vivid example of the limitations of men, monarchs, and monarchy.

In 2 Corinthians 8, Paul proffers a different model of wealth and of dealing with wealth, generosity. He describes a wealth of generosity in distributing wealth to meet the needs of the community.

Jesus's rejection of "an eye for an eye" opens this section that reads as a non-violent resistance manual and is consistent with rabbinic teaching that called for financial restitution in cases of bodily injury. Jesus says to yield to those who strike or force you and to give to those who ask and to those who take. That was Abigail's strategy and it saved her life and the lives of everyone on her estate. However, it can be easily twisted by those with power to victimize the vulnerable. Often neglected is the end of the unit articulating a model of extravagant generosity: *Give to those who ask from you, and those who want to borrow from you, do not refuse.* The objections are easy to imagine, "He can't possibly mean that." "Then I would have nothing left." That is the point. Nothing you have is yours. Everything belongs to God and should be used for the betterment of the kin-community of God.

FEAST OF ALL SAINTS, NOVEMBER 1

Isaiah 25:1, 4a, 6–10a; Psalm 67; Romans 15:7–13; Matthew 27:50–56

Isaiah 25:1 HOLY ONE OF OLD, you are my God;

> I will exalt you, I will praise your name,
> for you have worked wonders,
> ancient counsel, faithful and trustworthy.
> ⁴ For you are a refuge to the poor,
> a refuge to the needy in their distress,
> a shelter from the storm and a shade from the heat.
> ⁶ The COMMANDER of heaven's legions will make for all peoples on this mountain,
> a feast of rich food, a feast of well-aged wines,
> of rich food prepared with marrow, of refined well-aged wines.
> ⁷ And God will destroy on this mountain
> the shroud that shrouds all peoples,
> the veil that veils all nations.
> ⁸ God will swallow up death forever.
> Then the SOVEREIGN GOD will wipe away tears from every face,
> and will sweep aside the shame of God's people from the whole earth,
> for GOD WHOSE NAME IS HOLY has spoken.
> ⁹ It will be said on that day,
> Look! This is our God; in whom we hope, and who saved us.
> This is the CREATOR OF ALL in whom we hope;
> let us be glad and rejoice in God's salvation.
> ¹⁰ For the hand of the ANCIENT OF DAYS shall rest on this mountain.

Psalm 67

1 May God be merciful to us and bless us,
  show us the light of her countenance and come to us.
2 Let your ways be known upon earth,
  your saving health among all nations.
3 Let the peoples praise you, O God;
  let all the peoples praise you.
4 Let the nations be glad and sing for joy,
  for you judge the peoples with equity
  and guide all the nations upon earth.
5 Let the peoples praise you, O God;
  let all the peoples praise you.
6 The earth has brought forth her increase;
  may God, our own God, give us her blessing.
7 May God give us her blessing,
  and may all the ends of the earth stand in awe of her.

Romans 15:7 Accept one another, therefore, just as Christ has accepted you, for the glory of God. 8 I tell you that the Messiah has become a servant of the circumcised for the sake of truth to confirm the promises given to the mothers and fathers, 9 and in order that the Gentiles might glorify God on account of God's mercy. As it is written,

"Therefore, I will confess you among the Gentiles,
and sing praises to your name,"

10 and again it says,

"Rejoice, O Gentiles, with God's people,"

11 and again,

"Praise the Most High, all you Gentiles,
and let all the peoples praise God,"

12 and again Isaiah says,

"The root of Jesse shall come,
and the one who rises to rule the Gentiles,
in whom the Gentiles shall hope."

13 May the God of hope fill you with all joy and peace in believing, so that you may abound in hope by the power of the Holy Spirit.

Matthew 27:50 Jesus cried again with a loud voice and relinquished his spirit. 51 Then, look! The curtain of the temple was torn from top to bottom in two. And the earth was shaken, and the rocks were split. [52] And the tombs were opened, and many bodies of the saints who had fallen asleep were raised. [53] Then after his resurrection they came out of the tombs and entered the holy city and appeared to many. [54] Now when the centurion and those with him, who were standing guard over Jesus, saw the earthquake and what took place, they were terrified and said, "Truly this man was God's Son!"

[55] Now there were many women there, from a distance watching; they had followed Jesus from Galilee and had ministered to him. [56] Among them were Mary the Magdalene, and Mary the mother of James and Joseph, and the mother of the sons of Zebedee.

PROCLAMATION

Text Notes

Division of verses for Isaiah 25 varies among translations. I follow the Masoretic Text and Jewish Publication Society here. Similarly, the flexibility of Hebrew tenses can place God's salvific actions in the past or future. The past tense emphasizes God's past faithfulness laying the ground for a reasonable hope in continuing faithfulness.

Since *pateron* in Romans 15:8 can be inclusive of "ancestors" or "fathers" and God's promises were not and are not limited by gender, I use the most inclusive option. In verse 9, Christ takes up the same diaconal ministry with which the women who follow him are credited. Verses 9–12 quote Psalm 18:49, Deuteronomy 32:43, Psalm 117:1, and Isaiah 11:10 from the LXX. There are some variances between the Greek and Hebrew of Deuteronomy 32:43: In the Hebrew text, "the nations, God's people" are called to rejoice, while in the Greek, the heavens are called to rejoice *with* God's people. (For more on the divergence between the manuscript traditions on this verse, see the annotations and comparisons in *The Dead Seas Scrolls Bible*, ed. Abegg, Flint, and Ulrich.)

The women who "ministered" to Jesus, *diakoneo*, have been understood as providing for Jesus (NRSV), serving him (CEB), and ministering to him (KJV); all are viable, however, breadth in translation rather than specificity would seem to be called for.

Preaching Prompts

For the Feast of All Saints, this lectionary turns to declarations of God's faithfulness to all peoples and nations. This passage of Isaiah speaks repeatedly to "all peoples" and "all nations" in verses 6–7, all of whom will benefit from God's death-destroying salvific work. Similarly, in the psalm, God's salvation is for all nations with all peoples invited to join in the praise of God. The Epistle focuses on the acceptance of God's gift of salvation by the Gentile nations. The Gospel takes us back to that saving work in the life and death of Jesus, hinting at the resurrection to come with the resurrection of saints who preceded Jesus in death, at the moment of his death. Meanwhile, the saints who stood bearing witness would become second-class saints in the eyes of many, excluded from ministry, ordination, and leadership based on their gender. Perhaps ironically, and almost certainly intentionally, the reduction of their ministry to open checkbooks exploits and limits their gifts at the same time.

PROPER 26 (CLOSEST TO NOVEMBER 2)

2 Samuel 11:2–15; Psalm 32:1–7; 2 Peter 3:1–4, 8–9; Matthew 15:10–11, 15–20

2 Samuel 11:2 And it happened near the evening that David rose from his lying-place and went walking about on the roof of the palace and he saw a woman bathing from the roof; the woman was extraordinarily beautiful in appearance. [3] David sent someone to inquire about the woman. It was reported, "Is not this Bathsheba daughter of Eliam, the wife of Uriah the Hittite?" [4] And David sent messengers and he took her, and she came to him, and he lay with her. Then she purified herself after her defilement and she returned to her house. [5] The woman conceived, and she sent and had someone tell David, "I am pregnant."

[6] So David sent word to Joab, "Send me Uriah the Hittite," and Joab sent Uriah to David. [7] When Uriah came to him, David asked after the status of Joab, and the status of the people, and the status of the war. [8] Then David said to Uriah, "Go down to your house, and wash your feet." Uriah went out of the palace, and after him a gift from David. [9] Now Uriah slept at the entrance of the palace with all the slaves of his lord and did not go down to his house. [10] And they told David, "Uriah did not go down to his house." So David said to Uriah, "Have you not come from a journey? Why did you not go down to your house?" [11] Uriah said to David, "The ark and Israel and Judah dwell in temporary shelters and my lord Joab and the slaves of my lord are at the edge of the field, camping. Should I then go to my house, to eat and to drink, and to lie with my wife? As you live, and as your soul lives, I will not do this thing." [12] Then David said to Uriah, "Stay here this day also, and tomorrow I will send you." So, Uriah remained in Jerusalem that day and the next. [13] Then David called him to dine in his presence and he drank, and David got him drunk. Then in the evening he went out to lie on his couch with the slaves of his lord, yet he did not go down to his house.

[14] And it was in the morning that David wrote a [message] scroll to Joab and sent it in the hand of Uriah. [15] Now in the scroll David wrote, "Set Uriah at the frontline of the most intense battle and pull back from behind him, so he will be struck down and die."

Psalm 32:1–7

1 Happy is the woman or man whose transgression is forgiven,
whose sin is covered.

2 Happy is the woman or man
to whom the HOLY ONE does not reckon iniquity,
and in whose spirit there is no deceit.

3 While I kept silence, my bones wasted away
in my groaning all the day.

4 For day and night your hand was heavy upon me,
my strength melted away as by the heat of summer.

5 My sin I made known to you,
and my iniquity I did not hide.
I said, "I will make known my transgressions to the GRACIOUS ONE,"
and you forgave the iniquity of my sin.

6 Therefore let all who are faithful
offer prayer to you;
who are found at a such a time,
for a rush of mighty waters
shall not touch them.

7 You are a hiding place for me;
you keep me from distress;
you surround me with cries of deliverance.

2 Peter 3:1 Now this, beloved, the second letter I am writing to you all; in them I am trying to arouse your genuine understanding by reminding you all 2 that you should remember the words spoken in the past by the holy women and men who prophesied and the commandment of the Redeemer and Savior spoken through your apostles. 3 First of all know this, that in the last days will come scoffers scoffing and chasing after their own lusts 4 and saying, "Where is the promise of his coming? For, ever since our ancestors died, everything continues as from the beginning of creation!"

8 But this one thing, do not ignore, beloved, that with the Most High one day is like a thousand years, and a thousand years are like one day. 9 The Most High is not slow about God's promise, as some think of slowness, but is patient with you all, not wanting anyone to perish, rather all to come to repentance.

Matthew 15:10 Jesus called the crowd, saying to them, "Listen and understand: 11 It is not what enters the mouth that defiles a woman or man rather, it is what exits the mouth that defiles a person."

15 Then Peter said to him, "Explain to us this parable." 16 So Jesus said, "Are you all also still lacking understanding? 17 Do you not see everything that enters the mouth goes into the stomach and exits into the sewer? 18 But what comes out of the mouth comes forth from

the heart and this is what defiles a woman or man. [19] For out of the heart come evil intentions, murder, adultery, sexual immorality, theft, false testimony, slander. [20] These are what defile women and men, but to eat with unwashed hands does not defile a person."

PROCLAMATION

Text Notes

In 2 Samuel 11:7, *shalom* is used for the welfare check on the Joab and the people the war. Commentators understand the "gift" in verse 8 to be some largesse from David's table or holdings, agricultural stuffs, livestock, etc. In verse 11, *succoth* is the plural of "booths" or "shelters"; it is also phonetically the same as the city Succoth, which is how JPS understands it. In verse 13, Uriah's drunkenness is articulated with a verb form that lays the cause at David's feet: "he (made/got) him drunk."

In 2 Peter 3:1, *eilikrine dianoian* is "genuine" in the sense of both unadulterated and unpretentious, and "understanding" in the sense of comprehension and the intention to act on that understanding. In verse 2, "holy women and men who prophesied" renders and expands "holy prophets." "Scoffers scoffing" in verse 3 is a Hebraism; Hebrew (and Aramaic) roots form nouns and verbs—and sometimes adjectives. The nominal and verbal forms occur together but in inverse order, "they will come scoffing, scoffers." They're going "after their own lusts," here rendered "chasing after."

Preaching Prompts

In these lessons, David's most infamous act, the rape of Bathsheba, is held in conversation with later teaching on the ethical values and character traits that characterize the reign and realm of God. Psalm 32 is traditionally attributed to David. In terms of content, it is a good fit for a man whose recorded transgressions are legion, particularly in a text that is, at turns, hagiographic. It should be noted that the Hebrew formula commonly translated as "of David" actually means "to/for David." This may indicate "composed on behalf of" or "dictated by." The psalm offers assurance of the forgiveness of sin with repentance signified by confession in verse 5. The Epistle warns against all kinds of lust, lust for all kinds of things and promises a reckoning. In the Gospel, Jesus addresses many of the same undesirable characteristics as the Epistle, focusing on their origin in the human heart. He does so using ritual washing before meals as an object lesson, putting him at odds with the Pharisees in the text, a classic rabbinic disputation.

David's violation of Bathsheba's body is treated as a violation of her husband's rights to and over her body and as an offense against God. She is not treated as a victim or survivor. The extolling of her beauty has been weaponized—she (and other women) tempt men with their beauty by existing and conforming to some aesthetic standard. The construction of David's sin as adultery projects blame onto Bathsheba that neither the text nor Nathan assert on God's behalf. Indeed, Bathsheba is not charged with or punished for adultery; no sin is ascribed to her in the text. Rooftops often formed an extra room in Israelite households; Bathsheba's bathing there is also not critiqued in the text as it is in subsequent interpretation. The initial mention of her bathing in verse 2 did not mention "impurity," often read as menstruation, though that term is not used. She purifies herself from her impurity, "defilement" here, in verse 4 *after* David rapes her; that is a second cleansing. David's decision to gift (or pay) Uriah for a harm that he may not yet know he has suffered conjures men who after a sexual assault offer their victim money or something valuable for silence or just out of guilt. (For a detailed analysis of the passage, see the chapter on Bathsheba in *Womanist Midrash*.)

The Gospel portion intentionally omits the critique of the Pharisees as anti-pharisaic rhetoric in the Christian scriptures and its interpretation are often unnecessarily anti-Semitic. As always, contextualizing Jesus as a religiously observant Jewish scholar who respected the Pharisees even while disagreeing with them and agreed more than disagreed is helpful. Consider Jesus's overlooked instruction in Matthew 23:2–3: *"The scribes and the Pharisees sit on Moses's seat; therefore, do whatever they teach you and follow it."* The necessary prerequisite for understanding the following more familiar text to break with them only when they do not do as they themselves say. Jesus's dissent over ritual washing represents the normative variance in religious practice expected among any group, not a condemnation of the Judaism of his age or the authority of the Pharisees—though other texts will position them differently.

The ethical failures highlighted by these lessons continue; the Church has the responsibility to hear the victimized, which has not been the experience of most women or others abused by clergy. The Church needs justice in its own house and in the world without.

PROPER 27 (CLOSEST TO NOVEMBER 9)

1 Kings 5:1–6, 13–14; Psalm 72:1–4, 12–14, 18–19;
Philippians 4:1–7; Matthew 6:28–34

1 Kings 5:1 Now Hiram king of Tyre sent persons he enslaved to Solomon, for he heard that they had anointed him king in place of his father; for Hiram had always loved David. ² Solomon sent word to Hiram, saying, ³ "You know that my father David was not able to build a house for the Name of the ETERNAL ONE his God because of the warfare with which his enemies surrounded him, until the MOST HIGH put them under the soles of his feet. ⁴ Yet now the HOLY ONE my God has granted me respite all around; there is neither adversary nor ill fortune. ⁵ So look! I propose to build a house for the Name of the HOLY ONE my God, just as the HOLY ONE OF OLD spoke to David my father, 'Your son, whom I will set in your place on your throne, he shall build the house for my Name.' ⁶ Now then, command that they cut for me cedars from the Lebanon; my slaves will be with your slaves and wages for your slaves will I give you according to whatever you say; for you know there is no one among us who knows how to cut timber like the Sidonians."

¹³ And King Solomon imposed forced labor out of all Israel and the conscripts were thirty thousand men. ¹⁴ Now he sent them to the Lebanon, ten thousand a month in turns; one month were they in the Lebanon, two months at home and Adoniram was in charge of the forced labor.

Psalm 72:1–4, 12–14, 18–19

¹ God, give the ruler your justice,
and your righteousness to a ruler's son.
² May the [next] ruler judge your people with righteousness,
and your afflicted ones with justice.
³ May the mountains raise up well-being for the people,
and the hills, righteousness.
⁴ May the ruler do justice for the poor of the people,
grant deliverance to those born in need
and crush the oppressor.
¹² For the ruler delivers the needy when they call,
the oppressed and those who have no helper.
¹³ The ruler has pity on the poor and the needy,
and saves the lives of the needy.
¹⁴ From oppression and violence the ruler redeems their life;
and precious is their blood in the sight of their ruler.
¹⁸ Blessed be the FOUNT OF JUSTICE, the God of Israel,
who alone does wondrous things.
¹⁹ Blessed be her glorious name forever;
may her glory fill the whole earth.
Amen and Amen.

Philippians 4:1 Now then, my sisters and brothers [friends and kin], beloved and longed for, my joy and crown, thus stand firm in the Redeemer beloveds.

² Euodia I implore, and Syntyche I implore as well, to come to an agreement in the Savior. ³ Yes, and I ask you also, my faithful colleague, help these women, for in the work of the gospel, they have struggled beside me together with Clement and the rest of my coworkers, whose names are in the book of life.

⁴ [All of you] Rejoice in the Redeemer always; again I say, Rejoice! ⁵ Let your gentleness be known to every person. The Messiah is near. ⁶ Nothing should make you anxious;

rather in everything by prayer and supplication with thanksgiving let your requests be made known to God. ⁷ And the peace of God, which surpasses all understanding, will guard your hearts and your minds in Jesus the Messiah.

Matthew 6:28 [Jesus asked,] now why do you all worry about clothing? Consider the lilies of the field, how they grow; they neither labor nor spin. ²⁹ Yet I tell you all, even Solomon in all his glory was not clothed like one of these. ³⁰ Now if the grass of the field, which is alive today and tomorrow is thrown into the oven God so clothes, will not God do much more for you all of little faith? ³¹ Therefore do not worry, saying, 'What shall we eat?' or 'What shall we drink?' or 'What shall we wear?' ³² For all these the Gentiles strive and indeed your heavenly Provider knows that of you need all these. ³³ But strive first for the reign of God and God's righteousness and all these will be given to you all. ³⁴ So do not worry about tomorrow, for tomorrow has worries of its own. Sufficient is the trouble of this day."

PROCLAMATION

Text Notes

This portion of 1 Kings is numbered differently in Christian and Jewish texts and translations. What is 1 Kings 5:15 in the MT and JPS is 5:1 in NRSV, CEB, KJV, etc.; the LXX follows the Jewish numbering. In verse 1 (Heb. v. 15), Hiram's "love" for David should probably be understood as "loyalty," as in CEB; Everett Fox adds "in covenant." Solomon suggests that David was unable to build the temple because he was so busy fighting his enemies. He neglects to mention that God forbade David to build the temple because his hands were so bloody (1 Chron. 22:6–8, though it should be remembered that Chronicles represents an alternative reflection on Israel's story). In verse 4 (Heb. v. 18), "adversary" is *satan*; the term has no evil connotation in the Hebrew Bible, unlike the Pseudepigrapha (and subsequently, the Christian Testament) where the character first becomes God's adversary.

Throughout Psalm 72 I use "the ruler" for the monarch and his son and the many masculine pronouns for clarity and for the broader utility of this psalm beyond male monarchs. In verses 2 and 12, the people are afflicted (or oppressed) through a poverty that is imposed on them through unjust means, hence punishment of "the oppressor" in verse 4; Hebrew's lexicon of poverty has different words for different contexts. "Those born in need" replaces "children/sons of the needy" in the same verse. Hebrew uses "soul" for both the essence of a person's life, what we in the West tend to call a "soul," and a person's life. The language of saving and redeeming in Psalm 72:13–14 refers properly to lives; a leader's economic policies are matters of life and death.

In Philippians 4, *adelphoi* is inclusive; I translate it as "sisters and brothers" with the option of "friends and kin" (or all of these) for more inclusivity, specifically to include nonbinary and agender folk. In the same verse, "beloved" and "longed for" are adjectives counter to their portrayal as verbs in NRSV. The faithful colleague, *suguzu*, has occasionally been rendered as a proper name; however, no such name or a variant of the purported name has been found in the literature of the area.

Preaching Prompts

These lessons offer disparate models of community and the labor that sustains it. There is the monarchal model where the human monarch, Samuel predicts, will plunder the people and their resources; scholars understand this passage to be a critique of Solomon. Imaginatively, Psalm 72 is a response to that critique in the form of a prayer that Solomon might receive divine guidance to avoid the pitfalls of Samuel's prophecy. In the Epistle, women and men "struggle" together and sometimes against each other while building up the Jesus-following community, a familiar portrait in our own time. In the Gospel, it is God who does the work to provide for the needs of the community of believers, and all creation.

In the first lesson, David's time is past. His lineage will endure, though his throne will fall. Solomon inherits a wealthy stable country that he expands. He also inherits the divisions between their familial Judean supporters and the other tribes. In spite of his divinely granted wisdom, he lacks the charisma and savvy of David. His conduct, including his sexual excesses, would be his downfall, shattering the once united monarchy. Solomon's love for foreign women is often held as his primary failing, but his economic policies devastated his reign.

In the reading, Solomon conscripts able-bodied men to serve two months away and return for one month at home. Consider the impact on agricultural and pastoral work, the backbones of the Israelite economy. The effect of the conscription was so ruinous that when Solomon's son later tried to reinstitute it under the same taskmaster, the people stoned the overseer in 1 Kings 12:18 (there Adoram, understood to be the same as Adoniram here). As with all economic hardships, Solomon's policies would have been most devasting on women and children. The majesty of human monarchs always comes at a cost and those who pay it are most often those who can least afford it. Samuel's warning to the people of the cost of monarchy in 1 Samuel 8:11–17, understood by many as a retrospective on Solomon, lists all that a monarch would take from their subjects, including their daughters in verse 13.

Also often overlooked is that Solomon's expenditures of human and fiscal capital were to build a series of palaces that dwarfed the temple he built for God, including some for the foreign royal women he married. (One of David's wives was also a foreign royal, Maacah bat Talmi, the mother of Tamar and Absalom, who was the daughter of King Talmi of Geshur.) The temple was sixty by twenty cubits and thirty cubits high (1 Kings 6:2); it took seven years to build (1 Kings 6:38). In contrast, he spent thirteen years building his primary residence (1 Kings 7:1); a single hall in it was one hundred by fifty cubits, also thirty cubits high (1 Kings 7:2), a second hall was fifty by thirty cubits (1 Kings 7:6), and there were two more halls (1 Kings 7:7). His proper home was "the same construction" and he made a duplicate for the Egyptian princess he married (1 Kings 7:8). Perhaps, having exhausted his treasury, Solomon paid King Hiram of Tyre with twenty cities in Galilee (1 Kings 9:11).

The start-up Jesus movement is operating on a very different scale than the splendor with which Solomon surrounds himself. In the movement, Paul identifies a number of women who are his coworkers, "colaborers," deacons, and in one case, an apostle in Romans 16. Here are two more women on equal footing with him, Euodia and Syntyche. They are in artist disagreement over some matter and Paul is attempting to facilitate reconciliation for the greater good. But he does not chastise them or insinuate that there was a petty squabble or some matter of transgression. They are simply two women with their own differing opinions; two women who appear to be in positions of leadership of the larger community in Philippi, working beside Paul, not under nor subject to him. This passage is a reminder that disagreements are part of life and part of the life of the Jesus community, and are not an issue of sin.

This passage bids us trust God for what we need, a challenging proposition when there is so much inequity and so many do not in fact have what they need; women and children particularly, indigenous, black and Hispanic women and their children are as always most vulnerable. When read with the Epistle, it is a call to struggle together to ensure everyone has what they need.

PROPER 28 (CLOSEST TO NOVEMBER 16)

2 Kings 24:8–15; Psalm 79; Revelation 18:1–2, 4–8; Luke 7:11–23

2 Kings 24:8 Eighteen years was Jehoiachin at his reign; three months he reigned in Jerusalem and the name of his mother was Nehushta, daughter of Elnathan of Jerusalem. ⁹ And he did what was evil in the sight of the RIGHTEOUS ONE, just as his father had done.

¹⁰ At that time the slave-troops of Nebuchadnezzar, King of Babylon, came up to Jerusalem and the city was besieged. ¹¹ And Nebuchadnezzar, King of Babylon, came to the city, while his slave-troops were besieging it. ¹² Then Jehoiachin, King of Judah, went out [surrendering] to the king of Babylon: himself, his mother, his enslaved bureaucrats, his leaders, and his [most trusted] officials and the king of Babylon took him prisoner in the eighth year of his reign.

¹³ Thus Nebuchadnezzar brought out all the treasures of the house of the HOLY ONE and the treasures of the house of the king and he cut up all the vessels of gold in the house of the HOLY ONE which Solomon, King of Israel, had made; just as the ALL-KNOWING GOD

had said. [14] And Nebuchadnezzar exiled all Jerusalem: all the leaders, all the warriors, ten thousand exiles, all the artisans and the smiths; no one remained except the poorest people of the land. [15] So he exiled Jehoiachin to Babylon and the mother of the king, the women of the king, his [most trusted] officials, and the [men called the] rams of the land, Nebuchadnezzar took into captivity from Jerusalem to Babylon.

Psalm 79

1 God, the nations have come into your possession;
   they have defiled your holy temple;
   they have turned Jerusalem in ruins.
2 They have given the corpses of your slaves,
   women, children, and men,
   as food to the birds of the air;
   the flesh of your faithful ones,
   women, children, and men,
   to the wild animals of the earth.
3 They have poured their blood
   like water around Jerusalem,
   and there was none [left] to bury.
4 We have become a taunt to our neighbors,
   the scorn and derision of those around us.
5 How long, HOLY GOD? Will you be angry for all time,
   your jealous wrath burn like fire?
6 Pour out your anger upon the nations
   that do not know you,
   and upon the dominions
   that do not call on your Name.
7 For they have devoured Rachel's lineage
   and decimated their habitation.
8 Remember not the former iniquities against us;
   let your mother-love come speedily to meet us,
   for we are brought very low.
9 Help us, God of our salvation,
   for the sake of the glory of your Name;
   and deliver us and forgive our sins,
   for the sake of your Name.
10 Why should the nations say,
   "Where is their God?"
   Let it be known among the nations before our eyes,
   vengeance for the poured out blood of your servants.

¹¹ May the groaning of prisoners come before you,

according to the great [strength of] your arm;

preserve those destined for death.

¹² Now return to our neighbors sevenfold, into their bosom,

the taunts with which they taunted you, Holy One!

¹³ Then we your people, the flock of your pasture,

will give thanks to you for all time;

from generation to generation we will recount your praise.

Revelation 18:1 I saw [an] angel coming down from the heavens, one who had great authority and the earth was illuminated with its splendor. ² It called out with a mighty voice,

"Fallen, fallen is Babylon the great!

Now she has become a den of demons,

a bastion of every unclean spirit,

a bastion of every unclean bird,

a bastion of every unclean and hateful beast.

⁴ Then I heard another voice from heaven saying,

"Come out of her, my people,

so that you do not take part in her sins,

and so that her plagues you do not receive.

⁵ For her sins touch the heavens,

and God has remembered her iniquities.

⁶ Pay her back what she herself has paid out,

and pay her back double, double for her works;

in the cup she mixed, mix her a double.

⁷ Just as she glorified herself and lived running wild,

likewise give her just as much torment and sorrow.

Now then, in her heart she says,

'I sit a queen; I am no widow,

and sorrow shall I never see.'

⁸ Therefore in a single day her blows will come:

death and sorrow and famine.

And with fire shall she be burned;

for mighty is the Sovereign God who judges her."

Luke 7:11 The day after [healing a centurion's slave] Jesus went to a town called Nain, and his disciples and a large crowd went with him. ¹² He has just approached the gate of the town and suddenly, being carried out was a man who had died, his mother's only son and she was a widow; with her was a large crowd from the town. ¹³ When the Messiah saw her, he had compassion on her and said to her, "Do not weep." ¹⁴ Then Jesus came forward and touched the coffin, and the bearers stood still. And he said, "Young man, I say to you, rise!" [15] The dead man sat up and began to speak and Jesus gave him to his mother. [16] Fear seized all of them; and they glorified God, saying, "A great prophet has risen among us!" and "God visited God's people!" [17] This word about Jesus spread throughout Judea and all the surrounding country.

[18] Now the disciples of John reported about all these things to him. Then John summoned two of his disciples [19] and sent them to the Savior to ask, "Are you the one who is to come, or for another should we wait?" [20] When they had come to Jesus, they said, "John the Baptizer has sent us to you to ask, 'Are you the one who is to come, or for another should we wait?'" [21] In that hour Jesus healed many women, children, and men of diseases, afflictions, and evil spirits and gave sight to many who were blind. [22] Then Jesus responded, saying, "Go and tell John what you have seen and heard: *the blind receive sight*, the lame walk, the those with diseased skin are made whole, *the deaf hear, the dead are raised, the poor have good news brought to them.* [23] And blessed is anyone who is not scandalized by me."

PROCLAMATION

Text Notes

In 2 Kings 24:10–11, Nebuchadnezzar's soldiers are referred to simply as "slaves." The term is later used for one category of palace official. In verse 12, the king and the rest of the upper echelon "go out" in an inverse Exodus, using the same verb of the coming out from Egypt; "surrender" is clearly implied but not stated. The "most trusted" officials are either eunuchs or men who are as trustworthy as eunuchs, as the term has come to mean more than men with full or partial castration. It is not clear who or what is meant by the "rams of the land" in verse 15.

In verse 7 of the psalm, "Jacob" is replaced by his mother Rachel and her lineage.

At the heart of the verb *splagchnizomai*, "to have compassion," in Luke 7:13 is its root *splagchnon*, innards or guts, the locus of emotion. In verse 22, Jesus draws on the Isaiah tradition, including Isaiah 29:18, 42:18, and 61:1.

In the reading from the Revelation, I use the pronoun "it" for the divine being to signal that it transcends gender as we know it. In verse 3, *phulake*, "bastion," has the sense of prison and guard tower.

Preaching Prompts

In these readings, the fall of Jerusalem to Nebuchadnezzar and Babylon marks the end of ordinary time, preparing the Way for the feast of the majesty of Christ and Advent. The first lesson narrates the end of the continuous monarchy of Israel and Judah; in spite of the separation of the nations and violent upheaval and coups, a throne (or two) had been occupied since the time of Saul if not before. Babylon, Egypt, and Rome would install puppet kings; there would be a brief resurgence of autonomy under the Maccabees ending with the rule of Queen Salome Alexandra, also known as Shalom Zion, the Peace of Zion. The psalm is one of a small group that likely dates from the fall of Jerusalem and gives voice to the sorrow and terror of the people experiencing the abandonment of God if not the defeat of God, as it would have commonly been understood. The portion of the Apocalypse of John read for the Epistle recounts the cosmic defeat of Babylon, both the ancient evil empire and the amorphous evil that gets subsumed under her name. In keeping with the traditions of the ancient Afro-Asiatic world, Babylon like all cities, is grammatically feminine. "Babylon" as a trope for an overwhelming evil system of power endures into the present in Rastafari and in some preaching with fundamentalist roots. It is worth asking who/what/where is Babylon today? Some might well respond the United States. In the Gospel, Jesus is the one of Life, the one with resurrection power in his touch, who stands against the Babylon of his day—included as subtext as the Babylon in the Revelation. In raising a widow's child, Jesus demonstrated his power and authority over death itself; no empire could have the last word against him. He tells the disciples of John that he indeed is the one for whom they, we, have been waiting, preparing us for the season of waiting.

MAJESTY OF CHRIST (CLOSEST TO NOVEMBER 23)

2 Kings 24:8, 11–17; Psalm 47; Hebrews 1:1–9; Matthew 27:11–14, 27–37

2 Kings 24:8 Jehoiachin was eighteen years old at his reign. He reigned three months in Jerusalem and the name of his mother was Nehushta daughter of Elnathan of Jerusalem.

[11] Now King Nebuchadnezzar of Babylon came to the city while his troops were besieging it. [12] Then King Jehoiachin of Judah surrendered to the king of Babylon, himself and his mother and his slaves and his officers and his officials. The king of Babylon took him [captive] in the eighth year of his reign.

[13] He brought out from there the treasures of the house of the HOLY ONE OF OLD and the treasures of the king's house; he cut up all the vessels of gold in the temple of the HOLY ONE which King Solomon of Israel had made, just as the HOLY ONE had spoken. [14] Nebuchadnezzar took into exile all Jerusalem, all the officials, all the warriors, ten thousand exiled women and men, all the artisans, and the smiths; no one remained except the poorest people of the land. [15] He took Jehoiachin into exile to Babylon; the king's mother, the king's women, his officials, and the elite of the land he took into exile from Jerusalem to Babylon. [16] The king of Babylon took into exile to Babylon all the valiant warriors, seven thousand, the artisans and the smiths, one thousand, all of them strong and fit for war. [17] The king of Babylon made Mattaniah, Jehoiachin's uncle, king in his place and changed his name to Zedekiah.

Psalms 47

¹ All you peoples clap your hands;
   shout to God with a joyful sound.
² For the SOVEREIGN GOD, the Most High, is awesome,
   a great governor over all the earth.
³ She subdued peoples under us,
   and nations under our feet.
⁴ She chose our heritage for us,
   the pride of Rebekah's womb whom she loves.
⁵ God has gone up with a shout,
   SINAI'S FIRE with the sound of a trumpet.
⁶ Sing praises to God, sing praises;
   sing praises to our Sovereign, sing praises.
⁷ For God is Sovereign over all the earth;
   sing praises with a psalm.
⁸ God is ruler over the nations;
   God is seated on her holy throne.
⁹ The nobles of the peoples gather,
   the people of the God of Hagar and Sarah;
   for to God belong the shields of the earth,
   she is highly exalted.

Hebrews 1:1 Many times and in many ways God spoke to our mothers and fathers through the prophets, female and male. ² In these last days God has spoken to us by a Son, whom God appointed heir of all there is, and through whom God created the worlds. ³ The Son is the brilliance of God's glory and reproduction of God's very being, and the Son undergirds all there is by his word of power. When the Son had made purification for sins, he sat down at the right hand of the Majesty on high, ⁴ having become as much greater than the angels as the name he inherited is more excellent than theirs.

⁵ For to which of the angels did God ever say,
   "*You are my Child; today I have begotten you*"?

Or this,

   "*I will be their Parent, and they will be my Child*"?

⁶ Then again, when God brings the firstborn into the world, God says,

   "*Let all the angels of God worship him.*"

⁷ On the one hand of the angels God says,

   "*God makes winds into celestial messengers,
   and flames of fire into God's ministers.*"

[8] But of the Son God says,

> "*Your throne, O God, is forever and ever,*
> *and the righteous scepter is the scepter of your realm.*
> [9] *You have loved righteousness and hated lawlessness;*
> *therefore God, your God, has anointed you*
> *with the oil of gladness beyond your companions.*"

Matthew 27:11 Now Jesus stood before the governor and the governor questioned him, saying, "Are you the King of the Jews?" Jesus said, "You say so." [12] And when he was accused by the chief priests and elders, he did not answer. [13] Then Pilate said to him, "Do you not hear how many accusations they make against you?" [14] And he did not answer him, not one word, so that the governor was greatly astonished.

[27] Then the soldiers of the governor took Jesus into the governor's command post, and they gathered the whole cohort around him. [28] They stripped him and put a scarlet robe on him. [29] And having woven a crown from thorns, they put it on his head along with a reed in his right hand and they knelt before him and mocked him, saying, "Hail, King of the Jews!" [30] And they spat on him, and took the reed and struck him on his head. [31] After mocking him, they stripped him of the robe and put his clothes [back] on him. Then they led him away to be crucified. [32] Now going out, they found a Cyrenian man named Simon; this man they conscripted to carry his cross.

[33] And coming to a place called Golgotha (which means Skull Place), [34] they offered him wine mixed with vinegar to drink; but when he tasted it, he would not drink. [35] And when they had crucified him, "*they divided his clothes*" among themselves by "*casting lots.*" [36] Then they sat down and kept watch over him there. [37] Now they placed over his head his charge, written as, "This is Jesus, the King of the Jews."

PROCLAMATION

Text Notes

Nebuchadnezzar's troops are called "slaves" in 2 Kings 24:11. The king's surrender in verse 12 is articulated ironically with the primary verb of the exodus, *y-tz-'*. Likewise, Nebuchadnezzar "bought out" the riches of the Jerusalem temple in verse 13 just as God brought out the Israelites. The ranks of deportees include women and men. The first accounting includes the Queen Mother, second in authority to king (listed in that order verse 12) and the entire senior administrative team, which would have likely included women in some roles (indicated by seals from royal women and female administrators before and after the fall of Jerusalem). The second reckoning in verse 14 repeats and numbers the officials and warriors at ten thousand, as well as craftspersons and smiths; the former would have included women, as potting and weaving were traditionally female occupations. A third reckoning in verse 15 circles back to the surrendering of the Queen Mother and adds the royal women, wives, and other women, including royal daughters and likely the surviving wives of previous monarchs, then repeats the officials a third time and adds all of the nobles. A fourth accounting in verse 16 numbers the warriors at seven thousand and one thousand war-ready artisans and smiths. These different accountings suggest chaos and confusion rather than specificity in spite of the recorded numbers. The broader sense is that everyone who was anyone was exiled except the almost overlooked "poor of the land," tucked away at the end of verse 14, not mentioned again.

In Psalm 47:4, the "pride of Rebekah's womb" is "the pride (or majesty) of Jacob." In verse 9, "the God of Hagar and Sarah" is "the God of Abraham."

In Hebrews 1:1, the explication of prophets as female and male reminds the reader/hearer of the diversity in Israel's prophetic ranks.

"Astonished" in Matthew 27:14 can also mean "impressed." Verse 31 ends "to crucify" with no object; some translations add "him" there. Verse 35 quotes the LXX language for dividing garments and casting lots in Psalm 22:18 exactly.

Preaching Prompts

The liturgical year ends with a reflection on the Majesty of Christ as the Church prepares to begin a new year, remembering his first advent while preparing for his next. As the weeks reviewing the rise and fall(s) of Israel's monarchies during Ordinary Time have made abundantly clear, monarchy is, as all human institutions, an enterprise that is doomed to fail. Yet monarchy and its conventions have given us language for God, imperfect but familiar, as the psalm amply demonstrates. Jesus takes that language and those conventions and inverts them; the reign of God and its majesty are very different from the splendor of the world's sovereigns.

To the fallen Judean monarchy and their Babylonian colonizers and occupiers, Jesus says the poor of the land who were deemed not worth the labor to even deport are at the heart of the reign of God. The majesty of Christ is not found in treasures of temple or palace, burgled and broken apart, but in a crown of thorns beaten in by bullies and in his battered and denuded body. This human, mortal, woman-born Jesus is the glory and majesty of God; in the words of the Epistle to the Hebrews, *"the brilliance of God's glory and reproduction of God's very being."* That humanness, shared with every girl and woman, boy and man, nonbinary child and adult, is also the majesty of Christ and our own.

APPENDIX:
DIVINE NAMES AND TITLES[*]

FIRST TESTAMENT

AGELESS GOD

AGELESS ONE

ALL-KNOWING GOD

ALL-KNOWING ONE

ALL-SEEING GOD

ALMIGHTY

ANCIENT OF DAYS

ANCIENT ONE

ARK OF SAFETY

ARCHITECT OF HEAVEN

AUTHOR OF LIFE

BREATH OF LIFE

COMMANDER of heaven's legions

COMMANDER of heaven's vanguard

COMPASSIONATE GOD

COMPASSIONATE ONE

CREATOR

CREATOR OF ALL

DREAD GOD

ETERNAL

ETERNAL ONE

EXALTED

EVER-LIVING GOD

EVER-PRESENT GOD

FAITHFUL ONE

FAITHFUL GOD

FEARSOME GOD

FIRE OF SINAI

FOUNT OF JUSTICE

FOUNT OF LIFE

FOUNT OF WISDOM

GENEROUS ONE

GLORIOUS ONE

GOD WHO DWELLS ABOVE THE CHERUBIM

GOD WHO HEARS

GOD WHO IS HOLY

GOD WHO IS MAJESTY

GOD WHO IS MYSTERY

GOD WHO PROVIDES

GOD WHO REDEEMS

GOD WHO SAVES

GOD WHO SEES

GOD WHO THUNDERS

GOD WHOSE NAME IS HOLY

GRACIOUS GOD

GRACIOUS ONE

HEALING ONE

HEAVENLY MIDWIFE

HOLY GOD

HOLY ONE

HOLY ONE OF OLD

HOLY ONE OF SINAI

HOLY PROTECTOR

HOLY SHEPHERD

INSCRUTABLE GOD

INCANDESCENT ONE

INDOMITABLE GOD

---

[*] This list of divine titles intentionally exceeds the number of those used in this volume (and perhaps by the fourth and final volume, this series). These titles are offered to enrich the liturgical lexicons of those who pray, preach and preside, in public or in private.

JUDGE OF ALL THE EARTH

JUDGE OF ALL FLESH

JUST GOD

JUST ONE

LIVING GOD

LOVING GOD

MAGNIFICENT ONE

MAJESTIC ONE

MAJESTY

MAJESTY OF THE AGES

MAJESTY OF THE HEAVENS

MAKER OF ALL

MERCIFUL GOD

MERCIFUL ONE

MIGHTY GOD

MIGHTY ONE

MOST HIGH

MOTHER OF ALL

MOTHER OF CREATION

MOTHER OF THE MOUNTAINS

MOTHER OF WISDOM

ONE

ONE GOD

ONE WHO IS

REDEEMER

REDEEMING GOD

REDEEMING ONE

RIGHTEOUS GOD

RIGHTEOUS ONE

ROCK WHO BIRTHED US

ROCK WHO GAVE US BIRTH

RULER OF ALL

RULER of the Multitudes of Heaven

SAVING GOD

SAVING ONE

SHELTERING GOD

SHEPHERDING GOD

SHE WHO BIRTHED THE EARTH

SHE WHO HEARS

SHE WHO PROVIDES

SHE WHO IS

SHE WHO IS DELIGHT

SHE WHO IS EXALTED

SHE WHO IS FAITHFUL

SHE WHO IS GLORY

SHE WHO IS GOD

SHE WHO IS HOLY

SHE WHO IS MAJESTY

SHE WHO IS MIGHTY

SHE WHO IS PEACE

SHE WHO IS POWER

SHE WHO SPEAKS CREATION

SHE WHO IS STRENGTH

SHE WHO IS WISDOM

SHE WHO IS WORTHY

SHE WHO REIGNS

SHE WHO SAVES

SHE WHO SEES

SHE WHO SPEAKS LIFE

SHE WHO THUNDERS

SINAI'S FIRE

SOURCE OF LIFE

SOVEREIGN

SOVEREIGN OF ALL

SOVEREIGN-COMMANDER of winged
warriors

SOVEREIGN GOD

SOVEREIGN ONE

SOVEREIGN of heaven's vanguard

SOVEREIGN of the vanguard of heaven

THE I AM

TOO HOLY TO BE PRONOUNCED

THUNDER OF SINAI

THUNDERING GOD

WARRIOR PROTECTRIX

WELLSPRING OF LIFE

WISDOM

WISDOM OF THE AGES

WOMB OF CREATION

WOMB OF LIFE

WORTHY ONE
YOU WHO ARE

SECOND TESTAMENT
Jesus/Christ

Anointed
God-born
Messiah
Rabbi
Redeemer
Savior
Son of Woman
Teacher
Woman-Born

God

Creator
Creator of All
Dread God
Faithful One
Father
Holy One
Living God
Majesty
Maker
Most High
One Parent
Provider
Reconciler
Shepherd-Of-All
Sovereign
Weaver (of lights)

BIBLIOGRAPHY

Abegg, Martin, Peter Flint, and Eugene Ulrich. *The Dead Sea Scrolls Bible: The Oldest Known Bible*. San Francisco: HarperSan Francisco: 1999.

Aland, Barbara, Kurt Aland, et al. *Novum Testamentum Graece*. Stuttgart: Deutsche Bibelgesellschaft, 2017.

Alter, Robert. *The Hebrew Bible: A Translation with Commentary*. New York: W.W. Norton and Company, 2019.

The Anchor Yale Bible Commentaries. Garden City, NY: Doubleday, 1964–Present.

Ariel, Israel. *Carta's Illustrated Encyclopedia of the Holy Temple in Jerusalem*. Jerusalem: Coronet Books, 2004.

Arndt, William, F. Wilbur Gingrich, Frederick William Danker, and Walter Bauer. *A Greek-English Lexicon of the New Testament and Other Early Christian Literature*. 3rd ed. Chicago: University of Chicago Press, 2000.

Aymer, Margaret, *Acts of the Apostles*. Edited by Carol A. Newsom, Sharon H. Ringe, and Jacqueline E. Lapsley. *Women's Bible Commentary*. 3rd ed. Louisville: Westminster John Knox Press, 2012.

Barth, Markus. *Ephesians. Introduction, Translation, and Commentary*. The Anchor Bible, vol. 34. Garden City, NY: Doubleday, 1974.

Bassler, Jouette M. "First Corinthians." In *Women's Bible Commentary*, edited by Carol A. Newsom, Sharon H. Ringe, and Jacqueline E. Lapsley, 558–566. 3rd ed. Louisville: Westminster John Knox Press, 2012.

Berlin, Adele, and Marc Zvi Brettler. *The Jewish Study Bible*. 2nd ed. Oxford: Oxford University Press, 2004.

Bloch, Ariel, and Chana Bloch. *The Song of Songs: The World's First Great Love Poem*. Modern Library Classics. New York: Random House, 1995.

Briggs Kittredge, Cynthia, and Claire Miller Colombo. "Colossians." In *Philippians, Colossians, Philemon*, edited by Mary Ann Beavis, 124–201. Wisdom Commentary, vol. 51. Collegeville, MN: Liturgical Press, 2017.

Brooten, Bernadette. *Women Leaders in the Ancient Synagogue*. Brown Judaic Studies 36. Chico, CA: Scholars Press, 1982.

Brown, Raymond F. *The Epistles of John: A New Translation with Introduction, Notes and Commentary*. The Anchor Bible, vol. 30. Garden City, NY: Doubleday, 1982.

Byron, Gay L., and Vanessa Lovelace. *Womanist Interpretations of the Bible: Expanding the Discourse*. Atlanta, GA: Society for Biblical Literature, 2016.

Clines, David J.A. *The Dictionary of Classical Hebrew*. Rev. ed. Sheffield: Sheffield Phoenix Press, 2018.

Common English Bible. Nashville, TN: Common English Bible, 2011.

Cooper, Kate. *Band of Angels: The Forgotten World of Early Christian Women*. New York: Overlook Press, 2013.

Dickerson, Febbie. *Luke, Widows, Judges, and Stereotypes*. Lanham, MD: Lexington Books/Fortress Academic, 2019.

Edelman, Diana. "Mephibosheth." *The Anchor Bible Dictionary, Volume 5*. Edited by David Noel Freeman et al. New York: Doubleday, 1992.

Falk, Marcia. *The Song of Songs: Love Lyrics from the Bible*. Brandeis Series on Jewish Women. Waltham, MA: Brandeis University Press, 2004.

Fitzmyer, Joseph. *The Acts of the Apostles: A New Translation with Introduction and Commentary*. The Anchor Bible, vol. 31. Garden City, NY: Doubleday, 1998.

———. *First Corinthians: A New Translation with Introduction and Commentary*. The Anchor Yale Bible, vol. 2-2. New Haven, CT: Yale University Press, 2008.

———. *The Gospel According to Luke I-IX. Introduction, Translation and Notes*. The Anchor Bible, vol. 28. Garden City, NY: Doubleday, 1981.

Fox, Everett. *The Early Prophets: Joshua, Judges, Samuel, and Kings: A New Translation with Introductions, Commentary, and Notes by Everett Fox*. The Schocken Bible, vol. 2. New York: Schocken Books, 2014.

———. *The Five Books of Moses: Genesis, Exodus, Leviticus, Numbers, Deuteronomy: A New Translation with Introductions, Commentary, and Notes*. The Schocken Books, vol. 1. New York: Schocken Books, 1995.

———. *Give Us A King!: Samuel, Saul, and David: A New Translation of Samuel I and II, with an Introduction and Notes by Everett Fox*. 1st ed. New York: Schocken Books, 1999.

Freedman, David Noel. *The Anchor Bible Dictionary*. New Haven, CT: Yale University Press, 1992.

Freeman, Lindsay Hardin. *Bible Women: All Their Words and Why They Matter*. Cincinnati, OH: Forward Movement, 2014.

Frick, Frank. "Israel? A People and a Land: Joshua and Judges." In *A Journey Through the Hebrew Scriptures*, 240–262. Belmont: Wadsworth Publishing, 2002.

Gafney, Wilda. *Daughters of Miriam: Women Prophets in Ancient Israel*. Philadelphia, PA: Fortress Press, 2008.

———. *Nahum, Habakkuk, Zephaniah*. Edited by Barbara E. Reid, OP. Wisdom Commentary, vol. 38. Collegeville, MN: Liturgical Press, 2017.

———. *Womanist Midrash: A Reintroduction to the Women of the Torah and the Throne*. Lexington, KY: Westminster John Knox Press, 2017.

Henderson, J. Frank, Jean Campbell, Ruth Fox, and Eileen M. Schuller. *Remembering the Women: Women's Stories from Scripture for Sundays and Festivals*. Chicago: Liturgy Training Publications, 1999.

Huizenga, Annette Bourland. *1–2 Timothy, Titus*, Wisdom Commentary Series. Collegeville, MN: Liturgical Press, 2016.

Ilan, Ṭal. *Mine and Yours Are Hers: Retrieving Women's History from Rabbinic Literature.* Leiden: Brill Academic Press, 1997.

The Inclusive Bible: The First Egalitarian Translation. Lanham, MD: Rowman and Little-field, 2007.

Johnson, Luke Timothy. *The Letter of James: A New Translation with Introduction and Commentary.* The Anchor Bible, vol. 37. New York: Doubleday, 1995.

Kol HaNeshamah. Elkins Park, PA: Reconstructionist Press, 2000.

Kramer, Ross. "Nympha." In *Women in Scripture: A Dictionary of Named and Unnamed Women in the Hebrew Bible, the Apocryphal/Deuterocanonical Books, and the New Testament,* edited by Carol L. Meyers, Toni Craven, and Ross Shepard Kraemer, 132–133. Boston, MA: Houghton Mifflin, 2000.

Lamsa, George. *The Holy Bible from the Ancient Eastern Text: George M. Lamsa's Translations from the Aramaic of the Peshitta.* San Francisco, CA: Harper and Row, 1985.

Levine, Amy-Jill, and Marc Brettler. *Entering the Passion of Jesus: A Beginner's Guide to Holy Week.* Nashville: United Methodist Publishing, 2018.

———. *The Jewish Annotated New Testament.* New Revised Standard Version. Oxford: Oxford University Press, 2011.

Magiera, Janet. *Aramaic Peshitta New Testament Translation: Messianic Version.* San Diego, CA: LWM Publications, 2009.

Marcus, Joel. *Mark 1–8: A New Translation with Introduction and Commentary.* The Anchor Bible, vol. 27A. Garden City, NY: Doubleday, 2008.

———. *Mark 8–16: A New Translation with Introduction and Commentary.* The Anchor Yale Bible, vol. 27B. New Haven, CT: Yale University Press, 2009.

McCarter, P. Kyle. *II Samuel: A New Translation with Introduction and Commentary.* The Anchor Bible, vol. 9. New York: Doubleday, 1984.

Meyers, Carol L., Toni Craven, and Ross Shepard Kraemer. *Women in Scripture: A Dictionary of Named and Unnamed Women in the Hebrew Bible, the Apocryphal/Deuterocanonical Books, and the New Testament.* Boston, MA: Houghton Mifflin, 2000.

Moore, Carey A. *Tobit: A New Translation with Introduction and Commentary.* The Anchor Bible, vol. 40, part 1. New York: Doubleday, 1996.

Murdock, James. *Murdock's Translation of the Syriac New Testament. Translated into English from the Peshitto Version by James Murdock.* Boston: Scriptural Tract Repository, 1892.

New Revised Standard Version. Washington, DC: National Council of Churches, 1989.

Newsome, Carol, Sharon H. Ringe, and Jacqueline Lapsley. *Women's Bible Commentary.* 3rd ed. Louisville: Westminster John Knox Press, 2012.

Page, Hugh. *Israel's Poetry of Resistance: Africana Perspectives on Early Hebrew Verse.* Minneapolis, MN: Fortress Press, 2013.

Rashkow, Ilona. *Taboo or Not Taboo: Sexuality and Family in the Hebrew Bible.* Minneapolis, MN: Fortress Press, 2000.

Scholz, Susanne. *Introducing the Women's Hebrew Bible: Feminism, Gender Justice, and the Study of the Old Testament*. New York: Bloomsbury T & T, 2017.

Smith, Mitzi J. *I Found God in Me: A Womanist Biblical Hermeneutics Reader*. Eugene, OR: Cascade Books, 2015.

Soggin, J. Alberto. *Judges: A Commentary*. Translated by James Bowden. Philadelphia: Westminster, 1981.

Stamm, Johann, Ludwig Köhler, and Walter Baumgarner. *The Hebrew and Aramaic Lexicon of the Old Testament*. Leiden: Brill Academic Press, 1994.

Stein, David. *The Contemporary Torah: A Gender-Sensitive Adaptation of the JPS Translation*. Philadelphia, PA: Jewish Publication Society, 2006.

Tal, Abraham. *The Samaritan Pentateuch*. Tel-Aviv: Tel-Aviv University, 1994.

Tanakh: The Holy Scriptures: The New JPS Translation According to the Hebrew Text. Philadelphia, PA: Jewish Publication Society, 1985.

Thurston, Bonnie. *The Widows: A Women's Ministry in the Early Church*. Philadelphia: Fortress Press, 1989.

Trible, Phyllis. *God and the Rhetoric of Sexuality*. Overtures to Biblical Theology, no. 2. Philadelphia: Fortress Press, 1978.

———. *Texts of Terror: Literary-Feminist Readings of Biblical Narratives*. Overtures to Biblical Theology, no. 13. Philadelphia: Fortress Press, 1984.

Westbrook, April D. *"And He Will Take Your Daughters . . .": Woman Story and the Ethical Evaluation of Monarchy in the David Narrative*. New York: Bloomsbury T & T Clark, 2015.

Wills, Lawrence M. "Mark." In Levine and Brettler *The Jewish Annotated New Testament: New Revised Standard Bible Translation*. Oxford: Oxford University Press, 2011.

Winter, Miriam Therese. *The Gospel According to Mary: A New Testament for Women*. New York: Crossroad, 1993.

———. *WomanWisdom: A Feminist Lectionary and Psalter: Women of the Hebrew Scriptures, Part One*. New York: Crossroad, 1991.

———. *Woman Witness: A Feminist Lectionary and Psalter: Women of the Hebrew Scriptures, Part Two*. New York: Crossroad, 1992.

———. *WomanWord: A Feminist Lectionary and Psalter: Women of the New Testament*. New York: Crossroad, 1990.

Wisdom Commentary Series. Collegeville, MN: Liturgical Press, 2015.

Witherington, Ben. *A New English Translation of the Septuagint (and Other Greek Translations Traditionally Included Under That Title)*. New York: Oxford University Press, 2000.

SCRIPTURE INDEX